EUNOMIA

New Order for a New World

Philip Allott

Oxford   New York
Oxford University Press
1990

Oxford University Press, Walton Street, Oxford OX2 6DP
Oxford New York Toronto
Delhi Bombay Calcutta Madras Karachi
Petaling Jaya Singapore Hong Kong Tokyo
Nairobi Dar es Salaam Cape Town
Melbourne Auckland
and associated companies in
Berlin Ibadan

Oxford is a trade mark of Oxford University Press

Published in the United States
by Oxford University Press, New York

British Library Cataloguing in Publication Data
Allott, Philip
Eunomia: new order for a new world.
1. International relations
I. Title
303.402
ISBN 0–19–825599–3

Library of Congress Cataloging in Publication Data
Allott, Philip.
Eunomia: new order for a new world / Philip Allott.
Includes bibliographical references.
1. International organization. 2. International law. I. Title.
JX1954.A42 1990 341.2—dc20 89–71045
ISBN 0–19–825599–3

Typeset by Hope Services (Abingdon) Ltd.
Printed in Great Britain by
Bookcraft Ltd., Midsomer Norton, Avon

EUNOMIA

For Dorothy Allott (*née* Dobson)
Alma animarum mater

Contents

List of Figures

O chestnut-tree, great-rooted blossomer,
Are you the leaf, the blossom or the bole?
O body swayed to music, O brightening glance,
How can we know the dancer from the dance?

> W. B. Yeats, *Among School Children* (in *The Collected Poems of W. B. Yeats*, 2nd ed., London [1950], 244).

* * *

As a mark is not set up for men to miss it, so there is nothing intrinsically evil in the world.

> Epictetus, *The Manual* (in *Epictetus, The Discourses and Manual*, tr. P. E. Matheson, Oxford [1916], II, 224).

Preface

The unusual nature of this book calls for some preliminary explanation.

The book has its origin in the period (1960–73) which I spent as a legal adviser in the British Foreign Office (latterly Foreign and Commonwealth Office). That position enabled me to observe more or less closely all significant aspects of international government, as well as the international aspects of national government. It was an experience which left me with a settled moral conviction—that the nature of so-called international relations must be changed fundamentally and, with it, the nature of international law.

Into the Foreign Office in London, in those last years of British world power, there flowed a torrent of dispatches and letters and telegrams from our diplomatic missions and conference delegations abroad, reporting and evaluating the international activities of public authority everywhere, sometimes taking broader, more thoughtful views of the state of what were called Britain's *relations* with this country or that. Out from the Foreign Office there flowed a steadier stream of official reactions and instructions. And, connecting the one to the other, there was the collective ratiocinating of Her Britannic Majesty's Government, which normally took the form of rather languid *minutes* contributed to the relevant file by members of the different departments within the Office which had a special interest in the matter. The accumulating thought gained mass and momentum as it ascended through the hierarchy of the Office until some recommendation for action or inaction was accepted, with or without the involvement of a Minister of State or the Secretary of State himself, with or without the involvement of other Government departments or of some Cabinet committee or of the Cabinet itself.

Such were the tangible signs of the intangible frontier which divides the past from the future. For specialists in diplomatic history, they are the formless material from which further chapters of that history are formed. But for the British Government, as for any government, with the human power and responsibility to choose which future will form part of the past, such activity is the very substance of the process of choosing, applying a preformed set of concepts and values to a perceived reality with a view to altering that reality.

The British Government was an exceptionally diligent government, watching everything with a compulsive seriousness engendered by a long-matured sense of its world-wide responsibilities. The British diplomatic system, whatever the political and moral merits of particular decisions, seemed then to be a system of wonderful elegance and efficiency, operated by people of exceptional qualities of mind and character.

The reality, I came to understand, was quite other than the appearance. British diplomacy had for centuries played a leading part in making a world-system whose peculiar rationality could also be seen as a form of madness. Politicians and diplomats were privileged inhabitants of a world of unreality, an unreality which was life-threatening on a grand scale, a world which nevertheless seemed to its inhabitants, in characteristic paranoid fashion, to be perfectly real and natural and inevitable and right. It followed that specialists in the study of so-called international relations were studying a form of pathological behaviour. And it followed also that the role of international lawyers had been to seek to rationalize and regularize pathological behaviour.

The disorder of the old world order and the possibility of a new world order were ideas which formed themselves throughout my time in the Foreign Office, but especially through my experience of four particular areas of international government, areas which happened also to be four of the most significant in the development of the post-1945 international society.

(1) I was present during part of a regular session of the UN General Assembly for the first time in 1963. During the early 1960s I was concerned with the economic aspect of UN action, including the establishment of UNCTAD, and the beginning of the long negotiations on development policy which would reach their climax in the 1970s in two odes in honour of

hopeless hope, known as the Declaration on the Establishment of a New International Economic Order and the Charter of Economic Rights and Duties of States. I also followed the work, and attended some of the meetings, of the UN committees which were composing two sinister epics of international mythology, known as the Definition of Aggression and the Declaration on Principles of International Law concerning Friendly Relations among States.

After I had left government service, I attended sessions of the Third United Nations Conference on the Law of the Sea between 1976 and 1980, as a member of the United Kingdom delegation. That Conference, with the United Nations Law of the Sea Convention which it adopted, was the most important event in the development of modern international law, showing the way to a new form of law-making in international society and to a new set of international social expectations. It could have been predicted that the Conference and the Convention would themselves in the end be life-threatened by the anti-social attitudes of certain governments caught up in the fantasies of the old world order.

I thus had the opportunity to experience at close quarters the grim ambiguity of the United Nations—an international social system of a new kind trying to organize a new kind of international society but still trapped in the folk-ways of the theatre of ritualized cynicism which is the world of the old diplomacy.

(2) I was in Berlin from 1965 to 1968, as Legal Adviser to British Military Government. I came into close contact with the consequences of the two World Wars and the historical origins of the modern world system. The Government of the Soviet Union was no longer represented on the Legal Committee of the Allied Kommandatura. But the three Western legal advisers had a peculiar form of contact with Soviet representatives, military and civilian, in the context of the four-power responsibility for the Allied Military Prison (for so-called major war criminals) at Spandau.

Two Germanies, an isolated and divided Berlin, the distasteful paraphernalia of military occupation, the absurdities of the Cold War—to anyone who had lived in Europe during the Second World War, to anyone who admired the contribution of the German people to the making of European culture, to anyone who knew something, if only from Russian literature, of the special qualities and the long suffering of the Russian people, the folly of the post-War situation was a conclusive demonstration of the worthlessness of the old international order.

(3) I advised the Arabian Department of the Foreign Office during the period of British withdrawal from the Gulf (1969–71). The states which had been in special treaty relations with Britain for periods of up to 150 years were required to adjust, within two or three years, to their full political independence. And, with their responsibility for controlling one of the world's greatest concentrations of natural wealth, they had to find their own place in an ever-more dynamic, not to say chaotic, world economy. Their situation illuminated the situation of all other newly independent countries, some of which did not even have any substantial natural resource, other than the resilience and the simple hopes of their poverty-stricken people, to bring to the world economy.

I had also participated, as Assistant Agent for the United Kingdom, in the *Northern Cameroons Case* in the International Court of Justice (1963) and had followed from a distance, and occasionally more closely, the work of the Fourth (non-self-governing territories) Committee of the UN General Assembly, during the years when it was sifting angrily through the remains of an extinct epoch of world history.

There was hardly an organized society anywhere in the world which had been left unaffected by the international activities of the European powers. For better and for worse, that fact had to be recognized as the first fact of the international society which would replace the international society of imperialism. Representatives of the United Kingdom, as a former colonial power, had to persist in the defence of British positions because those positions still seemed to reflect British interests. But, for some of those representatives, the problem was to reconcile the future with the past, to respond to a sense of moral and social responsibility for the way the world had become—a sense which included pride as well as regret—while contributing to international action, especially international economic action, leading to a new world order.

(4) In 1972–3, when the United Kingdom became a member state of the European Communities, I was the first British Legal Counsellor in the Office of the British Permanent Representative to the European Communities in Brussels, at the time when we were establishing our initial positions on very many new and complex issues.

The ethos of the European Community is a lively mixture formed from the world-historical vision of those who created it, the extreme complexity of its day-to-day legal and administrative substance, and the arduous interacting of national governmental systems as they try to drag themselves beyond diplomacy into the realm of what can only be called communal government.

History attends every European Community meeting. In day-to-day discussion and confrontation and co-action among representatives of the countries of Western Europe, each with the distinct and proud traditions of its own peoples, it is impossible to forget all that has happened to those peoples, all that they have been to each other. For two or three thousand years, their representatives had met in other circumstances, often before or after yet another resort to public violence. And now they were engaged in the business of trying to create a new form of society, a community, a *Gemeinschaft*, complementing and completing their national societies, in the spirit of a culture which they had always made communally. It seemed then, as it seems now, that the self-transcending nature of the European Community, rudimentary and pre-democratic as it still is, has significance for the making of the new self-transcending international society of the whole world.

The conclusion I came to during my time in the Foreign Office was that the old international order was neither a natural phenomenon to which humanity had simply adjusted its behaviour nor a fortuitous aggregation of countless past events of human interaction. The old international order determines the possibilities perceived by, and hence available to, politicians and governments and, so far as they play any part in the system, members of the general public. But the international system itself is nothing other than a structure of ideas; and it has been made nowhere else than in the human mind. The international order forms the minds of those who make the international order. The masters of the world of tomorrow are the slaves of yesterday's ideas.

In withdrawing to the cloisters of Cambridge in 1973, I thus had the quite specific intention of finding a way to understand and then to change the systematic structure of international society. I knew that the problem had two aspects—philosophy and history. It was necessary to determine how we come to have present within our minds the particular social and moral and legal ideas which we find there. And it was necessary to determine how the present world system developed, as a matter of social and intellectual history.

My work on these two aspects lasted for fifteen years. It was work which could not have been sustained professionally without a tenured academic appointment. It was also difficult to sustain psychologically, as one area of study led on to another and there seemed no prospect of ever reaching an overall view of a kind which could be communicated to others. It is a ramshackle castle of self-reflection which the human mind has constructed over the last four or five thousand years, made from the material things, especially books, which happen to survive from one generation to the next. It is a place of interconnecting rooms, echoing with discordant voices, rooms with more or less arbitrary names on their half-open doors—Theology, Metaphysics, Epistemology, Moral Philosophy, Aesthetics, Philosophy of Science, Political Theory, Social Theory, Economic Philosophy, Legal Philosophy, Constitutional History, Economic History, Social History, Diplomatic History, and so on and strangely on.

In the end, it was the stimulus of discussion with graduate students at Cambridge which caused me to begin in 1984 to give a series of lectures which sought to explore a possible philosophical background to a new international order. The task was also facilitated by a sabbatical year which was spent mostly, with financial assistance from the Leverhulme Trust, in the library of the Hoover Institution for the Study of War, Revolution and Peace at Stanford University.

The response to those lectures, and to another series of lectures which I have given since 1976, taking a synoptic view of the history of social and legal philosophy, encouraged me to believe that it might now be possible to propose a general theory of society and law appropriate for a new international order.

The intellectual endeavour was not to contribute yet another book, or more journal articles, on specific topics in the field of social and legal philosophy but to create a new total view of society and law. And the task was always a practical one—to form a view which could become the normal content of consciousness of all those involved, closely or distantly, in national government and in international society, eventually replacing the existing theoretical structures completely.

I rejected, almost from the beginning, the theories of so-called international relations and, indeed, the legitimacy of such a field as a field of study. I regarded the very phrase *international relations* as the hallmark of the corrupt old order. Whether or not they ever have any effect on the substantive decisions of those whose activities they study, specialists in international relations conspire with those decision-makers by reassuring them with the idea that a transcendental rationality and validity can be found within the strange patterns of their behaviour.

The moral and social situation of international lawyers, practitioners, and academic specialists, seemed to me to be no better. Law constrains or it is a travesty to call it law. Law enters decisively into the willing of its subjects or it is a travesty to call it law. Law transcends the power of the powerful and transforms the situation of the weak or it is a travesty to call it law. A legal system which does its best to make sense of murder, theft, exploitation, oppression, abuse of power, and injustice, perpetrated by public authorities in the public interest, is a perversion of a legal system. Moral indignation, which certainly had not lessened through the years of my practical experience of international law, expressed itself in such preconceptions.

There had been two modern theorists of international law who had sought to elevate international law on to a plane appropriate to a true legal system.

Hans Kelsen had sought to create a philosophical basis for international law which, in the Kantian tradition, grounded legal obligation in the coherence of a closed system of obligation, in such a way that all law, including international law, could be regarded as a single, self-entailing system. The formalism of Kelsen's theory, its isolation of the formal validity of law from the social and moral valuing of its substantive content, meant that, as has been the fate of other such positivist theories of law, it was not able to enter into the minds of international lawyers, still less into the minds of international decision-makers, as a consciousness-transforming structure of ideas.

Myres McDougal (with his collaborators) had sought to integrate the conceptualizing of international society and law into the conceptualizing of social process in general. In particular, he sought to integrate the value-processing of international society into general social value-processing, law being perceived as an aspect of such value-processing. His work was prophetic, in two senses of that word. He was ahead of his time. He was preaching a new dispensation to a recalcitrant group of human beings who were almost beyond redemption, the participants in international relations.

For three reasons, perhaps, McDougal has failed to transform the nature of international society and its law. In the first place, his terminology and conceptual structures were those of a particular school of social theorizing which was unfamiliar and unappealing to most of those who were necessarily his primary audience. Secondly, although as value-rich as Kelsen had been, formally at least, value-free, he seemed to be assuming or asserting substantive values which were controversial or even culturally specific to a culture such as that of the United States or of post-Renaissance Europe. Thirdly, and most significantly, his theory seemed to threaten what little law-character international law might be said to possess without being able to rebuild it on any new, stronger foundation. Law-making seemed to tend to become a permanent process of negotiating. To rest the law-character of law too much on social process is liable to weaken that law-character if, and to the extent that, the social process is itself weak. And no one could doubt the pitiful weakness of the international social process, especially when compared with the social process of complex modern democracies.

The task of anyone seeking to fashion a new international

order thus seemed to me to be, certainly, that of providing, in the spirit of Kelsen, a basis of philosophical coherence for international society and law, and also that of integrating, in the spirit of McDougal, the international social process into social process generally. But the real burden of the task was to achieve both, and to do so in a way which could be assimilated not into the consciousness of members of any particular cultural or socio-political camp but into human consciousness generally. I soon realized that this was not a task to be completed by one person or at any one time. But it is a task that must at least be initiated by someone at some time.

The main purpose of the book is thus to propose a general theory of society and law which is potentially universal, that is to say, a theory capable of being the theory acted upon by all participants in international society.

Such an endeavour faces the most serious intellectual problem of all—how it is possible to produce general social theory in the late twentieth century, when it might reasonably be supposed that general social theory is no longer possible. This view would be based, in the first place, on practical grounds—because the volume of material to be assimilated (ideas and information about human social experience) is now beyond the capacity of a single human lifetime. It is a task which, in their different and distinctive ways, defeated (and tried the sanity of) Nietzsche and Tolstoy and Weber, and which Marx can be said to have achieved, if at all, only if account is generously taken of the creative work of his apologists.

But, also from a practical point of view, if we cannot produce new general social theory, then we are doomed to live out old social theory. In the case of international society, this means that we are doomed to live out, or to be destroyed by, the theory of an unsociety.

But the impossibility of general social theory might also be asserted on theoretical grounds. The philosophical obstacles facing a general theory of society and law are perennial. The human mind has been aware of them since it first began accumulating thought about the human situation. But it is only very recently that it has become possible to specify them in the following kind of way, crude as it still is. Each is formidable. Together they oblige anyone who wishes to propose general social theory to insist categorically on the tentative nature of the proposed theory.

(a) Plato, Rousseau. How can the social order be reconciled with the moral order, if the moral order is an aspect of being and the social order is an aspect of knowing?

(b) St Paul, St Augustine, Nietzsche, Freud (and aspects of Eastern religions and philosophies). To change humanity you must change human nature, but how can human nature change human nature?

(c) Marx (and social anthropology and structuralism). How can we transcend society in consciousness when our consciousness is created by the society which we create?

(d) Locke, Hume, Kant. We make the world in thinking it. How can we think about our thinking about the world of which we form part?

(e) Aristotle, Wittgenstein (and hermeneutics, phenomenology, linguistics). Leaving on one side mathematics, how can language (and, therefore, an idea expressed in language) make of itself something more than a form of human behaviour?

Theories of society and law must now take account of these problems. If they do not, they are worth very little. It is for this reason that a general social theory must contain, as the book seeks to do in its first part, a theory of itself—that is to say, a theory which would make possible the theory itself.

The book seeks to propose or to imply ways of dealing with all the perennial problems noted above, separately and together. However, it does so without addressing them directly or explicitly. In particular, it does so without discussing any of the written sources in which such problems have been proposed or discussed, over long centuries and in a superabundant literature. The unusual form of the book—entirely without footnotes, entirely without discussion of previous writings—is dictated by its overall intention.

In the first place, the book does not seek to be taken up into the academic mill of reinterpretations of previous interpretations of thought about social and legal philosophy. The preparation of the book had an almost empirical aspect, involving as it did a study of as many particular societies as possible, from the city-states of ancient Mesopotamia to societies of the present day, with a view to determining, in particular, how they conceived of themselves theoretically and how they changed over time, through revolution and through sustained and piecemeal social development.

Also, the theory as presented will seem to some readers to have leading features which might be described as Marxist (the social creation of consciousness and of value), religious (the integration of the individual and society within a significant universe), liberal (the subjection of society to its own transcendental values). And, it is to be hoped, there will be other leading features recalling long-evolved social self-theories going beyond those three currently familiar complexes.

Again, readers who are so minded may find echoes of many ideas associated with other names. Plato and the Good as social reality, Aristotle and purposive social becoming, Confucius and the moral authority of the past, Lao-Tzǔ and human self-ordering within an ordering universe, Cicero and the right reason of the law, Augustine and the non-autonomy of the morally good, Aquinas and the natural origin of human law, Leibniz and the presence of the whole universe in every part of the universe, Rousseau and the spiritual identity of the individual and society in the act of willing, Kant and moral rationality, Burke and the evolutionary constitution, Hegel and the self-creating of society at the level of spirit through struggle, Mach/Craik and scientific world-modelling, Nietzsche and human self-surpassing, Dilthey/Weber and the social construction of reality, Fustel de Coulanges and the religious roots of organized societies, Wittgenstein and the functional validity of language, Cassirer and the organic rationality of societies, Teilhard de Chardin and the human transcending of evolution—and many more.

The theory was not constructed in any synthesizing fashion, however. It is simply that, at least for the time being, it seems impossible to think abstractly about such matters without giving to such thought these familiar idea-forms. We may hope (or fear) that in due course, sooner or later, humanity will find, perhaps with the aid of electronic machines, radically new ways of conceptualizing itself and its aspirations.

The second reason for the unusual form of the book, for its lack of external points of intellectual reference, is to be found in its governing intention—to propose a universal theory. It is designed to be accessible to anyone who is inclined to think abstractly and constructively about the human social condition, whether or not they may be familiar with any particular previous thinking on the subject and whether or not their personal experience of the human social condition and their store of information about it are similar to those of the author. The points of reference which the book relies upon are not the external points of reference of any particular culture but the internal points of reference of each developing human mind. The reader is asked to assent, if possible, to the ideas proposed hereafter in response to the prompting of the internal system of intellectual coherence which we all possess but which works in a unique way for each one of us.

The third reason for the unusual form of the book is simply that its ambition is to find a place in the tradition of the most general works of social theory of the past: that is to say, it contains a theory; it is not a book about theory.

The book contains a structure of ideas, put forward as a hypothesis, that is to say, as a possible structure. The author accordingly invites the co-operation of those who read it, by way of comment and criticism and by way of the communication of relevant material, either in the form of references to sources in social and legal and general philosophy, general history, cultural history and traditions, the fine arts and literature, or in the form of the product of personal insight and experience. All such contributions should be related, where appropriate, to a particular numbered paragraph of the book.

The intention is that, in this way, a co-operative effort may be initiated, focused as precisely as possible, and bringing together as many different traditions and perspectives as possible from every part of the world.

To the extent that a new general international theory were established, it would lead to a reforming of the fundamental conceptions of international law and also, in due course, to the gradual creation of a new kind of substantive international law. Given the scale and the complexity of the events of international society, it is obvious that the law of that society must, sooner rather than later, form itself into a legal system at least as rich and complex as the more advanced national legal systems.

But the hope must go beyond the mere reforming of

international law. The hope must be that the fundamental conceptions of international society itself and, in due course, the very substance of the international social process of the whole world, may be changed fundamentally, leading to new policies and new behaviour not only on the part of governments and politicians and diplomats but also on the part of every human society and every human being, since all of them have an equal stake in the future of humanity as a species.

The necessity and the urgency of a universal theory of human society are plain to see. There is no one who is now unaware of the overwhelming interdependence of human societies. That awareness has developed in three phases. There was the phase of the development of the grotesquely named strategic nuclear weapons, as if mass murder and mass destruction could be strategies adopted by rational human beings. Then there was the phase of economic interdependence, as we became aware that economic decisions taken anywhere in the world can have immediate and substantial effects all over the world. The third phase has been the phase of environmental awareness, as we have become aware of the power of the human species to transform the Earth as a total natural system.

Far-sighted world leaders have already drawn attention to the next phase in the developing awareness of human inter-dependence. President Gorbachev of the Soviet Union, in his remarkable address to the United Nations General Assembly in 1988, and Pope John Paul II, speaking during his visit to Scandinavia in 1989, have both called for a new vision of the world. It is hoped that this book will make a contribution to the illumination of this fourth horizon of human awareness, a spiritual horizon, the horizon of the interdependence of the human spirit, as human societies and human beings everywhere at last begin to take moral and social responsibility for the survival and prospering of the whole of humanity.

The manuscript was completed in January 1989. No altera-tions have been made to take specific account of the major political developments, especially in Eastern Europe, which have taken place since then.

Trinity College,
Cambridge.

Part One *Society*

The mind of the Whole is social.

Marcus Aurelius, *Meditations*, V. 30.
(ed. and tr. A. S. L. Farquharson, Oxford [1946], i. 93).

*

Man takes his law from the Earth; the Earth takes its law from Heaven; Heaven takes its law from the Tâo. The law of the Tâo is its being what it is.

Tāo Têh King (Tāo Tê Ching), ch. 25.
(tr. J. Legge, in *The Sacred Books of the East*, Oxford [1891], xxxix. 68).

1 Society and Words

1.1. (1) *Society is the collective self-creating of human beings.*

(2) *International society is the society of the whole human race and the society of all societies.*

(3) *Law is the continuing structure-system of human socializing.*

(4) *International law is the law of international society.*

1.2. These are the definitions, the axioms, the premises, the conclusions, the theorems, the formulas, the theories, the ideas, the ideals with which we may construct a new kind of future for the human race, a future which is something other than a mere continuation of the recent past, a future which is a realization of unused potentialities, of theoretical and practical possibilities which are already available to us, but which cannot be made actual without an unprecedented theoretical and practical effort, a special effort of imagination and reason and will, a fundamental change of human consciousness. They are the instruments for initiating a new stage in the strange story of human existence, that is to say, in the strange process of human self-creating. They are the instruments for a form of human self-discovery which will be both a rediscovery and a new departure—in short, a revolution.

1.3. To assert the proposition (1), that society is the collective self-creating of human beings, is to deny the commonly accepted propositions that society is an illusion masking only the behaviour of human individuals, or that society is an organism of which individual human beings are merely component parts.

1.4. To assert the proposition (2), that international society is the society of the whole human race and the society of all societies, is to deny the generally accepted proposition that international society is the society of the nation-states of the world. And it is to deny a commonly accepted proposition that, in any true sense of the world *society*, there is no such thing as a society beyond the societies of the nation-states, let alone a society of the human race.

1.5. To assert the proposition (3), that law is the continuing structure-system of human socializing, is to part company with an unbounded set of propositions, including propositions to the effect that law is the wisdom of the ancestors, law is the wisdom of the elders, law is the voice of Justice, law is the voice of Nature, law is the voice of the judges, law is the will of God, law is the will of the people, law is the spirit of the nation, law is the actualizing of practical reason, law is the social pursuit of the Good, law is a set of self-entailing social norms or rules, law is a mask worn by power, law is the command of a sovereign, law is a set of theoretical epiphenomena of practical social phenomena, law is the operating principles of social engineering, law is custom, law is what law does.

1.6. To assert the proposition (4), that international law is the law of the society of the whole human race and of the society of all societies, is to deny the generally accepted proposition that international law is the law made by and for the nation-states of the world. And it is to deny the proposition that, in any true sense of the word law, international *law* is not a variety of law at all, let alone a law applying to human beings in general.

1.7. Such controversies seem to turn merely on the meaning of words, especially the words *society* and *law*. Agree some definitions, and the controversies will surely disappear. Agree to differ on the definition of words, and the controversies will surely cease to matter. But, for the human animal with its own special capacity to communicate within and beyond itself, words are not merely a form of self-expression. They are a form of life.

1.8. We live many lives—as a series of electromagnetic events in a universe of electromagnetic fields; as biochemical structures and systems organizing the stabilization and transformation of chemical compounds; as biological systems composed of neuro-physiological sub-systems; as living organisms exhibiting patterns of behaviour activated by instinct, reflex, and sensation; as animals of the genus *Homo* and the species *sapiens*; as individual persons with an identity and a history; as autonomous moral agents making life-determining choices; as social beings formed and conditioned by our interaction with each other in societies; as legal persons participating in legal relations; as embodied spirit, if we are among those who conceive of a spiritual reality beyond the world of physical and psychological phenomena; as creatures and servants of super-natural powers, if we are among those who believe that there are supernatural powers which concern themselves with our existence.

1.9. And, among our many lives, we live a life which is made of words. It is a life which we live within our individual consciousness, where consciousness can present itself to itself in the form of words which are spoken to an audience of no one other than the speaker. It is a life which we live in the social consciousness which we share with others, in the sharing of words within personal relationships, within social groups, as members of the undifferentiated human race.

1.10. The life we live in words is, as we know from the whole of recorded human history, a life of tremendous energy. We live and die for words; we create and kill for words; we build and destroy for words; wars and revolutions are made for words. *Sovereignty, the people, the faith, the law, the father-land, self-determination, nationality, independence, security, land, freedom, slave, infidel, tyranny, imperialism, justice, right, rights, crime, equality, democracy.* Words of love and faith and loyalty may inspire acts of self-surpassing courage and generosity, when spontaneous human goodness is focused in the aural and visual signs of a single word—the name of a nation, a word which signifies some supernatural reality or some deep interpersonal bond, the attractive and binding energy of some idea compressed into a word. Words of hate and intolerance and contempt may inspire acts of bestial cruelty, acts of genocide and persecution and oppression and murder, ignited by the name of a nation, a race, a faith, a class, a deviant group, or by some word exploding with the power of an idea. We do our best and worst with and for words.

1.11. The reality within which a life is lived in words is a world of its own. Our words make our worlds. To choose our words is to choose a form of life. To choose our words is to choose a world. To oppose words is to oppose a form of life and a world. To change words is to change a form of life and a world. We can make new forms of social life, new social worlds by choosing new words communally, including the new words constantly created through the redefinition of old words. To make a new word or to alter the meaning of an old word is to make possible new realities. We have made and remade unceasingly words which contain our most profound and general human experiences. *God, universe, spirit, life, death, change, matter, atom, cell, self, consciousness, mind, body, the void, nothingness, natural, supernatural, immortal, the good, truth, custom, law, morality, rule, duty, right, wrong, crime, punishment, family, race, nation, tribe, city, citizen, state, society, humanity, justice, democracy, the people, freedom, equality, class, will, love, power, interest, myth, the market, demand, welfare, philosophy, metaphysics, science, history, ideology.*

1.12. There could be no end, short of a universal lexicon and a universal grammar constantly revised, to the list of the words from which we make our worlds. We presume that there is no limit, in principle, to the capacity of the human imagination to create new words and new meanings for old words. But we are also achingly aware that the words and meanings actually available to each of us at any given time is finite. We can find within us so much, and no more, with which to express ourselves in words. We know that our vocabulary is not enough to contain all that we feel and think, all that we want to be, all that we can imagine ourselves becoming. We feel disempowered by the relative poverty of our vocabulary, by our relative incompetence in the expression of our potential selves. We feel trapped by the words and meanings into which we are born and educated, which act like a genetic and social destiny which we must accept and which we may overcome, to a more or less limited extent, only at the cost of struggle and a kind of suffering. But our servitude is also our means of escape. We can change our words and our meanings, and thereby we can change ourselves and our worlds. To change our words and meanings—including the meanings of words like *society* and *law*—is to change ourselves and our worlds by and for ourselves. To change our words is to change our minds. To change our words is a dying in order to live.

1.13. The constraining effect of our limited vocabulary is especially a constraint upon our imagination. Our imagination seems to be immeasurably fertile. We know of no limits to our imagination, and we feel entitled to suppose that, in principle, the imagination could not imagine its own limits. Our imagination is an aspect of the dynamic physiological capacity of the human brain, as an electrochemical sub-system. Through imagination the creative capacity of the brain presents an endless stream of new products within what we call our *mind* or *consciousness*—the activity of the brain as it is presented by the brain to the brain.

1.14. Imagination generates connections within the contents of our minds, making available to us a series of connections from among the infinity of possible connections, establishing electrochemical pathways connecting mental contents of all kinds. And the products of the imagination are not only a series of events in time. They seem to have a kind of spatial dimension. They form a growing, ever more dense, network which enables the products of the imagining brain to interact with each other, and then enables the products of that interaction to interact, and so on and on. Abstract thought may be seen as the process whereby such interaction establishes such networks of the most extensive kinds. Thus imagination is the mind in its creative aspect, creating itself from itself, combining and constructing and co-ordinating, providing the contents of the process of consciousness.

1.15. Consciousness-creating-consciousness may act in a relatively unconscious mode—that is to say, with the minimum of presentation of the activity of the brain to the brain itself, the minimum of self-observing, closest to the physiological phenomena of instinct, reflex, and sensation. And it may act in a relatively conscious mode, including the mode in which the brain presents its products to itself in the form of the particular sounds and signs which we know as *words*. And it may act at any level in between or with any mixture of levels. And it may act in co-operation with the physical impulses of the human body, attaching powerful energy in the form of so-called *feelings* to individual words and their uses.

1.16. Our current store of available words, with their current meanings, is thus a reflection of the current state of our consciousness-creating-consciousness. The meanings of our words determine their practical utility to us, the uses to which we may put them within the continuing process of consciousness. They are, for the time being, a practical limitation on our capacity to present the creative products of the imagination to ourselves in the form of words. When we come to communicate with other people, sharing our consciousness with theirs, words may have a still more limiting effect. In communicating with others, we have not only words at our disposal but also a complex repertory of symbols, gestures, and other non-verbal signs—a national anthem, a flag, a portrait of the leader, a style of dancing or marching, conventional forms of art and craft, a salute, a hand-shake, a seal and a signature, a raised fist, a smile. But all signs and symbols, and especially words, are limited in their communicative capacity by the fact that, to be effective as communication, they must have significance not only for us but for those with whom we intend to communicate.

1.17. The shared significance of signs is thus a further important limitation on the capacity of the imagination to communicate its profusion usefully, to organize the sharing of consciousness between human beings. For others, we may be more than all that we can say to them. Certainly we are less than all that we would want to say to them, had we an unlimited capacity to communicate. The human capacity to communicate sets limits on our social possibilities.

1.18. A shared language, in the widest sense of the word *language*, is thus a splendid inheritance, making available comunally the products of the infinitely fertile human imagination. To share a language is to share a wealth of possibilities. To acquire a new language is to acquire a wealth of new possibilities. The words of a shared language contain within themselves a past, all the accumulation of meaning and association which they have collected over their social lifetimes. Like rocks or plants or animals, they carry within them the whole of the past that has formed them. Words of the most extreme power—such as *God* or *Custom* or *Law* or *Love* or *Death*—illustrate at the limit not only the capacity of any word to concentrate within itself an immeasurably long and dense past but also its capacity to survive as a form whilst its substance changes endlessly. The permanence of a word is a powerful illusion, as powerful an illusion as the permanence of a rock or a plant or an animal or a human being, mysteriously retaining an identity through all the unceasing change. Words, like all other material things, are able to unite, within one form, stability and change, to carry the past into the future while allowing the future to be different from the past.

1.19. Social history is thus as much the history of words as it is the history of deeds. The history of words has as much explanatory power as any history of politics or diplomacy or law or economic life. As persons and as societies, we are what we were able to be, and we will be what we are now able to be. So it is with the history of words. We are what we have said; we will be what we are now able to say. Words contain social history, distilled and crystallized and embodied and preserved, but available also as a social force, a cause of new social effects. Each succeeding generation is a regenerating of words and in words and by words.

1.20. We cannot know the words which have not survived and the words which might have existed. We may know something of meanings that have not survived, but of many, if not most, past meanings of surviving words we know nothing. We can know only that their loss deprives us of possibilities which we might otherwise have, including possibilities of self-knowledge and possibilities of self-expression, and hence possibilities of individual and social existence. We are thus rich in the words which have survived as our inheritance. We are poor in the words and meanings which have disappeared from that inheritance. There are countless worlds we could have lived in, had we created other words and other meanings. It is possible to feel two conflicting forms of regret: that humanity has not taken greater care of its inheritance of consciousness, so that it has had to keep re-experiencing in order to reformulate and hence to relearn; and, on the other hand, that humanity has allowed itself so often to be enslaved and entranced by dead words and dead meanings.

1.21. It is reasonable to assume that those words and meanings which survive have some fitness for suvival, that is to say, that they are appropriately adapted to the social conditions in which they survive. For that reason, we must respect words which survive. They must convey some unit of consciousness which human beings have found to be usefully conveyed as a unit of communicated consciousness. They must convey some distinction which human beings have found useful to make and to communicate, since a word has the effect of isolating something from within the vast mass of consciousness, giving it a second existence within the capsule that is the word.

1.22. In particular languages and at particular times, there may be words for *the one* and *the all* and *the whole*, for *spirit* and *matter*, for *breath* and *spirit* and *soul* and *mind*, for *the brain* and *the mind*, for *knowing* and *knowing how* and *knowing that*, for *consciousness* and *conscience*, for *intelligence* and *understanding*, for *the real* and *the right* and *the true*, for *the idea* and *the ideal*, for *the good* and *the beautiful*, for *the person* and *the citizen*, for *person* and *personality*, for *law* and *custom* and *legislation*, for *society* and *community*, for *nation* and *people* and *state*, for *necessity* and *need* and *want*, for *love* and *friendship* and *affection* and *desire* and *lust* and *sex*. In such cases, it is possible to deny the truth, the rationality, the utility, the desirability, of such distinctions. It is not possible to deny the fact that such distinctions have been made or that, in some cases, they have been made throughout the whole course of recorded human history.

1.23. We may further reasonably assume that the making of the distinctions which the existence of given words implies must serve some purpose, however unfathomable, and to whatever extent that purpose may be a mixed product of imagination and reason, of the less conscious and the more conscious processes of the mind, of intention and happy accident, of particular social circumstances and developments. So it is that words acquire power and prestige. So it is that words rule our minds and our lives. For a given word to have survived, and especially to have survived through all the turbulent history of human social existence, with whatever changes of meaning, is to have defeated time and circumstance, to have demonstrated a virtually supernatural power. To seek to understand the power of long-surviving words—such as *society* and *law*—is to cross the boundaries of the occult.

1.24. The biological function of language is analogous to the biological function of buildings and social institutions. We live within the structures made from words as we live within our other human habitations and as we live within our other social structures. As with our buildings so with our language, we make our word-structures to shelter us from the hazards of a world which threatens to overwhelm us, to isolate ourselves from our neighbours, to provide a hearth at which we may establish our personal lives and worship our household gods, to provide a space in which to organize our communal lives, to contain the comforts and conveniences of our prospering, as persons and as societies. As with our other social institutions —of government, defence, religion, education, the economy, the law—so with language, we make our word-structures to staunch the flow of the stream of consciousness, to channel it into persisting forms, more or less of our making, which allow us the comfort and convenience of relatively settled expectations, which allow us to use our past experience in order to take some control over the otherwise unknowable and uncontrollable future by preparing the form in which we will receive the future, the form in which we will embody it within consciousness and in which we will communicate it to each other.

1.25. Language is humanity's first self-ordering. With language we ward off the fearful spirits of formlessness, aimlessness, and disintegration. Language is a magic to control our minds. Language is a magic to control the worlds made by consciousness. Language is a magic to control the world through consciousness.

1.26. The great expansion of social consciousness over the last five hundred years, which has increased immeasurably the productivity of collective thinking, has been matched by a greatly increased capacity to store and retrieve our past experience including, above all, past states of consciousness. The invention of movable-type printing in the fifteenth century has meant that words became the privileged medium for the retention and communication of past consciousness. With the intense development of visual means of communication in the twentieth century—photographs, cinema, television —and the development of computers, with their special languages and their capacity to transmute word-consciousness into number-consciousness, words no longer have an unchallenged dominance in the retention and communication of consciousness and may, in due time, be surpassed in importance by visual and quasi-mathematical forms of representation and by other, as yet uninvented, forms of communication. However, it seems safe to predict that the last stronghold of words will be the very place with which we are here most concerned—the self-conceiving and the self-ordering of society.

1.27. Such efficiency in the storage and retrieval of information in the form of words has given to us a vastly increased store of information about ourselves. We have an overwhelming abundance of information about past states of our consciousness and about our past social experience. We have an overwhelming abundance of information about the consciousness and social organziation of peoples all over the world, over relatively long periods of time, in diverse forms of society. And now, heirs of all the frenetic social and intellectual activity of recent centuries, and of the present century in particular, we are in a situation which is unlike that of any previous generation. In seeking now to understand the society of the whole human race, we have benefits and burdens which are unlike those possessed by any of our predecessors.

1.28. We know so much and we know too much and we know less and less. We have resources of unprecedented richness, offering new possibilities of human self-conceiving, of human self-knowing, of human self-ordering, of human self-transcending. But the volume and the intensity of our social experience and intellectual activity are exceeding our capacity to assimilate it and to make use of it. And this at the very time when the problems of personal and social self-ordering are greater than ever before, in scale and complexity and threat and urgency. There is, at the end of the twentieth century, the possibility that we may drown in the flood of our own words, falling into a sort of collective dementia under the stress of problems which seem to be beyond our capacity to formulate, let alone to resolve.

2 Society and Reason

2.1. *Society is a sharing of words. Society is also a sharing of reason. Reason is the self-ordering of consciousness. Society is communal consciousness-ordering-consciousness.*

2.2. The limitless profusion of the unending stream of consciousness is trapped by consciousness in the form of words. But consciousness has the further capacity of connecting words in forms which have a new and specific significance for consciousness. Consciousness can create ideas, in the following specific sense of the otherwise imprecise word idea: an idea is a bringing-together of units of consciousness which has an effect within consciousness greater than the sum of the effects of the individual units which it contains. When words are brought together in a certain way they create an idea which is *complex*, in terms of its constituent words, but is *simple*, in terms of its total effect. The constituent elements of an idea can be other ideas; in which case, the effect of the resultant idea is, once again, greater than the sum of the effects of the words contained in the constituent ideas. In this way, the human mind can construct significant idea-structures ranging from the minimal (*the sun is shining*) to the most far-ranging, up to and including, for example, the vast idea-structures of mythology and religion and science and law.

2.3. A word is itself a concentration of mental energy, in the sense considered in Chapter 1 above. It is capable of releasing its energy to produce great effects within consciousness. It follows that an idea, in consisting of several words, necessarily contains the potential energy of its component words. The five words—*all, are, born, free, men*—are words of great and fundamental power within human consciousness, each word an immeasurable accumulation of human experience, of consciousness-creating-consciousness. When the energy of the individual words is totalized in the idea—*all men are born free*—the total energy of the idea is a function of the energy of the individual words but is greater than simply their arithmetical addition. The individual words can be used in any number of other relationships with other words. But when they are brought together in the particular structure in question, they have a particular effect. It is the fusion energy of an idea. It will be our concern to consider where the fusion energy of idea comes from, since societies are constructed and maintained and developed by using the fusion energies of many ideas. Societies are energized by ideas. Societies are generated by the attractive energy of ideas. Societies are sustained by the binding energy of ideas. Societies are destroyed by the explosive energy of ideas.

2.4. The prescriptive definition of *idea* set out above is not confined to structures of words. Significant structures can be made from other units of consciousness, especially from material at the less-conscious levels of consciousness, where the mind does not present its contents to itself, does not observe itself acting. An aesthetic experience, a dream, an access of emotion, a moment of intuition—such units of consciousness are themselves complex structures containing many constituent elements brought together in a particular way and having an effect which is more than the sum of the effects of their constituent parts. They may be called *non-verbalized ideas*. They may themselves contain verbalized and non-verbalized ideas among their constituent elements.

2.5. It is also the case that a single word—or even a single sensation or image or feeling—may have the effect of an idea, if it is associated by the mind with a context, containing a network of other words and ideas, with which it is then integrated by the mind into a single whole. A national flag—the word 'charge!'—the smile of a loved one—a scream in the night—a mushroom-shaped cloud—a trade-mark. Such things can give rise to very complex *ideas-by-association*, ideas which may be capable of being expressed in words, but which often will not be capable of adequate expression in words. Human beings differ in the proportions in which they habitually order their consciousness in the form of verbalized ideas, non-verbalized ideas, and ideas-by-association. But all human beings experience, at least, these three forms of consciousness-ordering-consciousness.

2.6. Such a view of ideas as integrated structures necessarily implies four things: (1) the mind (the human brain presenting its functioning to itself as consciousness) has operational systems which are capable of generating totalized ideas by means of integration; (2) the mind is itself capable of responding to ideas so formed, so that they may themselves become active participants in the generation of further ideas; (3) there is something in the particular arrangement of the constituent elements in an idea which gives rise to the special fusion energy of the idea; (4) the something which gives rise to the special energy of the idea is a function both of form and content, the particular form (grammatical and syntactical and semantic or other) in which particular contents are put together. And there is a fifth fundamental aspect of the mind's capacity to form ideas, which is not so much a corollary of the definition as a hypothesis based on observed fact: (5) ideas are communicable between minds, can be shared between consciousnesses. This in turn implies: (6) the mind is capable of generating ideas of a kind and in a form to which other minds can respond; and (7) the mind is capable of making use of ideas generated in other minds. This, finally, leads to the inference: (8) there is an identity of functioning among human minds, parallel to the hypothetical identity of structure and functioning among human brains—at least to the extent necessary to allow for such communication and reception of ideas. The sharing of consciousness which is a society is thus not only a sharing of the power of words. It is a sharing of the mysterious power of ideas.

2.7. A striking feature of consciousness is its *reflexive character*. It can observe itself in action. It can purposively examine its own activity as if it were examining the activity of something separated from it. The mind has the remarkable capacity to examine itself examining itself. It can use the process which it is studying to study that process. It can form ideas about ideas and about the formation of ideas. This has meant that the mind is not merely a passive arena within which events occur, including the generation of ideas and the reception of generated ideas. The mind is an active participant in its own functioning. Furthermore, the mind is capable of storing the products of its own activity, so that it need not always start from the beginning. It can retain and retrieve, in particular, what it is useful to it, useful to the whole bodily system into which it is integrated, and what is useful to the societies in whose shared consciousness it participates. The wonderful consequence of all this is that the mind is capable of *ordering its own activity*. And this means, in turn, that, through the sharing of consciousness, it can share in the process of the communal ordering of consciousness in society. Society is a communal ordering of consciousness.

2.8. The self-ordering capacity of consciousness has traditionally been called *reason*. Human reason continues to be problematical for human reason. It may be that, in principle, reason will never be able to explain itself to its own satisfaction, since that would presumably require consciousness to overcome a Gödel limit and explain itself satisfactorily to itself. And yet, in the meantime, humanity has not been able, on the contrary, to convince itself that the activity of human consciousness is, in the final analysis, arbitrary and random, merely passive and mechanical. Consciousness seems to be capable of manipulating its ideas and thereby of ordering its ideas—assembling them, disassembling them, reassembling them—as a normal part of its functioning.

2.9. Reflexive consciousness has, over the whole course of accumulated human thought, devoted as much effort to convincing itself to doubt as to convincing itself to believe. Reason has sought, over and again, to doubt reason. It is as if it were a necessary part of the functioning of reason that it should constantly oppose itself. As an aspect of self-ordering, consciousness has unceasingly constructed great idea-structures in which it makes affirmations with a sufficient measure of certainty to provide the sufficiently settled basis for its individual and social existence. And it has unceasingly constructed idea-structures which question the validity of such affirming idea-structures, question the possibility of certainty, question even the possibility of such self-ordering.

2.10. The busy reflexive activity of consciousness over the last five thousand years, as evidenced by the record of that which happens to have survived, has been a process of human self-exploration. It has been a dialectical process, a constant interaction, dialogue, struggle, between the integrating and the disintegrating tendencies of the mind. The result has been that humanity has never achieved a state of unquestionable certainty on any matter, has never fallen into any settled and total uncertainty, and has experienced an incalculable number of degrees of certainty and uncertainty between the two extremes.

2.11. These facts have had a decisive effect on human social history. In the first place, force has been used again and again to compensate for the apparent limits on the power of reason and to enforce claimed certainties, especially religious certainties, but also racial, social, and moral certainties. In the second place, the certainties attained by individuals and societies have enabled them to resist, to the death if need be, those who seek to deny those certainties, meeting force with force, if need be, in the defence of some cherished certainty. Thirdly, human beings have been left, for everyday purposes, in an average state of uneasy equilibrium, of relative certainty/relative uncertainty, giving rise to a compensating tendency to make judgements intuitively, empirically, and pragmatically, rather than through the application of the reasoning capacity of the mind. This has meant that for most human individuals, most of the time, spontaneous action accompanied by rudimentary calculation has seemed to be the most appropriate response to the endless, and endlessly changing, challenges of the human condition, perhaps punctuated by moments of self-surpassing certainty and self-disabling doubt. And such has been the average response of most human societies at most times to the human social condition.

2.12. At the end of the twentieth century, we have overabundant evidence of the human capacity to believe and the human capacity to doubt. We have an overwhelming volume of information available to us about philosophies from many different periods of history, from many different cultures, formed by and for many different personality-types and society-types. It is a danger of our times that we are liable to be overwhelmed by the profusion of ideas available to us, their diversity, their uncertainty, their contradictions. There is the danger, faced by too much evidence of human certainty and uncertainty, that we will surrender ourselves to a sort of despair, despair in the face of the fundamental capacity of human consciousness to order itself. To despair of a fundamental human capacity— loving, hoping, believing, reasoning—is the most disabling form of despair.

2.13. But there is another possibility. The richness of experience retained in human consciousness and available to us today gives us an unprecedented opportunity to take stock of the activity of human consciousness throughout the long history of consciousness-considering-consciousness, as it has asserted and doubted its capacity to transcend itself and to order itself. And the overwhelming impression to be drawn from all the structures of ideas (philosophies) created by consciousness-considering-consciousness and which have survived within accumulated social consciousness, so that we can examine them today as ideas within our own consciousness, is not one of hopeless uncertainty and confusion. On the contrary, they demonstrate vividly, in themselves and by their effects within our minds, the wonderful power of reflective and reflexive human consciousness—consciousness reflecting on the universe in which it finds itself and consciousness reflecting on itself. As reason doubts reason, reason reasons.

2.14. There are seven general types of those philosophies whose tendency has been to question the capacity of human consciousness to order itself by its own effort. They are among the greatest achievements of self-transcending and self-ordering human consciousness.

2.15. These philosophies which have stressed the illusoriness of the self and of individual consciousness have themselves been impressive illustrations of the self-organizing power of the illusion. They recognize that we are condemned to live our present lives as conscious beings, even if we take it to be our essential objective during this lifetime to surpass, or to escape from, the illusory character of our consciousness. The purpose of such philosophies is precisely to enable us to become conscious of our consciousness, such as it is, whatever it is, in the light of all that which transcends it, at least to the extent of seeking to make our self-consciousness conform to the reality of all that transcends it.

2.16. Those philosophies of human psychology which have stressed the active and decisive role of the unconscious in the working of the conscious levels of consciousness, are themselves products of consciousness reflecting upon itself and ordering its reflections. Indeed, they assert, by example and even by intention, the ordering capacity of reflexive consciousness in relation to that part of consciousness (inappropriately termed *unconscious*) which is not specifically communicable by consciousness to itself or between consciousnesses. They are depth-philosophies of psychology. They assert the capacity of consciousness at least to reach down into the unconscious and to present in a communicable form (words, works of art, or other forms) some part of its unconscious activity, in such a way that the communicable presentation of the uncommunicable can influence conscious action. They even assert that consciousness can thus liberate itself, in some sense, from what they see, strangely, as a self-oppression of consciousness by its own unconscious activity (as if consciousness could be some kind of enemy to itself). And they have recognized that the vast structures of society, let alone the small structures of our daily lives, must proceed on the basis, however self-deceiving, that they can be the arena for the activity not merely of the unconscious mind but also of the conscious self-ordering mind, including its capacity to enlighten itself by some understanding of its unconscious activity.

2.17. Those philosophies of knowledge which have been radically sceptical of all grounds of certainty on which human beings rely so fervently to organize their lives are themselves impressive illustrations of an ordering capacity of reflexive consciousness, even if they assert or imply that the limit of its ordering capacity is the recognizing of its own ultimate and essential disorder. They suggest that consciousness is capable of ordering itself at least to the extent of recognizing the limits of its self-ordering capacity, of recognizing the inherent relativity or the mere probability of its supposed certainties. And they apparently believe also in the capacity of consciousness to share such a recognition with other consciousnesses through communicated words and ideas. And, finally, they apparently believe in the therapeutic effect, for both individual and social consciousness, in recognizing the uncertainty of our certainties. They are philosophies of the uncertainty of philosophy.

2.18. Those anti-philosophies of language which stress the opaque and illusion-filled nature of language as a medium and hence the illusoriness of all the ideas that we express in language, including ideas which purport to be ordered by reason, are themselves expressed in the form of structures of verbalized ideas, structures designed to be stored within consciousness, to be effective as ideas in modifying other ideas, and to be communicated between consciousnesses. They are philosophies of the impossibility of philosophy. They are apparently put forward with a view to modifying the self-conceiving of consciousness, modifying behaviour deriving from such self-conceiving. Apparently, therefore, as with sceptical theories of a general kind, their objective is therapeutic rather than nihilist—not requiring us simply to remain silent on all matters which call for explanation, but enabling us to understand ourselves better, even to enrich our mental experience, by better understanding the nature and the limitations of the linguistic forms in which our consciousness frequently expresses itself.

2.19. Those philosophies of acceptance or resignation or silence in the face of the unalterable unfolding of the universe in which we find ourselves seek to affect the knowing and the choosing and the acting of the humble centre of consciousness which is the human being. Whether they perceive the universe as a realm of all-embracing order or as a realm governed by the ineffable will of a supernatural power or as a mystery hidden behind an impenetrable cloud of unknowing, they assume that their philosophical ideas are not wasted on the human being who takes them as ideas into consciousness. They accept, explicitly or implicitly, that human consciousness is at least capable of transcending itself sufficiently to enable it to formulate and reformulate its ignorance and its impotence in ways which may be communicated between consciousnesses and which may lead to appropriate modifications of ideas and behaviour, individually and socially. They are philosophies of the impotence of philosophy.

2.20. Those philosophies which assert the overwhelming power of social circumstances over the very consciousness of the members of society, and which assert an unfolding of social processes in which individual consciousness is carried along in a social stream of cause and effect, nevertheless do not deny the capacity of consciousness to form an understanding of the processes in which it participates and, indeed, to take a hand in the future development of those processes. Nor do they deny that society is a dynamic process in which human willing and acting are the form in which social energies have their effect. They recognize, and rely on, the role of self-ordering consciousness, individual and social, in the progressive development of society and thereby of all consciousness. In other words, they are not nihilist in relation to the endeavours of human consciousness. Indeed, they are not appropriately described as materialist or determinist. They are philosophies of the sociality of philosophy.

2.21. There remains a seventh form of philosophy which seeks to demonstrate that the very idea of mind or consciousness is an unnecessary fiction, that there is nothing to consider or to explain other than the physical functioning of the physiological phenomenon which is the brain and nervous system or the functioning of a biological organism whose brain-activity is merely one of its forms of behaviour. For such a philosophy, such functioning is to be considered and explained within the forms of study appropriate to physical and physiological and biological phenomena. But consciousness is itself an aspect of the functioning of the physical and physiological and biological phenomenon in question, namely the human brain and nervous system. Consciousness of consciousness—the presentation of the brain to itself as consciousness of the presentation of itself to itself as consciousness—is precisely a fact of the physical functioning of the animal known to itself as a human being. And consciousness presents itself to consciousness precisely as *something other than* merely the physical functioning of the brain and nervous system. And such a mind-denying philosophy is itself conceived in, and addressed to, that self-conceiving consciousness.

2.22. There seems to be no possibility that, in the foreseeable future, a physical explanation of the brain and nervous system or of the whole organism of the human being will be able to fix itself within the brain in such a way as to be able simply to displace the phenomenon of consciousness as the brain's systematic presentation to itself of its own activity. In the meantime, philosophies which question the separate existence of consciousness throw light on the acute problems caused by the fact that the brain, in philosophizing, is doing what it is studying. They are philosophies of the self-transcending of philosophy.

2.23. In summary, it may be said that the long and complex story of consciousness-considering-consciousness implies the following common ground. (1) Human reflective consciousness has recognized in itself a process of self-ordering which calls for an explanation, an explanation which must ultimately imply, if it cannot ever wholly articulate it in words, a general theory of consciousness itself and probably a general theory of the nature of all reality (whether or not the rest of reality is conceived as being ultimately the same in nature as consciousness or different from it). (2) It is also a process which is evidently intended, or expected, to issue forth in action in the conduct of everyday life, including the life of societies. That is to say, reason is liable to affect human willing and acting, to the extent that ideas are involved in any particular human action. (3) The formation of an idea, from words and from other ideas and from other units of consciousness, clearly involves some process which is internal to consciousness and yet which involves consciousness in seeking to transcend itself, allowing consciousness to take itself by its own effort into new states of self-embracing consciousness.

2.24. In the light of all that consciousness has thought about itself in its long efforts at self-understanding, we may propose a hypothetical explanation of self-ordering consciousness, a hypothesis which seeks to identify the *necessary system of reason* as a particular mode of functioning of consciousness. Such a hypothesis should cover not only the reasoning of the mind of the individual human being but also the social aspect of reason, the communal ordering of consciousness in society.

2.25. What seems to be the case is that consciousness orders itself by two related processes, which concern respectively the formation and control of ideas in general (*reasoning*) and the formation and control of large integrated structures of ideas, which will here be called *theories*. The first process is a process which occurs in each individual consciousness but which can be conducted socially, in the sharing of consciousness which is a society. The second process is a process which occurs primarily in the shared consciousness of society, as the consciousnesses of human individuals participate in the communal self-ordering which is a society. They are the means by which society constructs an ever-developing, never-to-be-completed, reality-for-itself, an ideal reality within which it seeks to survive and prosper.

2.26. Reasoning is a process of integration. Reason structures. The integrating of ideas is an integration in relation to three co-ordinates, analogous to the three phases (past, present, future) in which time is presented by consciousness to itself.

(1) Consciousness relates a particular idea to the units of consciousness from which it is derived. This co-ordinate will here be called the *genetic* co-ordinate.

(2) Consciousness relates the idea to other coexisting ideas. This will here be called the *actual* co-ordinate.

(3) Consciousness relates the idea to possibilities, including possible ideas. This will here be called the *potential* co-ordinate.

2.27. The *genetic* co-ordinate of an idea is hypothetically necessary because: (1) an idea does not come fully formed out of nothing. Its constituent elements are an intrinsic part of its effect. Part of its effect is due to a background or context from which it emerges, its genetic material, as it were. Every idea has its origin in other ideas or in other events within consciousness, especially words and their extraordinary accumulated power. A verbalized idea depends on the functioning of words, considered in Chapter 1 above, that is to say on the ability of words to fuse within themselves, and to communicate, units of consciousness abstracted from the general stream of consciousness. A non-verbalized idea and an idea-by-association generally depend on a still denser and more obscure background and context, more intricate genetic material, from which they are generated and as a function of which they have their effect.

2.28. The genetic dimension of an idea is hypothetically necessary also: (2) as a mechanism of analysis. It enables the mind to see the integrated idea not only as a totality but also as an aggregation of its components. It can present the idea's components to itself in their individuality and hence present them to itself in their integration. And, if the components are themselves ideas, it enables the mind to disintegrate their integration, to unravel their components and the components of their components, and so on. And it enables the mind to present to itself the components of the idea, and all its sub-components, in relation to units of consciousness not included in the integrated idea. Every idea is a presence and an absence, the shadow-presence of all that which is not contained in the integrated idea.

2.29. And the genetic dimension of an idea is hypothetically necessary also: (3) as a mechanism of synthesis. An idea is not merely an aggregation; it is a structure. The mind must be able not only to unravel the component ideas and to know the context from which they came, but also to see the way in which the component ideas are brought into relationship with each other in the integrated idea, the programme of the idea's formation.

2.30. The inductive method of science, the analytical processes of mathematics, the deductive processes of logic, the norms of translation from one language to another, the principles of perspective in drawing, the aesthetic conventions of art in general, the registering and reporting of sensations and feelings, the recognition of obligation, the recognition of the certainty which is classed as 'belief'—all these are examples of genetic programmes which affect the judgement of the ideas which they generate. Each such genetic programme not only enables the ideas to be constructed and communicated. It is also a judging or controlling mechanism. We judge ideas not only by their content but also by the process of their formation.

2.31. The *actual* co-ordinate of an idea is hypothetically necessary because ideas, once formed, must come into contact with other ideas stored in consciousness. The mind must have ways of dealing with the interaction between co-existing ideas. What seems to be the case is that the mind has, in particular, a tendency to seek to reduce conflict, incoherence, contradiction, and incompatibility, as it finds them within itself. Having formed an idea within itself, the mind relates it to any number of other ideas, whether or not derived within the same genetic co-ordinate. A sort of anguish or pain or noise accompanies a finding of conflict, incoherence, tension, contradiction, or incompatibility.

2.32. Three qualifying principles seem also to apply, however, to such a tension-reducing process. (1) The first is that the mind cannot, at least at any conscious or near-conscious level, conduct a total search of all other potentially conflicting ideas. No doubt a large part, probably the larger part, of the searching process is conducted at the least conscious levels of the mind, so that it is impossible to know, at the conscious level, how far the searching has gone, especially after its conscious traces have faded away. But it seems to be clearly the case that the anguish or pain or noise caused by conflict in the mind can be the result of a wholly non-conscious finding, so that, in such cases, we *just know* that something is not true, not right, not good, without being able to formulate in words what the conflict is. What are called 'intuition' and 'experience', on which we, as individuals and societies, sometimes rely in making judgements, are thus aspects of a sorting process in the mind which occurs autonomously and more or less beyond our conscious control.

2.33. (2) A second qualifying principle is that the mind seems to be capable of living with a certain degree of conflict among ideas, even when conflict has been found to be present. No doubt, some conflicts cannot be lived with, especially conflicts relating to genetically similar ideas—a belief that God exists and a belief that no God exists; an inductive hypothesis that the physical universe is explicable on Newtonian principles and a hypothesis that it is not wholly so explicable. And even conflicts between genetically different ideas may give rise to too much pain, at least for some people, at least at some times—an idea that human beings are free moral agents, and the hypothesis that every effect in the universe has, in principle, an assignable cause; the hypothesis that the human being is evolved from the higher primates, and the idea that human beings are a special creation of God; the idea that love between human beings is essentially a metaphysical uniting and the idea that love is an epiphenomenon of human physiology.

2.34. (3) A third qualifying principle is that conflict among ideas can be productive. Faced with some incoherence or incompatibility within its contents, the mind may seek neither simply to eliminate the conflict nor simply to tolerate it. Consciousness may seek to surpass it, using the conflicting ideas to generate a new idea which is more than the sum of the conflicting ideas, but which does not simply negate those ideas. In this way, consciousness as a whole can grow absolutely in density and complexity, and not merely by the rearrangement of existing content. In particular, imagination can feed reason with incompatible ideas which are nevertheless fertile sources of further ideas formed by reason.

2.35. In short, therefore, we may say that self-ordering consciousness has a tendency to seek to resolve internal conflict and to seek states of integrated equilibrium within itself, a tendency to tolerate a measure of internal conflict, and a tendency to use internal conflict as a means of self-enriching.

2.36. This endless pattern of conflict and equilibrium leads to the hypothetical necessity of the third co-ordinate, the *potential* co-ordinate. The mind is not a thing or a state but a process. It is a constant stream of states, an endless process, never the same from one moment to the next, throughout the whole course of a human life. It follows that an idea found in the present state of mind is a constantly re-enacted vanishing-point between the genetic material from which the idea in question has come and the incalculable richness of potential states of mind which the imagination could conceive. Every actual idea is a possible component of countless possible ideas. In judging and controlling and ordering its ideas, therefore, consciousness knows that what *is* within the mind *will be* within it, either as a more or less altered presence or as an absence. We may modify or reject or forget an idea. But even if we retain it, apparently unaltered, it changes necessarily in its total effect because its effect is always relative to all the rest of the ever-changing contents of consciousness.

2.37. We know also that our ideas are part of a reality we make for ourselves. They are part of what our consciousness is for us and hence of what all-that-is is for us within our consciousness. In forming our ideas we form our reality. In forming our reality we form our consciousness. In forming our consciousness we form ourselves.

2.38. The ordering of consciousness as potentiality is thus a sort of pragmatic self-control, constantly aware of the possible effects for us of retaining the given idea as a possible cause of effects within us. To adopt a particular religious belief may involve an adjustment of countless other ideas, some of which may appear to be only remotely connected with that belief; for example, it may affect aesthetic ideas or moral ideas or social ideas. To adopt a particular idea about a particular person or a group or class or race of persons may affect every subsequent moment of our thinking and behaving in relation to such persons and other persons. And to fail to adopt a particular belief or idea or attitude, to fail to make the mental effort to resolve some conflict in consciousness, may modify all the possibilities of all our subsequent states of consciousness.

2.39. Conceived in this hypothetical fashion, reason—the self-ordering of consciousness—is thus a process by which consciousness, from the moment when the brain is sufficiently formed to begin ordering its own contents until the moment when the brain ceases to function, unceasingly works on its contents, ordering them in relation to their origin, their coherence and their possibilities. It is a process which is autonomic, spontaneous, natural, inevitable—in the sense that, like our breathing or the beating of our heart, it continues whether or not we present its activity to the conscious level of consciousness. It is a process which can be conducted at any level of consciousness, from the seeming oblivion of the unconscious levels to the most fully conscious levels, including the level of verbalized ideas.

2.40. Reasoning is a process which, if it is hypothetically the self-ordering process of the individual brain, is a also a process which may be conducted by more than one brain, through the communication of ideas from the consciousness of one individual to the consciousness of another individual. And it may be conducted socially through the sharing of ideas among the members of society and through their retention within the reality-for-itself of society. It is a process which must presumably serve a biological function at the level of the individual, at the level of society, and at the level of the species.

2.41. The biological function of the self-ordering of consciousness, like the biological function of words, is presumably connected with the evolutionary history of the human species. Reason has presumably served to get humanity to the situation in which it finds itself as a participant in the total life-system of the planet Earth. A remarkably efficient form of life among other living things. A notably successful animal among successful animals, in terms of multiplication and adaptation to habitat. An exceptionally socialized animal among socialized animals. An exceptionally capable animal among capable animals, especially in the use of other living and non-living resources otherwise than merely for food, and in the use of tools made therefrom. Above all, the human animal, by its amazing development of the capacity to communicate, has been enabled to share consciousness to a significant extent and hence to share the ordering of consciousness. That in turn has meant that humanity had acquired a collective capacity of ordered consciousness which gives it what is presumably a unique status among all communicating animals.

2.42. The great idea-structures of religion, mythology, art, philosophy, history, science, economy, morality, and law are creations of the collective ordering of consciousness. The process within consciousness of integrating ideas within the three co-ordinates of self-ordering has been extended to include any number of other persons and, even more importantly, has been extended indefinitely in time, beyond the life-span of human individuals. To extend the process of consciousness-ordering-consciousness to include the consciousness of indefinitely large numbers of people and over indefinitely long periods of time is to increase immeasurably the potential energy of human consciousness and hence the potential energy of the human species.

2.43. Of all the achievements of the human animal, one of the most remarkable has been the creation of a human reality, beyond the reality of the physical world, beyond the reality of the self-consciousness of each individual human being. That new reality of accumulated social consciousness exists tangibly and intangibly. Its tangible existence is in all the forms in which consciousness is made to endure—language, books, works of art and craft, ceremonies and rituals and signs and symbols, modern electronic media. Its intangible existence is in the human minds within which such phenomena have life and act as the causes of dramatic effects. Social reality is humanity's reality-for-itself. We are what we think.

2.44. The new, social reality created by the self-ordering power of human consciousness is a place where human beings live their lives, a world which, though made entirely out of ideas within consciousness, is so substantial that spatial metaphors seem hardly to be metaphors. The making and using of *words* is, as it were, the *mechanics* of self-ordering consciousness. The making and using of *ideas* is the *engineering* of self-ordering consciousness. The making and using of what will here be called *theories* is the *architecture* of self-ordering consciousness. Theories are the great public buildings, designed by consciousness for humanity's orderly, comfortable, and prosperous living.

2.45. A theory is a structure of ideas designed to serve as the explanation of other ideas in such a way that those other ideas can be regarded as a necessary inference from the theory.

2.46. A theory is a structure of ideas which has a pre-determining effect on the generation of further ideas. A theory is a pre-set programme of operation of the three co-ordinates of rational self-ordering (genetic, actual, potential). The result is that the ideas generated in accordance with the theory give rise to relatively little tension or noise within consciousness. A theory makes theory-conforming ideas seem naturally reliable, naturally coherent, naturally fruitful.

2.47. Theories reflect what is no doubt a further biological feature of consciousness—namely, that consciousness cannot work out its most general structures of ideas again and again, as each life-challenge presents itself, whenever a human being or a society is called upon to will and act. A theory is thus an evolved mechanism of consciousness which enables a human being and a society to generate ideas efficiently after a relatively small amount of preliminary self-ordering activity with a view to willing and acting effectively. Theory optimizes the operation of human reason as a function of human needs. Theory gives to theory-conforming ideas a self-assurance analogous to that of the ideas of intuition and experience.

2.48. It is evident that theories are liable to have very large practical consequences in the life of societies. A society's theories are liable to be seen as part of society's settled structure because they form a major part of society's reality-for-itself, the way it sees its own world and the society-transcending universe of all-that-is. All society's willing and acting, including the willing and acting of and under legal relations, is shaped by society's theories. A society's theories are the atmosphere it breathes.

2.49. Theories are constructed as an interacting of three different kinds of theory, which will be referred to here as *practical theory, pure theory, and transcendental theory. Practical theory* is the set of ideas on the basis of which actions are willed. *Pure theory* is the set of ideas which are used to explain practical theory. *Transcendental theory* is the set of ideas which are used to explain pure theory. They are three *dimensions* of a single process of high-level self-ordering within consciousness.

2.50. The *practical* importance of making the distinctions proposed in paragraph 2.49 is that they are often, normally even, overlooked or obscured, at the cost of great and unnecessary confusion and conflict, suffering, and misery. In relations between human beings and in relations between societies, especially relations between so-called *states*, much has flowed, including blood and tears, from the asserting and the defending of practical theories (say, about practical steps to promote human survival and prospering) which seemed to involve a conflict of pure theory (say, about the nature of society or the purpose of human life) and which have seemed sometimes even to involve a conflict of transcendantal theory (say, as to the social formation of ideas or the status of the ideas of religion or science).

2.51. The *hypothetical* significance of distinguishing among different kinds of theory is that, to understand the self-creating of societies, that is, to establish a pure theory of society such as that proposed in the present volume, it is necessary to understand the genesis and the function of the different kinds of theory.

2.52. *Practical theory is the theory of willed action.* It is the explanation of willed action which the actor would use if the actor had the capacity to articulate at the fully verbalized level the theory of that willing. It integrates such willing with alternative choices which might be made in accordance with the same practical theory and it integrates choices which might not be so made and which, if they were to be explained in terms of practical theory, would involve a modification of practical theory. Practical theory tends to prove itself in action, tends to develop dialectically by interaction with its own implementation. It is not necessary that all actions taken on the basis of practical theory should explicitly be explained or even be justified or justifiable by reference to the content of the theory. Its function is both more formal and more utilitarian.

(1) The practical theory is available to provide a common point of reference in debates as to its implementation, including debates in political and judicial forums (*practical theory as shared ideology*).

(2) The practical theory may be relied on by actors in society when they need to present to themselves the *justification* for the actual arrangements of society and for their action in society (*practical theory as legitimation*).

(3) The practical theory also provides a basis for *explaining* what happens in a society, when that explanation is sought by an outsider or by an insider seeking to *understand* the society rather than to *act* in the society (*practical theory as pure-theory hypothesis*).

2.53. *Pure theory is the theory of practical theory.* This does not mean that any particular practical theory is the only possible inference from a given pure theory. On the contrary, a pure theory is liable to be capable of generating a variety of practical theories. What it does mean is that the given pure theory is available as an explanation and justification of the practical theory and hence, indirectly, of social arrangements made, and actions taken, on the basis of the practical theory. The function of pure theory is, again, both formal and utilitarian.

(1) The pure theory is available to provide a point of reference in debates as to the content or meaning or implications of the practical theory (*pure theory as shared philosophy*).

(2) The pure theory may be relied on by actors when they need to present to themselves the *justification* for the practical theory, thereby reinforcing the justification of the arrangements of society and actions taken in society (*pure theory as legitimation*).

(3) The pure theory also provides a basis for *explaining* the practical theory, when that explanation is sought by an outsider or by an insider seeking to *understand* the society rather than to *act* in the society (*pure theory as pure-theory hypothesis*).

2.54. *Transcendental theory is the theory of theory.* It answers the question: what set of ideas would make possible a set of ideas explaining other ideas? Just as practical theory bridges the gap between human willing and human action, so transcendental theory bridges the gap between particular ideas or structures of ideas and the nature of consciousness itself. Transcendental theory is, as it were, the genetic co-ordinate of both practical and pure theories, reason functioning meta-rationally. It is in this sense that transcendental theory is focused on the genetic dimension of the ordering of consciousness. It is concerned with the way in which ideas are formed from ideas and become part of the great idea-structures of theory. It is apparent that it would, in principle, be possible to have a transcendental theory explaining all practical and pure theories. It remains open to question whether there could, in principle, be a meta-transcendental theory of all theory, explaining all practical and pure and transcendental theories, including itself. The presumption is that there could not be such a theory of all theories, at least at the present stage of the evolutionary development of human consciousness, since consciousness apparently cannot, as at present constituted, get outside itself and express itself in something which is not consciousness.

2.55. The function of transcendental theory within society is, as in the cases of the other dimensions of theory, both formal and utilitarian.

(1) The transcendental theory is available to provide a point of reference in debates as to the validity, and hence as to the content and meaning and implications, of the practical and pure theories (*transcendental theory as shared epistemology*).

(2) The transcendental theory may be relied on by actors when they need to present to themselves the *justification* for their acceptance of the practical and pure theories, thereby reinforcing the justification of the arrangements of society and actions in society (*transcendental theory as legitimation*).

(3) The transcendental theory also provides a basis for *explaining* the practical and pure theories, when that explanation is sought by an outsider or by an insider seeking to *understand* the society rather than to *act* in the society (*transcendental theory as pure-theory hypothesis*).

2.56. The following two diagrams illustrate the relationship of the different dimensions of theory.

WILLED ACTION	PRACTICAL THEORY	PURE THEORY	TRANSCENDENTAL THEORY
Religion (observance)	Religion (doctrine, ethics)	Metaphysics (theology etc.)	Bases of belief or enlightenment
Artistic activity	Principles of technique, style	Aesthetics physiology, psychology	Philosophy of judgement
Legislation adjudication, exercise of legal powers	Constitutional theory, legal theory	Philosophy of society	Philosophy of obligation
Scientific research, technology	Principles of respective branches of science	Philosophy of empirico-hypothetical science	Philosophy of knowledge

Fig. 1. The theoretical dimensions of certain kinds of action

PRACTICAL	PURE	TRANSCENDENTAL
Liberal democracy	Social contract, idealism, natural law, utilitarianism	Logical and ethical rationalism
Communism	Historical determinism, materialism, socialism	Logical and ethical rationalism
Common-law	Constitutionalism, theory of adjudication	Logical and ethical rationalism

(The world *rationalism* is used here to refer to a belief in the possibility of orderly activity within shared consciousness using the capacity here considered under the name of *reason*.)

Fig. 2. The theoretical dimensions of certain particular theories

2.57. Seven aspects of such a theory of theory should be noted. (1) Such a hypothesis places theory as an intermediary between consciousness and action. Before and after theory, there is willed action. Before and after theory, there is consciousness.

There is, in particular, the imagination and reason from which all ideas, including theories, derive. So it is that all theories depend ultimately on some transcendental theory, articulated or unarticulated, explaining the working of consciousness (mind) itself.

2.58. (2) The three dimensions of theory are mutually inter-dependent. They are not in a simple hierarchical relationship. None is theoretically prior to any other. They mutually sustain and reinforce each other, hypothetically and practically. For example, the ritual requirements of a given religion may sustain the idea of doctrinal authority (say, the magical powers of a priesthood extending to the speaking of truth as well as to the doing of sacred actions) or they may sustain the idea of belief (say, the rote-learning of sacred texts or catechisms of belief being both a ritual action and the achieving of a form of knowledge-bearing enlightenment). Or, as a further example, the pure theory of liberal democracy or of communism may have the effect of causing participants in the system to see and judge the working actuality of the system as containing the very phenomena which the practical theory seeks to promote (say, the consent of the governed or the absence of class-oppression).

2.59. (3) A given practical theory may generate a wide variety of possible courses of willed action which may be regarded as required by it, as being in conformity with it, as being explicable or justifiable in accordance with it. For example, the everyday political life of a liberal democracy is supposedly organized, in accordance with the practical theory of liberal democracy, to provide as open a debate as possible about such matters. The practical theory conditions the debate; it does not make inevitable any particular outcome of the debate.

2.60. (4) Similarly, the inference from pure theory to practical theory, and vice versa, and the inference from transcendental theory to pure theory, and vice versa, is not unequivocal and necessary. A given theory is capable of supporting a wide range of possible inferential theories. In particular, a given practical theory may be supported by a number of different and overlapping pure theories. It seems that it is not necessary to reach agreement on the 'true' theory of a given practical theory. However there may be pressures of a practical kind within a particular society to establish an orthodoxy on such matters and to discourage dissent on matters even of pure theory (through education, the criminal law, censorship, exile, ostracism, witch-trials, inquisitions, killing of heretics and dissenters).

2.61. (5) A society's theories may well be shared with other societies. In the case of *transcendental* theory, this is liable to be the case, since transcendental theory comes close to an explanation of the functioning of a major aspect of consciousness (its capacity to order itself), and consciousness is evidently, at least seen at some level of generality, a common possession of members of all societies. However, insofar as a given society accommodates different religions (say, Hinduism and Buddhism), it may accommodate different theories as to the nature and functioning of consciousness, even if, for practical social purposes, it must presumably operate on the basis of a shared hypothetical theory of those aspects of consciousness which affect action in society.

2.62. (6) In the case of *pure theory*, it is more likely than not that a society's pure theory will be shared with some other societies, since a pure theory will precisely seek to transcend actual and practical social arrangements in terms of something which is above and beyond those arrangements, to give to a particular society a non-contingent, virtually supernatural, basis for its existence and its institutions. For example, it could be shown that liberal democracy and communism not only rely on a shared transcendental theory of rationalism but also share significant elements of pure theory. The reasons for this are to be found in the historical development of the theoretical ideas from which both are derived. By identifying the different theoretical dimensions of liberal democracy and communism (and any other social theory), it is possible to determine rather precisely the area of disagreement between them—an area of disagreement which would be found to be substantially different from that presented through the willed action (public decision-making, political dialogue) of those relying on the one practical theory or the other.

2.63. (7) The pure theory of a given society may tend to be exclusive and particularist in nature if it postulates the membership of the very society as an instance of the society's pure theory—for example, if the society is based on a concept of race, ethnicity, cultural specificity, religious specificity. The characteristic example is to be found in certain forms of theocracy, where the formation and the identity of the society is seen as the direct work of a god or gods or other supernatural powers or events. Other forms of theocracy, especially those based on a non-exclusive universalist religion, do not have this effect. The religion-based pure theory is, in those cases, available to be used to explain and justify the practical theories and social arrangements of any number of societies.

2.64. Societies live within the theories they make. A society generates a theory-filled reality which shapes its willed action which, in turn, shapes its actual everyday living. In the remainder of Part One, it will be considered how this endlessly self-sustaining social cycle allows a society to create itself as it socializes itself, to socialize itself as it creates itself.

3 Society Self-creating

3.1. *A society is not a thing but a process. Any society—from the society of a family to the society of the whole human race—is a process of continuous self-creating.*

3.2. We are born into societies. The first consequence of this fact is that we do not choose the societies we are born into. The second consequence is that we cannot know what we would have been, had we been born into other societies. The third consequence is that we enter at once into a relationship of mutual interaction with societies, an interaction which we do not leave until we die. The fourth consequence is that our participation in every other society is conditioned by our participation in the societies into which we are born.

3.3. Our interaction with a society to which we belong is mutual in the sense that we form the society as it forms us. The shared consciousness of the society is modified by our sharing in that consciousness. Our individual consciousness is modified by participating in the shared consciousness of society. As we learn *words*, we learn the way in which reality is presented to the shared consciousness of the society whose language we learn. The dual effect of socially formed words, considered in Chapter 1, begins to affect us. By one and the same process, our capacity to communicate expands as the social constraints on our imagination increase. As we begin to learn socially-formed *ideas*, we become subject to the dual effect of ideas, considered in Chapter 2. We begin to submit ourselves to the social ordering of consciousness which has occurred before we became a member of the society and which is contained in the very fabric of the society when we become a member. And, at the same time and by the same process, we begin to acquire the capacity to participate in the further development of society's ideas.

3.4. The process of education, which we undergo in each society to which we belong, transforms us into the persons needed by that society. By education we are socialized, civilized, citizenized. We are enabled to share in the reality which society has made for itself, especially the reality-forming theories of the kinds considered in Chapter 2. And, at the same time and by the same process, we become able to participate in all of society's reality-forming.

3.5. Education aims to produce people who are both submissive and creative. In order to provide for the continuing of the process of society's self-creating, the members of society must share in that society's reality, must make it their own; and they must learn its possibilities, must make its aspirations their own; and they must be trained to use their natural power, and to share in society's power, to take socially useful action. By education society takes power over our consciousness. By education we take power over society's power. Knowledge takes power over consciousness. Consciousness takes power over knowledge.

3.6. From the earliest moments of our life until the moment of our death, we live the equivocal nature of our individual existence, as cause and effect, subject and object, creator and created, free agent and servant of our servant, that is to say, of society.

3.7. So it is that the existence of every individual modifies every society to which that individual belongs. In this sense at least, every individual is immortal. The universe is altered for all time by the existence and the acting of every human individual. To exist as a human being is to change the world as a human being.

3.8. As much would be true of human beings as sets of electromagnetic events. Every physical event is an alteration in the state of the universe. But, in the case of human beings, to change the world is to choose to change the world. Consciousness enables us to present possibilities to ourselves before we take action. Before the future becomes actual in the world of physical reality, it may be present in the reality-made-by-consciousness as a possibility. For physical reality the future is a mirror reflecting the past. For physical reality there is nothing in the future which was not in the past, even if the route from the past to the future may pass through events which can only be conceived within consciousness in probabilistic terms. However, for the reality-made-by-consciousness the past and the future are equally present. The history of a society is its future only to the extent that it is its present. The future is the set of possibilities created by consciousness out of past states of consciousness, any one of which has a presently-existing potentiality to become actual. The imagining and ordering capacities of consciousness can create things which the physical universe could not create by the process of physical causation. In the reality-made-by-consciousness, consciousness can make the possible actual by choosing and then acting. We not only alter the state of the universe by existing; we can *choose* the future of the universe. *To live is to choose the future. To exist as a human being is to choose to change the world.*

3.9. Human beings thus intrude into the causation of the physical world. They act as causes within the reality-made-by-consciousness and they act as transcendental causes within the physical world, as the causes of causes. Such is the substance of social life. Social life is the communal creating of a reality-made-by-consciousness and the communal organizing of human causation.

3.10. In order to organize human causation, consciousness has had to create a conception of the operation of human causation. It has had to create ideas not only to express the ultimate structure of the physical universe but also to recreate hypothetically within consciousness the ultimate structure of the world of consciousness. And it has done so by means of ideas which correspond to the ideas which it uses to explain *change* in the physical world. The becoming of consciousness and the becoming of non-consciousness are reconstructed side-by-side within reality-made-by-consciousness.

3.11. *Desire* and *obligation* are the counterparts within the reality-made-by-consciousness of the *impulse of life* and *necessity* which consciousness conceives as the determinants of the action of living things in the physical world, including the action of the human body acting as a living thing in the physical world. *Will* and *action* are the counterparts within the reality-made-by-consciousness of the *cause* and *effect* which consciousness conceives as the contents of change in the physical world, which constitute the becoming of things, including the becoming of the human body as a thing in the physical world.

3.12. The term *impulse of life* is used here, in a special usage, to refer to the way in which living things behave specifically as living things, using a specific form of potential energy contained within a specific kind of systematic structure. The distinction between animate and inanimate things lies in this characteristic, that the living thing uses the potential energy of life stored within it as a cause of its own future. The application of such energy is not the sole cause of its future. It is subject to the effects of many other causes which determine its future (climate, terrain, environment, other co-operating and competing living things). But, to whatever degree it may be affected by other causes, its internal sub-systems continue to generate events which are specifically connected with its own individual future as a system. Such events focus and direct and apply the energy of life into physical impulses of various kinds, instinctive and reflexive and electrochemical impulses. In animals and plants which reproduce sexually, the sexual drive is an instance of such an impulse. Each plant and each animal, every living organism of whatever degree of simplicity or complexity, is thus able to transform its surroundings in ways which contribute to the survival and development, including the reproduction, of that particular organism as a system and of that particular species of organism as a system of organic systems.

3.13. Consciousness, having formed the idea of *impulse of life*, to recreate within consciousness the application by living organisms to the physical world of the potential energy of life, then conceives of itself as a living organism within the physical world, but a living organism which has consciousness, a living organism which can not only apply the energy of life to its survival and development, but can present that process to itself in consciousness. It translates the idea of physical impulse into the idea of *desire*, the form which the impulse of life takes within the reality-made-by-consciousness. So the word *desire* is used to express a corresponding impulse within human consciousness, an impulse which allows and impels a human being to act as a cause of its own future, transforming its world in ways which contribute to its survival and development and to the survival and development of the human species. Through desire a human being chooses a future. By desire a human being draws itself into its chosen future.

3.14. The word *necessity* is used to refer to the idea, formed within consciousness, that all things in the physical world, including animate things, are held within the grip of the order of the whole universe. No thing which is part of the physical universe can escape the systematic functioning of the whole universe. Human consciousness may yet surpass its present ideas of the order of the physical universe, especially the ideas which it has formed of that order in religion, mythology, the natural sciences, and mathematics. It may find itself able to form another idea of the totality of the physical universe. It may yet surpass the tendency in its ideas to isolate the physical universe, for the purposes of investigation and understanding, from consciousness itself and from some putative non-physical universe. But, for the time being at least, the integrating function of reason, considered in Chapter 2, has generated the fundamental idea of an interconnecting structure-system of the whole physical universe, the interconnecting of all physical events with each other.

3.15. *Necessity* is an idea which expresses the controlling effect of that hypothetical universal structure-system. It is the idea of *necessity* which expresses the phenomenon that, among all the many conceivable futures of the physical universe, that future happens which, because it happens, was the only possible future. It was the only possible future, always on the assumption that everything is connected in and through the structure-system of the universe. The planet, which might have followed another course, is held by the sun, and it could not have been otherwise. The tree, which otherwise might have lived, is destroyed by the wind, and it could not have been otherwise. The animal which would otherwise have killed prey is itself killed as prey—and it could not have been otherwise. *Necessity, in the physical world, is necessary after the event.* The possibility which becomes actual is the only possibility. The possible event which becomes actual is the necessary event. All else that seemed possible has become impossible. After the event, all the countless other possibilities have been excluded by necessity. After the event, there could only have been the event. The possible becomes inevitable; what was otherwise conceivable becomes impossible. It is the function of the natural sciences to enable consciousness to foresee physical necessity before the event.

3.16. Having conceived of the *necessity* of the physical universe, consciousness conceives of itself as part of the physical universe and, as such, held in the grip of the necessity of universal order. The human body will grow to maturity and decay and die. Every physical world made by human beings will be a world permitted and governed by universal necessity. But consciousness conceives of itself not only as the consciousness of a part of the physical universe but also as the consciousness of a physical thing which is possessed of consciousness, able to present to consciousness the unlimited number of possibilities which its future might contain, and able to choose among those possibilities, under the impulsion of *desire.* Within that reality-made-by-consciousness, the idea of *necessity* is translated into the idea of *obligation. Obligation is necessity before the event, when that event is an event within consciousness.*

3.17. Obligation is the necessity which consciousness makes for itself, from within itself, to enable it to act as a system. It reconciles four considerations. (1) Consciousness has the capacity through imagination and reason to conceive of unlimited possibilities within the reality-made-by-consciousness, going far beyond those available in the physical world ruled by necessity. Consciousness can create something from nothing.

Consciousness can dream. Consciousness can cause things to happen which would not otherwise happen. (2) Yet consciousness is an aspect of the functioning of physical structures (the brain and nervous system) which are part of the physical world. (3) And yet the *necessity* of the physical world does not extend to the world of consciousness. In the world of consciousness, consciousness can set aside the laws of physics, set aside the constraining framework of time and space. (4) And yet necessity in the physical world, as conceived by consciousness itself, is that which enables the physical world to act as an interconnected system. Necessity gives rise to order, resisting order's tendency to decline into disorder. If the physical world acts as a system, it is due to necessity. If the physical world is governed by necessity, it can act as a system.

3.18. So consciousness recognizes obligation as a constraint on its creative capacity, as that capacity creates possibilities. It is a constraint which, like necessity in the physical world, enables it to function as a system. *Obligation is the integrating constraint of the totality of consciousness, designed to enable consciousness as a total system to function as a system.* Obligation reminds choosing consciousness of what is necessary, if it is to survive as an integrated system. Just as necessity in the physical world determines that the possibility which becomes actual is the only possibility consistent with the universe-as-system, so obligation in the world of consciousness excludes possibilities from the possibilities which consciousness may make actual through its choosing, if consciousness is to act as a system within the human system. Like necessity also, obligation connects an individual event with the totality of the system. Not knowing *the totality of the physical universe*, we cannot know *necessity* other than hypothetically, finding its traces within the choices which it makes between those conceivable events which turn out to be possible and those events which are not the possible event, the non-possible events. Not being able to be conscious of *the totality of consciousness*, we cannot know *obligation* other than hypothetically, as the forming pattern of our choosing. Obligation, like necessity, is the hypothetical pattern of all constraints on our possibilities.

3.19. Desire is the necessary structural category of a *living* system with consciousness. Obligation is the necessary structural category of a living *system* with consciousness. Desire and obligation together are the ultimate structural categories of the human being as a *living system with consciousness*, that is to say, of the human being as a self-creating structure-system. All living things, including human beings, act within the physical world on impulse within the structure of necessity. Human beings, within the reality-made-by-consciousness, act on desire within the structure of obligation.

3.20. *Cause* and *effect* are ideas formed by consciousness in its effort to understand *change* in the physical world. To the eye of consciousness, the physical world seems to be a never-ending process of *becoming*, one state of affairs emerging from another. The relationship between related states of affairs is conceived as a relationship of cause and effect. The relationship is one of the most difficult for consciousness to explain to itself, even as hypothesis, since it requires the brain to present to itself in consciousness its own ultimate systematic functioning. In default of any better explanation, it seems that an explanation of the relationship must at least contain the idea that one state of affairs (the effect) is potentially contained within the interacting of two other states of affairs (the state of affairs on which the cause acts and the state of affairs which is conceived as being the cause).

3.21. It may be that consciousness will eventually surpass such conceptions of change, of cause and effect. But, for the time being, they are ideas emerging from the work of imagination and reason, integrated within the co-ordinates of reason (genetic, actual, and potential) discussed in Chapter 2. This is to say: they have been formed by a particular process of interaction with the physical world (especially, observation through the physiological systems known as senses); they cohere with countless other related ideas (especially the ideas of classical mechanics); they enable consciousness to act in the physical world as if they were, indeed, features of the physical world. They reconcile the otherwise formless becoming of the universe with what consciousness conceives to be the necessity of the integrated systematic order of the universe. Cause and effect are the necessity of the universe actualizing itself in particular events.

3.22. For the purposes of explaining itself to itself, consciousness has conceived itself also as containing change. For consciousness, consciousness is also a becoming. And it has conceived itself as having a capacity to act as cause within the reality-made-by-consciousness, and to act as a transcendental cause in the physical world, a cause of causes. It has conceived this capacity as being a capacity to *choose action* by a so-called *act of will*. Will and action in the reality-made-by-consciousness correspond to cause and effect in the physical world. Will is to cause as action is to effect.

3.23. Will is the process within consciousness by which the energy of the human being is focused with a view to action. It is desire which has been processed within consciousness with a view to action. All and any of the contents of consciousness are liable to intervene in the formation of the will. In particular, the will is affected by the processes of both individual and social consciousness in the course of their mutual interaction. The act of will is both an individual and a social act.

3.24. Similarly, the action which follows from willing is individual and social, both because it is affected by events within both individual and social consciousness and because the action of an individual or of more than one individual or of a society affects other individuals and groups and societies. The action can take an infinite variety of forms—from a kiss or a curse to the planting of seed or the bombing of a city. When the action is taken, it not only alters the physical world. It re-enters consciousness to join in the processes within conciousness, including the processes through which further willing and action occur.

3.25. It is interesting to speculate, but difficult to speculate usefully, on the question whether such a conceptual approach by consciousness to the explanation of the actualization of necessity in the becoming of the physical world (and the actualization of impulse and necessity in the physical world of living things) came before or after its corresponding conceptual approach to the explanation of the actualization of desire and obligation in the becoming of the world of consciousness. In other words, did *cause and effect* in the physical world suggest *will and action* in the world of consciousness, or vice versa?

3.26. The relationship of these various ideas may be tabulated as follows:

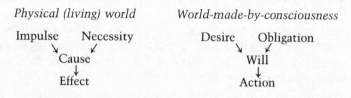

Fig. 3 The active principles of the physical world and the world of consciousness

3.27. To mediate between ideas and action, consciousness uses the idea of *value*. A value is an idea which serves as a ground for choosing between possibilities. As an idea, its formation is subject to the three integrating co-ordinates of reason considered in Chapter 2—the genetic, the actual, and the potential. It is liable to be judged in terms of its origin, its coherence, and its consequences. As a ground for choosing, it is an inference from and to society's theories, also considered in Chapter 2. In other words, society's values are integrated into idea-structures which extend up to explanations of the ultimate nature of the universe and of consciousness.

3.28. A value enables consciousness to move from desire and obligation to will and action in conformity with the rest of consciousness. By being so integrated, the move is explained and justified. In this way, a particular act of willing can be made to conform with the *necessity* of the physical world (as conceived within society's theories as to the nature and functioning of the physical universe) and with the *obligation* of the world-of-consciousness (as conceived within society's theories as to the nature and functioning of individual and social consciousness). By this means, society is able to organize the action of all consciousness in pursuit of the biological function of the living organism in both its capacities, as a system within the physical world and as a system within the world of consciousness.

3.29. Desire and obligation and will and action are *hypothetical categories of consciousness*. They are not themselves substantive values. They are transcendental in relation to all substantive values, just as impulse and necessity and cause and effect are transcendental in relation to the substance of the physical world. In other words, even if they are not themselves substantive values, they are not empty categories. Given their biological function as the expression of the integrating totality of consciousness as a system, they affect the formation of every value. Every value is, therefore, contingent, in relation to the structural categories of consciousness and in relation to the possibilities of its substantive content.

3.30. Values are expressed in different grammatical forms—as adjectives, adverbs, and nouns: good, well, the good; just, justly, justice; useful, usefully, utility; free, freely, freedom. The availability of these different grammatical forms suggests that the underlying value is something which is only reflected in such words. They do not contain it, still less embody it. Each value is a hypothetical resultant from the whole process of consciousness which gives rise to the words in question, each word being a unit of consciousness, in the sense considered in Chapter 1, each word being capable of forming part of an infinite number of ideas and of the great structures of ideas which have been called theories in Chapter 2.

3.31. When we speak of *the good*, for example, we are using not merely words, not merely ideas-by-association (the good things to which we have heard the words applied). We are making use of a residue, a distillation from a particular activity of consciousness as it operates under the impulsion of desire and within the constraint of obligation. We can only explain a value in tentative and approximate terms, precisely because a value necessarily surpasses our capacity to express it in words. It is so much more complex than anything we can say, its complexity being ultimately that of consciousness as a total system. In such tentative and approximate terms, we can say that, in speaking of *the good*, we are speaking of something which has a relatively high probability of generating a will to action, of something which more or less balances desire and obligation. But that probability has to be set against the probabilities attaching to countless other things—our physiological impulses as living organisms (which may lead us to action which is not good), competing values (of utility, comfort, generosity, antipathy, and so on), and the imperfections of the processes within our consciousness, including failings of imagination and reason.

3.32. Value-words are thus the occurrence at the most conscious level of consciousness (consciousness verbalized, normally with a view to possible communication with other consciousnesses) of events which are connected with countless other events at all levels of consciousness, all the events in question being products of consciousness working as a totality on the task of will and action. The existence of particular value-words reflects the long experience of consciousness in dealing with that problem, an experience accumulated not merely during one human lifetime but during the long history of the shared consciousness of the human race. Particular value-words reflect the distinctions which that human experience has found to be necessary and useful for the survival and development of human consciousness as a system. As products of consciousness, those distinctions, and the corresponding values and value-words, are produced under the impulse of desire and within the constraint of obligation. Values integrate consciousness with a view to willed action.

3.33. The relationship of value to action may be tabulated as follows.

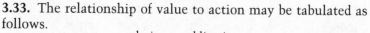
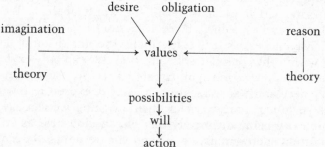

Fig. 4. Value and the generation of action

(There might be added to this figure lines connecting *action* with *theory* and *will*, to indicate the reciprocal effect which action has, as theories and values and acts of willing and action are modified in the light of information fed back into consciousness about the effects of possibilities actualized through action.)

3.34. The self-creating of a society is a multiple dialectic of exponential complexity. (1) A society interacts with itself in all of its socially organized becoming. In organizing its becoming, society not only generates the reality-made-by-consciousness but also generates the values which, within that reality, enable the movement from desire and obligation to will and action. Such an organizing is, in social consciousness as in individual consciousness, an endless cycle of interaction, every aspect interacting with every other, modifying every other, all of them interacting with the rest of reality-made-by-consciousness, including all the words and ideas and theories and values of the given society.

3.35. (2) And the total social process of a given society interacts with the world-beyond-consciousness, the physical world of non-human causation (through physical action willed by consciousness and through the action of the physical world on consciousness). The becoming of society-in-consciousness and the becoming of society-in-the-physical-world co-determine each other.

3.36. (3) And the self-creating of the given society interacts with the self-creating of other societies outside itself, other societies to which it belongs as a member and in whose self-creating it participates, and other societies of which it is not a member and whose willing and acting as societies, and the willing and acting of whose members, affect the becoming of the given society, including the forming of its reality-for-itself.

3.37. (4) And the self-creating of the given society interacts with the self-creating of the societies which it contains within itself, its subordinate societies. All the overlapping societies to which its members belong are creating themselves as they participate in the creating of the societies to which they themselves belong: the family, the tribe, the clan, the school, the university, the sports club, the social club, the commercial or industrial company, the public enterprise, the professional or trade association, the political party, the government department, the executive branch of government, the legislature, the courts, the church, the regiment, the nation-state, the inter-governmental organization, the non-governmental international organization or association, the multinational company or group, the state-trading enterprise, the international commercial market-place, international society.

3.38. (5) And the becoming of the given society interacts with the becoming of the individual human beings who are among its members, as they form their own realities-for-themselves within the reality-forming of the given society, as they participate in the self-creating of the societies to which they belong, including the given society.

3.39. (6) And these five forms of interacting interact with each other.

3.40. So it is that the process of social self-creating is as energetic and complex and dense and continuous as the process of life itself. Society is a self-creating structure-system for the socializing of desire and obligation and will and action through the mediation of value. And all such self-creating is the work of consciousness, using imagination and reason to generate society's self-creating words and ideas and theories and values. And all such self-creating is a struggle, as society struggles with all that it is and all that it is not and all that it could be.

4 Society Socializing I: Dilemmas of Identity and Power

4.1. Society is struggle. Every society is on its way to becoming what it could be, what it will be. Every society, from the society of the family to the international society of the whole human race, is a socializing.

4.2. Consideration of self-creating social consciousness in Chapters 1, 2, and 3 has already made clear that the human condition is rooted in duality. In the first place, consciousness conceives itself as present in the human body, a physical object among physical objects, a set of electromagnetic events within a material world of electromagnetic events, a set of biochemical systems within an organic world of biochemical systems. But consciousness also conceives itself as not being simply a slave of the body, and conceives the body as not being simply a slave of consciousness. Each seems to have its own life, its own story. And yet they are fated to live their lives together. Each is a system of the other's system. But, in conceiving of their participation in each other, consciousness, by the same act, separates them.

4.3. Secondly, consciousness conceives of its reality-for-itself as distinct from the reality of the physical world. The reality-made-by-consciousness is a reality formed through the contact of consciousness with a reality conceived by consciousness but not made by consciousness, the reality of the physical universe to which the human body belongs. And yet reality-made-by-consciousness and physical reality are, from the point of view of consciousness, intrinsically different realities—one a world of necessity and causation, the other a world of the possible and of human responsibility for the actualization of the possible through willing and acting. Reality-made-by-consciousness is not simply carried on the stream of physical reality, nor vice versa. They are two mirrors reflecting a hypothetically single universe, but mirrors set at an angle to each other.

4.4. Thirdly, the human being is evidently an animal among animals, a living organism among living organisms. And the human being is evidently not the only animal which conceives of the world in consciousness before it acts as part of the world. The human being is evidently not the only animal with a reality-for-itself. And yet a difference of degree has come to seem to be a difference in kind. Human consciousness, and especially the exceptionally efficient sharing and storing of consciousness through communication, has allowed human consciousness to develop in complexity to a point which detaches the human being, within the conceiving of its own consciousness, from the rest of the living world. But it is a semi-detachment. The human being, in its behaving as well as in its self-conceiving, never allows itself to forget for long that it is the human animal.

4.5. Fourthly, each human being is alone and not alone. We are born in company and we die alone. We live alone with our own consciousness, our own private life-story, and yet we cannot live without other human beings, to whom we owe our life and with whom we must share not only our labour but also our consciousness. We live alone in the company of society.

4.6. Fifthly, human beings, half-natural and half-supernatural, are able to conceive themselves as being in a middle state between inanimate matter and a universe of all-that-is which contains both matter and consciousness. They are able to conceive of a universe which is not simply made by consciousness but which contains consciousness. And that conceiving can take more specific forms in religion and mythology and philosophy, as they conceive of a supernatural order of non-contingent being, neither merely physical nor merely conscious, neither merely rational nor merely random, an order of god or gods or other superhuman powers and personalities, an order of the ultimate, unfathomable but significant, superhuman reality of all-that-is.

4.7. It is as if an ingenious and inquisitive Creator had chosen to conduct an experiment in one small corner of the universe—an experiment in which a piece of matter would be given a certain measure of control over its changing states, a living organism would be given a special kind of choice over its own life. But two possibilities of control and choice would be withheld—the possibility of simply submitting entirely to the necessary order·of the physical universe and the possibility of acting entirely independently of the necessary order of the physical universe. The human experimental subject would be allowed to be both matter and consciousness, but would be prohibited from being only matter or consciousness. And one possibility of knowledge would be withheld—the possibility of knowing the reality of reality, the reality of the reality which contains within it both matter and consciousness. The human experiment is an interesting and tantalizing destiny.

4.8. All the grandeurs and all the miseries of human history, and all the small struggles of everyday life, stem from the ambiguous duality of the human condition, a duality which is not quite a duality. Human beings can behave as matter and as animals; and they can behave as earth-born gods. Human beings can treat each other as matter and as animals; and they can treat each other as creatures of unique and priceless value. Human beings can find wonder and delight in the physical universe, a source of inexhaustible physical power; and they can find danger and disease and terror and pain and death. Human beings can use the wonderfully energetic impulse of physical life to form and inspire their desire, in love and generosity and creative activity; and they can use it to pervert and distort their desire into aggression and destruction and indignity. Human beings can find unlimited opportunities for self-fulfilment and self-giving in society; and they can find unlimited opportunities for selfishness and cruelty and oppression.

4.9. Social life is a perpetual struggle with the obscure duality of the human condition. Human beings live the human condition in society. In social life we find the human condition not only as a theoretical hypothesis but as actuality, as lived life. In every word and idea and theory and value, in all willing and in every action, humanity lives the duality of the human condition. In the history of the actual social life of the societies whose histories are known to us, there is humanity's accumulated experience of the duality of the human condition.

4.10. It is possible to present the whole of human social experience hypothetically as a series of dilemmas in which the ambiguous duality of the human condition is lived socially. Such dilemmas are more than mere lived duality. They are proposed as the patterns of the pattern of all social becoming. They are the form in which societies become the particular societies that they become. They are the system of all the systems of socializing. The five perennial dilemmas of human society may be called—the self and the other; the one and the many; unity of nature, plurality of value; justice and social justice; new citizens, old laws.

4.11. The word *dilemma* is here used to refer to a situation in which consciousness is presented with possibilities which are seemingly in conflict, contradictory, incompatible, irreconcilable, and which cannot finally be resolved or eliminated, but which can never be evaded.

4.12. The hypothesis of the perennial dilemmas of society is intended to discover in the apparently amorphous dialectic of social life a regular and symmetrical and systematic pattern shaping the whole course of accumulated human social experience. The contention is that in their simplicity, their ubiquity, and their perenniality they are the social manifestation of the ultimate creativity of the human condition.

4.13. The hypothesis is thus the following: All human societies, from the society of the family to the international society of the whole human race, are a process of socializing, conducted within the reality formed by social consciousness. And, within that reality, the social process is a struggle. And that struggle is a struggle dictated by the ultimate nature of the human condition manifested in a set of creative dilemmas.

DILEMMA 1: *THE SELF AND THE OTHER*

4.14. The dilemma of the self and the other is the dilemma of identity. We are what we are not. We make our identity in relation to all that which is not us. It is apparent from what has been said above that, to the extent that our identity is a matter of our consciousness, its boundaries are neither clear nor fixed. Our consciousness flows into and out from the consciousness of the societies to which we belong, and the boundaries of our personal identity are affected to a similar extent. The extent of this effect is obviously greater even than the effect of the participation of our bodies, including brain and nervous system, in the physical world. Our bodies are continuous with the physical world and, for us to have life and to continue to have life, we depend on the flow of the physical world into and out from us. But we define our physical identity systematically. As with other material objects in the physical world, we find it overwhelmingly appropriate and useful to make the more or less arbitrary isolation of systems which we can regard as more or less closed, that is to say, the body and its sub-systems.

4.15. The involvement of our identity with society goes much further. (1) We obtain important parts of our identity from the identities of the societies to which we belong; for example, our family, our religion, our nation, the human race. (2) The societies to which we belong establish their identity by being identified with their members and also, and more so perhaps, by distinction from the identity of their members. Societies are precisely designed to survive changes of membership. Societies contain their members by being other than their members. (3) The societies to which we belong obtain important parts of their identity from the societies to which they themselves belong; for example, a sports team and the city or nation which it represents, a government and the state-society of which it is a constitutional organ. (4) The societies to which we belong obtain essential parts of their identity by contrast with other societies, the societies which they are not and to which they do not belong, but whose identity is sufficiently similar to constitute a specific 'other'; for example, political parties, state-societies, linguistic groups, religions, religious sects.

4.16. The frenzy of the human search for identity, which spreads from the individual human being to all the myriad societies which human beings form, is a major cause of the very high energy levels of social life. The struggle for survival in the reality-made-by-consciousness is not merely a struggle for physical survival; it is a struggle to survive as an identity. Human beings transfer the desperate life-preserving energy of their self-consciousness to their society-consciousness; perhaps also, they learn something about the making and defending of identity from the energetic self-preserving energy of the societies to which they belong. The survival of our societies becomes as important to us as the survival of our selves, because our societies are part of our selves.

4.17. The result is, historically, that societies have been able to accumulate high levels of life-preserving energy—with a series of fateful consequences. (1) The willing necessary for the preserving of the society becomes part of the public willing and acting of the society, that is, willing and acting on behalf of society as a whole. (2) Those who control, or predominantly control, the public willing of a society take control over the willing which is necessary for the preservation of society. (3) The life-preserving of society may come to take precedence over the life-preserving of its members. (4) The lives of the members may be sacrificed to preserve the life of society. (5) Those who control, or predominantly control, the public willing of the society may will the sacrificing of the lives of its members, perhaps not willing, at the same time, the sacrifice of their own lives. (6) The lives of the members of one society may be sacrificed to preserve the life of another society. (7) Those who control the public willing of the one society may will the sacrifice of the lives of members of the other society, perhaps not willing, at the same time, the sacrifice of their own lives or the lives of members of their own society.

4.18. Such is the sane-insane logic of what is called *war*.

4.19. It is apparent that very much turns on the societies to which we perceive ourselves as belonging. And very much turns on the societies to which we perceive ourselves as not belonging. We will kill for the one. We will kill the other. And, if we do not kill, we will maim. We will obtain for ourselves, at the expense of other selves, the conditions of life which we consider necessary for ourselves—conditions of dignity, nutrition, health, education, self-government, self-fulfilment. And we may fail to seek for others, who do not belong to our societies, the same conditions of life. We may deprive others or leave others deprived.

4.20. What came to be referred to as the *nation-state* has come to be seen as the apotheosis of the self. Those who have controlled the public willing power of the so-called nation-state have chosen to identify certain kinds of society as nation-states and have then chosen to identify *the other* as other nation-states. They have found their own so-called statehood mirrored in the will-controlling classes (governments and other organs and persons) and in their aggregated, depersonalized members (so-called citizens).

4.21. And they have ordered the consciousness of their societies in such a way as to cause their citizens to accept value-forming theories to the effect that the ultimate identity of other human beings is not their humanity but their national identity— ultimate, in the sense that, as members of one nation-state, we may be required to act, preferably of our own willing (and, if not, under the compulsion of the willing of others), to kill or maim human beings who are members of other nation-states. It is an eloquent demonstration of the power of human consciousness to control human consciousness that people have sacrificed themselves by the million, and continue to sacrifice themselves by the million, in the name of such theories. It is an eloquent demonstration of the power of human consciousness to resist human consciousness that human beings in general, to this day, do not believe, in the intimacy of their own hearts, that the ultimate identity of their fellows human beings is not their humanity but their national identity.

4.22. The dilemma of the self and the other is the struggle of a society to become what it might be, to be what it is. It is a struggle, never won and never lost, because life is an endlessly self-creating process. The consciousness which gives us the power and the burden of willing our future never lets us cease the forming of our selves, in company and in competition with all other self-forming selves. As long as we live, as long as society survives, our struggle and society's struggle goes on, the struggle to become our selves.

4.23. Consciousness presents to itself its struggle with the dilemma of the self and the other in words and ideas and theories and values. Powerful words which are used as weapons in the struggle include the following: *aboriginal, alien, apartheid, autochthonous, autonomy, believer, caste, chosen people, class, colonialism, colour, country, discrimination, the elect, the enemy, equality, ethnic, the faith, the fatherland, foreign, freedom, heretic, home, homeland, imperialism, independence, indigenous, infidel, integrity, intervention, liberation, marginal, member, the nation, nationality, native, non-member, outlaw, outsider, pariah, the people, prejudice, the race, self-defence, self-determination, self-government, sovereignty, territorial integrity, traitor, tribe.*

DILEMMA 2: *THE ONE AND THE MANY*

4.24. The dilemma of the one and the many is the dilemma of power. A person is a single structure-system. A person is also a collection of organs and systems and a series of electromagnetic events and a set of biochemical structures. A society is a single structure-system. A society is also a set of subordinate structures and systems. It is also a collection of human beings. It is also a series of historical events. A person and a society are one and many. The dilemma of power is the struggle to create a systematic relationship between the one and the many.

4.25. A person and a society are also one and many in another sense. Each is a multiple unity. The component parts are systems of component parts. A person is a system which integrates subordinate physiological systems and it integrates those sub-systems with the system of consciousness. A society is a system which integrates both its own subordinate systems (for example, decision-making bodies) and the systems of systems which are individual persons. And it includes in its systematic integration any subordinate societies which are contained within it.

4.26. Consciousness synthesizes as readily as it analyses, generalizes as readily as it particularizes, integrates and unifies as readily as it separates and multiplies. Once again (compare paragraph 3.25), it is interesting to speculate, but not easy to speculate usefully, as to whether consciousness has tended to use its conceiving of the unity-in-multiplicity / multiplicity-in-unity of the physical universe to pattern its conceiving of the human person and human society, or vice versa. Whichever, if either, is the case, the outcome is that there is a close identity between the conceiving within reality-made-by-consciousness of the physical universe and the conceiving of human and social experience.

4.27. The dual functioning of consciousness—disintegrating and integrating—has had dramatic effects in the natural sciences as they take the physical world apart and then put it together again in the form of hypotheses as to its functioning. The hypothetical structures made by science are hypothetical unities formed as theory from the isolation of particular multiplicities. The explanatory power of this process stems from the fact that, if the hypothetical unities of theory are made the basis of willing and acting in the physical world, the physical world seems to recognize them, as it were, to treat them as its own. The physical world responds to the predictions of science. The consequence is that consciousness conceives itself as lifting one corner of the veil hiding the necessity of the physical world. The necessary order of the physical world seems to be revealed as containing, in some way or other, partial and intermediate unities of order corresponding to the unities in theory of the scientific hypothesis—*partial*, in relation to the universal order-of-everything; *intermediate*, as between that universal order and the undifferentiated infinity of particulars of the physical world from which scientific theory makes its unifying selection.

4.28. Societies are partial and intermediate unities made by consciousness within the reality-made-by-consciousness. So are persons. As with the fruits of science, the benefits which individual persons gain from considering themselves to be persons, hypothetical unities-in-multiplicity, are immediately apparent. So also are the burdens, especially the inescapable and endless responsibility to will and act as an identity, to be a single focus of the impulse of life within the necessity of the universe, to be a specific agent of the reconciling of desire and obligation.

4.29. In society, the person is repersonalized in the personalization of society; the unity-in-multiplicity of the individual person is reproduced in the unity-in-multiplicity of society. The social is personalized. The personal is socialized. Society takes on the unity of a person. A person becomes one part of the multiple unity which is a society.

4.30. What might have been merely a metaphor or a theoretical construct has become the most substantial of realities. Societies have acquired within consciousness the personalities of individual human beings. Individual human beings have acquired, in their identity as members of societies, the dispersonalities of atoms or cells. The abstracted unities formed within theories have become actual focuses of will and action, intense concentrations of energy at every energy level, up to the massive energies of the willing and acting of the so-called nation-state and the massive energies of international society.

4.31. From the viewpoint of the individual human being, the consciousness focused in that individual, connected with that human body, is the primary and irreducible unity of consciousness; the consciousness of society is a derivative, an accumulation, an amalgamation. From the point of view of a given society, the consciousness focused in that society is the primary unit of consciousness; the consciousness of the society's members are a multiplicity within that unity. A remarkable consequence of this is that the human individual comes to have two identities, generating two kinds of willing and acting. There is the willing and acting as an individual human being and there is the willing and acting as a society-member. The social arrangements of a given society determine the extent and the form of the involvement of each of its members in the willing and acting of the society. All members participate in the willing and acting of society. All participate in different ways, to different degrees.

4.32. What we know of human history suggests that important consequences have followed from this double life of members of society. Those consequences relate, in particular, to the operation of society's theories and values. It has proved surprisingly easy for the theories and values of a society to have different effects on the willing of a person acting as an individual and the willing of a person acting as a social unit. In particular, the ethical aspect of a society's theories may be one thing for social willing and acting, another thing for individual willing and acting. If the person acting as a social unit is an absolute monarch, a dictator, a military leader, an oligarch, a high-priest, a judge, a revolutionary, or a terrorist, then the ethical disparity will be open and obvious. If the person acting as a social unit is a member of a corporate government, some other corporate political body, a ruling political party, a military general-staff, the management of an industrial or commercial enterprise, or the governing body of other kinds of social institution, the ethical disparity is no less real for being less apparent.

4.33. Even at the level of an individual member of society having no extraordinary social power, participation in the social process as a citizen is liable to involve a disjunction of theory and value, a disjunction of behaviour as a human being and as a member of society. The explanation is that a society has a socionomy which permeates every moment and every corner of its life and the life of its members.

4.34. The term *socionomy* is here intended to refer to the way in which the words and ideas and theories and values of the society are present as a *totality of obligation* in the social consciousness of that society, and hence in the individual consciousness of each of its members (subordinate societies and individual human beings). The socionomy of a society, of any society from the society of the family to the international society of the whole human race, includes its constitution and its legal system, but it includes also all those other kinds of reality-forming (in particular, religion and mythology and philosophy and morality and economy) which impinge on the reconciling of desire and obligation in the willing and acting of a society and its members. A socionomy is a society's reality conceived in the mode of obligation.

4.35. While we are subject to the socionomy of a society, we are possessed and entranced by it. In our everyday life, we pass in and out of many societies. When we are within some subordinate society, say, the society of the family, we enter its socionomy and share in its obligation-reality. But, in so doing, we do not free ourselves from the socionomy of the superordinate societies to which that society itself belongs, up to and including a state-society and international society. If we travel outside one of the societies of which we are a member, we enter into the socionomy of any other society which we enter, carrying with us inevitably the socionomies of our own societies.

4.36. The result is that we can will and act differently in the different societies to which we belong, willing to do things in one context that we would be unable to will in another context. We can put on and take off obligation, as the general changes out of his uniform at the end of the working day, the judge takes off his robes, the persons of power return to the society of their families. We can do things out of duty in the name of a society which we would not allow ourselves to do as a matter of desire when we act as individual human beings. We can weep as human beings for what we feel obliged to do as citizens.

4.37. So it is that a society can come to be seen as having not only a will of its own, but also its own needs and interests and rights and duties. So it is that all the amazing power of reason and imagination can be harnessed in the service of a society, generating words and ideas and theories on behalf of that society, generating action of unlimited energy in its name. So it is that a society can come to be loved and feared as if it were a human individual. And so it is that societies can come to have a fantasy life, full of the power of unreasoned imagination. So it is that societies can come to have so-called *relations* with each other, as full of feeling and calculation as the relations between any human individuals—societies seducing and cheating and conspiring; societies caring and sharing and protecting.

4.38. So it is also that the struggle within the dilemma of the one and the many comes to be seen as a struggle for the control of something conceived in the word *power*. The word refers to some form of energy conceived within reality-made-by-consciousness which corresponds to some form of energy which consciousness finds in the world of non-consciousness, the physical world. The effect of the word used in the one sense flows freely into its use in the other sense. Neither is metaphorical in relation to the other; each vigorously sustains the strength of the other. Human power is evidently full of the very impulse of life itself, full of self-creating energy, which flows from the physical world into the world of willing and acting.

4.39. Power is the energy which transforms desire, through willing, into action. Society, in organizing the willing and acting of human beings, organizes the energy of human beings in the form of power. Society is an organizing of energy in the form of social power.

4.40. It follows that societies are partial and intermediate systems for the organization of willing and acting: *partial*, in that they do not organize the whole of the willing and acting of all their members (citizens and subordinate societies); *intermediate*, in that they themselves are liable to form part of superordinate societies which also organize willing and acting, up to and including the international society of the whole human race, the society of all societies.

4.41. It follows also that the socionomy of a society manifests itself as a sort of *acting* in relation to the *willing* of its members. By the systematic operation of the social process, the willing of society acts, as obligation, to modify the possibilities of the members of society, when they come to choose among their possibilities in the process of willing. The reality-for-itself of society in becoming reality-as-obligation becomes the reality within which the member of society must conceive of the possibilities of willing and acting. The socionomy of a society makes a sort of world of necessity for the society's members.

4.42. It follows also that the struggle of power is a struggle which is never won and never lost, never ending, because the impulse of life obliges all societies and all human beings to will and to act in order to live, and their willing and acting takes place within the realities which the societies conceive and the realities which are conceived by their members. Human beings and their societies are locked in a necessary struggle of the one and the many, as each empowers the other by disempowering itself, as each empowers itself by disempowering the other.

4.43. Consciousness presents to itself its struggle with the dilemma of the one and the many in words and ideas and theories and values. Powerful words which are used as weapons in the struggle include the following: *absolutism, bourgeois, capitalist, caste, citizen, civil liberties, class, collective, collectivism, communism, consent, constitution, custom, democracy, divine right (of kings), due process, equal protection, equality, exploitation, freedom, free market, general will, government, human rights, the individual, individualism, interest, labour, land, land reform, the law, the leader, legality, legal person, legitimacy (of kings, of institutions), liberation, market forces, master, the nation, national interest, national security, natural rights, the Party, the Peace, peasant, peon, the people, the plan, planning, power, privilege, proletariat, property, public interest, public order, public safety, representation, right, the Rule of Law, self-government, separation of powers, serf, servant, slave, social contract, society, solidarity, sovereignty, the state, supremacy, tyranny, worker.*

5 Society Socializing II: Dilemmas of Will and Order

DILEMMA 3: *UNITY OF NATURE, PLURALITY OF VALUE*

5.1. The dilemma of unity of nature, plurality of value is the dilemma of will. The Earth is one world among countless worlds in an immeasurable universe. It is a world with a finite physical history. It is a world of which there now hardly remains a single square metre which has not been possessed by human consciousness. We are one species among many species. It is a species with a short history by comparison with the history of the universe, the history of the Earth, the history of some other species. It is a species with a known social history of a duration which is hardly significant in relation even to the history of the human species. And we are a species which has counted and named all of its members, a species of which there is presumably now hardly a single family which has not been integrated into superordinate human societies, no society whose consciousness has not been modified by the consciousness of more energetic societies.

5.2. We are organisms which are formed and which develop in accordance with principles and processes which are no different from those which form and develop uncountable other forms of life on the planet Earth. By the interaction of matter in atoms and cells in various specific circumstances, we are caused to live and die, effects of causes, like the effects of any other causes in the physical world. Every moment of our lives is a transient pattern within fields of energy which extend to the ends of the universe and in which we are a set of events of equal significance with any other set of events of similar duration and energy. Our duration and energy are considerably greater in scale than many events of which we know, immeasurably smaller than many others. We are something more than a spark of fire, something less than the movement of continents.

5.3. But this collection of atoms, this collection of cells has created something which is not atoms or cells, something which we have here been calling the world of consciousness. It is a world made from within the consciousness of each individual human being; and it is a world made by human beings acting collectively in societies. It is a world which is situated in the physical world and which flows into and out of the physical world. But it is a world whose dimensions are not those of time and space, a world containing the whole planet Earth and everything beyond, to the limits of the universe and beyond those limits. And it is a world which surpasses the lifetime of each individual human being, which survives the birth and death of particular societies, which connects each currently existing human being with every human being who has lived and who is yet to live.

5.4. It is a world in which the human being has been condemned and empowered to take responsibility for making the future, sharing that responsibility with the necessity which governs the physical universe. As joint master of its own world, human consciousness transforms its worlds, the physical world and the world of consciousness, by its willing and acting. By its willing it chooses to act in response to its own desiring, its life-filled impulse of self-creating, within the constraints of the necessity of the physical world and the obligation which is the self-acknowledged necessity of human consciousness as an orderly system. In society, social consciousness organizes its willing in order to organize the acting of society and its members. The dilemma of unity of nature, plurality of value is the struggle to organize the willing of human consciousness—the willing of individual consciousness and the willing of the shared consciousness of societies. And the organizing of willing involves the social formation of the values which consciousness, individual and social, uses as the basis of its willing.

5.5. If we consider the relatively brief record of human social history, if we consider all that the human species has created and done during that brief period, we are struck by an extraordinary uniformity in the midst of so much diversity. If we consider the total accumulation of religion and mythology and philosophy and the plastic arts and literature, the whole story of agricultural and commercial and industrial life, the whole story of the so-called public life of societies, the whole story of the so-called private life of human individuals, we are easily led to the hypothesis that there is a pattern of human existing which transcends time and place, a pattern which has traditionally been characterized as a human nature and a human condition.

5.6. We look with familiar eyes on the ancient civilizations of Egypt, Mesopotamia, India, China, Greece, Persia, Israel, and Rome, and on their medieval and modern successors. However exotic it may be, none of it is alien to us. Always and everywhere, the struggle of human life and the responses of socializing humanity have a family resemblance. It is not only a matter of the physiological responses of life-making and life-preserving reflex and instinct, not only the spontaneous responses of feeling and imagination, but also the responses of self-ordering consciousness, as it makes the words and the ideas and the theories and the values needed to carry humanity from desire and obligation to will and action. We see ourselves as if we were looking in a more-or-less clouded mirror when we look at those who have lived before us, who have struggled with the same ultimate human nature and the same ultimate human condition, and who have left the imprint of their lives within our living consciousness. In our many languages we speak one language. The human enterprise is apparently a single enterprise.

5.7. And yet, we have only to change the focus slightly and we see nothing but division, dispute, dissent, strife, conflict, enmity, hatred, aggression, and their wretched servants, murder and devastation. Great religions divide into fratricidal sects. Great empires collapse into warring states. Great civilizations fall into the hands of disputing and unworthy heirs. And the worst wars of all seem to be the wars fought by close relations, religious wars within a single religion, cultural wars within a single culture, local wars within a single region, civil wars within a single nation, feuds and vendettas of blood relatives. We are impressed by the evidence of the wonderful integrating power of human consciousness. We are appalled by the human power to make disorder.

5.8. The irony is the more painful for being so apparent. The limitless power of human imagination and reason can as well construct social words of order, progress, and prosperity as it can invent the means to destroy them. And the irony has in recent centuries become more painful and more apparent than ever. The development of the natural sciences since the fifteenth century has demonstrated two things. (1) Human consciousness can create theories which give humanity very great power over the physical world through orderly willing and acting. (2) Human consciousness is capable of creating theories (natural science) which are universal, in the sense that they have precisely equal intellectual value and practical potentiality in every continent, region, culture, and nation of the world. But the same development has also raised two anguished and urgent questions. (1) Will humanity apply, through imagination and reason, the physical power which it is gaining from natural science to integrate or to disintegrate humanity, for the survival and prospering of humanity or for its destruction? (2) Will humanity learn from the universality of natural science how to universalize its willing and acting in the human world, especially in the social world of value?

5.9. The dilemma of unity of nature, plurality of value thus arises from the fact that it is of the essence of the process of self-ordering reason, considered in Chapter 2 above, that ideas are caught up in an endless process of comparison, modification, surpassing, as they are integrated in the three integrating co-ordinates of reason. The price of the creative power of imagination and the ordering power of reason is that consciousness can not only entertain conflicting ideas but, indeed, must contain conflicting ideas, as it generates possibilities from within itself and from its contact with the physical world and with other consciousnesses.

5.10. It is by surpassing itself that human consciousness develops. It is by opposing itself that consciousness creates itself. To be able to affirm, consciousness must be able to deny. From conflicting ideas come new ideas and new theories, new willing, and new action, endlessly responding to the changing challenges of the physical world and of the world of consciousness, endlessly enriching and empowering human life. But from conflicting ideas can also come conflicting values, and from conflicting values can come conflicting will and conflicting action. And conflicting will and action can take every form and degree, from a disagreement between friends to world war. Such is the social dilemma of value. Society must contain conflicting ideas if it is to survive and prosper. Society cannot bear too much discord.

5.11. It has been the privilege of natural science, in the period since the fifteenth century, to have as its professional co-worker, so to speak, the physical universe, having excluded from its laboratory the dubious assistance of religion and magic and metaphysics and politics. In natural science, the integrating co-ordinates of reason can operate in relation to something which does not contain consciousness, something which responds to the endless changing ideas of consciousness with absolute detachment. By conceiving of the physical world, for its own purposes, as something which is other than consciousness, human consciousness, in natural science, has been able to use imagination and reason in a way which does not exclude conflict and dissent among scientists but which allows a third party, the physical world, to intervene in all their controversies, a third party which has no imagination and so has no need of reason.

5.12. When reflective human consciousness considers anything other than the physical world, and especially when it considers humanity itself, its consciousness, and its social life, then it has no such privilege. When humanity considers humanity, it is matching changing words and ideas and theories and values with changing words and ideas and theories and values. Natural science, using the third integrating co-ordinate of reason (the potential co-ordinate), is able to generate regular events in the physical world in order to eliminate incoherent ideas and thereby to produce a coherence among its ideas which is, for the time being, total.

5.13. Society is a permanent experiment. Human consciousness can teach itself by its own social experience. But there are reasons why the effect of social experimenting, and hence the success of society's self-educating, is radically uncertain. (1) Social experiment may be costly. A period of tyranny or decadence is interesting, but may be expensive in human happiness and lost opportunities. (2) Social experiments cannot easily be organized as experiments. Society cannot easily isolate itself, or one part of itself, in a self-contained environment, cut off from its past and from the inextricable interacting of the total social process. (3) The evidence obtained from social experimenting is subject not merely to measurement and formalization and abstraction. A social hypothesis is an interpretation, invoking unlimited areas of surrounding human consciousness, subject to all the creative and discordant possibilities of imagination and reason. (4) Any apparent increase in the coherence of consciousness learned from the permanent social experiment is liable to become simply the first term of a new contradiction, as consciousness unceasingly works on itself to surpass itself.

5.14. So it is that consciousness has had to find other means of bringing order to its own self-understanding, of bringing order to its own value-forming, as it forms and endlessly re-forms the values which will cause its willing and acting to carry it from its past to its future, as it seeks its own survival and prospering. Society uses five practical strategies to control the overabundant fertility of imagination and reason as they generate an unending stream of conflicting and changing values.

5.15. (1) Society seeks to enforce an idea-unity in society by incorporating ideas in the *identity* of the society. (2) Society seeks to enforce an idea-unity by incorporating ideas in the *distribution of power* in society. (3) Society incorporates arenas for controlled disagreement within the structure of society, including the arenas which are called *politics*, *public opinion* and *private life*. (4) Society seeks to increase the volume of *information-ideas* at the expense of value-ideas. (5) Society creates semi-permanent sub-systems (constitutional organs and other subordinate societies) within the general reality-made-by-consciousness, realities designed to condition the functioning of large areas of the total social process.

5.16. (1) It is one of the gravest of all problems in the social history of humanity that societies have tended to incorporate ideas in their identity, especially in the struggle with the dilemma of the self and the other considered in Chapter 4. Membership of the society thereby comes to involve acceptance of, and unquestioning allegiance to, certain ideas, so that the self-preserving energy of the society may be directed to preserving its ideas. Self-defence is also idea-defence. Such preserving relates both to a society's own members, who may have to be compelled to remain loyal to those ideas, but also to non-members and to other societies, who may be seen as a threat and whose ideas may be seen as incompatible. The result is that ideas which are otherwise subject to the integrating co-ordinates of reason, and hence always liable to be surpassed or negated, take on the character of objects in the physical world. They cease to be a reconciliation of the impulse of desire and the constraints of obligation, and take on a sort of necessity.

5.17. Judging from the whole story of human social experience, some such objectivization or reification of ideas is evidently a necessary feature of any society. A society's theories cannot be reconsidered and reconfirmed every day of the week in open debate. A society must be able to assume a great deal of theory if it is to survive from day to day as a society. Similarly, the values derived from the application of imagination and reason to its theories cannot be re-formed every day of the week in open debate. A society must be able to assume very many values if it is to survive from day to day as a society. In particular, society responds to the need to establish relative stability in the midst of change as it struggles with the dilemma of new citizens, old laws, which will be considered in Chapter 6 below.

5.18. But the story of human social experience also shows that the price of stability is oppression and stagnation and aggression.

Every society is necessarily a form of oppression, since to be a member of a society is to accept, as a matter of behaviour if not as a matter of conviction, a necessary minimum of its ideas. Every society is necessarily a form of stagnation, since a society must embody a necessary minimum of ideas which persist. Every society must necessarily be more-or-less aggressive, since a society must preserve its identity, its self, and the ideas contained in its self, not only in relation to its members but also in relation to non-members and to other societies. The struggle with the perennial dilemma of value is precisely a struggle to determine how much unity of value must be purchased at the expense of how much plurality.

5.19. (2) It is a major task of the distribution of power within a society to organize a necessary unity of ideas, a necessary unity of value, and the necessary defence of those unities. And the necessary structures of power include not only structures of policy-making and legislation, the social processing of ideas with a view to willing and acting. They include also educational institutions, religious institutions, courts, bureaucracies, agencies for the protection of law and order.

5.20. These structures of power necessarily involve, as in the case of the incorporation of ideas and values in the identity of society, oppression, stagnation, and aggression. But they lead also to the possibility of the use of physical and mental force to enforce unity of ideas and values. In this way society takes over the reality-made-by-consciousness and seeks to ensure that it coincides with the consciousness of the given society. For the average member of the society, reality comes to coincide, more rather than less, with the socially determined reality. The average member may not know much of the structures which support the values of the society—the practical theory, let alone the pure and transcendental theories. The average member of society may not know much about the special nature and functioning of words, ideas, and theories, and so may not be in a position to reconcile deviant or dissident ideas with the social reality other than by either simply submitting to the social reality or else retreating into privacy, into individual consciousness, into a self-imposed inner exile.

5.21. (3) Societies have always known that an important part of their functioning is to organize their relationship with individual consciousness. They have always known that the social consciousness which creates them must be shared with the individual consciousness of their members, of non-members, and of other societies and their members. Different societies are a series of experiments with different solutions to the problem of the relationship between social and individual consciousness. Many different kinds of solution are familiar to us from social experience.

5.22. Over recent centuries, society seems to have learned, or relearned, a lesson to be learned from human social experience, a democratic lesson in four parts. (*a*) Individual consciousness is ultimately irrepressible. To silence all public dissent requires the constant use of extreme physical and mental force. And, even then, private dissent will always remain. (*b*) For the reasons already considered above, alternative ideas are inevitable. The nature of words and ideas and theories is such that, in fields other than that of natural science, every word and idea and theory co-exists with an alternative. Words and ideas, and theories exist by interacting. This does not mean that all ideas are of equal value. The actual is not necessarily rational. On the contrary, reason permits the modification and surpassing of ideas, by way of the three co-ordinates of reason considered in Chapter 2. But it does mean that consciousness is irrepressibly creative of conflicting ideas.

5.23. (*c*) The unity of the human condition, of human nature, transcends the diversity of socially organized ideas. It is not possible—at least, it is no longer possible—to isolate a society from other societies. It is thus not possible to prevent the members of a society from recognizing what they share and do not share with the members of other societies. (*d*) The most dramatic lesson of all is that the fusion energy of a society depends on the fusing of the energies of all its members. If one part of society, especially one economically homogeneous part of society, monopolizes control of the social process, it may lead to a diversion of energy into non-productive conflict. But, worse, the more individual consciousness is suppressed, the more depressed will be the total energy level of the society.

Desire, reflecting the life-impulse of the human beings who are members of the society, must be organized, necessarily involving some suppression of that energy. But the generation of socially productive ideas by desire must also be encouraged and inspired and amplified and channelled and co-ordinated by society. That task is as important for the survival and prospering of a society as the maintenance of its identity and of its structures of power. Ideas are potential energy. Society is an organization of energy. Society is a generation of energy through the structures and systems of society.

5.24. These lessons have been learned through countless different experiments, but especially with institutional experiments of three kinds—(a) institutions allowing the participation by society-members in the willing of society, especially through the process called politics and institutions called political institutions; (b) the socialization of education with a view not merely to the conditioning of children to the words, ideas, theories, and values of society, but also to their development as persons, with a view to their personal self-fulfilment, and with a view to their energetic participation in society, in whatever form of social activity is theirs in that society's division of labour; and (c) the establishment of boundaries between a private realm, of more or less non-socialized life, and a public realm of social willing and acting by organs and subordinate societies acting on behalf of society as a whole. It has become a leading function of law to define and defend such boundaries. The development of constitutionalism since the eighteenth century (to be considered further in Part Two) has enabled these experiments to be installed within the structure-systems of society.

5.25. (4) It is probably not a coincidence that the lessons from social experience considered in paragraphs 5.22 and 5.23 have been learned in the period in which natural science has developed so dramatically. At one time, it seemed that it might be possible to extend the method of science to the study of society. But the special character of social study, noted in paragraphs 5.12 and 5.13, has reasserted itself to make the method of natural science only a distant analogical inspiration to social study. But the apparent universality and neutrality of science has had a more specific effect within social consciousness. It has inspired the idea that it would be desirable to increase the volume of *information* in society and reduce the volume of ideas of other kinds.

5.26. Information is value-neutralized ideas. No idea, not even an information-idea, can be value-neutral. Any idea can be used by consciousness as a ground for willing and acting, so that every idea is liable to be judged in value terms. But an idea may be said to be an information-idea if and when it is an idea which is formed for a purpose other than to serve as a ground for willing and acting. Like any other idea, its presence within consciousness depends on the theories which support it, a practical theory which determines how it might be used, a pure theory which integrates it with other related ideas, a transcendental theory which explains, in terms of the functioning of consciousness, the possibility of the theory which makes it possible. Thus even an information-idea is no more effective than the theories which support it. If they are essentially value-generating theories, then the idea is relatively less value-neutral. Even science depends on its pure and transcendental theories, that is to say, on particular views of the nature of reality and particular views of the nature of consciousness. And science may be conducted in pursuance of theories whose function is to generate values, to support a political cause or a religious belief or a social theory, or a national identity, for example.

5.27. So it is that information is value-neutralized rather than value-neutral. But this relative neutrality may have an important effect on the status of the idea within consciousness. It means that the idea is likely to be relatively widely accepted without debate, without having to prove itself beyond demonstrating, or showing on its face, either its genetic co-ordinate or its potential co-ordinate, its methodological origin and its possible consequences. The more an idea is perceived as information, the less it is liable to generate debate. The less it generates debate, the less it invites negation, modification, supersession by other ideas. Within a given society, ideas which are a straightforward derivation from the necessary theories of that society are liable to be treated by members of that society as if they were information. So it is that, for example, within a sports club or a federation of sports clubs, events which are an application of the rules of the given sport are collected as information. There may be debate about the application of the rules (was a certain referee's decision unfair?), but otherwise the information is value-neutral. Within a given economic system, information about economic events, especially statistics, tend to be accorded the same status. Within a given religion, theological ideas and even moral ideas may come to have a status which is virtually that of an information-idea, not requiring proof or justification.

5.28. Within a given legal system, such an approach has important effects. Forensic decisions as to the veracity of a witness, the reasonableness of behaviour, the foreseeability of risk, human expectations of future events, human intentions, have to be treated as if they were matters of information which can be determined by comparing the facts of a case with some value-neutralized standard. So-called *evidence* in a court is treated as the collection of information, resting on a theoretical basis which is simply assumed. When that theoretical basis relates to the functioning of the physical world (especially in regard to physical causation), such assumptions may be relatively innocent. When they relate to human behaviour (for example, as regards foresight or reasonableness), they necessarily involve some degree of deception, since humanity cannot judge humanity other than within the reality-for-itself of the given society, including its values.

5.29. Whatever the inherent conceptual difficulties of the process of idea-neutralization, it is a leading feature of the modern social process. Given the overwhelming complexity of large-scale modern societies (especially commercial and industrial enterprises, bureaucracies, the law, state-societies, international market-places), more and more reliance has to be placed on information as opposed to other forms of ideas. Given that information-ideas are less strongly related to desire and the impulse of life, to social identity and the distribution of power, it may be reasonable to welcome a corresponding reduction in areas of consciousness liable to give rise to violent conflict. If kings will not aspire to be philosophers, it may be no bad thing that they should aspire to be machines.

5.30. (5) Society's fifth strategy for unifying value (the creation of realities through social institutions) will be considered in Chapter 6 below. In the meantime, it may be noted that, surprising as it may seem, the struggle of society with the dilemma of unity of nature, plurality of value turns out to be a struggle for the ordering of society's energy. Ideas are potential energy. Values are ideas with especially high potential energy. Society, in unifying and multiplying values, is organizing its survival as a system of energy.

5.31. Consciousness presents to itself its struggle with the dilemma of unity of nature, plurality of value in words and ideas and theories and values. Powerful words which are used as weapons in the struggle include the following: *abnormal, absolute values, allegiance, anti-social, archetype, authority, barbarism, belief, blasphemy, the Book, catholic, civilization, class consciousness, class enemy, conditioning, conscience, contemplation, conversion, crusade, culture, custom, customary, deviant, dissenter, dissident, doctrine, dogma, ecumenism, education, enlightenment, equality, ethos, evil, the Faith, fetish, folkway, freedom, general will, ghetto, good, heresy, history, Holy War, humane, humanism, humanitarian, humanity, knowledge, the Law, legend, liberalism, loyalty, madness, mankind, meditation, mental illness, morality, mystery, mysticism, myth, nature, opposition, orthodoxy, persecution, policy, privacy, prophecy, protestant, reform, relativism, revelation, revisionism, rite, ritual, sect, sin, stereotype, taboo, toleration, tradition, treason, tribe, the Truth, universal, universalism, values, the Way, way of life, worship.*

DILEMMA 4: *JUSTICE AND SOCIAL JUSTICE*

5.32. The dilemma of justice and social justice is the dilemma of order. A society is a microcosm. It is not the universe. Every society is a system within systems, a structure within structures. It forms part of a universal system of the physical world as conceived by natural science. It forms part of the world of consciousness which knows no frontiers of time or place, which embraces all societies and all human beings, and which includes the human species-characteristics of imagination and reason, of desire and obligation, without which a human society could not form itself as a human society. It forms part of the system of superordinate societies within which it is formed, within the reality of which, and within the constitution of which, it conducts its self-creating and its self-socializing. Those superordinate societies include, inevitably, the system of international society, the society of all societies.

5.33. A society forms part of the system of the transcendent totality which is the more-than-hypothetical totality conceived by all its theories—practical, pure, and transcendental —and by which it knows for itself the totality of all-that-is, including all of the physical universe and all of the universe conceived by and in consciousness. And a society forms part of the universal system of *supernatural reality* conceived by its religious theories, to the extent that its reality-for-itself contains such specific religious theories.

5.34. So it is that every society has an external aspect as well as an internal aspect. Society has an inside and an outside. Both are necessary parts of its specific structure-system as a society. The external aspect is part of the *other* without which it could not form its identity, without which it would be different in its self. Its identity being a resultant of its *self* and its *other*, a society is a system which unites its internal and its external aspects within a single idea of itself. (The word *resultant* is used here, and elsewhere in the present study, on an analogy with its use in mechanics, where it refers to a force of a certain magnitude acting in a certain direction which is composed of two or more other forces of other magnitudes acting in other directions.)

5.35. The internal aspect of a society—its total social process, including all its willing and acting in its struggle with the perennial dilemmas—is what its structure is structuring and its system is systematizing. The willing and the acting of the society is the society socializing itself. The external aspect of a society, on the other hand, is not within the field of society's self-ordering system. In its external aspect, society meets other societies, the rest of the world of consciousness, the rest of the physical universe, the rest of the reality-made-by-consciousness which is formed by its theories, insofar as it relates to that which is external to society.

5.36. All such externalities are capable of being taken into society's reality-for-itself. (1) They are all capable of being conceived by society within and in the light of its own theories. (2) Society participates in such externalities, itself an actuality contained within that which is external to society, especially as the society participates in superordinate societies. (3) Society's reality-forming in relation to externalities and its consequential willing and acting in relation to them affect the systematic development of those externalities. (4) And, merely by being conceived as externalities, externalities are internalized in the self-creating and the self-socializing of society. They are present in their absence. They are inside by being perceived from inside as outside.

5.37. Externalities may cease to be external. A society may choose to internalize externalities—for example, when one person acquires ownership of the property of another; or when an industrial or commercial enterprise acquires and absorbs another; or when one religious sect merges with another; or when a member of one family marries a member of another family; or when territory is transferred by one state-society to another by force or agreement. And a society may seek to lessen the externality of externalities—for example, when industrial or commercial enterprises agree on a market strategy; or when neighbouring tribes or cities or families agree on the joint use of an area of land; or when a religious society joins in communion with another religious society; or when a sports club joins in organized competition with other sports clubs; or when nation-states agree to co-ordinate their willing and acting in a given matter. And such internalization may take the form of the creation of a new society, wholly or partly absorbing the pre-existing societies—for example, a joint-venture corporation, a unitary state-society, a federation, a central government agency, a state enterprise, an intergovernmental organization, a league, a union, a holding company, a trust.

5.38. By a contrary process, internalities and part-internalities may become externalities or may become less internal—as a society divides into more than one society, a territory and its people separate to form an independent society, a federation is dissolved, a contractual or treaty relationship is terminated, a marriage is terminated, a corporation is dissolved, a religion or a church suffers schism.

5.39. At any particular moment, therefore, a functioning society is an actual and particular relation between its internalities and its externalities. The internal order of a society and the order of that which is external to a society are united in a third order which integrates the two. The systematic order of a society is a unique order integrating the order of that which is internal to the society and the order of that which is external to the society. To be a society is to be a third order.

5.40. Justice is the order of the third order which is society. Justice is the pattern of order which is reflected in all the self-ordering of a society, as it creates itself in socializing itself. Justice is that without which the systematic order of a particular society could not be conceived, but which itself cannot be conceived as any particular system of order. Justice is the ordering of a society conceived as theoretical possibility. Justice is the mathematics of society. As mathematics seems to be an order underlying the order of the physical world, but not subject to the ceaseless becoming of the physical world, an order discovered by and in consciousness, but seemingly not merely made by consciousness, so justice is an order underlying the order of society. Justice is the systematic possibility of the systematic possibilities of society.

5.41. Justice itself has no substantive content. Its effect is to draw society into order. Justice is always one step beyond the specific ordering of a given society, beyond the specific order of all societies, beyond the specific order of international society, as the society of all societies. Justice is the possibility of order which makes possible the possibility of ordering in society, which social consciousness actualises as it chooses each reconciliation of the impulse of life and physical necessity, each reconciliation of desire and obligation.

5.42. Such an approach to justice is intended to be anything but mystical, or merely an affirming by the way of negation. It is simply to acknowledge within the hypothetical self-conceiving of consciousness, and within the theoretical self-conceiving of societies, that thing without which they could not be systematic structures, but which itself cannot be a systematic structure. But if justice has no substantive content and can be conceived rather than known or perceived, it does not follow that justice is without substantive effect. On the contrary, its effect is perceived in every event of every society. There is nothing in society which does not reflect the idea of justice.

5.43. Justice is present in its presence; and it is present in its absence. Social consciousness would be formless and inactive, were there no idea of justice. The rankest injustice would not be injustice, were it not for the forming effect of justice. The most pragmatic and utilitarian and short-term of social organizing would not be organizing, were it not for the forming effect of justice. Even the decay and the dissolution and the destruction of societies—the overthrowing of a tyranny, the withering-away of an empire, the collapse of a tribe or a state-society into self-destroying strife or anarchy, the shameful descent into the crime of war—are events formed within human consciousness as it struggles to order itself socially within the possibilities offered by imagination and reason, desire and obligation, the impulse of life and the necessity of the physical universe.

5.44. Justice gives society its direction, an orientation, a tendency, a pole of attraction. Love, in all its forms from the most physical to the most spiritual, is so similar to justice in its effect that it is hypothetically tempting to suppose that each is the other, that justice is love, love is justice. Love as lust, love as longing for physical union, love as self-decentering, love as longing for the welfare of the other, love as self-giving, love as motiveless giving, love as self-annihilating, love as identification with the other, love as self-absorption in the other, love as willing in the interest of the other, love as longing for the supernatural, love as longing for self-annihilation in the supernatural, love as longing for union with the supernatural. No form of love is merely an impulse, merely a means, merely a rationalization of purpose. Love, like justice, is complete in itself. Love, like justice, is found within consciousness but comes from elsewhere. Only its effects differ, as its forming effect meets the possibilities of human willing and acting. Like justice, too, love is powerfully present in its countless forms of absence, in all the many forms of disdain, contempt, hatred, discrimination, cruelty, and aggression. As justice is the possibility of the possibility of order in social consciousness, so love is, perhaps, the possibility of the possibility of order in individual consciousness. Love is, perhaps, the mathematics of being human.

5.45. It is justice which makes society intrinsically progressive. It is the possibility not merely of order but of ordering. Justice fuels society's engine of progress. Society, as a system of willing and acting, is always on the move, never for two moments the same. Justice, like love, draws society towards itself by drawing society towards what it could be. All the striving and the struggling of society, including the struggle with the perennial dilemmas of society, is not aimless activity. The aims of societies are as various as human imagination and reason can devise. Ths aims of a given society are as complex, obscure, and changing as the rest of the fabric of social reality. But societies are not systems for destroying themselves; they are not systems for de-societizing themselves. They are systems for socializing themselves. And socializing means a movement in the direction of society's possibilities. Justice, as the order of the order of that system, is constantly tempting and encouraging and inviting society to be better, to become itself, to fulfil itself. As love, in all its forms, holds out to us the possibility that we might, for a while or for ever, become more ourselves in becoming more than ourselves, so justice holds out the permanent possibility to society that it might become more than itself, might continually surpass its successive selves.

5.46. Justice is society seeking to be a structure within the structure of all structures, seeking to be a system within the system of all systems.

5.47. Thus arises the perennial dilemma of justice and social justice. A society is what it can be. It will never be what it might be. Justice, which enables it to be what it is, unceasingly condemns it for not being what it might be. Justice is what society might be. Social justice is all that society is seeking to become.

5.48. Justice is the constructive critic who never will be silenced. For society, justice is the court jester, not deceived by the pomp of the court, always reminding the pompous of their fallible humanity. Justice is permanent revolution. But it is the permanent revolution without which nothing can be permanent.

5.49. Social justice is justice taking effect within and for a given society, within the reality-for-itself of a given society. As a member of an animal species, the human being has what is presumably a natural tendency to seek its own survival, individual survival, perhaps group-survival, perhaps even species-survival. As a member of the specifically human species, the human being seems also to have a natural tendency to generate wants that exceed its biological needs. That is to say, the human being, individually and in societies, seeks not only survival but also prospering. Whether or not such a seeking is a species-characteristic and a matter of so-called human nature, or merely a by-product of the actual social history of the species, the phenomenon now seems ineradicably rooted in the actual human condition. By conceiving of what it is to prosper, and not merely to survive, human consciousness transforms the whole universe into a realm of value, a realm of justice, the value of all values.

5.50. The modern world is gripped in a frenzy of self-improvement, as individuals and societies labour, with mind and body, to improve their condition of life. The seeking may be for a tin roof that does not leak, a water supply that does not fail or spread disease, a nutritious meal once a day or once a week, employment or regular employment, a living wage, some land of your own, a fair price for your crop or your animals, some basic health-care for your family, some primary education for your children, a loan to stock a farm or buy a house or set up a business, a police force that is not corrupt, local officials who are not abusive or venal, local politicians who are not only self-interested, freedom to worship in your religion, equality of social and economic opportunity, the end of a war, the avoidance of war, a husband or a wife, a horse or a car, happy and healthy children, a holiday, less stress, a bigger house, a modern kitchen, a better job, a university degree, recognition and reward for a skill or a talent, much more money, a second home, another yacht, a pure heart, higher states of consciousness, mystical union with God, eternal life in heaven, nirvana.

5.51. Whatever we particularly want, desire ensures that our wanting always exceeds our having. Such is the impulse of self-creating life in a world of consciousness. It is the function of obligation to make us desire only the possible, to desire only that which is possible for us as self-ordering system. Such is the consequence of our being self-ordering systems, within the physical universe and within self-ordering consciousness, and of our belonging to a network of self-ordering systems, up to and including the system of all-that-is. Justice presents the possibility of the reconciling of desire and obligation as the necessity of our systematic self-ordering. It generates the idea of the possibility of reconciling our prospering with our surviving. Social justice presents to society the possibility of reconciling the survival of the society with the prospering of the society and its members.

5.52. So it is that society, a tributary of justice, is also permanent injustice. It is desire actualized but frustrated, diverted, deferred. It is disorder in order, order in disorder. In enabling human beings to be more human, it constantly violates their humanity. Society, in actualizing perfection, is permanent imperfection. These apparent paradoxes flow from four considerations:

(1) The impulse of life, the necessity of the physical universe, and justice being all external to society, they are not themselves a product of society's self-ordering; they are prior

to society; it is for society to incorporate them by and in its self-ordering.

(2) The individual human being and the societies to which the individual belongs, and the societies to which societies belong, are forms of order which are part of an order which always and necessarily transcends them.

(3) A society, as a self-ordering through willing and acting, transforms what might be into what is, possibility into actuality; but every actuality is another possibility; society is a process not a state.

(4) The order which transcends a society (the order of superordinate societies, the order of the universe of all-that-is) is also not a state but a process, itself an ordering of that which it contains, including all subordinate societies; it is an ordering constantly drawing them on, to surpass themselves, to surpass imperfection in the name of perfection, to surpass social justice in the name of justice.

5.53. So it is that the dilemma of justice and social justice must be fought out in society through its social willing and acting. Because consciousness, through imagination and reason, can conceive of possibilities which are impossible, in terms of the causation of the physical world, and unjust, in relation to the perfect ordering of justice, it is possible for a given society to organize its willing so as to cause actual injustice. Human social history has a shadow side which is a testament to the self-creating power of human consciousness, the same power which has caused the bright side of human social history. It is in the actual struggle of given societies with all the perennial dilemmas of a society that the actualization of social justice is determined. Justice haunts society in all its self-ordering. The struggle of social justice haunts all of society's willing and acting, all of its struggle with all of its perennial dilemmas.

5.54. Human consciousness cannot escape from justice, without ceasing to be consciousness. To have the power of reason and imagination, by which societies are formed and ordered within and by self-creating consciousness, is to be unable to escape from justice. Justice is unequivocal, irreducible, and irrepressible.

5.55. Justice is unequivocal, because human consciousness knows justice and injustice with a directness and a certainty comparable only with its awareness of love. Justice is a reason which surpasses reasoning. Justice imposes coherence on consciousness, even when consciousness is at its most disordered and frenzied. The certainty of justice and injustice resists every argument and all doubt.

5.56. Justice is irreducible, because justice is a form of ordering rather than a set of principles or ideas and hence needs no explanation in terms of anything else (God or pleasure or utility or subjectivity or behavioural conditioning). Justice is an explanation that needs no explanation.

5.57. Justice is irrepressible, because it flows from the order of our consciousness within the order of the universe of all-that-is. It is possible to reject justice, to do injustice, to submit to injustice. It is impossible for human consciousness to extinguish justice. To be human is to know justice.

5.58. Consciousness presents to itself its struggle with the dilemma of justice and social justice in words and ideas and theories and values. Powerful words which are used as weapons in the struggle include the following: *asset, balance, benefit, burden, capital, collective, common heritage, commonwealth, co-operative, cost, crime, deficit, demand, development, discrimination, distribution, duty, economy, equality, equal rights, equity, equitable, exchange, exploitation, expropriation, fair, fairness, fraud, freedom, free market, income, injustice, interest, investment, just, labour, land, liability, minimum, money, need, opportunity, peasant, penalty, plan, planning, policy, power, poverty, price, privilege, profit, progress, progressive, property, punishment, reactionary, redistribution, reform, responsibility, revenue, revolutionary, right, saving, scarcity, security, share, social, solidarity, supply, surplus, taxation, theft, unequal, unfair, unjust, value, wage, want, wealth, welfare, worker, wrong.*

6 Society Socializing III: Dilemma of Becoming

6.1. The dilemma of new citizens, old laws is the dilemma of becoming. Society is dynamic. In its struggle with the perennial dilemmas of society, in all the work of imagination and reason, in all the forming of words and ideas and theories and values, in all its willing and acting, society is an endless stream of happening, an endless stream of becoming. And yet something persists. Something which is the society persists through all the process of becoming. It is society which becomes in all the becoming of society. It is society which does not change in all the changing of society. Society is stability as well as change. Society is stability in change, change in stability. Society's never-ending struggle with the dilemma of new citizens, old laws is a struggle to reconcile conserving and creating, combining the past and the future in the present.

6.2. Through its struggle with the dilemma of identity, society forms the changing pattern of its identity. Through its struggle with the dilemma of power, society forms the changing pattern of its systematic structure. Through its struggle with the dilemma of will, society forms the changing pattern of its values. Through its struggle with the dilemma of order, society forms the changing pattern of its relationship to the order of all-that-is. Through its struggle with the dilemma of becoming, society forms the reality-for-itself of all its changing patterns.

6,3. All such patterns are changing in the sense that they change under the combined pressure of all the energetic forces to which the total social process of a society is subject—the pressures of its internal life, the pressures of its externalities, up to and including the pressures of the universe of all-that-is.

The externalities include not only the pressures coming from other societies but also the pressures of the physical world, the necessity of the physical universe, the natural environment, natural events—all the pressure which come from the ordering and the disorder of the universe of all-that-is. The internal pressures stem from society's whole internal life acting as a reciprocal, self-causing cause, causing changes to its own identity, power-structure, willing, and ordering, and thereby modifying, by its own action, the possibility of its own possibilities and of its own willing and acting.

6.4. Society struggles to achieve stability-in-change / change-in-stability by embodying its reality in its structure, embodying its structure in its reality. Society struggles to socialise itself as a structure-system by struggling to create the reality within which it exists as a society. Society forms the reality which it needs to survive.

6.5. Society exists nowhere else than within the reality-made-by-consciousness, that is to say, within the second world made by consciousness through the work of imagination and reason. Without the capacity of consciousness to make a world of its own, there would be no society. But society does not merely exist within reality-made-by-consciousness. Society *lives* within a world of consciousness which it is also *making*. Society is a living thing, like any other living thing: it chooses to transform the world as its mode of becoming.

6.6. To create relatively permanent structures and to form its own reality, social consciousness has found a mode of functioning analogous to the mode of functioning which it finds in the physical world—a mode of functioning which includes consciousness but also non-consciousness (just as the physical world must include consciousness as an aspect of its systematic functioning), a mode of functioning which can be conceived as a system by conceiving it in the temporal co-ordinates of consciousness (past, present, future—the co-ordinates within which the physical world is conceived by consciousness), and a mode of functioning which contains possibilities and which contains the transforming of some possibilities into actualities (just as the physical world seems to be full of events, of caused effects).

6.7. In other words, society seeks to create something which is capable of being conceived apart from the actual state of the total social process, apart from the actual becoming of society, but which is, at one and the same time, a product of that becoming and a source of that becoming and the place of that becoming. Given that, unlike our conception of the physical world of non-consciousness, such a continuing reality is also something which can exist only in and for consciousness, the task of society to create its continuing self—of-itself and yet for-itself—evidently calls for an exceptional effort of imagination and reason.

6.8. A living thing makes itself in the process of living. Society does no less. The body of an animal is formed in the living of its parents and, separated from its parents, forms itself as a particular and unique animal in and through existing as an animal. Society does no less. The forms (objects and processes) of the physical world of non-consciousness, at least as they are conceived in human consciousness, are formed from that which they are not by the very action of that which they are not (matter formed from energy by the action of energy; matter as energy formed in patterns which are not the patterns of energy, but without ceasing to be energy). Society does no less.

6.9. Society does no less. And society does much more, since society must do such things, and more, within human consciousness. Human consciousness makes itself in making itself within each individual human being. In society social consciousness makes itself by forming human consciousness not merely as the self-presented system of a physical system (brain and nervous system), but as the self-presented system (society in and for social consciousness) of many self-presented systems (the consciousness of human individuals). Society, by its own activity, makes the structure-system in and for the consciousness of many structure-systems.

6.10. All systems, conscious and non-conscious, are thus a becoming which is always a self-surpassing—that is to say, the becoming is always a *surpassing* of self but also a surpassing of *self*. We die daily in order to live tomorrow. We are what we were by not being what we were. We will be what we are by not being what we are. A society is what it was by not being what it was. A society will be what it is by not being what it is. Such is the dilemma of society's becoming, the dilemma of *new citizens, old laws.*

6.11. Society's struggle with the problem of its continuing reality is a second dimension of all social activity, all of society's self-identifying, power-structuring, will-forming, self-ordering. In living from day to day, society is inevitably living also for yesterday and tomorrow. The greatest achievements of consciousness have been the reality-forming by-products of society's struggle with the dilemma of its becoming. In religion, mythology, art, philosophy, history, natural science, economy, morality, and law, society creates stability-in-change through controlled self-transcendance. Such continuing idea-structures are secreted and accreted in the endless social process like amber or wax or honey or coral, or like silt. Conceived in the permanently present time of the minds of the actual members of society, they are nevertheless fruits of the past and seeds of the future. They speak the words of the past in the voice of the present into the ear of the future. They take hold of the future by taking hold of the past in the present. They re-form the past, form the present, pre-form the future.

6.12. As words and ideas and theories, they are formed by reason and imagination in the manner considered in Chapter 2. There is no limit to their possible content other than the limits of the imagining power of consciousness, no limit to their structural coherence other than the limits of the reasoning power of consciousness. But they have a special power attributable to their reality-forming function. Since they are reality-forming, affecting the way in which consciousness sees the whole of reality, they inevitably affect every aspect of the social process, the pattern of every social possibility, and hence all willing and all acting in society. In particular, having been formed as a by-product of the whole social process, they re-enter the social process to affect all society's work on the perennial dilemmas, powerfully affecting its identity-forming, its power-structuring, its value-forming and its self-ordering. They take part in an endless cycle of reciprocal action between the past and the present of society, from which emerges its future. The mind of society feeds on the mind of society.

6.13. Because the reality-structures of society are relatively permanent (relative to the impermanence of everyday social activity), because they have the prestige and authority of survivors in the evolutionary social struggle, and because they are often surrounded by mind-flooding signs, symbols, rituals, and ceremonies, they acquire a power within consciousness which is great and which is constantly reinforced by their repeated reaffirmation in heightened word and in numinous deed. They are liable to concentrate within themselves great resources of potential social energy, including the varied energies of impulsive feeling—of love and loyalty and joy and exaltation and self-preservation and self-abnegation and terror and anxiety and submission.

6.14. There is always the possibility, therefore, that a society may lose control of its relatively permanent reality-forming idea-structures, may succumb to them. There is the danger that they may lead it into a world of unreality, a world of fantasy, a world which, when it is experienced in the world of *individual* consciousness, is the world of alienation, of mental abnormality, of self-endangering and other-endangering behaviour. The consciousness of societies may become pathological. Transcendance may become possession.

6.15. The development of such a state of affairs may be imperceptible to members of the society itself, or to the majority of its members. It may be perceptible only to outsiders, other societies and their members. And their perception must, as in the perception of mental abnormality in individual consciousness, depend on their own theories, their own self-formed reality, their own conception of the normal, which, in turn, depends on their own self-formed reality, which might also be more or less pathological in the eyes of a third society and its members.

6.16. And what if the reality-forming of the international society of the whole human race were to become pathologically possessed by unreality? There is no human society beyond international society. Human social experience suggests that reality-forming pathology is liable to arise in two places—in the minds of single individuals, who make their own pathology into the pathology of a whole society, and in the fused minds of masses of human beings, the social consciousness of the crowd. The social energies of the whole of humanity are very great in volume and humanity is a very large crowd.

6.17. Within the capacity of the mass media of communication to unite the whole of humanity in a single process of reality-forming, the dangers are now as great as the opportunities. The burden of responsibility placed on those who watch, in the name of reason, at the frontier between reality and fantasy has never been greater.

6.18. Among all the processes of social reality-forming, it has been *religion* which, throughout all the recorded history of human socializing, has had the most powerful effects on individual and social consciousness, and on the practical products of that consciousness. Religion seeks to integrate all value with all reality. Religion seeks to connect an order of the whole universe with the willing and acting of the individual human being. The religious instinct is a reflection of the capacity of imagination to form possible reality and the capacity of reason to bring order to possible reality; and it is a reflection of the individual human being's sense of the mystery of self and of an individual's mysterious responsibility for the becoming of self within the mysterious becoming of all-that-is.

6.19. Religion is as natural to a human being as thinking. To will and to act is, for a human being, to will and act through consciousness in accordance with value under the impulsion of desire and within the constraint of obligation. It is natural, therefore, that reflexive and reflective consciousness will seek to find a theory to reconcile, within a single structure of significance, all willing and acting, all values, all desire and obligation, all of the impulse of life and all of the necessity of the universe. Such is the function of religion.

6.20. Religion is inevitable. Human consciousness is able to conceive of the problem of conceiving of the totality of all-that-is. It is able to conceive of any number of theories in relation to the problem. It is able to ignore the problem. Human consciousness is unable not to conceive of the problem of conceiving of the totality of all-that-is.

6.21. In considering the problem of the totality of all-that-is, religion is seeking to transcend itself, to provide for consciousness a theory of consciousness within the reality of all-that-is. Imagination is more than capable of the task. Reason is not. The result is that there is not religion but religions. And there is not only belief in religions but unbelief. And, since religion is one of the reality-forming theories in society, the self-conditioning effect of such theories applies to religions. They may lead a society into a world of fantasy and unreality, into a sort of madness. That unreality may come to play a major part in the society and in the society's relations with other societies. And since religions are liable, in their constant self-reinforcing, to generate the highest possible levels of social energy, they are liable to lead to violence on a great scale, and the most destructive of conflicts, up to and including major so-called wars.

6.22. So it is that religion is liable to dominate all the willing and acting life of individuals and whole societies. So it is also that religion may not alway be socially beneficial, that it may even be dangerous to societies and to individuals. Humanity would be able to dispense with diverse religions only if it were possible to create a single transcendant religion whose effects were only beneficial. The possibility of such a religion may exist already, but there is little prospect that that possibility could be actualized as a universal religion of international society within the foreseeable future. Humanity would also be able to dispense with religion altogether if humanity were more or less dehumanized, either by conditioning itself not to seek a universal reconciliation of all value with the reality of all-that-is or if machines were to take over higher-level thought and were instructed to stop short of ideas above a certain level of abstraction or generalization, and to filter out ideas liable to lead to the formation of such more general ideas. Both of these developments are possibilities contained in the future of humanity. Each is, perhaps, more likely than the generation of a single transcendant religion-of-religion.

6.23. In the meantime, while religions continue, with all their sublime and unsublime consequences, it is for human individuals and societies to monitor existing religions and their social effects and, as another part of the work of imagination and reason, to seek to improve religions and to moderate the effects of those religions which prove harmful in terms of the willing and acting that they generate.

6.24. In *art*, consciousness makes consciousness part of the physical world. The art-object is a part of the physical world filled with consciousness. The painting, the drawing, the building, the music, the vase, the pot and the dish, the sculpture, the poem, the play, the novel, the film—physical things (pigment, stone, paper, clay, sounds, visual images, lines, forms, shapes) are transformed by willing-and-acting consciousness into things existing in and for consciousness. They then become the causes of powerful effects within consciousness, where they become internalities, participating in all the processes of consciousness. Art-objects are things external to consciousness whose function is to be internal. Art is consciousness-creating-consciousness.

6.25. Consciousness emerges into the physical world by the creating of the art-object in order to re-enter consciousness in the art-object. The art-object takes on four important qualities of the physical world. (1) It becomes relatively permanent. (2) It becomes a possible object of contemplation for any consciousness into whose field of perception it happens to enter. (3) Its significance is at least as manifold as the number and diversity of those who perceive it. (4) Its only objective significance is that it must at least be a thing which is capable of having those specific significances for those specific people.

6.26. By this means a complex unit of consciousness is made to transcend time and to transcend the artist's consciousness in which it was formed. From cave-paintings to soap-operas, humanity has chosen to recreate physical reality within consciousness by recreating consciousness within physical reality. It must be supposed that such behaviour serves some specific biological function.

6.27. Anything within consciousness—words and ideas and theories and values, all accumulated human experience, instincts and impulsive feelings—can be placed by the artist in the vehicle of the art-object, however obscure, however complex, however unspeakable they may be—from a reaction to the physical world itself to a reflection on the nature of a god or gods, from a cry of pain to the joy of living. In particular, the contents of consciousness which lie at the so-called unconscious levels, not communicated by consciousness to consciousness, can readily be projected onto and into the art-object by its creator and by the audience.

6.28. The art-object becomes a possible object of contemplation for an audience which is indeterminate in number and identity. It is an audience which may contemplate the art-object after, perhaps long after, its creator has died. It is an audience which may be part of a society other than that within which the object was created, with different aesthetic standards and expectations, different social circumstances in which interpretation and evaluation take place. It is an audience which brings its own consciousness, and hence its own realities, into contact with the object, so that the object ignites untold numbers of different effects within consciousness, at every level of consciousness. The art-object, once created, lives countless lives.

6.29. Art is the union of physiology and philosophy. Passing from consciousness to consciousness by way of the physical world, the art-object detaches consciousness from itself and enables it to contemplate itself. Consciousness contemplates itself in the art-object as something other than itself but which comes from itself. Consciousness-considering-consciousness (philosophy) is made into a physiological event, as the object is apprehended through the senses, through the participation of the human body in the physical world. Art criticism and literary criticism and music criticism are a form of philosophy. They are consciousness-considering-consciousness-creating-consciousness.

6.30. Art is philosophy at play. It contemplates the world-for-consciousness, including the world as value and the world as obligation, without calling for any willing or acting on the part of the spectator. Art presents possibilities to the spectator, but does not demand that the spectator make any choice. Being a product of imagination, the art-object can thus present possible worlds *ad libitum*, rewrite history, re-form human nature, remake society, all without any form of commitment, free of consequences.

6.31. But play is a serious business. Play is never for play's sake. Play is an exploring of the world which is liable to have permanent effects on the ordering of the consciousness of the players. Aesthetic pleasure is a simultaneous pleasure of the mind and the body, as physiology responds to philosophy and philosophy responds to physiology. So it is that the pleasure we take in the fine arts at their finest is akin to the pleasure we take in the great idea-structures of natural science, the theorems of mathematics, a sublime landscape, a beautiful person. When the mind becomes aware of an order which is an order shared by the mind and the physical world, then the totality of the human system, mind and body, the whole of self-presenting human life, feels joy. And when the order is the order of our own lives, human experiences and human feelings, presented to us in circumstances of moral freedom, contemplation without commitment, then we are not merely elated; we are enlightened.

6.32. So it is that art, at its finest but also as entertainment, acquires a supernatural character. Art says things we cannot say, but are interested to hear. So it is also that art takes its place in reality-for-consciousness alongside the place occupied by religion. So it is also that art has a pathological tendency within it, similar to the pathological tendency within religion. There is always the danger that the unreal reality of art may overwhelm the rest of the reality-made-by-consciousness and generate a world of fantasy, alienation, mental abnormality. In the art of mass entertainment, perfected in the twentieth century through the concentration and application of great quantities of social energy, there lies the danger of mass hallucination, a danger quite as great as the mass alienation which may be caused by religion. As in the case of religion, the forming and re-forming through art of a transcending reality is an inevitable and never-ending social struggle. As in the case of religion, it is fraught with danger.

6.33. In *mythology*, a society seeks to relate itself to the order of all-that-is. Mythology is, therefore, a religion-for-society.

Mythology relates a society to its origin, relates the society to that which transcends it (the rest of physical reality and a supernatural reality), establishes the society's purposes, finds its future in its past. In mythology a society constructs its own genetic inheritance.

6.34. Mythology thus seeks stability in change by deriving society's significance from its past but in such a way that the past is perpetually present. The mythology is present in the consciousness of the members of society. But it is also present in all the processes of society, affecting all the words, theories, ideas, and values, all the willing and acting, of the society. As such, it gains reinforcement through the conditioning effect of social consciousness, through education, through the decision-making and decision-enforcing of social institutions, through rites and taboos and rules derived from it. Legends and superstitions and laws learned at the mother's knee become the reality of the adult's reality, the reality of society's reality-for-itself.

6.35. Mythology is particularly effective in organizing the unconscious aspects of society's consciousness. As much as any individual human being, human society has unspeakable areas of its consciousness which, even if they cannot be formulated in words and ideas and theories, nevertheless have a relentless effect on the generation of words and ideas and theories, and on the feelings, the impulsive energies, which may accompany those words and ideas and theories. As noted in Chapters 1 and 2, consciousness is able to integrate more than it can articulate. In mythology society is able to present to itself, often in symbolic and indirect and artistic forms but also in the form of words and ideas and theories, material of every conceivable kind, material which is of fundamental importance to it in constructing its own reality, in bringing a relatively stable order to the torrent of change in which it is immersed. It can present to itself ideas about the creation of the universe, the creation of the society, the identity and character of its founders (whether gods or heroes or wise men), their purposes and aspirations, the unfolding story of the society, the power of its origin and its past over the present and the future of the society.

6.36. The biological function of mythology—like the biological functions of religion and art—is thus to enable the human being, and especially the human society, to appropriate a transcendental reality, that is to say, to place within society's present reality-for-itself a reality which transcends society in its present condition. A mythology is an hypothesis of society's transcendental existence beyond its existence as a constitutional structure-system, the pattern of its becoming, the identity of its identity, an explanation of itself for itself. For this reason, mythology enters powerfully into a society's socionomy (its internal reality conceived as obligation), haunting all obligation, as obligation tempers desire in the name of society's systematic totality. A society's mythology may demand conforming behaviour.

6.37. Mythology is present not only in uncomplex societies. It remains as a sort of secular religion in the most complex of societies. When a society reaches a certain level of complexity, mythology changes its name to *history*. History takes the form of a presentation by a society to itself of its past. Since there is no way of knowing all that has happened in a society's past, society must itself choose from what remains of its past what it will carry into the future. And, in writing its own history, it is society itself which must determine the significance of its self-selected past. But, in studying its past, society is studying itself. Since society in its present state is a resultant of all the actualities of its total social process, history is the past studying the past. But society in its past and in its present is also a resultant of society's conceiving of its possibilities. So history is also the present studying its future. A society's future is in its past; its past is in its future. It is the function of history to conceive of society's future and its past as part of its present.

6.38. Like art, history seeks to present consciousness of society's past as if it were part of the physical world. It treats the past of a society as if it were the past of a natural system, susceptible to retrospective ordering, explanation, justification. But, because the past of a society is composed not only of the effects of physical causes but also of the effects of the willing and the acting of consciousness, history, like art, must perform a transformation on units of consciousness in order to give them this quasi-physical status.

6.39. History makes the past into an hypothesis. It gives to the past a second existence, giving it a capacity to influence the present not only as actuality—the possibilities which have survived from past activity of the total social process—but as hypothesis. In this way, the past re-enters consciousness, but now with a transcendant quality. The past of consciousness acquires, through history, a relatively permanent form, and it acquires a relatively objective form, in the sense that it becomes available, in the form imposed by history, to be an object of contemplation for anyone into whose field of perception it happens to enter. History makes the human past behave like an unhuman past within the human present.

6.40. Because history may have a powerful effect on the present and the future of society and because history is not observation of the physical world but consciousness-explaining-consciousness, it is not surprising that the writing of history can be a scene of social struggle. It is not surprising that it is a main arena for the struggle within all the perennial dilemmas of society here under consideration—as society struggles to identify itself in terms of its past, as society struggles to order its structures of power by reference to its past, as society struggles to order its values by reference to its past, as society struggles to determine its relationship to transcendant order in the light of its past, as society struggles to become what it might be as a product of what it has been. It is not surprising also when, in a particular society, history becomes collective fantasy, when history tends to madness, as a society conceives of the possibilities of its future in the unhealthy light of an unnatural past.

6.41. The historian stands guard at another of society's key frontiers of reality. History cannot escape from the social consciousness in which history is formed. But the historian is exercising a special form of social power in participating in the reality-forming by which society orders its becoming, reconciles social stability and social change. With special social power comes special social responsibility. The historian's first responsibility is to society and its purpose. Any responsibility to the actual holders of public power in society is subordinate.

6.42. International society must also come to terms with its past, its mythology and its history, which means coming to terms with the pasts of all its subordinate societies and with the past of all their turbulent interaction. International society has a past which humanity makes as it becomes the human society. International society will come to form the reality of its history as it comes to conceive of itself as a society. It will have its own international historians. The task of the international historian is an exceptionally difficult one. The responsibility is a responsibility owned to international society as a whole, that is, to humanity as a whole and to the future of humanity which is in its past.

6.43. In *natural science*, society creates a theory by which consciousness is enabled to will and act in the physical world as if it understood it. Science is concerned with the world which consciousness conceives to be a world which is not the world of consciousness, a world from which consciousness, and therefore value, is absent. It is an *other* world which consciousness makes in making the world of its *self*. The function of science is to create piecemeal within consciousness a theoretical structure whose *real* relationship to the *real* reality of the physical world is scientifically unknowable, let alone its real relationship to the real reality of all-that-is. That is to say, it is not the biological function of science to propose solutions to metaphysical questions about the nature of reality, nor even to propose solutions to philosophical questions about the nature of consciousness.

6.44. The biological function of science is to use imagination and reason in a particular way: imagination, to create theoretical models—including mathematical structures, models of systematic functioning, models of classification—which contain in symbolic form some part of the physical world as conceived by consciousness; reason, to control the process of theoretical structuring, within the integrating co-ordinates of reason (genetic, actual, potential) considered in Chapter 2.

6.45. Science creates a third reality between the reality of the physical world and the reality of consciousness. It is a reality-within-consciousness but a reality-from-physicality. Science makes a new world, a world made by the mind from a world which the mind did not make. The success of science since the fifteenth century has been the success of constructing such a third reality. Because of the prestige of its amazing practical achievements, science has succeeded in gaining an unquestionable and apparently permanent place for its third reality within the general structure of reality-made-by-consciousness. Science is a magic by which we seek to control the physical world through consciousness. Among forms of magic, it is uniquely effective.

6.46. Although scientific reality is value-free, in the sense that science does not seek to integrate the world of consciousness and its values in its hypothetical structures, it is a work of human consciousness and, therefore, a work not only of imagination and reason but also of desire and obligation, and hence a world of willing and action mediated by value. To do science is to act as a human being not as a machine.

6.47. The relation of science to human willing and acting is thus a complex one. There are four particular respects in which it plays an important part in social reality-forming and thereby in society's self-forming socializing. (1) Science enters as a privileged participant into the willing and acting of individuals and societies. Any act of consciousness which involves any contact with the physical world is liable to be decisively influenced by scientific reality. It is possible to act in ignorance of science. It is possible to act in opposition to science, preferring, for example, to act within a magical or a mythological or a religious or an artistic reality, preferring the products of free imagination to the products of imagination ordered by reason in accordance with the pure and transcendental theories of science. But it is not possible to act with the intention of altering the physical world with a degree of probability akin to certainty and, at the same time, to act contrary to the relevant hypotheses of science. This means that science can have a determining effect on the ideas and theories and values of society, and on individual acts of willing, individual value-decisions, which is unlike the effect of any other kind of idea. Scientific ideas tend to the condition of information.

6.48. (2) But the effect of scientific reality goes further. It has had a general philosophical, not to say metaphysical, effect. It has made possible a sort of universal materialism. Although science itself can say nothing scientific about the ultimate nature of reality (God? Spirit? Mind? Matter? Illusion? Unknowable?), it behaves, as an essential part of its successful functioning, as if the physical world of energy in the form of matter were self-contained, self-explaining, even self-justifying. This has led, in turn, to a natural inference that, especially given the actual capacity of science to transform the physical world, including the physical aspects of the human world, there is little or no need to consider further the nature of reality, to consider further the matter of transcendance, of what lies behind and beyond the material world. And this inference has seemed, in its turn, to have obvious value-implications, tending as it does to suggest that human willing and acting would become orderly if and to the extent that human consciousness, including social consciousness, were to behave as if it were ordered by pragmatic and non-transcendant theories, like those of science. Science has suggested the idea that human beings would be more orderly if they were less human.

6.49. Scientific reality seems obviously to be an orderly reality or a potentially orderly reality. Non-scientific reality, especially human and social reality, seems by comparison to be rather disorderly. The realities made by religion, mythology, art, history, philosophy, economy, morality, and law seem to be not only fluid and partial. They also seem to have a built-in incoherence, especially given that there are different religions, mythologies, arts, histories, philosophies, moralities, and laws, at different times and in different places. In this way science has seriously unsettled and weakened the other realities and thereby the ideas and theories and value-systems which they generate.

6.50. As magic, astrology, medicine, and psychology gradually succumb to its possibilities and disappear into the scientific reality, so consciousness forms the idea that there may be no area which is, in principle, beyond the reach of science, no other reality which will not in due course merge into scientific reality. Even consciousness itself, so it may seem to consciousness, could lose any special quality which it still has. This sense of the possible death of non-material human reality has had a significant effect on human self-confidence in recent centuries and thereby on human confidence in human values.

6.51. (3) Science is intensely progressive, constantly extending the reach and the quality of its hypothetical ideas. The idea of *progress* had never established itself finally in human consciousness before the modern age of science. Hypotheses of becoming, especially social becoming, had included ideas of natural decay and degeneration, periodic rise and fall, cyclical regeneration, rebirth and reincarnation, ineffable change, the wheel of fortune, supernatural determination. Science has now succeeded, where religion and mythology and history and philosophy had failed, in installing the idea of natural progress in the depths of human consciousness. It now seems certain that, at least in a particular sense of the word, we will *know* more tomorrow than we know today. It now seems certain that, in a particular sense of the word, we will have greater *power* over the physical world tomorrow than we have today. Since knowledge and power are important in society's struggle to survive and prosper, it seems to follow necessarily that, in a particular sense of the word, we will have more *successful* societies tomorrow than we have today. It is a purpose of the present study to suggest that society is, indeed, naturally capable of being progressive, able to achieve its survival and prospering by the appropriate willing and acting of human beings.

6.52. (4) The products of science are anything but value-free when they enter into the total social process of society. They may be used to do great good. They may be used to do great evil. The flood of the products and by-products of science is uncontrollable and overwhelming. Society is not able to assimilate so much progress. Social progress is surrendering to the progress of science, becoming a dependency of science, as science compels society to come to terms with all that it produces, to convince itself that it needs or even wants all that science is providing. Science-led social reality could become a tyranny of the non-human over the human.

6.53. Such is the harsh paradox of science. Science submits itself humbly to the physical universe by reducing it to something which can fit inside human consciousness. Science gives human beings ever-greater power over the physical universe as it tends to reduce human beings to the scale of the merely material.

6.54. Scientific reality has now established itself throughout international society. There is no corner of the world which is not subject to it. This means, in particular, that the intensely stabilizing effect of scientific reality, its capacity to take control of the endless flood of change, is now available to the whole of the human race and to all human societies. It means that the precious lesson of scientific objectivity and universality, the possibility of transcending value and conflicts of value, is heard throughout the world. It means that the whole human race now has available to it the splendid world-transforming power of natural science, a power to transform the world through the willing and acting of self-ordering human consciousness, especially as it struggles with the dilemma of justice and social justice. And it means also that the materializing, de-humanizing tendency of society's scientific reality-for-itself, when scientific consciousness spreads beyond consciousness of the physical world into the world of human value, is now felt through the world, modifying every other form of human reality.

6.55. In *morality*, society creates a relatively permanent structure of value. Morality is a practical theory of value based on a pure theory of order and a transcendental theory of reason. Morality creates a social reality in which the world is presented not in terms of the *justifying is* of religion, the *possible is* of art, the *was-is* of mythology and history, the *hypothetically is* of science, the *shall-be* of law. In moral reality, the world is presented in terms of *ought*. In morality, consciousness creates a system of obligation ordered by reason. Morality is obligation seen in the perspective of the total order of society.

6.56. As with the other forms of social reality, morality is thus a way of seeing the world. Everything in the world—the physical world and the world-of-consciousness—has, within moral reality, its own moral significance. Nothing is without moral significance—no word, no idea, no theory, no value, no willing, no acting. Morality presents the world to consciousness as obligation. And, since obligation is for the world-of-consciousness what necessity is for the physical world, morality is the constraint on desire which reflects the conception by consciousness of the requirements of consciousness as a system. To act as if effects in the physical world were the orderly outcomes of causes is to accept the obligation of necessity in the physical world. To act as if action in the world of consciousness were the orderly outcomes of willing is to accept the necessity of obligation in the world of consciousness.

6.57. Obligation has its constraining effect on desire in many other ways—in particular, in the generation of values, in the application of values to willing and acting. Between obligation and acting there lies the whole process of social and individual consciousness. All of society's reality-forming forms the reality within which willing takes place, and so forms the terms in which obligation presents itself to consciousness. As we see the social world, so we see its order. As we see the order of the social world, so we recognise obligation. As we recognise obligation, so we will and act.

6.58. Morality presents the socionomy of society (society as a totality of obligation) not only as a voice of society-as-system but also as a voice of society-as-continuity. Morality carries the past of society-as-obligation from society's past through its present into its future. Morality is value in the perspective of permanence. The function of moral reality is to collect in systematic form the experience of human consciousness of its world as a system of order. Its function is not, like that of law-reality, to form society as a system of order. Morality legislates; morality is not legislated.

6.59. Each society has its own moral reality. A society is a moral reality. But the tendency towards moral plurality is matched by an at least equal tendency to moral unity. In the first place, individual human beings are members of more than one society (for example—family, religion, state-society) and are liable to carry moral experience from one to the other. Secondly, societies, other than international society, are subordinate societies of superordinate societies (for example—a family within an organized religion, an industrial or commercial corporation formed under the legal system of a particular state-society, a state member of a federation of states). In such circumstances, the moral reality of one society is liable to flow into the others.

6.60. Thirdly, the integrating power of reason is common to all human beings and all societies. The systematic functioning of consciousness is a species characteristic. Fourthly, the systematic ordering of societies is common to all societies. The self-creating and the socializing of societies are the systematic products of the species characteristics of the human race. It follows that, whatever the differences of actual social experience between one society and another, there is likely to be a substantial concordance in their experience of the self-ordering process of society as society, the experience which manifests itself in the reality of morality, the reality of systematic social obligation.

6.61. Finally, it must be said that, were international society to conceive of itself as society, to become aware of its own reality-forming processes and of its own realities, then the moral experience of the human race, at all times and in all places, would be available as a moral reality of international society, as the society of the whole human race and the society of all societies.

6.62. *Economy* is the physical world seen as a world of potential human transformation, the world of consciousness seen as a world-transforming system of willing and acting. In forming its reality as economy, social consciousness chooses to see the world-for-consciousness as a world-made-conscious, a world of the word-made-thing, a world of the thing-made-word. In the perspective of economy, the physical world becomes the arena for the actualizing of human possibilities. In the perspective of economy, both the physical world and the world of consciousness become a world of human potentiality, where the actual, whether or not it is the product of human willing and action, becomes at once a possibility within the self-conceiving of human consciousness, individual and social. Everything is a possible object of human will and human action.

6.63. In the economy, the world is seen in the light of desire, as consciousness focuses its will with a view to acting on the world as object of desire, and in the light of obligation, as consciousness acknowledges the systematic constraints on obligation flowing from the necessity of the physical world and from the socionomy of society (society as a totality of obligation). Words and ideas and theories and values are generated to organize the working of consciousness on the world-as-economy. Practical and pure theories of the economy integrate ideas into structures within which desire and obligation may be reconciled with a view to the survival and prospering of society and its members (subordinate societies and human individuals).

6.64. Within all the other realities of society's reality-forming, economic reality shares in the values of society, using them as the basis for willing and acting. But the specific reality-forming of economy generates its own idea of value, *economic value*. Economic value is the world valued with a view to its transformation by human willing and acting. Within all the evaluating and distributing performed by society as it struggles with the dilemma of justice and social justice, society evaluates and distributes in the light of economic value, reconciling the socializing order of society with its self-conceived order of all-that-is, reconciling its economic transforming of the world with all its other socializing.

6.65. So it is that economy is a reality which depends directly on all the rest of society's reality-forming, reshaping society's reality into the willed action by which society continues its existence in the physical world and the world of consciousness. Economy depends particularly on law. It is in the law-reality that economic reality and economic distribution are carried from the past to the future, in the form of legal relations, especially in the legal relations of so-called property. It is through the law that the economy distributes social power to transform the world to serve the purposes of society, for the survival and prospering of society and its members.

6.66. The nature and functioning of economic reality will be considered further in chapter 17.

6.67. In *law*, society accumulates its self-creating. Law is the self-directed becoming of society. Law is the purposive self-ordering of society. In the law-reality, the reconciliation of impulse and necessity, desire and obligation, is actualized as possibilities which may then be actualized in willing and acting. In the law-reality, social identity is actualized as possibilities which may then be actualized in willing and acting. In the law-reality, structures of power are actualized as possibilities which may then be actualized in willing and acting. In the law-reality, values are actualized as possibilities which may then be actualized in willing and acting. In the law-reality, justice is actualized as possibilities which may then be actualized in willing and acting.

6.68. Law actualizes possibilities in the form of legal relations, that is to say, relations established within the law-reality of consciousness which relate individual human beings to each other, relate individual human beings to the societies of which they are and are not members, and relate societies to each other and to individual human beings. Legal relations are possibilities, since it is by an act of willing that a possible legal relation is chosen and may give rise to action.

6.69. The legal relations are created by the law from the possibilities made available by values, and hence indirectly from the possibilities made available by the words, ideas, and theories contained in that society's reality-for-consciousness. The law wills and acts to create legal relations. Its willing and acting take place within the general social process and, in particular, within society's struggle with the perennial dilemmas of society. Thus law is an integral part of the total social process. Its specificity is the form in which its willing and acting actualizes the products of the total social process—namely, as legal relations.

6.70. All law is old law. All law is potential law. Law is idea not fact. At a given moment in time, law does not exist except as a possibility from the past, a possibility for the future. It is a constraining possibility by reason of the non-possibilities which it excludes. It is an empowering possibility in all the actualizations which it makes possible. The legal relations which law creates are the resultants, actualized outcomes, of past states of the social process. They are the potential content of future states of the social process. It is in this way that law helps to mediate between stability and change, enabling the past of the social process to be carried into its future without excluding the possibility of willing and acting in the present.

6.71. Law is privileged among the social structures which are generated by a society's struggle with the dilemma of new citizens, old laws in that it has as its explicit function the mediation of stability and change. Religion may strongly affect the content of legal relations, may affect its forms and procedures and rituals. Art may affect the form in which the law conceives the physical and human world imaginatively. Legislation represents human and social events and relations in symbolic, abstracted, and generalized forms but, like the visual arts or literature, in a code which the spectator can translate into the recognizable particularities of everyday life. A statute is a complex image of human and social possibilities. A case decided by a court is a story of a story. A reported case is a story of a story of a story. Mythology and history affect the way in which the law conceives of the human past, individual and social, as being something explicable in terms of human motivation, significant in terms of human purposes having an organized continuity in relation to the seeming transience of actuality. Natural science affects the creation and the actualization of legal relations, to the extent that the law accepts the science-reality of cause and effect in a world of necessity. Legal relations assume that events in the physical world and events in the world of human consciousness which act on, and are acted upon by, the physical world are events in science-reality, even if they are also events in reality-for-consciousness.

6.72. Morality is law's privileged co-worker. Morality inspires the law to attribute willing and acting to individual persons (human beings and societies), to attribute freedom, understanding, foresight, purpose, guilt, responsibility, to think in terms of redress and punishment. Morality has supplied the law with many of its words and ideas. Morality has shared with the law much of its potential social energy, concentrating even impulsive human feelings into the creating and the actualization of legal relations. And law has fed back into morality, causing morality, in some societies and at some times, to be conceived of as a moral system, a sort of diffuse legal system.

6.73. Law thus substantially shares not only in the products of the general social process, including the products of the social struggle with the other perennial dilemmas. Law also shares substantially in all the self-stabilizing realities created by society within the perennial dilemma of becoming, to form part of the self-prolonging reality-made-by-consciousness. It acquires a metaphysic from religion, an imaginative technique from art, historicity from mythology and history, materialist objectivity from science, subjectivity (responsibility and motivation) from morality.

6.74. Law is idea not fact, but it is idea tending to the condition of fact. As one of the self-stabilizing realities of societies, law shares in their characteristic strategies of forming a special reality within consciousness by creating something relatively independent from actual consciousness, something transcendant in relation to actual consciousness, something echoing the independence of objects in the physical world. The particularity of law's quasi-independence is in relation to willing. Law retains within social reality acts of *past willing* with a view to the control of *future acting*.

6.75. Any act of will determines that among all available possibilities a certain possibility or certain possibilities will be actualized. An act of will says *it shall be*. The general function of acts of will is to transform a possibility into an actuality. But law creates acts of will with a special function. Law is a set of acts of will retained as possibilities within social reality.

6.76. Thus law is not merely a set of possibilities—models of behaviour that *may* constitute a crime or a civil wrong or a contract or a marriage or a corporation, models of behaviour that *may* constitute the response to a crime or a civil wrong or a contract or a marriage or a corporation. It is a set of possibilities of a special kind. They are possibilities which are *already* acts of will. This behaviour *shall* constitute a crime or a civil wrong or a contract or a marriage or a corporation. This behaviour *shall* constitute the response to a crime or a civil wrong or a contract or a marriage or a corporation. The future tense of the law is not a prediction, but an action-in-advance.

6.77. Law is a set of retained acts of will. Society has already performed an act of will when it has made law. The willed action which follows from that given law is action following from that given retained act of will. There may be many intervening acts of will. The actor or actors must will the relevant behaviour (crime, civil wrong, contract, marriage, corporation) and the relevant behaviour in response to those things (implementation, compliance, indictment, civil suit, judgement, conviction, sentence, exaction of the penalty). But in all the network of willing and acting relating to the behaviour in question, law stands as a quasi-independent, quasi-objective, quasi-permanent, quasi-fact, quasi-datum.

6.78. The *quasi-ness* of the materiality of law stems from the fact that law is a phenomenon within consciousness, perceived by consciousness, not a phenomenon of the physical world perceived by consciousness. The perception of law is part of the total social process. Those whose behaviour comes within the field of possibilities covered by law are themselves willing and acting in consciousness within the reality-made-by-consciousness, in particular in all the consciousness-forming realities considered above. Law is consciousness aspiring to be mechanism but doomed to be consciousness.

6.79. Perhaps by association with the reality which is morality, law is sometimes conceived and presented as if it were a set of legal rules or norms, echoing the commandments, precepts, prescriptions, dictates, in which morality is sometimes conceived and presented. And the reciprocal effect of law on morality has been that morality has sometimes in some societies, under the influence of certain formalizations of law, tended to be formalized as a set of moral rules. Law is not a set of rules or norms. Law is will. And the willing of the law is a willing of the action of one person in relation to another. Law is a set of legal relations.

6.80. In summary, therefore, it may be said that law-reality is one of the transcendental realities created by society in its struggle with the dilemma of new citizens, old laws, a reality with five leading characteristics. (1) It is, like the other transcendental realities, a reality transmitted from the past of society to the future of society with a view to determining the content of that future. (2) It is, again like those other realities, a reality which is itself subject to change, subject to never-ending modification under the influence of all the pressures of the total social process. (3) But, unlike those other realities, it is generated by society not merely as a theory or as a form of conceiving. It is generated as willing by willing. Law pre-forms the future by willing it in advance. (5) Past acts of will are retained in the form of legal relations which restrict the possibilities available for actualization by subsequent acts of willing, thereby restricting the exercise of social power in the physical world and in the world of consciousness.

6.81. The generation of law within social consciousness may be illustrated by Figure 5.

6.82. The nature and functioning of legal reality will be considered further below, especially in Part Two.

6.83. Consciousness presents to itself its struggle with the dilemma of new citizens, old laws in words and ideas and theories and values. Powerful words which are used as weapons in the struggle include the following: *act, authority, beautiful, binding, cause, commandment, constitution, convention, correct, creator, crime, culture, custom, decision, decree, deed, discretion, duty, effect, establishment, evidence, evil, faith, form, formality, god, gods, good, guilt, illegal, immunity, intention, invalid, judgement, justice, law, lawful, legal, legislation, legitimate, liability, moral, natural, nature, new, obligation, old, penalty, person, possession, power,*

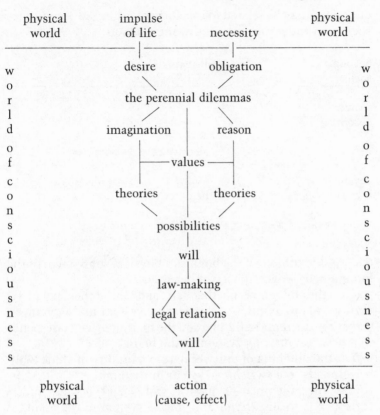

Fig. 5. The generation of law within social consciousness

precedent, privilege, proof, property, punishment, responsibil-ity, reform, retribution, revolution, right, rule, sin, statute, tradition, true, unlawful, valid, void, voluntary, will, wrong.

6.84. It is possible that, in due course, scientific hypotheses concerning the functioning of the human brain and nervous system, as a physical sub-system of the human body (and of the physical universe), will propose physical processes corresponding to the interlocking and interacting but separable processes within social consciousness which have been identified here as the five perennial dilemmas of socializing society. These dilemmas may be related to each other within the becoming of society in the form of the following diagram.

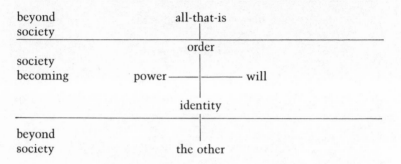

Fig. 6. Society's becoming as a system of dilemmas

6.85. A hypothesis of the brain as a physical sub-system of the human body might conceivably suggest:

that the dilemma of the self and the other (identity) corresponds to an *internal integrating* system in the brain;

that the dilemma of the one and the many (power) corresponds to a *network-forming* system in the brain;

that the dilemma of unity of nature, plurality of value (will) corresponds to a *switching* system in the brain;

that the dilemma of justice and social justice (order) corresponds to an *external integrating* system in the brain;

that the dilemma of new citizens, old laws (becoming) corresponds to a *storing and sorting* system in the brain.

6.86. It should always be borne in mind that, since human consciousness, whatever else it may be, is at least an aspect of the functioning of the system of systems which is the human brain, all its activities, up to and including the making of societies, must also be an aspect of that functioning, whether or not the particular hypothesis suggested above, of the correlation of brain-function and society-function, is anything more than a primitive fancy.

7   Society and Humanity

7.1. *A single species. One humanity.* Humanity shares the species-characteristics, the species-history, the species-potentiality of the human species. Humanity shares human physiology, the capacities and the limitations of the human body and of its sub-systems, the brain and the nervous system. Humanity shares the human condition. Humanity shares human consciousness. Humanity shares the world-made-by-consciousness. Humanity shares desire and obligation, imagination and reason, willing and acting. Humanity shares the capacity to make words, ideas, theories, values. Humanity shares the planet Earth, its abundant and finite resources. Humanity shares the strange, mind-surpassing universe. Humanity shares the unalterable necessity of the physical universe and the inexhaustible impulse of life.

7.2. *One humanity. Five billion human beings, each one unique.* Each human being an individual consciousness, the centre-point of an individual universe, the meeting-point of a unique set of worlds-of-consciousness. Each individual human consciousness the focus of its own desire, the focus of its own obligation, the focus of its own values, the focus of its own possibilities, the focus of its own will, the focus of its own action. Each of unique value to itself. Each a unique purpose for itself. Each its own becoming—self-fulfilling, becoming what it might be, becoming what it is. And each human being is born as every other and dies as every other. Each human being is a human being for every other. Each human being is as much a human being as every other. Each a co-habitant, co-user, co-worker, co-builder, co-enjoyer on the one planet Earth in one small corner of the same universe.

7.3. *One humanity. Uncountable intermediate societies.* Between humanity and the human beings, uncountable intermediate societies. Families, villages, tribes, communities, cities, autonomous regions, religions, churches, sects, clubs, ethnic groups, language-groups, nations, peoples, states, federated states, republics, federal states, companies, corporations, enterprises, organizations, associations, leagues. And each is a world-of-consciousness, each a complex web of realities-for-consciousness. Each is the focus of its own desire, the focus of its own obligation, the focus of its own values, the focus of its own possibilities, the focus of its own will, the focus of its own action. Each of unique value to itself. Each a unique purpose for itself. Each is its own becoming—self-fulfilling, becoming what it might be, becoming what it is. And each is a co-habitant, co-user, co-worker, co-builder, co-enjoyer on the one planet Earth in a small corner of one and the same universe.

7.4. *One species. One humanity. One planet Earth within one universe. Every single human being an integral part of a single physical universe.* Every atom and every cell of every human body, every neurone of every human brain, connected directly and reciprocally with all the energy of the universe. Every human being thereby connected with every other living thing that ever was or ever will be. Sharing in the energy of one universal system of order. Sharing the energy of the one planet Earth, the small by-product of small events in an inconceivable totality of events.

7.5. *One humanity. Five billion human beings. One society. One social struggle embracing the willing and the acting of one humanity, of every single human being, and of every intermediate society.* One social struggle within the agonizing and wonderfully fruitful dilemmas of the human condition—self-forming through other-forming; unifying power through multiplying power; unifying value through multiplying values; seeking the order of all order in continual re-ordering; creating stable realities through the making of an inexhaustible profusion of new realities. The life of every human being locked into the life of every other human being, as they all seek to survive and prosper through the transforming-through-consciousness of the small planet Earth and its small resources.

7.6. As humanity learns of its insignificance in a mysterious universe, its potentiality as a self-creating species increases. As humanity learns of the vulnerability of the Earth and its resources, its power to use those resources increases. As humanity learns to respect the dignity of every human individual, the potentiality of human society increases. Fruitful and hopeful paradoxes of the human condition.

Part Two   *Constitution*

It is not surprising if ignorance of the principle of its order makes people think a thing is unplanned and chaotic.

Boethius, *The Consolation of Philosophy* (tr. V. E. Watts, Harmondsworth [1969], 133).

*

Zeus therefore, fearing the total destruction of our race, sent Hermes to impart to men the qualities of respect for others and a sense of justice, so as to bring order into our cities and create a bond of friendship and union.

Plato, *Protagoras* (tr. W. K. C. Guthrie, Harmondsworth [1956], 52).

8   The Dimensions of Reality

8.1. *Time* and *space* are words. They are powerful words which are members of a large family of related words and ideas-by-association and which imply theories of great generality about the nature of consciousness and the nature of the universe. Words and ideas and theories of time and space haunt the whole of human language and, beyond language, the whole of human consciousness. Time and space, made by consciousness as it contemplates itself and its relationship to that which is not consciousness, have taken possession of consciousness. They have come to seem *necessary* ideas, without which, so we believe, we would be unable to conceive not only of the physical world, but even of the world of consciousness, of the functioning of individual and social consciousness within a universe which transcends them. Time and space have come to seem the inherent dimensions not only of reality-for-us but of reality itself.

8.2. Time and space enable us to present to ourselves a privileged version of reality which we call *the present*. The present seems to be the here and now, where and when we conceive ourselves to exist. In being conscious that we live, we conceive ourselves as living in a continuous present. And yet we cannot watch, observe, examine, measure, describe, or know the present. The here is no-where. There is no particular place that is here. There are as many heres as there are not-heres. The now is no-when. There is no particular moment that is now. There are as many nows as there are not-nows. The present is a no-thing. The *now* which seems to be a fixed point in time is ever-changing. The *here* which seems to be a fixed point in space is ever-moving. The present has the strangely discordant characteristics that it is the place where we live and yet it is a place which we can never find. The present is the hypothesis which we inhabit.

8.3. So fundamental and apparently so necessary in the structure of our consciousness, the present evidently performs some essential and distinctive function within the process of consciousness. Evidently it reflects some ultimate structural relationship within our consciousness and between our consciousness and all that is beyond our consciousness. In conceiving ourselves to exist in the here and the now we conceive a present in and for our own consciousness. We conceive of time and space in order to make possible our willing and acting.

8.4. The present-as-now is an idea formed from our ideas of the past and the future. It is the past and the future presented to consciousness in willing and acting. It is the past and the future contained in our willing and acting. We conceive as past that which is actuality, realised possibility. We conceive as future that which is possibility, capable of being transformed into actuality by our willing and acting, and by countless other transforming processes, including the unfolding of the physical world and the willing and acting of other individuals and of societies.

8.5. The arrow of time which we conceive as perpetually condemning the future to become the past, irretrievably and irreversibly, echoes our conception of the transforming process which is our willing and acting. We present our willing and acting to ourselves as the unceasing actualizing of possibilities through the choosing activity of consciousness. We project onto the rest of the universe a similar transforming activity. We watch the universe ceaselessly becoming, and we interpret its activity as the transforming of possibility into actuality, as energy is constantly reorganized, as matter endlessly integrates and disintegrates, as life ceaselessly develops, decays, and regenerates. Offering ourselves alternative explanations of such intense but apparently orderly activity, human consciousness may choose causation rather than chance, inherent order rather than external destiny. By so choosing, we have chosen also to regard the future of everything as being contained potentially in its past, the possible as latent in the actual, the actual as realizing the possible. And we conceive of a present-now which is the frontier between the future and the past, between the possible and the actual, the imperceptible crossing-point, the transformation which is not itself transformed.

8.6. We use time to put the universe into a form which makes possible our willing and acting. We arrange the universe so that it is the kind of universe in which the kind of being that we are can conceive of itself as a cause of causes, as a being which can present to consciousness a future which contains possibilities of choice, a present which contains our choosing through willing, a past which contains, among other things, the actualities which we attribute to our acting through willing.

8.7. In arranging the universe in the dimension of time, in making a reality-for-us which is time-structured, we do not exclude the possibility that the universe might be arranged in other dimensions or no dimensions at all, that there could be another reality for other forms of consciousness and for non-consciousness. We do not exclude the possibility that our own level of consciousness, which seems to demand a structure of time to make possible our willing and acting, will be *surpassed* by the consciousness of our genetic successors, through human effort or through the unfolding of the universe as physical universe. Nor do we exclude the possibility that humanity will *lose* even its present level of consciousness and cease to be a self-creating cause of causes, will rejoin the seemingly undifferentiated mass of the physical universe.

8.8. If the future provides the possibility of transformation available for our willing and acting, and the present contains the transforming which is our willing and acting, the past provides that which is transformed by our willing and acting. The past, irreversible and irretrievable as it may be, nevertheless contains the actual whose only function is to be transformed. So it is that we conceive of permanence by conceiving of change. It is the function of the past to subsist pending change. So it is that the possibilities of the future are limited by the past which contains that which may be changed by the future. So it is that the subsisting of the past is forever at risk of the actualizing of the possibilities of the future. And so it is that the present acquires its dramatic signifiance in our lives, as the hypothetical place where the past gives way to the future and where the future collapses into the past. The stage of that drama is our own consciousness, individual and social. And the drama is reality-for-us, a drama in which we human beings have assumed leading roles.

8.9. If the dimension of time enables consciousness to grasp the universe as possibility and actualized possibility, the dimension of space enables consciousness to grasp the universe as non-consciousness. Space organizes reality into states of actuality from which consciousness can conceive of itself as separated and on which consciousness can focus its willing and acting. The present-as-now enables consciousness to intervene between the future and the past through willing and acting by presenting the future as possibility and the past as actuality. The present-as-here enables consciousness to intervene between the future and the past through willing and acting in a universe which already contains co-existing actuality, realized possibilities in the present-as-now.

8.10. Time paradoxically enables consciousness to conceive of stability in grasping hold of change, making of *duration* the image of both change and stability. By a corresponding paradox, space enables consciousness to conceive of non-consciousness in grasping hold of its own co-existence with that which is not itself, making of *location* or *extension* the image of both integration and separation. Presence-here entails an integration between consciousness and that of whose presence it is conscious. And presence-here entails a separation between consciousness and that of whose presence it is conscious. To locate something is to acknowledge its nearness and its distance, that it is here and also there.

8.11. To locate something is also to create something. Just as time isolates manageable portions of reality and gives to each a duration, a becoming, a history, a future and a past, so space isolates manageable portions of reality, giving to each a location, an extension, an individual field of causation. It gives them not only an existence but also a unique existence. It is an existence which is unique whilst participating in the existence of all that shares presence in some given *here*. Space constructs the universe as a single structure whose centre is here. All-that-is has its existence in relation to the centre of the universe which is always here.

8.12. So it is that we form our reality, constructing a reality around a presence-here which is the hypothetical focus of all conceivable presences-here. The effect for me of the present sentence as a visual impression is an effect which I may situate as an event occurring in the physical location which is my brain, and as an event occurring outside my brain (in the elements of the physical world which I conceive of as being connected with that occurrence). The present sentence as seen on the printed page is here as compared with other sentences on the page and other pages. The place where I am reading this sentence is here as compared with other places—up to and including the place which is the universe and the place, if I conceive of any such, which is beyond the universe. The effect for me of the present sentence as an idea is one which I am able to express metaphorically, in words and ideas borrowed from the dimension of space, as being an effect within (present-here) in consciousness.

8.13. The effect of such things for other consciousnesses is communicated in space-language in ways which, on the one hand, seem to justify a belief in similar shared experiences within consciousness of a reality-in-the-dimension-of-space, and, on the other hand, tend to the establishment of a shared reality-in-space which is the hypothetical sum of all such experiences and the hypothetical cause of all such experiences. Individual and social consciousness constructs its space-based reality within which to conceive of its existence, individually and socially, to make possible its existence, its survival and its prospering. Consciousness constructs a hypothetical universe whose nature is to be the *there* of an infinity of *heres*.

8.14. Unlike the future and the past of the present-as-now, actualities can enter and leave and re-enter the present-as-here. Nothing is irrevocably *there*, necessarily beyond the reach of our willing and acting. There is no arrow of space pointing in a single direction, by which we put actualities beyond the reach of our willing and acting. However, time, with its arrow, intersects with space in two fundamental respects. From here to there is conceived as being inevitably a distance in time as well as a distance in space. The space between here and there is also a space in time. And, secondly, actualities which are conceived as remaining in, or re-entering, the present-as-here (the print on this page, this page, this book, this room, this planet, this universe) are yet also conceived as events, ceaseless becomings, unceasingly changing, never the same, even if they are changing in such a way as to be able to be conceived as being present-as-here, for some period of time— the lifetime of a tree or a human being, the period of the conceiving and the construction and the demolition of a building, a rainbow, or a spark.

8.15. So it is that the interaction of present-as-now and present-as-here presents to us the actuality which is held in the past and held in the present-here and is thereby made available to be transformed in realization of the possibility which we find in our future and which, through our willing and acting (our actualizing choice) becomes a new actuality, which is itself then held in the past and is available (if it is still present-here) for transformation by our willing and acting. We not only construct the reality which we need by conceiving it in time and space; we also construct reality by our willing and acting in relation to the reality which we have conceived.

8.16. Time and space are thus a consequence of the human being's ability to conceive the world in consciousness and to conceive of it as a world of possible willing and acting. If human beings were merely part of the physical universe, with a brain which did not present its activity to itself in consciousness, then the brain would not have needed time and space. In recreating the universe in time and space as a universe fit for consciousness, human consciousness has made an interlocking structure in which the universe is made to contain actualities which are yet possibilities (duration as change and duration as stability) and to contain actualities which are not consciousness itself (location as one-with-consciousness and that-which-is-not-consciousness).

8.17. The conceiving by human consciousness, in its actual state of development, of the dimensions of time and space, of a reality formed from a present-as-now and a present-as-here, is allied to and powerfully reinforced by our impulsive *feelings*, which seem to vindicate and validate our special way of grasping reality-for-us. Feelings are events in the human body, conceived as part of the physical world, which are also events in the world of consciousness. By a series of dualities, but also by an infinite range of intermediate states within those dualities, we respond to our existence in the dimension of feeling. Pleasure and pain, hope and fear, love and hate, hunger and satiety—such states of consciousness, and all the intermediate states, have their effect on us because they seem to be part of the present conceived as here-and-now. They happen to this body here: they are happening to this body now. In the feelings, consciousness feels the passage of the future into the past as a simultaneous presence, feels the here and the there as a coterminous presence.

8.18. We are both active and passive in relation to our feelings. They happen to us. They would not happen to us if we were not as we are. We are as we are because we have created ourselves as we are, through our willing and acting. We do not will and act to produce all the feelings that we experience. We could not will and act to avoid all the feelings that we experience. We place our feelings in the human body, as well as in their effects within consciousness, because they present themselves to us as actualities, actualities which form a more or less substantial part of the possibilities available to our willing and acting. Our feelings are constantly passing from our present into our past and, in so doing, are constantly influencing our choice of possibilities from the future, constantly present in the actualities which the future must transform into still more actualities of the past.

8.19. We see that non-human animals experience physical events which correspond to the physical events which, in the human body, generate the feelings we know (for example—attacking, defending, hunting, fleeing, mating, nurturing, sharing). We see responses in such animals which seem to correspond to the feelings which we know (fear, pain, pleasure, fatigue, affection). We also see that such animals can recall past events in a form which affects their future willing and acting (learning patterns of behaviour, recognizing situations of threat and opportunity, recognizing mates and offspring and co-members of a social group) and that they can identify places in a form which affects their future willing and acting (migration routes, nests, hunting-grounds, camouflage). We do not know the form in which such animals conceptualize such experience. In the absence of such knowledge, we use words such as *instinct* and *reflex*. And we tend to use the same words of ourselves, indicating the extent to which our possibilities, and our choosing of possibilities, are presence-there in the world of non-consciousness.

8.20. The alliance of feelings with our ideas of the present-now and the present-here has had a dramatically affirming effect on the structure of reality which we use to make possible our survival and prospering as conscious animals. Feelings seem to speak imperiously, beyond the possibility of negation. Ideas, by contrast, seem to be fragile, malleable, vulnerable, challengeable, controvertible. That we (and possibly other animals) experience so directly and so unequivocally the here-and-now of pleasure and pain, fear, desire, disgust, and so on, makes it difficult for us to accept the idea that the present-here-and-now is a convenient hypothesis of a conscious self-creating animal, human consciousness contemplating itself and its situation, and ordering its reality.

8.21. The reality of our universe-for-consciousness of time and space seems also to be affirmed powerfully by natural science. The hypotheses of science seem to relate to events, happening somewhere, happening sometime. Every physical event, from the beginning of the universe to the release of energy from this printed page, seems to be identifiable by reference to the co-ordinates of time and space. The becoming of the universe, its ceaseless change, seems to be change occuring in a place-here (my universe) at a time when (now or then). And with the successful application of science as a world-transforming instrument, its hypotheses have become completely and comfortably a part of human willing and acting, producing amazing effects in response to causes willed by human consciousness. Twentieth-century science has begun to suggest that, sooner or later, a physical universe structured on the basis of the human subjectivity of time and space may prove to be an inadequate hypothetical reproduction of the reality, whatever that may be, of the physical universe. In the meantime and for the foreseeable future, human consciousness is able to generate as many wonders of science as humanity can need or want.

8.22. With time and space consciousness has made a world fit for consciousness. But it has done more. With time and space consciousness makes a consciousness fit for consciousness. It makes of itself a system whose function is to will and act. Because we conceive of a future which contains possibilities, and a present-now which contains the choosing among possibilities with a view to action, and a past which contains actualized possibilities, and because we conceive of a present-here which relates us to everything which we regard as not-us, so we find ourselves, through our genetic inheritance as a species and through nurture and education, to be systems whose function is to transform the world through willing and acting. Objects in an undifferentiated universe, we become subjects in our own universe. Subjects in our own universe, we become makers of our own world.

8.23. It has been one of the biological functions of religion to absorb our ineradicable sense that the universe cannot be merely a universe-for-us, that the universe must be something which includes human consciousness but is not simply contained in human consciousness. In religion, we construct, through imagination and reason, the theory of a possible universe which is not a universe of time and space, a universe which is not simply an arena for human willing, a universe in which humanity is merely an incident. The hypothetical universe of religion is thus one about which we cannot speak in the way we speak about the universe of human subjectivity, of time and space, unless we speak of it metaphorically. For religion the universe of all-that-is exists in order to transcend the physical universe of time and space, it exists in order that we should not be able to speak of it, except metaphorically, and in order that we should not be able to will and act in relation to it, except in total submission. It is a universe in which the necessity of the physical universe and the obligation of the world of consciousness are contained in, and surpassed by, something which also contains and surpasses all life and all desire. So it is that the theory of religion may find a God beyond time and space.

8.24. Consciousness, by the amazing power of imagination and reason, allows us to stop the endless flood of becoming and call it the present here-and-now, in order that, through our willing and acting, we may be able to take responsibility for our future, to participate in making the future out of the past, the past out of the future.

9 The Dimensions of the Constitution

9.1. The constitution of a society is the fruit of a society's contemplation of itself in time and space. In the constitution society takes responsibility for making its future by making its past, takes responsibility for making its past by making its future. It does so by giving itself a continuing present-here-and-now.

9.2. Society is a sharing of consciousness and a sharing of willing and acting. Society participates in the creation by consciousness of a reality in the dimensions of time and space and so shares in the possibility of willing and acting. An individual human being has a personality. A society has a constitution. The constitution is for society what personality is for the human individual—the unique structure-system which confers a unique present-here-and-now on a unique individual enabling that individual to make a future from the past, a past from the future, possibilities from actualities, actualities from possibilities.

9.3. The constitution and the personality make possible the willing and acting of the uniquely constituted and personalized individual (society, person). They make possible also the presence of that individual in the consciousness of other individuals, to form part of all reality in space and time, an actuality among other actualities, having duration in time-structured reality, having location in space-structured reality. A constitution, like a personality, makes possible existence-for-self in making possible existence-for-others, makes possible existence-for-others in making possible existence-for-self.

9.4. Since a personalized human individual and a constituted human society are works of, and in, consciousness, it follows that their reality-forming is an application by consciousness to itself of the reality-forming process through which consciousness establishes its relationship to non-consciousness in the dimensions of time and space. In creating the person and the society, consciousness creates them as actualities, virtual things, virtual objects of the world of time and space. Since reality-forming by consciousness in relation to non-consciousness enables consciousness to carry out its characteristic function of willing and acting, it follows further that, in the person and the society, consciousness is enabled to act in relation to itself, to make of itself that which is capable of willing and acting in, and in relation to, the reality which it has formed for that purpose. The unique person and the unique society are unique sources of willing and acting.

9.5. The constitution of a society, like the personality of an individual person, enables society to have an existence in the hypothetical present-now, which contains the willing and acting, and in the hypothetical present-here, which is modified by the willing and acting. To live is to exist in a present-here-and-now formed by consciousness in willing and acting. A society and a person live, have existence, in a present-here-and-now which contains their willing and acting and which are modified by their willing and acting. In their present-here-and-now, the past is transformed into the future and the future is transformed into the past, the there becomes here and the here becomes there. By their constitution and their personality they organize the becoming of their universe.

9.6. The constitution of a society is accordingly one and three at the same time. It is continuously and uniquely present-to-itself through all its becoming. And yet it has three faces, three aspects, three perspectives, three moments, three internal dimensions. The constitution is three constitutions in one— the legal, the real, the ideal. That is to say, society has a constitution which presents its past as an actuality, a constitution which is contained in its willing and acting, and a constitution which contains the possibilities of its future. Through· its constitution society creates itself, as a function of what it is as willing consciousness (real constitution), of what it conceives itself to have become (legal constitution), and of what it conceives that it could be (ideal constitution).

9.7. The *legal constitution* is the constitution as law, a structure and a system of retained acts of will. Retained acts of will which are concerned with the distribution and use of social power are carried in the legal constitution. Power is thereby made available as social power in the real constitution, in the actual willing and acting of society. The legal constitution determines the categories of person holding the categories of social power; it determines the contents and limits of social power. It determines the methods of implementing and enforcing social power. It determines such things by acts of will and then retains those acts of will as law, as actualities within the possibilities of further acting and willing.

9.8. The *real constitution* is the constitution as it is actualized in the current social process, a structure and a system of power. It is the constitution as it takes effect in the present-here-and-now, as actual persons exercise the social power made available by the legal constitution to realize the possibilities of the ideal constitution, as actual persons will and act in consciousness as the makers of their own future from their own past, their own past from their own future. It is the constitution as it meets the rest of the present-here-and-now of the social process, as it meets every form of power, not merely legally formed social power but also natural power (physical power, and the power of consciousness itself working through imagination and reason, working through individual and social consciousness). The real constitution is the pattern of the actualization of society's possibilities-for-itself, the pattern of the relationship between the constitution and the personalities of individual human beings and the constitutions of other societies.

9.9. The real constitution is thus the scene here-and-now of society's perpetual self-creating, as it struggles, in its willing and acting, to create its unique social identity, to organize the interaction of all the power of its members, to reconcile its internal order with the order of the rest of reality, to conceive of its potential self within its actual self, to convey itself into its future as the society of its future members. Within the systematic willing and acting of the real constitution, society creates itself for itself, in accordance with its words and ideas and theories and values, making its reality-for-itself within the reality of all-that-is.

9.10. The *ideal constitution* is the constitution as it presents to society an idea of what society might be. In the ideal constitution, society organizes desire and obligation with a view to its own becoming. In the ideal constitution, society conceives of its other selves, possible selves which conform to its idea of itself as society. In willing, society chooses to make an actual self out of one of its possible selves. Its possible selves are possibilities inherent in the legal constitution and the real constitution, but they are also possibilities which shape the legal and the real constitution. Power which is made into social power by the legal constitution and which is applied as social power in the real constitution is power which makes possible the actualization of the ideal constitution. From the ideal constitution come the aims and objectives of social power. The ideal constitution is the pattern of society's self-conceived possibilities-for-itself and thereby the pattern of society's possible self-creating through willing and acting.

9.11. The total social process includes an integration by society of the three dimensions of its constitution, moment-by-moment in every aspect of the life of the society. The continuous present of the constitution is a constant re-presenting. The constitution is a constituting of its constituents. Each face of the constitution integrates the others. The *legal* constitution contains the present distribution of social power, but is itself a product of the past work of the social process, including the continuing effects of all the past work of the real constitution and of the ideal constitution. The *real* constitution contains the actual willing and acting of actual persons, including subordinate societies, but works with the self-willed actualities of the legal constitution and the conceived possibilities of the ideal constitution. The *ideal* constitution contains the potentialities of society, but as an extrapolation of the actualities of the legal constitution and the possibilities of the real constitution.

9.12. And the constitutional integration, a perpetual juggling by society with the dimensions of its own reality, is also an integration of perspectives which are themselves constantly changing. The legal constitution is not merely a survival from the past. It is constantly being remade, through the willing and acting of the social process, with a view to being the legal constitution of tomorrow. The real constitution is not merely a given state of affairs (such specific persons actually holding such power and exercising it in such a way). Power is exercised in relation to the rest of reality, social and extra-social and physical reality, which is constantly changing, constantly modifying the actualities which determine the possibilities for the exercise of power. The ideal constitution is not a fixed star towards which society steers a fixed course. It is constantly being remade as society's words and ideas and theories and values alter society's idea of its potential self through all the intense activity of the total social process.

9.13. The constitution is a changing resultant of the changing resultants of changing forces. In its constitution, society builds from its own substance the structure of its own structure, and builds its own system by the operation of its own system. Through its own system it builds the system of its own system. By willing and acting under its constitution, society makes possible its willing and acting under the constitution.

9.14. The overwhelming difficulty which consciousness has experienced in understanding the working of society stems from this self-interacting of society, its *intra-acting*. Its structure and system make its structure and system. Its constitution makes its constitution. It makes itself in making itself. And since all this creation takes place within consciousness, social consciousness is making itself in contemplating itself. In contemplating itself, society is making itself. In making itself, society is remaking itself. In constituting itself, it is constituting its self.

9.15. The intra-acting of society within itself accounts for the otherwise strange social phenomenon that, when the constitution itself comes to be explicitly in issue within the dialectical struggle of society, it seems to become, at one and the same time, an actual thing and a potential thing and a merely hypothetical thing. It seems to be an actual thing if the society has a constitutional instrument (the written constitution of a nation-state, the charter or the articles of incorporation or association or the statutes of a corporate legal person, the rule-book of some other form of society). And, even if there is no specific constitutional instrument, the constitution seems to be an actual thing in particular forms of the self-conceived con-stitutional reality-for-consciousness (laws, customs, traditions, taboos, rites, rituals, ceremonies, legends, stories, poems, songs, chants). The actuality of the constitution enables members of society to speak of the constitution as if it already existed. They may say: *such-and-such is unconstitutional! the constitution is under attack! defend the constitution! punish the violators of the constitution!*

9.16. And yet, at the same time, other members of society may sharply dispute such a view of the constitution, speaking as if the constitution were something quite other than that presented by its expounders and defenders. They may speak of quite different possibilities as being constitutional. They may declare themselves to be defending the true constitution, to be justified in their action and behaviour by the true constitution. Such a situation arises when fundamental choices are presented in the social process, as possibilities for social willing and acting. It is a situation which arises in its most striking form before and during times of intense social contention, so-called revolutionary times, when those wielding power under the real constitution may be condemned as violators of the constitution by revolutionaries who may claim to represent the true constitution, who may seek to overturn the real constitution by the use of unconstitutional power (power not distributed by the legal constitution), who may rely on the ideal constitution to justify their willing of a new legal constitution. And, in normal non-revolutionary times, there may have to be a system under the constitution by which social power is conferred on some authority precisely to determine constitutional questions, social power to will and act that such shall be constitutional.

9.17. This phenomenon—a constitution which is worth dying for but which can also be seen as merely potential or even hypothetical—is a direct consequence of the fact that the members of society are making the constitution as they contemplate it, as they dispute about it, as they will and act under the constitution, as they live and die for it. To be seen as a constitution is to become a constitution. To become a constitution is to be seen as a constitution.

9.18. There is another respect in which the constitution seems to be as much potential as actual. The legal constitution socializes power in the form of abstract categories (the organs of the constitution and other subordinate societies, legal persons, legal powers, legal rights, legal duties, public offices, forms of property, crimes, wrongs, legal transactions). In so doing, it creates actualities (social power), but actualities which present themselves as possibilities within the real constitution, as possible patterns of willing and acting. Between the actualities of the legal constitution and the possibilities of the real constitution there is the whole social process which determines the actual outcomes of the exercise of the abstracted forms of social power. Similarly, contemplation of the ideal constitution is articulated in terms of words and ideas and theories and values (incorporating society's practical theory, invoking its pure and transcendental theories). Once again, therefore, the ideal aspect of the constitution seems to be mere patterns of possible willing and acting. Between the abstracted possibilities of the ideal constitution and the actual possibilities of the real constitution (actual social power) there is the whole social process, which determines the actual outcomes of the realization of the abstracted possibilities of society's future.

9.19. The integrating of the three constitutions, the interacting of the three ceaselessly changing perspectives of the constitution, the intra-acting of society socializing, generates a process of generation. The constitution is a process not a state of affairs. The constitution is a becoming not a being.

9.20. However, if the constitution of a society is a process, it is a particular process, the process of a particular society. The constitution is not *merely* potentiality. It is the particular potentiality of a particular society, the product of its particular willing and acting throughout the whole social process, within its unique continuous present. All three constitutions involve and embody particular choices among the immeasurable range of possibiliities made available by imagination and reason, willing and acting in response to the impulse of life and in response to desire, willing and acting under the constraint of the necessity of the physical world and the obligation discovered within consciousness.

9.21. It is the given social process of a given society which generates the particular actualities of that society's legal constitution (the organs of the constitution, the distributing of social power, the control of social power), which generates the particular possibilities of that society's ideal constitution (the particular economic theories, the particular conceptions of the relationship of the individual to society, the particular conceptions of the relationship of the society to other societies, the particular conceptions of the relationship of social reality to universal reality). And, still more clearly, it is the given social process of a given society which generates the particular possibilities of the real constitution, the particular possibilities for individual members of society (including all subordinate societies) to make use of the legal and ideal constitutions (to acquire and exercise public power in public offices, to acquire and use property, to form subordinate societies, to participate in all reality-forming social processes, such as teaching, research, art, entertainment, the media of communication).

9.22. To act under the constitution or in relation to the constitution is to *make* the constitution. But it is also to make *the constitution*. The actuality of a given constitution is the potentiality of that constitution. The potentiality of a given constitution is the actuality of that constitution. A constitution is the becoming of *that* constitution. A constitution is the constituting of *that* constitution.

9.23. The particularity of a given constitution is thus a function of the given social process within which that constitution is being generated. The struggle of a constitution with the perennial dilemmas of society, considered in Part One, includes the struggle to generate the particular constitution of that society and to make the society which that constitution makes possible.

9.24. In the struggle of the self and the other (the dilemma of identity), society needs to give substance to its self and to give substance to all the others in relation to which it is becoming its self. The constitution, in its three forms, provides the kinds of substance which this need calls for. Its actuality is substantial enough to carry the substance of the actual self. Its potentiality is enough to allow for the becoming of the potential self. And the constitution of an *other* society is substantial enough to help form the *self*-perception of the given society. But the constitution is also potentiality enough to allow for the becoming of the potential self—and not only to allow for it. It also conditions the potentiality of the self, by shaping the possibilities within which self-development may occur. A society forms its constitution to bear its identity. But it also forms its constitution to shape its identity. Once again, there is a cycle of mutually reinforcing energy between the identity of the society and its constitution.

9.25. Thus the constitution, in all its forms, is an essential part of the self-identifying of society. The constitution is able to receive and contain and retain the constantly forming identity. The identity is able to discover its own image in the making of the constitution, to reveal itself to itself in the mirror of the changing constitution.

9.26. In the struggle of society with the one and the many (the dilemma of power), society needs to give substance to the endless succession of its resolutions of the unity and multiplicity of society—the unity/multiplicity of its own internal structure; the unity/multiplicity of its own membership of other societies. The structure of a society is a structuring, and society needs some form in which to retain the outcomes of that process of structuring, a form which is able to treat those outcomes as both actualities and possibilities. They are *actualities* to the extent that they restrict the range of possibilities which may be turned by further acts of will into action. The relations of power (governmental power, property, economic power, patriarchal power, ecclesiastical power) restrict the range of possibilities available to the power-holder and those affected by the absence of power and by the exercise of power. The outcomes of the process of social structuring are *possibilities* to the extent that they are themselves inevitably part of the continuing social struggle, liable to be negated and modified and surpassed by other outcomes.

9.27. Thus the constitution, in all its forms, is an essential part of the self-structuring of society, its organization of power. The constitution is able to receive and contain and retain the constantly forming structure. The structure is able to structure itself by reference to the constitutional structure.

9.28. In the struggle with unity of nature, plurality of value (the dilemma of will), society needs to be able to give substance to its temporary and partial unities of value as provisional actualities. Provisional they may be, but, while they last, they fundamentally affect the willing and acting of society and all its members, including subordinate societies. All the willing of society, from the willing of society at the most general levels to the willing of individual human beings, involves a choice among possibilities, the possibilities and the choice being conditioned by the words and ideas and theories of society, inspired by desire and constrained by obligation. Society's partial and provisional unities of value mediate between desire /obligation and will/action. To do that they must be carried in the structure of society—not immune from the possibility of change, but substantial enough to have their effect on will/ action.

9.29. Thus the constitution, in all its forms, is an essential part of the organization of society's willing. The constitution is able to receive and contain and retain the constantly evolving transcendental willing of society, its acts of will about willing and acting. Society, in willing and acting, is able to will and act its willing and acting under the constitution.

9.30. In the struggle with justice and social justice (the dilemma of order), society needs to be able to give substance to its endless re-ordering of its relationship to the order of all-that-is. The microcosm of society must for ever establish and re-establish its relationship to all that transcends it (cosmos) to societies of which it is a member, including the international society, to the physical universe and its necessity. But the microcosm of society is also a cosmos. Most urgently of all, society must establish and for ever re-establish its relationship to its own order as a structure and a system. As a totality, an integrated structure, a self-coherent system, society must constantly integrate its willing and acting, its struggle with all the perennial dilemmas, in relation to that totality. In seeking the order of social justice it must seek the order of justice. The results of that seeking, from day to day, must be able to be integrated with the results of past order-seeking and the possibilities of future order-seeking.

9.31. Thus the constitution, in all its forms, is an essential part of society's self-ordering. The constitution is able to receive and contain and retain the outcomes of society's self-ordering, as society orders itself as a total structure and system. Society is able to submit to the self-willed order it finds in its constitution.

9.32. In the struggle with new citizens, old laws (the dilemma of becoming), society needs to be able to give substance to the self-created realities which it treats as reality. The constitution obviously plays an especially significant role in the drama of the dilemma of becoming. Because the constitution is three-in-one, creating an indissoluble relationship between the past and the present and the future, and because the constitution is actuality and potentiality, it is able to offer the most effective means for organizing the stability-in-charge/change-instability which society needs to prolong its existence, to ensure its survival and prospering. The great social idea-structures of religion, mythology, art, philosophy, history, science, economy, morality, and law are themselves wonderfully efficient vehicles for taking society from its actualized past through its actualizing present into its actualizable future. They do so by becoming the reality of all consciousness as it wills with a view to acting. But they themselves depend on the constitution. They depend on society's having a structure-system which is more solid and more stable than they are, but which also has an inexhaustible capacity to change.

9.33. It is in this respect that the three-in-one constitution is most like the personality of an individual human being. Our personality is the compendium of our past, our powers, and our plans. At the moment when we are called upon to will and act, the totality which is our personality organises our personal reality so that the outcome of our willing and acting is not only a product of the circumstances in which we are called upon to act; it is a product of our personality interacting with those circumstances. Our own personal becoming is the resultant of that interaction, of all the interactions between our personality and the becomings of all other human beings and all of all societies to which we belong or which have the power to affect us. Similarly, the becoming of a society is the resultant of all the interactions between that society's constitution and the becomings of all other human beings and all other societies which have the power to affect that society.

9.34. The present here-and-now of the world of human consciousness is thus the sum total of the becomings of all human beings and all societies as their consciousness takes responsibility for willing and acting in exercise of their powers, as permitted by their past, as proposed by their plans. The constitution of a society and the personality of an individual human being impose that responsibility, generate the possibilities for willing and acting in exercise of that responsibility, but leave the willing and acting as a choice which the society and the individual human being make as a function of the whole content of their world of consciousness, including all their words, ideas, theories, and values. It is in this sense that the constitution, like the human personality, is the structure and the system of society. The culture of a society, its life, is something greater. It is the totality of all that that society has made of itself, timeless and spaceless. Within that totality, the constitution retains society's reality in the form necessary for it to take responsibility for its becoming, its self-creating, through its willing and acting as a society.

10 The Social Exchange

10.1. Society, as a structure and a system within consciousness, creates itself by conceiving of itself within consciousness in the perspective of its constitution, by willing and acting with a view to the constant re-conceiving of that constitution, and by willing and acting with a view to actualizing the constitution. The structure-system of society contains an exchange of energy. The social exchange transforms natural power into social power, exchanges power for purpose. Social power created under the legal constitution takes the form of legal relations.

10.2. Systems which are structures defeat formlessness. Structures which are systems defeat aimlessness. Structure-systems are thus able to contain their past, from which they have become the structures that they are, and their future, which contains the possibilities which will be actualized by their systems and will become their past. In this way, structure-systems take hold of the future by means of the past and take hold of the past by working on the future.

10.3. And if a structure-system is a structure-system within consciousness, a structure-system for willing and acting, then it also has a present, that continuous present which, in the way considered in Chapter 8, is made by consciousness from its past and its future and in which it takes responsibility for willing and acting to generate its future from its past. A constitution, as a structure-system within consciousness, thus enables society to defeat formlessness and aimlessness, enables society to have a continuous present within which daily life can be lived, the life of willing and acting, the world of society socializing, of society self-creating.

10.4. A rock is a structure which contains structure-systems (atoms) and may contain structures (lattices, crystals). A motor car is a structure-system which contains structures (metals, rubber, man-made materials) and structure-systems (ignition, braking, lighting—as well as the structure-systems which are atoms). A tree is a structure-system which contains structures (cellulose, water) which contain structure-systems (atoms, cells). A legislature is a structure-system which contains structures (buildings and their contents) and structure-systems (human beings) which contain structures (flesh, bone) and structure-systems (the brain and nervous system and other bodily systems, atoms, cells).

10.5. Such a distinction between a *structure* and a *system* is a prescriptive distinction, proposed for the purposes of the present hypothesis. There could be other ways of representing in words and ideas the various forms of integration which seem to consciousness to be present in the physical world and in the world of consciousness. The distinction focuses on the *totality* of a structure and the *transforming capacity* of a system. That is to say, the description of a structure requires that its constituent elements be not only listed but also placed in relation to each other. The description of a system requires that, in addition to such a structural description, the interacting of its constituent elements be described.

10.6. It is apparent that features of the physical world and of the world of consciousness can be described at any number of structural levels—in the case of the physical world, from the subatomic level to the level of the structure-system of the whole universe; in the case of the world of consciousness, from the level of the smallest unit of consciousness (a word, a feeling, a non-verbalized idea) up to the structure-system which is the accumulated consciousness of the whole human race. Every structure-system in both worlds contains component sub-structures and/or sub-systems. Every structure-system in both worlds is a component sub-structure and/or sub-system of other structures and/or systems. For different purposes, the same features of the physical world and the world of consciousness can be described at different structural and systematic levels.

10.7. What we can say is that consciousness, for the purpose of its willing and acting, has found it useful to identify particular structures and systems. But no particular identification is exclusive or necessary or final. Structural identifications may be created, modified, abandoned. The struggle with the perennial dilemmas of society, considered in Part One above, is the main arena in which societies work out structure identifications for the purposes of their own particular willing and acting. Available words, ideas, theories, and values determine, directly or indirectly, the structures and systems within which society sees its realities. The great social institutions of religion, mythology, history, art, natural science, morality, law—themselves structure-systems full of subordinate structures and systems—play a leading role in the conceiving and sustaining of structures and systems. The dynamic character of the whole social process is reflected in the changing structures and systems which a society uses for its own purposes.

10.8. The *totality of a structure* is an internal and an external totality. It is internal in the sense that the elements of the structure are related to each other in a relation which can be expressed without reference to anything outside the structure —a given tree, a given motor car, a given legislature. The totality is external in the sense that the totality of the structure is precisely a separation from other structures. The given tree is separated from the earth in which it grows, from a neighbouring tree, from the human being who sees it. The given car is separated from other cars, from the road on which it travels, from the driver who enters it for the purpose of driving it. The given legislature is separated from other organs of the constitution, from the constitutional structure of which it forms a part, from the human beings who come and go as its members.

10.9. The interaction of the constituent elements of a system involves *transformations*. Transformations are transformations of energy in all its forms—unstructured energy (for example, electricity or kinetic energy), energy structured as matter, units of consciousness (words, ideas, theories, values), all other kinds of sub-structures. The transforming capacity of a system transforms the transformed materials so that they become new or different structures and systems through the functioning of the system.

10.10. The system of the living tree transforms light, carbon dioxide, water vapour, chemical substances taken from the earth, into its cellular substance. It retains some of that substance for a shorter period of time (leaves) and some for a longer period (wood), before its substance is again transformed by the operation of the living system of the tree, including the final transformation when the tree is said to die and its substance is transformed by other natural systems into new substances (timber, gases, earth, insects, plants, trees). The system of the motor car transforms gasolene, oil, stored electricity, air, and the stored energies of the driver (energy of his body, energy of his consciousness) into forms of energy which can be applied by its sub-systems to cause friction energy between its wheels and a road surface. The system of the legislature transforms the energies of human speech and writing, the energies of machine-systems (public address systems, typewriters, printers, lighting, heating), the energies of other social systems (law, morality, education, the media of public opinion) into the form of debates, recorded debates, legislative acts, decisions, which then undergo any number of further transformations in other systems.

10.11. Once again, it is apparent that all such transformations are themselves constituent elements of any number of more general systems, up to and including the transformation of energy which is the Earth-embracing and Earth-transforming star known as the Sun, and the all-embracing and all-transforming of energy which is the total system of the Universe. So far as consciousness is concerned, it is a feature of some religious philosophies to postulate a universal structure-system containing, but not limited to, all humanly known sub-structures and systems, including the structures and systems of the physical world and of consciousness.

10.12. So it is that a structure defeats formlessness. A structure enables consciousness to grasp the world, the physical world and the world made by consciousness, in forms which are intermediate forms between a hypothetical unity of everything and a hypothetical multiplicity of everything. Between the smallest conceivable unit of physical energy and the whole universe, between the smallest unit of consciousness and the whole of human consciousness, consciousness wills and acts by using the structure and the structures available to it, such as they are, such as they are capable of being. Grasped in the form of structures, the world has a present here-and-now in which consciousness can will and act to transform the future into the past. A structure carries the past (in which it was formed) into its future and enables the future (as it is formed as a structure) to become the past, through the operation of the present (the willing and acting which forms the structure). A structure locates some part of reality in relation to some part of consciousness.

10.13. So it is also that a system defeats aimlessness. A system enables consciousness to take hold of the process of forming as it is happening. Systems choose. The system transforms possibilities into actualities—the gasolene, the oil, the electricity, the air, the energy of the driver, could have been applied within other systems and caused other transformations. The ignition system of the engine, the braking system, the lighting system, could have been used as part of other structure-systems. And the system which is a motor car might not have worked as such. The engine might not have ignited, the lights might have failed, the brakes might have failed, the car might have travelled in the wrong direction through a fault in the steering system or in the gear system. So a system chooses to make transformations within a range of possible transformations. It is limited to a given set of possible transformations. But, within that set of transformations, its acting can produce a given set of possible outcomes. To be a system is to liberate, by allowing a choosing from among possibilities, and to constrain, by excluding the unchosen and the unpossible. To be a system is to choose one future out of many futures from within one past which was itself one future among many futures.

10.14. The concept of *purpose*, which seems to be so central to all human activity, all willing and acting, all social activity, is thus an expression of the systematic character of the structure-systems which are human beings and human societies. Human beings and human societies share the liberating and constraining aspects of all structures which are systems—the capacity to make actual some possibilities from among a limited set of possibilities. Our systematic structure makes us able to produce transformations, to make possibilities actual. Our systematic structure makes us able to produce only certain transformations, to make only certain possibilities actual. Human beings cannot jump over the moon. Human beings can make a rocket to propel human beings to the moon. Human beings cannot know the nature of all reality. Human beings can imagine and order partial pictures of the physical world which enable them to make rockets which take them to the moon. Human beings cannot make themselves into gods. But human beings can imagine and order pictures of the reality of their own world of consciousness which give them power, individually and socially, to live better and better as human beings, to make themselves better and better human beings, constantly to recreate themselves.

10.15. And human beings, having consciousness, can conceive of their own systematic capacity and can present to themselves their systematic activity within the dimension of the present, as they take responsibility for making the future through willing and acting. In short, human beings can form purposes. Purpose is choice seen before the event, when the event is consciousness as it chooses among the possibilities of its system.

10.16. If, as has been suggested in Chapter 3, desire is the impulse of life as conceived within the self-creating world of consciousness, and obligation is the necessity of the universe as conceived within the self-ordering world of consciousness, purpose is possibility conceived by consciousness within the dimension of the present-here-and-now, the dimension of its willing and acting. We cannot will and act in accordance with our system but contrary to our purposes. We can act without willing, in our so-called involuntary actions, where we do not present to consciousness the possibilities of our system. But if we will and act, we act in accordance with our purposes. The dimension of the present, considered in Chapter 8, is the form in which consciousness sees the future and the past as a function of its responsibility to will and act.

10.17. The motor car allows movement from places on land to other places on land at a given range of velocities. The tree allows the formation of wood and reproductive structure-systems (such as flowers and fruits and seeds) within a certain range of quantity and within a certain range of rates of growth. The legislature allows the holding of certain forms of public debate and the making of a certain range of legal acts with a certain range of substantive contents. Were the car or the tree to present its activity to consciousness, it might present that activity as purposive, actualizing its possibilities. The legislature, a product of human consciousness, is able to present to itself (and participants and spectators are able to present to themselves) the activity of the legislature as purposive, actualizing its possibilities in the making of legal acts. It is *purpose* that links the present of consciousness with its future by linking willing and acting to the possibilities contained in its future. But purpose has meaning only in terms of the system as a whole within which willing and acting occur as transformations of energy.

10.18. The word *power* will be used here to refer to the energy which a system uses to achieve its systematic effects. In the case of human beings, power is energy applied for a purpose. Potential power becomes actual power when it is applied within a structure-system to produce actualities from possibilities within the range of possibilities offered by, and within the limits imposed by, that structure-system. Every system depends on the application of power to initiate the process of its transforming effects, and the application of power to make available the materials which it transforms. The ignition of the car must be switched on; the gasolene and the stored electricity must be available in the right form, in the right place, at the right time. The seed of the tree must be germinated by the action of the sun and the presence of other necessary chemical elements; the constituents necessary for the growth of the tree must then be constantly provided. The buildings, the material systems, and the human beings must be brought together to form the legislature; the elements necessary for its day-to-day functioning must be constantly provided.

10.19. Power may thus take the form of what will here be called *natural power*—the power which comes from participation in the physical world and the power within the consciousness of an individual human being which exists independently of that individual's membership of a particular society. Power which is derived from participation in one society is natural power from the point of view of the systematic operation of another society, to the extent that it is external to the systematic operation of that latter society. The term *social power* will be used to refer to the power which comes from the systematic activity of a society. Social power may be the power of an individual human being or of a subordinate society within a society (say, an organ of the constitution, a commercial or industrial corporation). Social power comes from the nature and functioning of the society as a structure-system, capable of making transformations which turn its possibilities into actualities, which transform its future into its past, which achieve its purposes. Social power is energy transformed for the purposes which flow from the sytematic structure of the society. To achieve its purpose, society transforms natural power into social power and transforms social power into natural power. This is the *social exchange.*

10.20. Thus, in summary, it may be said that the constitution is the structure-system of a society which enables social power to be applied to make the transformations which enable a society to create itself from its possibilities, to actualize its possibilities through willing and acting in fulfilment of its purposes, to make the social exchange.

10.21. The functioning of the social exchange may be illustrated in diagrammatic form (opposite).

10.22. That is to say, natural energy is transformed into natural power by its dedication to a purpose (say, the building of a private house). Natural power is transformed into social power by its dedication to a social purpose (say, the decision to build a public highway). The social purpose is derived from the ideal constitution, which is itself as product of all society's reality-forming and contains society's idea of what it might become. The creation of the social power is the product of the

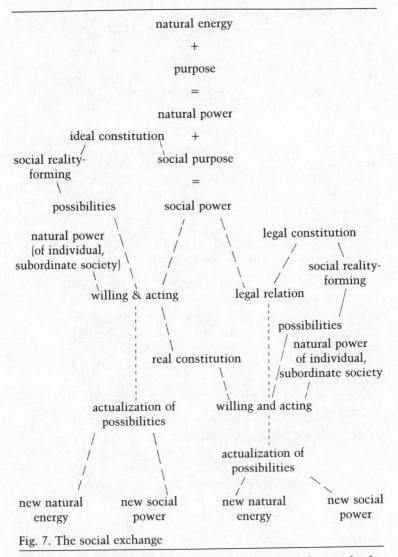

Fig. 7. The social exchange

total social process of the society, as it struggles with the perennial dilemmas of society.

10.23. If the social power is exercised, it is a coming-together of an appropriate possibility (selected as a matter of willing from among possibilities conceived in the light of all society's self-conceiving within its reality-for-itself) and the natural power of some member of society (individual human being or subordinate society, such as an industrial or commercial enterprise). The determination of the actual person to exercise the power is a matter for the real constitution under which social power is actually assigned in society's present-here-and-now.

10.24. If the relevant social power is a legal power (say, a power under a contract to build the public highway), then that power is part of a legal relation relating the power-holder to any number of other legal relators (say, the parties to the contract, other public authorities, subcontractors). The legal power has been created under the legal constitution which determines the way in which legal relations may be created. The legal constitution is itself a product of all society's reality-forming in the past of society (the past as seen from the time when the legal power is to be exercised).

10.25. If the legal power is exercised it is the coming-together of the legal relation and an appropriate possibility (selected as a matter of willing from among possibilities conceived in the light of all society's self-conceiving within its reality-for-itself) and the natural power of some member of society. Again it is the real constitution which determines who the holder of the relevant legal power and the other legal relators actually are in society's present-here-and-now.

10.26. The willing and acting which consists of the exercise of the social power in question (say, the building of the public highway) leads to new possibilities for natural energy (say, the use of the highway by members of the public) and for social power (say, legal powers to control the use of and to use the highway).

10.27. Such a schematic and mechanistic description of the social structure-system should not be allowed to obscure four aspects of it. (1) All social activity is part of an endless intra-acting cycle, since the actualization of possibilities, and the exercise of the natural and/or social power which results from it, in turn leads to further activity of the constitutional system, the further exercise of social power, including further development of the constitution itself. All social activity is not only social activity of the system of society but also social activity with a view to forming the system of society. As noted before, it is such intra-acting which makes social phenomena so intensely difficult to study and to rationalise, as society makes its structure-sytem in using its structure-system, makes itself in using itself.

10.28. (2) And all social activity is part of a network of inter-societal activity, as the activities of all societies interact with each other, both because each society may contain any number of subordinate societies and because one society may exercise its power in relation to another.

10.29. (3) And the functioning of the social exchange is as complex and dynamic as the total social process considered in Part One. That is to say, the functioning of the system contains all the work of society on words, ideas, theories, and values. And it contains all the struggle with the perennial dilemmas of society, including all the making and the functioning of the social reality-forming (religion, mythology, art, philosophy, history, science, economy, morality, law), each a complex system of many subordinate systems, all contributing to the formation of society's own reality, within which society constructs its own idea of itself as a system and thereby constructs the purposes for which all its transformations of power are carried out.

10.30. (4) And each such sub-system (religious institutions, legal institutions, economic institutions, educational institutions) is itself a system of sub-systems, all interacting with each other and with the sub-systems of other sub-systems.

10.31. The systematic activity of society—including the social exchange—is made possible by the legal constitution, which carries retained acts of will (law) from society's past to its future through its present and which transforms society's future into its past through willing and acting in the present in implementation of the law. Its present contains the application of law (the past making the future in the present) and the making of law (the present making the future's past). So the legal constitution makes possible the making of law, the application of law, the persistence of law.

10.32. The mechanism which the legal constitution makes available to society for embodying the social exchange as law is the *legal relation*. The legal relation—commonly, but too crudely, conceived as comprising so-called *rights* and *duties*— is a mechanism for integrating the willing and acting of members of society (including subordinate societies) with the willing and acting of society. In its elemental form, a legal relation establishes a relationship between two members of society (individual human beings and subordinate societies of all kinds). Its function is to modify the wills of those whose wills are related by the legal relation and who are hereafter refered to as *legal relators*.

10.33. The content of the relation is presented to the legal relators as an actuality in the perspective of their present-here-and-now, an actuality which modifies the possibilities of their future and which thereby modifies the transformation of their future through their present into their past. The legal relation presents itself as an externality to the legal relators. It is an externality which is *there* in relation to the present-here-and-now of the legal relators, that is to say, an externality which they cannot modify by their willing and acting here and now. But it is an externality which the legal relators internalize in the process of their willing and acting, as they will and act in relation to the possibilities of their future and the actualities of their present-here-and-now. A legal relation is society present-here in the present-here-and-now of the legal relators.

10.34. A legal relation thus presents itself to legal relators as part of the systematic structure by which their own future becomes their own past and yet, at the same time, as something which is the producer and the product of the willing and acting of others. It is in this sense that a legal relation establishes a relationship among the wills of the legal relators and with society in general.

10.35. I may make a legal contract with another person and that contract will modify our future willing and acting by becoming an actuality which enters into the process of our choosing among our possibilities, our willing and acting. But the effect of the contract on our willing and acting in turn depends on the willing and acting of those who have made the law governing contracts and the willing and acting of those who apply and enforce the law governing contracts. Our contract-forming behaviour, the contract itself, our contract-respecting (or contract-violating) behaviour, the contract-recognizing behaviour of others, their contract-applying and contract-enforcing behaviour—all of these are actual and potential presences within individual and social consciousness. It is the function of the legal relations involved in a contract to systematize all these relationships in forms which modify all our willing and acting in consciousness and, as the case may be, in the world-beyond-consciousness, including the natural physical world (if, for example, we carry out a contract to build a house or to make a film). The legal relations involved in a contract create a system of will-modification through creating a presence within the present-here-and-now of all those whose wills must be modified to make the contract effective.

10.36. A legal relation also establishes itself as a presence-there for those members of society who are not involved in the particular legal relation. If P, a public official, has a power to take possession of the property of person X but not the property of person Y, then the legal relation between P and X is also an actuality for Y, and the fact that Y does not participate in the legal relation is an actuality for P and X. That is to say, the legal relation is a presence for P and X and Y which is liable to modify their willing and acting as an actuality affecting their choosing among the possibilities presented to them by their future.

10.37. Legal relations take effect at two levels. They are *articulated* in an abstracted form, classifying persons and things by abstract category (plaintiff, defendant, trespasser, contracting party, person who kills another person, person who is married to another person, territory, land, contract, treaty, loss or damage, self-defence, public interest, public order, and so on). They are *applied* in individualized form; that is to say, they have effect on willing and acting to the extent that an individual person or thing falls within the abstracted category.

It follows that, although a legal relation is an actuality, a presence-there in the consciousness of the legal relators, beyond the possibility of modification by willing and acting, its individualization depends on willing and acting, both in the recognition by the legal relators that a given person or thing is within the abstracted content of the legal relation and in such recognition by those who must apply and enforce the relation. However, the function of a legal relation—to be an actuality rather than a mere possibility within the process of willing and acting of those affected by it—would not be achieved if the individualization were not itself a matter of law, that is to say, itself the content of legal relations.

10.38. In other words, the legal relation must be constructed so as to enable those affected by it to individualize it with sufficient certainty and regularity to enable it to succeed as a legal relation. And, to the extent that the legal relation cannot be made to be sufficiently certain in itself, sufficiently self-executing, it will be necessary to establish further legal relations (such as the powers of third parties, including public officials and courts of law) tending to ensure the successful individualization of the legal relation in question.

10.39. It is the legal constitution which determines the coming into existence of legal relations, including the legal relations governing the interpretation and application and enforcement of other legal relations. It is in the real constitution, the actual willing and acting of society and its members in fulfilment of the legal and ideal constitutions, that the legal relation is formed and performed, in the actual willing and acting of specific persons. It is then that the actualities of the past—acts of will retained as law—work on the possibilities of the future in the present-here-and-now, making a new past and thereby creating a future of new possibilities. So it is that society survives and develops through the mechanism of legal relations. So it is that society directs its becoming through the system of its law.

10.40. It follows from the above that, although a particular legal relation may be conceived as containing a relationship of two persons, every such elemental relationship forms part of other legal relations up to and including the whole of the legal constitution, itself integrated into the total structure-system of society. It may be possible to identify, and base actual willing and acting on, a simple legal relation between, say, the two parties to a bilateral contract or a bilateral treaty, a nation-state and its national, or plaintiff and a defendant, an arresting police officer and an arrested person, the prosecuting authority and an accused person, a sentencing judge and a convicted person, owners of adjacent land, a land-owner and a trespasser, a parent and a child, a wife and a husband. But it will also be apparent that such a relation involves *necessary relations* between those two persons and countless other members of society. All legal relations in a given society are legally related. A legal relation is a legal relation because it forms part of a seamless web of legal relations up to and including the whole network of legal relations which is the legal constitution of a society.

10.41. Since legal relations are designed to modify willing and acting in accordance with society's purposes, it follows that they act on those aspects of consciousness which have been identified in Part One as the essential constituents of willing and acting. In so far as they modify *acting*, legal relations incorporate the *impulse of life* (the dynamic self-creating power of living things) and the *necessity* of the physical world (the physical world conceived in consciousness as a structure-system). In so far as legal relations modify *willing*, they intervene in the operation of *desire* (the impulse of life transformed within the self-creating power of consciousness) and *obligation* (the necessity of the physical world transformed within the structure-system of consciousness).

10.42. The hallowed conceptualization of legal rights and legal duties as the two fundamental forms of legal relation flows from the connection between legal relations and the elementary forces of, respectively, desire and obligation.

10.43. Rights are conceived as that kind of legal relation which affirms the desiring and hence the willing of the right-holder. Duties are conceived as the kind of legal relation which constrains the willing of the duty-holder in the form of obligation. By a legal relation in the form of a right, society is considered to confer on the right-holder the benefit, the protection, the assurance, the individuality of the law. By a legal relation in the form of a duty, society is considered to impose on the duty-holder the burden, the order, the universality of the law. The right seems to enlarge the possibilities of the right-holder, by making certain possibilities into the actuality of a legal relation. The duty seems to diminish the possibilities of the duty-holder, by excluding certain possibilities in the actuality of a legal relation.

10.44. Such a straightforward conceptualization is now so deeply rooted in the words, ideas, theories, and values of societies that it must be presumed to have proved its evolutionary utility in the struggle of societies to create and socialize themselves. It echoes so many of the dualities which we use to structure every kind of reality—male and female, matter and consciousness, ying and yang, positive and negative electricity, the north and south poles of magnetism, left and right hands, inside and outside a mirror, time past and time future. Consciousness seems to need such fruitful dualities in its reality-forming. However, it is important to bear in mind that the facile conceptualization of legal relations into rights and duties conceals important aspects of legal relations and can have significant distorting effects on the understanding of law and society in general and of international society and law in particular.

10.45. In the first place, there are many forms of right and many forms of duty. Secondly, rights are as much a constraint as they are an empowering, and duties are as much an empowering as they are a constraint. Thirdly, different forms of rights and duties are mutually interdependent, but serve different legislative purposes. Fourthly, legal rights and legal duties are intimately connected with modifications of willing arising outside the law.

10.46. Following a line of thought traced by Jeremy Bentham (*An Introduction to the Principles of Morals and Legislation*, 1789; especially chapter XVI, footnote to paragraph XXV), and Wesley Hohfeld (*Fundamental Legal Conceptions*, 1919), it is possible to distinguish at least four significantly different forms of legal right. A *claim-right* enables the right-holder to invoke the law to obtain certain willing and acting from another person. A contract and a treaty include claim-rights (along with other forms of right and duties). A *freedom-right* enables the right-holder to invoke the law to avoid interference by other persons with certain willing and acting by the right-holder. Freedom of speech and freedom of navigation include freedom-rights (along with other forms of right and duties).

10.47. A *power-right* enables the right-holder to invoke the law to protect certain willing and acting by the right-holder which affects the legal rights of other persons. A power to legislate, to make a will, and to expropriate property are power-rights (also involving many other kinds of rights and duties). An *immunity-right* enables the right-holder to invoke the law to protect certain willing and acting from the application of the rights of other persons. State immunity, diplomatic immunity, and legal professional privilege are immunity-rights (supported by many other kinds of right and duty).

10.48. It is possible also to distinguish at least four significantly different forms of legal duty. A *requirement-duty* is an affirmative duty, a duty to act in a certain way. It seeks to cause conforming willing and acting by the duty-holder. A duty to act with care (non-negligently), a duty to pay a debt or a tax, a duty to provide public housing, and a duty to pay compensation for expropriated property are requirement-duties. A *constraint-duty* is a negative duty, a duty not to act in a certain way. It seeks to modify the willing and acting of the duty-holder so as to avoid such action. A duty not to trespass on another's land, a duty not to defame another person, a duty not to use force against another nation-state, and a duty not to use torture are constraint-duties.

10.49. A *liability-duty* is the corollary of a power-right. It limits the willing and acting of the duty-holder to the extent of the power of the right-holder. A liability-duty is thus a potential constraint so long as the power has not been exercised in relation to the liability-holder. It becomes an actual constraint if and when the power is exercised. Liability to arrest, to be summoned as a witness, to be ordered to pay maintenance for a child, and to the compulsory purchase of one's property by a public authority are liability-duties. A *disability-duty* is the withholding of a particular right, especially a power-right. It means that the holder cannot invoke the law to protect or give effect to certain willing and acting. Disabilities as to the holding of public office and the exercise of public rights, disabilities by reason of age or gender or nationality or religion or race, and disabilities arising from a surrender of a right by agreement (such as agreement not to contract with a third party, agreement not to take legal proceedings) are disability-duties.

10.50. Such different kinds of legal relations are not in any sense unique and mutually exclusive essences. It is obvious that the relationship between two legal persons can be analysed in many different ways and that an analysis in terms of one particular legal relation always implies the existence of many other supporting legal relations. In particular, it is important to see that rights necessarily involve constraint and duties necessarily involve empowering. Rights may protect a certain area of willing and acting but they protect *only that area* of willing and acting. The limits of a right are as significant as its content. The limits of a right amount to a peripheral duty (or, normally, a bundle of all kinds of duties) not to exceed those limits. To exceed those limits gives rise to rights of all kinds in other right-holders, either the coming into existence of new rights or the actual exercise of existing rights.

10.51. Contrariwise, duties may require willing which would not otherwise be chosen by the duty-holder. But duties have limits. The limits of a duty are as significant as its content. The limits of a duty amount to a peripheral right (or, normally, a bundle of all forms of rights) not to be required to go beyond those limits. The limits of a duty affirm our freedom beyond those limits, a freedom which can be specifically enforced as one or more forms of right.

10.52. There is another sense in which rights are constraining and duties are empowering. Since rights are conferred by society for the purposes of society by way of the social exchange of power for purpose, right-holders are serving society in holding and exercising their rights. They may will and act in their own interest but, if they will and act pursuant to a right, they will and act also in the social interest. Similarly, since duties are imposed by society for the purposes of society by way of the social exchange of power for purpose, society is giving the protection of the law to those who accept duties under the law, that is to say, giving them also the benefit of related rights under the law. This aspect, with its far-reaching implications, is considered further in Chapter 11.

10.53. Given that a given legal relationship could be presented in any number of different right-duty analyses, given that each legal relation depends on an unlimited number of (explicit or implicit) supporting legal relations (up to and including the whole structure-system of the legal constitution), and given that rights and duties are not mutually exclusive opposites, it is open to question why and how it is that the law chooses to achieve its will-modifying effects by conferring and imposing such-and-such particular rights and duties. This amounts to asking why law-reality is as it is, with legal relations corresponding to the more or less settled structures and systems which consciousness conceives within the temporal and spatial dimensions of its reality-for-itself, as it establishes its relationship to itself and to the world-beyond-consciousness, including the physical world.

10.54. There are four motivating factors affecting law-consciousness as it makes the law-reality. The first is *psychological or rhetorical*. To create a particular legal relation, a particular kind of right or duty, to produce a particular effect in the willing and acting of members of society, society as lawmaker judges that a particular legal relation, a particular kind of right or duty, would be effective, given the general nature of consciousness, and given the nature of that society's reality-for-itself, including all its words and ideas and theories and values. To legislate in terms of the individual's rights of property or the overriding powers of the state to act in the public interest, to legislate in terms of the rights of the individual or the limits on the powers of the state, to invoke the freedom of the individual or the responsibility of the state, these are among the unlimited number of legislative choices open to society as it wills and acts to create its self-creating law. The choice is made case-by-case pragmatically.

10.55. The second factor motivating the legislative choice of legal relation is that, in making its choice, society knows, that the particular way of formulating a legal relation to produce a desired modification of willing and acting is liable to have significant *practical implications*. It has functional effects within the legal system. It conditions the form in which legal relations are asserted and applied. For example, to confer a claim-right on X may have the same net effect as the imposing of a power-right or a duty on Y, so far as the net willing and acting of X and Y is concerned. But the legislative choice of one or the other may significantly affect the way in which such behaviour is ensured in practice. To confer a claim-right on X (say, a right to privacy, a right to housing or a minimum wage) will tend to place a legal burden on Y to justify an interference with X's privacy, a failure to provide housing, or a failure to pay a minimum wage. On the other hand, to impose merely a constraint-duty on Y not to interfere with X's privacy, or to confer merely a power-right on Y to provide housing, implying a duty to exercise the power in appropriate circumstances, or to impose merely a requirement-duty on Y to pay a minimum wage—these will tend to place a burden on X to show a failure by Y. A particular legal relation orientates the law in a particular direction, focuses the image of the law as it impinges on the actual willing and acting of society and its members.

10.56. The third factor affecting the legislative choice of particular legal relations concerns the total effect of the *law as a system* in a given society, the overall systematic or distributive effect of the choice of legal relations. The legal system as a whole is a central part of the overall distribution of power in society, among the members of society, including subordinate societies of all kinds. It will be necessary to consider in Part Three how social power is distributed to ensure not only the survival but also the prospering, the well-being, of society and its members. Central to that process is the overall distributive effect of law. Central to the overall distributive effect of law is the utilization by the law of the particular legal relations. A society sees itself reflected in its law. Society sees its image in the law. And, given the interaction of the three aspects of the constitution, society sees itself in its present-here-and-now, its real constitution, as the outcome of what it has been (the legal constitution) and what it might be (its ideal constitution). Fundamental structures of society are determined by the net position of the individual human being in relation to society as a whole, the net position of the organs of public power in relation to each other and to the members of society, the net status, in particular, of the family, the religious association, the trade union, and, above all, the net position in relation to control over property of all kinds.

10.57. Accordingly, the fourth factor affecting legislative choice is *educational*, the conscious self-creating of society's reality-for-itself. A society not only sees its image in its legal system. It forms its image in seeing its image in its legal system. The law plays so fundamental a part in the life of its members that their socializing, through formal education and through mere participation in the functioning of society, is an education in its law. So, in distributing the benefits and burdens of the law through the mechanisms of legal relations, society is not merely doing a particular sort of engineering. To legislate is to educate. To educate is to legislate.

10.58. The legal relations which society creates—rights and duties in all their forms—are intimately connected with rights and duties arising from society's other reality-forming systems. Those systems give rise to non-legal relations which are referred to, and not merely metaphorically, as rights and duties (religious duties, moral rights and duties, conventional duties of protocol and politeness, family duties). Legal relations and other forms of social relation sustain and reinforce each other, each an affirmation of, and an education in, the inherent interdependence of all social power, the mutality of all social willing and acting.

10.59. Society, by means of the social exchange, integrates the willing and acting of society with the willing and acting of its members, integrates the willing and acting of its members with the willing and acting of society. Individual willing and acting is socialized. Social willing and acting is individualized. Society, a system of constraints, is thereby a realm of freedom. Individual members of society can choose freely among the possibilities generated by the physical world of non-consciousness, by the dynamic world of social consciousness, by the energetic world of consciousness. And the individual members of society participate, by their participation in the structure-system of society, in generating the possibilities and the constraints. Society, a system of possibilities, is thereby a realm of duty. To be a member of society is to be a participant in the self-structuring and self-socializing of society, to be a participant in the organization of all willing and acting with a view to actualizing society's purposes. To be a member of society is to be called upon to be both a unique source of willing and acting and an agent of the willing and acting of society.

11 The Generic Principles of a Constitution

11.1. The constitution of every society is unique. The constitutions of all societies have in common their operating principles as systems.

11.2. A fish, a bird, a tree, an atom, a computer, a human being, a society—each is a particular individual, but each is also a member of a class of individuals united by their common possession of a particular system for transforming the world. That system is the system of their existing, the system of operation by which they actualize their possibilities. It is the particular actualization of the particular possibilities of a given individual which makes the uniqueness of the given individual, as the given individual creates itself by the interacting of its own structure-system with the structure-system of all-that-is. But it is the operating principles of its system which unite the given individual with other individuals which have the same system. The operating principles of a system are the generic principles shared by all structure-systems which contain such a system.

11.3. A constitution is a structure-system which is shared by all societies. The constitution of each society is unique, as a function of its own history, the story of its own actualizing of its own possibilities within the possibilities of a constituted society and within the structure-system of all-that-is. But the constitution of each society is also an instance of a system shared by all societies, operating according to generic principles which are shared by all the constitutions of all societies.

11.4. The generic principles of a constitution are thus those operating principles which make possible the social process of a society, its self-creating and its socializing, its survival as a society through time, as it transforms its future into its past by its willing and acting in its present-here-and-now. They are the principles which integrate the social process of a society into a total social process, a total structure and a total system, a whole. They are the principles which, like the operating principles of a living thing or of an organic system or a material system or of a machine, systematize the interacting of the sub-systems of society's constitutional structure, which organize their functioning relationship to each other. They are the principles without which the structure-system of a society could not be a structure-system.

11.5. It may be suggested hypothetically that the contents of the generic principles of a constitution—of any constitution of any society, from the society of the family to the international society of the whole human race, the society of societies—are the following:

1. *Law is part of the total social process.* Principle of integration.

2. *Law is dynamic.* Principle of transformation.

3. *All legal power is delegated power.* Principle of delegation.

4. *All legal power is limited.* Principle of the intrinsic limitation of power.

5. *All social power is under the law.* Principle of the supremacy of law.

6. *All legal power is power in the social interest.* Principle of the supremacy of the social interest.

7. *All social power is accountable.* Principle of social responsibility.

11.6. These proposed generic principles are analytical-synthetic generalizations. They are *analytical*, in the sense that they are general ideas which express the coherence of the other ideas used to explain the system of society. They are ideas without which the structure-system of society proposed in the present study would not be a coherent structure of ideas. They are, in other words, ideas made necessary by what has been called, in Chapter 2, the *actual* co-ordinate of human reason.

11.7. They are *synthetic*, in the sense that they are intended to make sense of human social experience, as societies have sought their survival and prospering through the systematic organization of the natural power of human beings, as individual human beings have sought to survive and prosper through their participation in the integrated structure-systems of societies. No doubt there could be many other synthetic generalizations of human social experience—so complex and varied and dynamic as social experience has been over many thousands of years. It is, above all, in the *potential* co-ordinate of reason, considered in Chapter 2, that the particular hypothetical pinciples, such as those suggested here, must be judged. How do such ideas relate to other ideas of society and its potentiality, to our social ideas and ideals? How do such ideas relate to other ideas of individual human existence and its potentiality, to our personal ideas and ideals as human beings?

11.8. The generic principles of a constitution are intended to perform a similar explanatory function to that of general hypothetical principles in the natural sciences—the principles of Newtonian mechanics, thermodynamics, relativity, quantum mechanics, genetics. They are offered as the ultimate equations relating to constituted power in society, the constitution of constitutions, as it were. What were at one time called the laws of science have an equivocal philosophical status, both as regards their *genetic* co-ordinate (inference from already-synthesized regularities/imaginative intuitions of possible forms of order?) and as regards their *actual* co-ordinate, that is to say, in particular, their relation to other ideas of the reality to which they refer (models of the essential features of that reality / apparently related to that reality but in an indeterminate way?)

11.9. From the consideration of social self-creating and socializing in Part One above, it is evident that three things may be said about such principles of science:

(1) that their coherence with the other ideas that we currently have about the physical world is such that we can say that there is a reality which at least has the characteristic that it can cause such principles of science to be generated in human consciousness.

(2) that the substantive content of the principles of science is

such that they allow human consciousness to will and act in the physical world as if it understood the principles of action of that world, even if only to certain limits of probability and subject to some ultimate threshold of indeterminacy;

(3) that the principles of science may be valid in these two senses, even if they are incapable, in principle, of amounting to an explanation of the whole of the physical universe as a total system, that is to say, incapable of transcending themselves in order to explain themselves.

11.10. Similarly, the generic principles of a constitution proposed here, if they are to be treated as the constitution of constitutions, the laws of law, must, like the general principles of the natural sciences, be generated by the theory-forming power of imagination and reason in such a way:

(1) that they leave nothing incoherent in our understanding of law-in-society and hence allow the possibility that social reality is at least such that it can generate such general principles in human consciousness;

(2) that they enable human consciousness to act in society as if it understood the nature and functioning of law as a self-ordering system of society, to act as if consciousness were the master of the structure-system which it has created for itself;

(3) that, whilst continually being surpassed by further hypothetical generalizations, they must always remain subject to the ultimate inability of human consciousness to transcend itself in consciousness, so that the principles remain ultimately hypothetical, ultimately indeterminate. Like the principles of natural science, the generic principles of the constitution give rise to a sense that they are seven ways of saying one and the same thing, of expressing some ultimate unified principle which would, no doubt, be analytically more satisfactory but would be substantively less fruitful than its seven-fold form.

(1) PRINCIPLE OF INTEGRATION

11.11. *Law is part of the total social process.* Analytically and practically, law is part of society. From an analytical point of view, its nature and functioning cannot be explained except in the context of a general explanation of the nature and functioning of society. From a practical point of view, the substantive development of law is determined within the development of general social reality through the total social process.

11.12. The consequence of this is that, through the total social process, law is an integral part of the whole activity of consciousness, individual and social. Law is part of the creator and part of the creature of the words and ideas and theories and values of society, responding to the impulse of life in the form of desire and to the necessity of the physical universe in the form of obligation. Law is a product of the process of society as it struggles with its perennial dilemmas to achieve its purposes, to survive and prosper as a society, including its struggle with the dilemma of justice and social justice. Law is connected with all the other reality-forming processes of society (religion, mythology, art, philosophy, history, science, economy, and morality), and hence is connected with society's total reality-for-itself, its self-forming relationship to consciousness itself and to its conception of all-that-is.

11.13. Law is an integral part, formed and forming, of the total social process in every kind of society, from the society of a particular family to the international society of the whole human race, and including every intermediate society.

(2) PRINCIPLE OF TRANSFORMATION

11.14. *Law is dynamic.* Society is not merely a structure. It is also a system, transforming the future into the past, the past into the future, in the continuing present-here-and-now of society, a system which is carried in society's constitution and in which actual willing and acting takes place. Legal relations, themselves the product of transformations arising in the total social process, give rise to transformations which form part of the functioning of society as a system. They systematically organize the willing and acting of the members of society, including human beings and all kinds of subordinate society.

11.15. Given that the structure-system of society is a structure-system within human consciousness, such transformations are the application of energy for a purpose. The social purpose is formed by the total social process. The transformation occurs through the willing and acting of the members of society. So it is that society creates itself through the socializing of human purpose, using legal relations as a means of organizing that socializing.

11.16. Legal relations are the product of social transformations. Legal relations are the source of social transformations. Society is a ceaseless becoming, but a becoming which is inherently self-ordering and self-directing and self-achieving. Law is an inherent part of the becoming of that becoming, in every form of society, from the society of a particular family to the international society of the whole human race, and including every intermediate society.

(3) PRINCIPLE OF DELEGATION

11.17. *All legal power is delegated power.* No member of society can claim to have legal power which is not power delegated from society. To claim legal power is to acknowledge its delegation. To act as a member of society is to acknowledge society, to acknowledge its structure-system, its constitution, including its legal constitution. All legal power is a form of social power, that is to say, it embodies within its very substance the social exchange of power for purpose. When natural power is transformed into legal power by being made subject to society's purpose, it is stamped and sealed with its origin and source.

11.18. But the process of delegation, the process of so-called law-making by which legal relations are created, is itself a process of willing and acting by members of society using delegated legal power. All law-making is also law-applying. The legal constitution carries into the present-here-and-now of society, among all the other legal relations, power-rights to make further legal relations. It is the total social process which generates, and may modify, those legal relations, like any others.

11.19. The society as delegator is the society acting under the real constitution in application of the legal constitution and in the light of the ideal constitution. The delegator in delegating is also a delegate, in every form of society, from the society of a particular family to the international society of the whole human race, and including every intermediate society.

(4) PRINCIPLE OF THE INTRINSIC LIMITATION OF POWER

11.20. *All legal power is limited.* The transformation of natural power into legal power is the transformation of a particular quantum of natural power and a transformation for particular purposes. To claim legal power is to accept its limits. A legal relation is a relation, in the sense that it is liable to modify the willing and acting of at least two members of society. One legal relator's power does not necessarily involve an exactly equivalent loss of power in another legal relator. The benefit and the burden may be shared in a complex legal relation, or a complex of legal relations. The burden may not be referable specifically to another legal relator—for example, if the legal power is to make use of natural resources. In such cases, a corresponding loss of power may be widely distributed in society. But what is certain is that all legal power is liable to constrain in some way other members of society, if only by imposing consequential liabilities in one form or another. The limits of legal power are inherently a matter of interest to other members of society.

11.21. To acknowledge the limits of legal power and the interest of other members of society in those limits is to accept that the limits of legal power cannot be self-determined. The law is an actuality so far as the willing and acting of a member of society is concerned, present-now in the legal constitution, but present-there so far as the real constitution is concerned, beyond the range of modification by the willing and acting which is to be modified by it. Legal relations are actualities which affect the possibilities of willing and acting. Thus even the power-right to make law, to legislate as it is called, is legal power with limits. Those limits are systematic and substantive. They are *systematic*, in the sense that the power-right to legislate is a power-right to will and act as part of society self-creating, of society socializing. To legislate is to act as society's self-ordering delegate. They are *substantive*, in the sense that legislation is part of the total social process, not an isolated and self-causing sub-system.

11.22. Natural power—in the energy of human consciousness, in the energy of the natural world, in the energy of the economic systems of society—has limits which may, however, be unspecifiable or unmeasurable. Social power and, in particular, legal power is, on the other hand, necessarily power quantified in the very process of becoming social power, in every form of society, from the society of a particular family to the international society of the whole human race, and including every intermediate society.

(5) PRINCIPLE OF THE SUPREMACY OF LAW

11.23. *All social power is under the law.* When natural power becomes social power in the form of legal power, it is transformed into something specific, the specifically legal. To serve its function in the structure-system of society, law has a specific character, like blood or muscle or cellulose in a living organism. In law potential energy is stored as acts of will. Society wills in advance of the event in the form of legal relations. The willing in advance is retained in the form of law.

11.24. To make possible its survival as a structure-system, society must be able to control its future from the point of view of its past, to control its future by willing and acting in the past of that future. It must be able to cause its future to be realized in its continuous present-here-and-now by placing into that present-here-and-now acts of will from its past designed to carry its substance, its structure-system, into its future. Given that society is a structure-system within human consciousness, applying energy to achieve purpose, society's making of its future substance by means of law is an endless seeking to achieve its purposes.

11.25. It follows that, in case of conflict between legal power and other forms of social power, legal power must, in principle, prevail. Otherwise, society would be acting, at one and the same time, to create itself and to destroy itself. It is evident that such a principle of legal supremacy, if it is not itself to become self-destructive and abusive, depends on all the other six principles of a constitution. But they equally depend on the principle of the supremacy of law, if they are not to be ineffective.

11.26. The ultimate human right, which is also an ultimate human need, is to be a member of societies under the law. In that way only can human beings, endowed with the capacity to will and act in consciousness, constantly create themselves in accordance with their purposes. Such a right, and such a need, is the human right and human need in every form of society, from the society of a particular family to the international society of the whole human race, and including all intermediate societies.

(6) PRINCIPLE OF THE SUPREMACY OF THE SOCIAL INTEREST

11.27. *All legal power is power in the social interest.* When natural power becomes social power, in the form of legal power, the willing and acting of the individual human being is systematically integrated with the willing and acting of society. When there is willing and acting in the present-here-and-now, the law modifies the willing and acting of human individuals and subordinate societies. At the moment of willing and acting under the law, the private interest cannot be invoked against the law, except to the extent that the law itself so allows.

11.28. The law modifies, in particular, the willing and acting of those who act in a public capacity, those whose specific function is to act explicitly in the public interest. When there is willing and acting in the present-here-and-now by such persons, especially by public officials, the public interest (state necessity, reason of state, or whatever) cannot be invoked against the law, except to the extent that the law itself so allows.

11.29. If private interest cannot be invoked against the law and if public interest cannot be invoked against the law, at the moment of willing and acting, it is because the law is necessarily in the social interest. This is a consequence of the fact that the law is a means of the systematic self-ordering of society, as it applies its purposes to transform natural power into social power. It also a consequence of the fact that the law is part of the total social process, so that the reconciliation of private and social interest is effected in the context of the total social reality, including society's words and ideas and theories and values. Last and by no means least, it is a consequence of the fact that, within a society, an individual member and the society do not have intrinsically conflicting interests. Each forms and is formed by the other. Each gives and receives value from the other. The individual member of society is the society individualized. The society is the individual socialized. Law embodies this transformation.

11.30. Thus it is not the function of law to reconcile intrinsically conflicting interests. Law is an expression of the self-interest of all members of society in the survival and prospering of the society and the self-interest of society in the survival and prospering of all its members. Law is the universalizing of private interest and the individualizing of social interest, in every form of society, from the society of a particular family to the international society of the whole human race, and including all intermediate societies.

(7) PRINCIPLE OF SOCIAL RESPONSIBILITY

11.31. *All social power is accountable.* When legal power takes effect to modify willing and acting, it alters society's reality-for-itself. That alteration may take every kind of form, from a modification which remains within consciousness (the creation of a new legal relation, a transfer of intangible property, ideas and feelings of all kinds) to a modification which takes a physical form (the holding of a public meeting, the transfer of tangible property, the handing-over of tangible property). As its constitution carries society from its past to its future, society for ever re-makes itself.

11.32. Nothing social is alien to society. Society cannot be indifferent about any aspect of its own functioning. Society cannot create itself unwittingly. It follows that the holder of legal power cannot claim that power, and yet claim to be immune from society's interest in the exercise of that power. Whatever the nature of the activity in which the power takes effect—political, economic, religious, educational, military, judicial, administrative—, it is power which is subject to all the principles of the constitution. It is part of the total social process and remains within the total social process even when it is exercised. It is dynamic—at its most dynamic in being exercised. It is power delegated by society, but delegated with a view to its effect when exercised. It is limited power and hence society has an interest in the respecting of those limits. It is power under the law, but the law does not merely create abstract powers; it creates power which will modify actual willing and acting in accordance with the law. It is a manifestation of the social interest, so that the holder cannot claim that its exercise is a matter of merely private interest.

11.33. Social responsibility can be asserted in two ways—as legal accountability and as social accountability. Legal accountability retains within the legal process the control of the implementation of legal relations, including the exercise of legal powers. Social accountability extends the arena of such control to include the rest of the total social process, including (but by no means confined to) the politics of society's public realm.

11.34. All legal power is shared power. All legal power, including both its exercise and the control of its exercise, is shared by the power-holder with all other members of society and with society itself, in every form of society, from the society of a particular family to the international society of the whole human race.

12 The Constituting of Modern International Society

12.1. Its constitution makes it possible for a society to create itself in socializing itself, to survive and prosper through the systematic organizing of power in the form of social power, including legal power. Its constitution does not make it certain that every society always wills and acts in its own best interest and in the best interest of its members.

12.2. A society is a structure-system whose structure and system enable it to survive and prosper as a society. Not all societies survive. Some societies promote not well-being but misery. A society is a structure-system which enables a society to create itself. Some societies destroy themselves. A society is a system which enables the willing and acting of its members to be integrated with the willing and acting of society. Some societies oppress and exploit their members. A society is a system which enables human consciousness to actualize its self-surpassing potentialities. Some societies dehumanize and degrade their members. A society is a structure-system which enables it, as a member of a society to which it itself belongs, to will and act in accordance with the law of that society, the law as universalizing of private interest, particularizing of social interest. Some societies act as law-breakers, maiming and destroying and plundering others. Through the whole course of recorded human history, there have been societies which demonstrate the wonderfully creative capabilities of the human race and there have been societies which demonstrate the disgracefully destructive capacity of the human race. The history of international society has contained much to bring credit and pride to the human race and much to bring disgust and dishonour.

12.3. Machines break down. Living things suffer disease, decay, and death. Any structure may fall apart. Any system may work badly or fail. The structure-system of society, considered in Part One and in the preceding chapters of this Part Two, is intrinsically dynamic, well-adapted to the task of promoting the ever-increasing well-being of itself and its members. But the structure-system of a society is also capable of doing harm to itself, to its members, and to other societies and their members. Society offers the possibility of unlimited well-being. If that possibility is actualized in a particular society over a particular period of time, it is through the particular efforts of that society and its members. To do well, in and through society, is a human potentiality. To do badly, in and through society, is an all-too-human possibility.

12.4. Since a society integrates its own willing and acting with the willing and acting of its members, its achievements are a product of willing and acting. A society may do harm through its *willing*. That is to say, a society may do harm through its conceiving of its possibilities, through the reality it forms for itself, through its words and ideas and theories and values. As it conceives its future, so it forms its will in its present-here-and-now. As it conceives its future, so it forms its past. It creates itself from its future as it conceives its future in consciousness. And a society may do harm through its *acting*. That is to say, a society may do harm as it actualizes its self-conceived and self-willed possibilities in its present-here-and-now, as it modifies its own consciousness and the consciousness of its members, and as it modifies the world beyond its consciousness, the physical world and the consciousness of other societies and their members. As a means of choosing the future, a society may do harm in and through its choosing.

12.5. The structure-system of a society, which enables society to promote the ever-increasing well-being of itself and its members, contains no guarantee that it will be so used or will be exclusively or always so used. Society contains no fail-safe mechanism to protect itself from itself. And, since all societies are members of other societies, up to and including the international society of the whole human race, the society of all societies, there is no overriding social mechanism protecting societies from each other's harmful willing and acting. All that can be said is that international society has the ultimate capacity to enable all societies to promote the ever-increasing well-being of themselves and their members, the ultimate responsibility to prevent societies from doing harm to themselves and to other societies. It is in international society that humanity's capacity to harm itself can achieve its most spectacular effects. And it is in international society that the ever-increasing well-being of the whole human race can, must, and will be promoted.

12.6. Human society shares with the individual human being the capacity to do harm. The capacity to do harm, like the capacity to do good, is a consequence of the human capacity, and the inescapable human responsibility, to choose, moment by moment, day in and day out. A human being contains a system for making choices. There are four features of the structure-system of a human being which give rise to the possibility that a human individual may do harm. They give rise, as a consequence, to the need for a constant effort—a moral effort—on the part of the individual to avoid harm. As a system integrating individual willing and acting with the willing and acting of society, a society shares in the features of the human system which give rise to the possibility of doing harm. They give rise, in the case of a society, to a corresponding need for a constant effort—social effort—to avoid harm. Life, individual and social life, is not only a constant struggle. It is a struggle which calls for unceasing effort.

12.7. (1) When an individual human being chooses a future in the present-here-and-now, that choice takes effect in relation to the past, to that which is actuality, the past of the given human individual. The past of that individual is an integration of a physical inheritance (including the genetic inheritance), a past retained as memory and to some extent capable of being presented to present consciousness, and a systematic past retained in the individual's personality as the resultant of all previous states of that individual's present-here-and-now. In actualizing a particular possibility, in choosing a future, the individual is, therefore, integrating a past as actuality and a future as possibility in the present-here-and-now of willing and acting. An individual human being cannot choose the past. Because it is past, it is beyond choice. It follows that the choosing of an individual human being is a choosing within a field of forces which contains forces which are beyond control.

12.8. (2) All the conceiving and willing and acting done by and through individual consciousness is not done in isolation. It is done within a world beyond consciousness, the physical world of the brain, the body, the rest of the universe. It is done in a world which also contains other self-creating persons, all other human individuals and societies, including all the societies to which the given individual belongs, up to and including the international society of the whole human race. We do not choose alone. Our choice interacts with the choices of others. The outcome of our choice, our acting, is a resultant of forces some of which are beyond our control.

12.9. (3) There is an accumulator effect, a principle of cumulative causation, which means that small events of willing and acting accumulate into large-scale complexes which would not be as they are without the willing and acting of the individual human being but which are not willed by that individual as a specific event of willing and acting. In particular, the personality of the individual includes the accumulated residues of the ceaseless willing and acting of the individual. The individual can present to consciousness, at the moment of choosing in the present-here-and-now, the possible effect of a particular choice within the long-term process of personality-accumulation. But the structure-system which is a personality is never offered to the individual as a totality to be chosen as such, to be made in a specific event of willing and acting. An individual human being is self-creating, but the self which is created is not a self which is itself chosen.

12.10. (4) At the moment of willing and acting, the individual human being conceives of a choice between possibilities. That conception and hence those possibilities are an integration in and by consciousness, an integration whose complexity far surpasses the capacity of the individual to conceive or to present to consciousness. Indeed, it is an integration which the individual consciousness could not, in principle, wholly conceive or present to itself, since that would require consciousness to transcend itself, to conceive of itself as merely *other*. And yet, in recognizing the possibility of choosing, individual consciousness takes upon itself the whole burden of choosing among its self-conceived possibilities. In conceiving itself to be human consciousness, human consciousness conceives itself to be choosing-consciousness. Human consciousness, in conceiving itself to be choosing-consciousness, must choose as if it were able to trancend itself, knowing that, by its choosing here-and-now, it will make a past which it has not chosen wholly or chosen alone, that it will make a self which is not chosen specifically, but a past and a self which will contain the unique choice which it makes and for which it is uniquely responsible. To choose a future is to choose a past. To choose a possibility is to choose an actuality. But they are a past and an actuality which we cannot know until after we have chosen them.

12.11. So it is that the structure-system of individual consciousness can do harm by its choosing. Individual consciousness cannot unchoose the past, cannot control the choosing of others, cannot control the totalizing effect of particular choosing, cannot know all the terms of the choice to be made. If the individual human being were able to do all these things, the human being would not be a human being but a particular kind of god. To be human is to be able to choose. To be able to choose is to be able to choose badly. But to be able to choose is also to be able, with effort, to choose well. And, above all else, to be able to choose is to be able to know that there is good choosing and bad choosing. Otherwise human living would not present itself as struggle, would not demand a constant effort of and in and through consciousness.

12.12. The structure-system of society, integrating its willing and acting with that of its members, shares in these features of individual consciousness. In society, the conceiving of the possibilities of the future is shared. The burden of choosing in the present-here-and-now is shared. The responsibility for the past is shared. The willing and acting of society takes place within the context of the constitution, society's personality, which society has made but which presents itself to society as actuality, which is never presented to society in its totality as something to choose. The willing and acting of a society takes place in a world which transcends society, not only the physical world, not only the world of other societies and their members, but also a world which contains the consciousness of the individual human beings who are that society's members. The accumulator effect is liable to be much more dramatic in its consequences than in the case of an individual human being, as society corporately and collectively achieves things which far surpass the capacity of any individual human being. And society, like the individual human being, is blessed with the burden of choosing, simply responding to the impulse of life which, for all its naturalness and inevitability, yet calls for an unending effort of self-creating.

12.13. So it is that so much of the effort of society, like so much of the effort of the individual human being, is devoted not merely to choosing but to preparing to choose. The great struggle of a society with the perennial dilemmas of society is a struggle not only to will and act in the present-here-and-now, to make a particular past from a possible future. It is a struggle also to find the best way to be ready to will and act. Much of the social effort of society, like much of the moral effort of the individual human being, is devoted to willing and acting in such a way as to become a particular system of willing and acting.

12.14. So it is also that society must devote so much of its effort to its reality-forming activities, so much of its effort to the forming of its words and ideas and theories and values, so much of its effort to making the consciousness that it needs to enable it to choose well, to enable it to avoid choosing badly.

12.15. As society conceives the world, so it chooses the world. Because society wills and acts in a world beyond consciousness, the physical world, it must remake that world, the rest of all-that-is, as a universe-for-itself within consciousness. Because society wills and acts in relation to the past which is actuality, it must remake that past as a past-for-itself within consciousness. Because society integrates its willing and acting with that of its members, so it must concern itself with the consciousness of its members, forming their consciousness as a consciousness-for-society. Because society must will and act in relation to the willing and acting of other societies and their members, society must concern itself with the nature of human consciousness in general, individual consciousness and social consciousness, forming humanity as a humanity-for-society.

12.16. Its reality-for-itself determines society's willing and acting. But this does not mean that society is doomed to be no better than the lowest common denominator of its actual consciousness. On the contrary, since society is a system for actualizing its self-conceived possibilities, it means that a society can choose to be all that it can conceive as possibility. A society can transcend its present self by actualizing its possible selves.

12.17. As it struggles with the perennial dilemmas of society, society forms its reality-for-itself and finds the means of its self-transcendance. Education is the means by which society causes its members to find and to actualize self-transcending possibilities—education at the mother's knee, at the father's side, in the circle of the elders, through the voice of the prophet and the poet and the priest and the teacher. Education in a society is not merely a passage into maturity to be achieved by a certain age. Society is a permanent self-education. The educating of a society is not merely an education in actuality, the pre-formed reality-for-society. The educating of a society is also an education in the future, in society's possibilities. It makes possible society's constant self-transcending. Society is a permanent self-education of the will. Society is a permanent self-education in virtue.

12.18. In law and morality societies embody their self-transcending self-educating within the structure-system of society. *Morality* is a concern of *society* because the development of the individual personality of its members, the education of their wills, is a determining factor in the survival and prospering of the society in which their willing and acting is integrated with the willing and acting of society. Morality seeks to modify the desiring of the individual human being at the moment of choosing, of willing and acting, by predisposing that individual to choosing well. Morality is society educating itself within the consciousness of its members. *Law* is a concern of the *individual human being* because the development of the constitution of society, the education of the will of society, is a determining factor in the survival and prospering of the human individual as a member of society, predisposing society to choose well. Law, as the universalizing of individual interest and the particularizing of social interest, modifies the desiring of society at the moment of choosing, of willing and acting. Law is society educating itself within the consciousness of society.

12.19. The generic principles of a constitution make possible the self-transcending self-education which is law. They are the means by which self-transcendance is built into the structure-system of law and hence into the constitution and hence into the structure-system of society and hence into the willing and acting of society and its members. Through law society can always will and act to promote the ever-increasing well-being of society and its members. The principles of the constitution guarantee that possibility to any society. But the substantive contents of the law, actual legal relations, are no pre-fixed programme. Law makes legal relations possible. Law does not embody any particular legal relations.

12.20. The substantive contents of the law—like the substantive contents of the other reality-forming systems of religion, mythology, art, philosophy, history, natural science, economy, morality—are determined through the whole life of society, through the total social process, and, in particular, through society's struggle with the perennial dilemmas of society. The total social process, including all society's reality-forming systems, determines the actuality of society, its actual achievements in ensuring the survival and prospering of itself and its members. And so arises the possibility of harm, the harming by society of itself and its members, the harming of other societies and their members.

12.21. It follows also that the harm done by society, including the harm done by law, can be caused by willing and acting at any level and any stage of the total social process. The experience of human social life through all recorded history shows that social harm, on the small scale and on the grandest world-historical scale, can be caused by everything from a particular theory as the nature of a god or gods down to the mentality (personality and ideas) of the most insignificant bureaucrat, and including the effect of every kind of word and idea and theory and value.

12.22. The humanity-shaming failures of international society through so much of its history, are failures in which the whole of humanity has participated. But they are not failures due to some supposed inherent weakness in some supposed human nature. They are failures in the actual activity of human consciousness, failures of imagination and reason, failures of willing and acting. It need not have been so. It need not be so. If international society had been otherwise, human history would have been otherwise. If human history had been otherwise, international society would have been otherwise. If human history had been otherwise, humanity would have been otherwise. International society can be otherwise. Humanity can be otherwise.

12.23. If we are now to will and act to choose the better future of international society at the end of the twentieth century, it is accordingly necessary to consider how and why it is that the structure-system of society, in the continuous present-here-and-now of international society through the centuries, generated actual willing and acting which has led to great progress in human well-being, to great and continuing human distress, and to an uncertainty amounting to despair as to humanity's future. In this way, we may determine what international society is, what it might be, and what it should be. We might, in other words, re-conceive the constitution of international society and so re-conceive the future of humanity.

12.24. For this purpose, we shall put on one side, in the first place, the part played in human social history by charismatic persons—tyrants, prophets, dictators, emperors, generals, statesmen—who have, at one time or another in one place or another, managed to turn the drama of their own personality into the drama of a whole society. They have managed to fuse the development of their individual consciousness with the development of the social consciousness of a whole society. As their armies, their ministers, their servants and agents have marched acoss the face of the earth carrying the leader's personality in their baggage, they have even, in some cases, managed to come close to subsuming the consciousness of the whole of then-known humanity into their own individual consciousness—a consciousness sometimes troubled by madness, generally abnormal, often harmful, self-destroying, other-destroying. The long-term effects of the socialization of the willing and acting of such exceptional individuals can often be very great. They may leave behind them, not only death and destruction and degradation and corruption and misery, but also new political systems, new world perspectives, new perspectives of the human capacity through willing and acting to transform the world. Above all, and most relevantly for our present purposes, they may generate new words and ideas and theories and values, by positive or negative example. So that, although we may place them at the side of the stage for present purposes, they haunt the whole drama of human social development.

12.25. We shall put on one side, secondly, human history as the serial account of events, of human willing and acting. Such history, in so far as it treats social development as a development of psychological and political and physical phenomena, seeks to find an explanation of those phenomena on their own terms. Inventing the past in the present-here-and-now, the writing of such history is itself a form of behaviour, a form of willing and acting which is not different in kind from the rest of the willing and acting which is the present-here-and-now of society. A major battle, a dynastic marriage, a civil war, the assassination of a tyrant, conspiracies and deceits solemnized in constitutions and treaties—these are events which certainly alter the structure-system of societies, often in far-reaching ways. But, from our present point of view, they are not even phenomena. They are epiphenomena, the appearances of appearances. It would no be possible to determine the future on the basis of such a description of the past. They are not events in the physical world which might be understood even according to the epistemological principles of the natural sciences. They are not events knowledge of which, generalization about which, using imagination and reason, can enable us to act in the social world in the future as if we understood that world.

12.26. Thirdly, we shall put on one side, but only for the time being, the economic aspect of social development, the story of the social transformation of the physical world through the systematic application of social power. It is apparent that that story comes closest to our present purpose, since the economic aspect of society comes closer than the charismatic behaviour of individuals and the system-building behaviour of actual societies to being the direct application of consciousness to the physical world of the whole planet Earth. It might seem to follow that, by studying the economic willing and acting of societies, one would come as close as possible to understanding the development of the social consciousness of the international society of the whole human race. However, the difficulty in the way of such an approach is that the formation of social consciousness, as considered in Part One and in the preceding chapters of this Part Two, has been seen to be a totalizing activity, one of whose leading characteristics, and most difficult characteristics, is what has here been called its intra-acting nature, its endless self-reflecting, self-interacting nature.

12.27. However fundamental the economic aspect of society may be to its self-organizing and, hence, to its self-conceiving, at the level of words and ideas and theories and values it becomes caught up in a much more general world of consciousness, integrating the most intimate events in the most unconscious parts of each individual consciousness within the most universal theories of social consciousness, as it struggles to situate itself in relation to all-that-is. To say that an individual's relationship with his mother or a society's conception of the genesis of the universe is explicable by an analysis of the development of economic willing and acting in particular societies is to have a faith in the generalizing power of imagination and reason not justified by its past performance. The universe may be contained in a grain of sand, a human life may be contained in a tear, and a whole society may be contained in a knapped flint. But we would have to make ourselves gods to know how.

12.28. Accordingly, our concern is with the development of social consciousness as it conceives itself, as it considers itself at the level of theory, as it forms its reality-for-itself, as it makes the pure and practical theories which will form all its willing and acting. To understand international society as it now is and as it can be hereafter, we need to know how international society has arrived at its present conception of itself as a structure-system. To conceive humanity and its future, we need to know what humanity has thought of itself as society, what humanity thinks of itself as society.

12.29. There is a constant in society's self-conceiving, a constant of the practical theories of societies, which may be called *the constant of the supersocialization of the social world*. It is a constant in two senses. It is present in the theorizing of all societies known to us through recorded human history. It provides a fixed point by reference to which society's struggle to theorize itself is conducted.

12.30. In its struggle with the perennial dilemmas of society, society necessarily sees itself in three perspectives —an *internal perspective* of its inner life, including the individual lives of its members; an *integral perspective* of itself as a totality, as a coherent structure-system; and an *external perspective* of itself in relation to that which is outside and beyond itself. Supersocialization enables society to have a theoretical view of itself which transcends each of these perspectives and integrates all of them. Like the theoretical strategy which may be called the *supernaturalization of the physical world*, supersocialization throws back the theoretical explanation of that which is to be explained onto something which is not subject to that explanation. It should be noted, in passing, that the supernaturalization of the physical world is not solely the work of religions and mythologies and the arts. It is the work of the natural sciences which create within consciousness that world which has a specific relationship with both the natural world and the world of consciousness but which is something other than both the natural world and the world of consciousness.

12.31. The root cause of the problem of the development of international society over recent centuries may be traced to a particular feature in the supersocializing of international society. The revolutionary recreation of international society as a means of promoting the ever-increasing well-being of the whole human race now depends on an effort at the theoretical level to reintegrate the constant of supersocialization into our understanding of international society, to re-constitute international society.

12.32. Consider the following:

Human nature—	natural goodness, natural evil;
	natural sociability, natural selfishness;
	natural sympathy, natural aggression.
Social nature—	natural freedom, natural law;
	natural equality, natural hierarchy;
	natural harmony, natural conflict.
Physical nature—	natural order, natural chaos;
	natural progress, natural decay;
	natural unity, natural relativity.

Fig. 8. The constant of supersocialization

Such are the commonest supersocializing elements in the long history of human self-understanding. The use of the words *nature* and *natural* in each case is designed to relate the possible to the ideal by way of the actual. That is to say, they seek to explain how reality could be (the possible) by postulating how reality is (the actual) in order to discover what reality should be (the ideal). In this way, the idea of the *natural* is able to perform two functions at one and the same time. It explains what is. It reveals what should be. The articulation of the possible and the actual in terms of the ideal is one of the greatest of all the achievements of human consciousness, giving to humanity the possibility of unlimited self-improvement.

12.33. The history of society's self-understanding is the history of these ideas as they participate in the total social process of one society after another, and, in particular, as they manifest themselves in one pure theory after another, designed to support the practical theories of the day-to-day functioning of the social process of given societies. By supersocializing the explanation of a given society this procedure allows unlimited acts of inference and deduction and implication and individualization, which are themselves part of the substantive willing and acting of the given society.

12.34. The oldest and the commonest form of supersocial theory is *religious*. The tribe, the clan, the city, the nation, the state, and humanity are conceived supersocially by integrating them into a religion which connects everything in the universe with the willing and acting life of every human individual. The three perspectives of such a society—the internal, the integral, and the external perspectives—are integrated within a single structure-system which transcends them all and subtends them all. Human nature, social nature, and physical nature are integrated in a unified view of all nature. The legal constitution, the real constitution, and the ideal constitution are integrated in a present-here-and-now which transcends all time and all space. Individual and social consciousness are integrated in a religious theory of consciousness which is the pure theory which subtends the practical theory of society. With a religious theory of society, the supersocial is the supernatural, and the supernatural is social.

12.35. A *mythological* explanation of society, occupying some intermediate and indeterminate ground between a religious theory and an historical theory, is a supersocial theory in the sense that the origin, the specificity, and the culture of a given society are connected with a reality which transcends that society, a reality of gods and demigods and heroes and spirits and evil spirits and miscellaneous powers and forces, of transmutations of matter and of persons. As has been noted in Part One, the obscurities, incoherences, and malleability of myths seem to serve only to heighten their effectiveness within human consciousness. The imaginative power of their content and their reason-beyond-reason combine to form a mysterious power which leaves consciousness intellectually disempowered to resist them. And it leaves the members of the given society politically disempowered in relation to the system and the systems of the mythologically-explained society. With a mythological theory of society, the supersocial is superhuman, and the superhuman is social.

12.36. An *historical* explanation of society is a supersocial explanation if it is also historicist. That is to say, if it contains a theoretical explanation of history, it is capable of using history as a theoretical explanation of society. As such, a historical explanation is liable to be only one variety of what may be called philosophical explanations of society. Theoretical explanations of history may be religious or mythological in character. If they are neither of those things, then they are liable to rely on philosophy of the most general kind, in order to explain how one particular form of knowledge—historical knowledge—not only can explain the nature and development of a society, especially the nature and development of the society within which that knowledge is generated, but also can be the basis of practical theories, connecting conceived reality through values with willing and acting. Historical explanations of society accordingly seek to show that all history, and not merely the history of a given society, is comprehensible as the unfolding of a systematic pattern, or as emergence through evolution, or as the actualization of a transcendant potentiality. History is then the story of a past and a future which are themselves a present-here-and-now. With an historical theory of society, the supersocial is supertemporal, the supertemporal is social.

12.37. Among supersocial theories of society, there remains the class which may be called *philosophical* explanations. To the extent that philosophy aspires to be universal, dealing with problems raised by consciousness which are not merely the problems of a given society, offering theoretical explanations which are not merely explanations valid for a given society at a given time, then a philosophical explanation of society is supersocial in seeking to explain the origin, the specificity, and the spirit of a given society by reference to such universalizing theories. A philosophical explanation of society is liable to make use of the most general of philosophical theories, including epistemology to explain the nature of knowledge about society and about the world beyond society, metaphysics to explain the nature of any form of being, including social being, and ethics to explain the nature of any form of obligation, including social obligation. A philosophical theory then gives rise, by a process which it can never transcend itself sufficiently to explain but which stems from the total social process of a given society, to practical theories in given societies, connecting reality, philosophically conceived, through values with willing and acting. With a philosophical theory of society, the supersocial is self-transcendence, the self-transcendant is social.

12.38. Seen in the light of actual historical experience, a striking feature of supersocial theories of society is that, for all that they are among the most obscure and complex works of human imagination and reason, they have dramatic real-world everyday effects within societies. The supersocial is also powerfully social. For supersocial theories of society, the supersocial is social, the social is supersocial. Supersocial theories internalize the external perspective of society, within the integral perspective of society's total structure-system. All that happens in society becomes an image or shadow or witness of that which is beyond society. The acted and witnessed drama of society is a puppet-show within a larger drama which is unseen. Every social event is also an event in a universe beyond society. Every social cosmos is merely a microcosm. As a consequence, every word and idea and theory and value generated within society has a second significance in and for a consciousness which surpasses that society, which surpasses all society, a transcendence built into all immanence.

12.39. It is this sense of the eternal significance of the most transient social event which has given to the social struggle of humanity such ferocious intensity. The struggle with the perennial dilemmas of society, society socializing, seems to the protagonists like an ultimate struggle engaging not only their survival and prospering but their very significance as human beings, the significance of the universe which they can conceive for themselves in consciousness, the significance of the universe which seems to surpass the capacity of imagination and reason, the universe which in the end and ineluctably transcends them. The fact of the supersocializing of social theory, through recorded human history, has meant that humanity has, by its own willing and acting, chosen to install the infinite within the relentlessly finite present-here-and-now of human willing and acting.

12.40. Supersocial theory, full of the most dynamic social power, may serve to consolidate a social order, to judge a social order, and to overturn a social order. The same theory at one and the same time may serve all these functions. Supersocial theory may be used in support of any number of competing derived ideas of pure and practical theory: the sovereignty of the people, the sovereignty of a monarch; tyranny and democracy; democracy of a hundred different kinds; the will of God, the general will, the consent of the governed; state power and *laissez-faire*; the sanctity of private property, the socialization of property; established and disestablished religion; slavery and emancipation; colonialism and self-determination; political pluralism and political centralism; intellectual and artistic freedom, censorship; free trade and protectionism; nationalism and internationalism.

12.41. To make theory is to make society. To dominate theory is to dominate social power. To defeat theory is to defeat a structure of power. To change theory is to change society. All social struggle is also a theory-struggle. The total social process of every society contains a struggle to control the commanding heights of theory. The history of every society is also a history of that society's theories. The history of international society, the society of all societies, is also the history of the theories of all the societies which have been contained within international society.

12.42. The infinitely various variables of actual social history over the last six thousand years are given a shared significance by the constant of supersocialization. The socionomies of different societies and of the same society at different times, that is to say, their structure-systems conceived as obligation within the willing and acting consciousness of the society and its members, share a family resemblance, thanks to the constant of super socialization. We recognize our social selves in pre-ancient societies (of the period ending in about the sixth century before the present era). We recognize ourselves in ancient societies (of the period ending in about the fifth century of the present era). We recognize our social selves in pre-modern societies (of the period ending in about the fifteenth century of the present era). We recognize our social selves in modern societies (of the period of the most recent five centuries). We recognize our social selves in contemporary societies all over the world. We know that, given the opportunity, we could have useful discussions about social theory with a pre-ancient Egyptian or a pre-ancient Mesopotamian or an ancient Chinese or an ancient Greek or a pre-modern monk or feudal lord or a Renaissance prince or a Japanese shogun or a nomad of the Mongolian plains or a member of a remote jungle tribe. We know that we are in unbroken line of descent from a social consciousness which extends back to the earliest days of human social organization—and possibly beyond. We contain within ourselves not only genetic physiological material but also genetic social material from time immemorial.

12.43. We can see the whole story as one long struggle of humanity to socialize itself, a struggle with countless episodes of tragedy and pathos, countless episodes of heroism and human self-transcending, of self-surpassing creativity and intelligence, as humanity has applied its gifts of head and heart and hand to its own self-creating. And we can recall that story with every appropriate feeling, from pity to wonder, from anger to delight, from intellectual curiosity to revolutionary impatience. But we are not merely spectators. The story of humanity socializing itself is our story. Social history is our social life. Humanity makes itself in knowing itself.

12.44. In the modern period, over the last five centuries, there has been a continuous and intense development in the super-social theoretization of society, a development which has come to have a determining effect on societies all over the world and a determining effect on the theory of international society. It is a process by which humanity has re-constituted itself as a society yet again, a process which has determined the current state of international society, and a process which now makes necessary and urgent, and almost makes possible, another re-conceiving and re-constituting of international society.

12.45. At the beginning of the modern period, and in a region of the world whose peoples were to play a major part, for better and for worse, in the social development of the whole world, a dominant supersocial theory of the pre-modern era which had been a religious theory was superseded by dominant supersocial theories based on philosophy and on a philosophical view of history. The social struggle of social theory was resumed in its full intensity, using the fruits of that struggle which had survived from the ancient societies, but including now also the fruits of social experience in the pre-modern period. Intense energy came to be applied to social development, both at the level of theory and at the level of willing and acting, with the theoretical aspect accompanying and generating and responding to dynamic developments in political and social and economic structure-systems in societies, ever-accelerating developments which came to affect the whole world and which are continuing in the intensely dynamic present-here-and-now of international society.

12.46. Pre-modern social theory had not been monolithic. There had been many rival formulations of pure theory vigorously asserted and vigorously challenged, many variations in practical theories leading to a patchwork of locally varying social structure-systems. And there had been many intense social struggles within and between societies (Papacy, Empire, kingdoms, republics, local magnates, local churches, sects, cities, guilds, corporations), in which pure social theory had played a leading part in the forming of practical theory. And there had been other societies in Europe which had been little affected by contact with either the Roman Empire or Roman Christianity. And there had been other societies elsewhere in the world, with ancient supersocial theories of their own. But, in most of western Europe, Roman Christianity had absorbed the attention of most of those who thought about social questions at the theoretical level and had provided a framework, however uncertain, and a world-view, however elusive, and a point of reference, however unstable. It had provided the essential elements of a readily available and practically effective reconciliation of the internal, the integral, and the external perspectives of any society.

12.47. The release of consciousness from the powerful hold of Roman Christianity was both a liberation and the resumption of an old and hazardous adventure. Lacking now a reliable, if imperfect, self-conception, social consciousness had to make an exceptional effort to re-conceive itself. It was left to find once again its own self-transcendence at the level of theory, to reconstruct its words and ideas and theories and values, in the middle of real-world social events which were unsettling the structure-systems of every kind of society, up to and including the international society of the whole human race.

12.48. At the end of the pre-modern period, it could not have been predicted with any justifiable sense of certainty that one particular form of social organization would come to dominate all the others. It could not have been predicted that the pre-modern kingdoms of Western Europe, the so-called barbarian kingdoms which had emerged from the decay of the Roman Empire, having come to conceive themselves as nations, would gradually re-conceive their structure-systems in the concept of the *state*. It could not have been predicted that the concept of the state would come to supersede the concept of the nation itself as a focus not merely of social organization but also of individual and social self-identification. It would not have been possible to foresee the overwhelming power which the concept of the state would acquire within social reality-for-itself, subjecting all other forms of subordinate society to itself. It would not have been possible to foresee the immense potentiality, for good and for harm, of the statally organized society.

12.49. At the beginning of the modern period, theoretical materials were to hand in the consciousness-legacy of pre-ancient and ancient societies and in the retained experience of the pre-modern societies. And theoretical materials were to hand in the conceptualized constitutions of societies which had survived from the pre-modern period, some with roots in the ancient period. There were societies of every kind—from empires and churches to craft guilds and universities—which still carried within their constitutions the fruits of the social struggle of generations and centuries. And there were kingdoms whose pre-modern constitutions had proved a match for the theories, structures and systems of the Roman Empire and the Roman Church, whose ideas they had assimilated without losing their own native specificity.

12.50. Among the theoretical elements which social consciousness has not lost in the turbulent social struggles of countless societies, extending back to the societies of the pre-ancient world, was the most significant of all—the idea of society itself, society as some form of entity, some form of structure, some form of system. The problem of society had continued to present itself as the problem of a society. The problem of society had continued to present itself as the problem of explaining the being of any given society, as some sort of entity belonging to a theoretical class called society. What have been called, in the present study, the perennial dilemmas of society are the form in which a society systematically explores that one underlying problem, the problem of the being of a society, the problem for any given society of how to conceive itself, and so create itself, as society. How can a society have its own identity, in relation to other societies and in relation to its members (dilemma of identity—the self and the other)? How can a society function as a unity, a system of all its subordinate systems (dilemma of power—the one and the many)? How can a society make choices as a society, providing itself with the grounds for *its* choosing, *its* willing and acting (dilemma of will—unity of nature, plurality of value)? How can a society integrate the system of its being with the system of all-that-is (dilemma of order—justice and social justice)? How can a society persist as a structure through all its ceaseless self-creating and self-surpassing (dilemma of becoming—new citizens, old laws)? A self which is internally organizing as a system to integrate the willing and acting of human beings, which is making itself able to will and act for itself, which is integrating itself with its conception of the worlds-beyond-itself, which is making itself able to turn its future into its past, to carry its past into its future—when you find these things together, you have a society creating itself as a structure-system, as an entity of some sort.

12.51. With the beginning of the modern period, there was also more than ever present to consciousness the long experience of supersocializing social theory—more than ever, because of the new availability and new attention paid to the consciousness-residues of ancient and even pre-ancient societies. Once again, the constant of supersocialization would manifest itself in the work of self-creating social consciousness. To reconcile the internal, the integral, and the external aspects of society, recourse was had, once again, to one set or another of the elements listed in Fig. 8 (paragraph 12.32 above).

12.52. As compared with significant supersocializing theories of the ancient period, including some of the leading theories of ancient Greece and China and Rome, the philosophical form of supersocialization of the modern period had, from the start, a mythological flavour of its own. As a residual effect of the dominant theological texts of Roman Christianity, the problem of supersocializing society tended to express itself in terms of the problem of the genesis of society and hence of the origin of authoritative willing in society, or, put in other words, the problem of the origin, and hence the authority, of law in society. The problem of understanding the becoming of a society would be posed as if it were a problem of how its being determines its becoming. To understand the being of a society would be posed as if it were a problem of how a society comes into being. As a consequence, the being of a society came to be seen as supersocial in relation to its becoming. To explain the willing of society expressed in its law, it was necessary only to explain the willing of that willing.

12.53. Put in the terms of the present study, the essence of this approach, adopted at the beginning of the modern period, was that the willing of law under the real constitution was willing by a will which had itself been willed under the legal and ideal constitutions. There remained the question of how society's will is itself willed. The will by which society's will is itself willed came to be known as *sovereignty*. Sovereignty is unwilled will. Sovereignty was a familiar word in supersocial theories of ancient Greece and Rome and even in the supersocial theory of one phase of Roman Christianity. It represented a closing term of an awkward series which was otherwise open-ended. Used in an authority-based view of society, it posited an ultimate authority—god, the monarch, the law, the people—which is the authority of authority. It was an aspect of the internal perspective of society. It was the closing term of an hierarchical series which was the willing system of society. But its own theoretical basis was regarded as supersocial. In the early modern period it was to depend on the theory-with-a-hint-of-mythology which offers to explain the genesis of society. Postulate a genesis of society which gives rise to sovereign authority, then all authority within society can be regarded as flowing from the source of sovereignty.

12.54. Two consequences of this authority-based approach to the conceptualization of a society were that it tended to make all society seem to be essentially a system of authority, and that it tended to make societies incorporating systems of authority seem to be the most significant forms of society, at the expense of all other forms of society, including non-patriarchal families, at one extreme, and international society, at the other.

12.55. And, in particular, it cut across the significance of one form of society—the nation—which was, and is to this day, difficult to reconcile with the systematic nature of society-as-state.

12.56. Among all the societies of which they are members, human beings are born into societies of which they consider themselves to be members by birth—the natural selves of their self. These subjective societies determined by birth will here be called *nations*. Nations may be based on any form of human distinction—place of birth, language, religion, art and literature, history, customs of all kinds (food, dress, coming-of-age, marriage). Membership of a particular nation does not exclude membership of other societies, that is to say, co-membership with members of other nations, nor co-membership of two or more nations in a third society in which they cooperate, up to and including co-membership of the international society of the whole human race, the society of societies. Membership of a nation may, in particular, be compatible with membership of other nations—one defined by place of birth, another by religion, a third by more specific customs, and so on. A family is itself a form of nation, connected by marriage in co-membership of other families, and participating in many other societies, including other nations.

12.57. Human beings are remarkably resistant to re-determination of their nations. They will tolerate extremes of force of all kinds to defend their self-conceived membership of their self-conceived nations. Feelings, among the most powerful feelings which human individuals experience, attach to our membership of the particular nations of which we are nationals and we conceptualize those feelings in theory-words which are also powerful value-ideas—freedom, independence, self-determination.

12.58. At the beginning of the modern period, human beings found themselves to be members of countless such nations, organized and connected and co-operating through countless forms of social organization of countless different degrees of complexity and sophistication. These included large-scale nations (the English, the French, the Chinese, the Japanese, the Turks, the Persians, and so on) which were ambiguous in their territorial and political and linguistic and cultural and religious and economic bases.

12.59. They were ambiguous territorially in that, in the pre-modern period, their territories had altered constantly, were at no stage clearly delimited, and were under constant threat from neighbours. They were ambiguous politically in that there were subtle and contested and mutually misunderstood systematic links between them (hegemony, suzerainty, lord-ship, protection, personal union). They were ambiguous linguistically in that they might contain more than one language, and their predominant language was always in a state of development, never settled in structure or vocabulary. They were ambiguous culturally in that they had rudimentary views of their own history, often in more or less legendary form, and because the high culture of the pre-modern period (universities, theology, philosophy, literature, visual art, architecture) had been notably inter-national. They were ambiguous in religious terms because religion united and divided nations, with religions which transcended nations and nations which contained sects. They were ambiguous economically in that production-beyond-subsistence was locally and regionally organized for both agricultural and manufactured products but there was also a striking volume of inter-national trading, at international fairs and along long-distance trade-routes.

12.60. There had also been much inter-national power-competition, at least at the level of monarchs and their courts, competition in prestige and display and possessions and even in territorial and legal control. The monopolization of social consciousness, in education and religion and law and other reality-forming processes, by those closer to the monarch led to a magnification of the role of the monarch in such nations, the self-creating of the nation as a society coming more and more to embody the self-interested fantasies of those close to the monarch. The self-identification of such large-scale nations, over the last centuries of the pre-modern period, came to be more and more the self-recognition of membership in a society presided over by such-and-such a monarch. It should be said that a similar process was occurring in non-monarchical systems, especially in cities and small republics where those with most control over social consciousness, including occasional individual and collective tyrants, behaved very much as monarchs in their contribution to the self-creating of the society, especially the self-creating of the society in relation to the *other*, other national societies, through power-competition.

12.61. The concept of sovereignty came to the aid of the self-creating of the large-scale nations. From the obscure womb of the nations was born the prodigy of the state. The state is a particular form of social organization. A state is an organization of society in which: (1) the willing and acting of the society is conducted through sub-systems which are regarded as an objective manifestation of the willing and acting of the society itself, rather than as a mere aggregation of the willing and acting of members of the society; (2) those sub-systems will and act, under the constitution of the society, with the authority of the whole society; and (3) the willing and acting of such sub-systems comes to be perceived as a *governing* of the society in a *public realm* of social willing and acting—the *commonwealth* or *public affairs* or the *public thing*. A nation organized as a state is thus a nation in which a government conducts the social willing and acting of the society with the authority of the whole of society. It is a nation in which the members of society have taken on a second existence as *citizens*.

12.62. The concept of sovereignty came to the aid of this form of social development in three corresponding ways: (1) by enabling the members of society to conceive of their society as a systematic unity; (2) by enabling members of society to conceive of their society as containing an ultimate source and locus of social authority; (3) by enabling members of society to conceive of a separation between the willing and acting of their individual lives and the willing and acting of the society as a whole (including the willing and acting in which they participate in a *public* capacity). In particular, the sovereignty-theory of a monarchy prepared the ground for later developments by offering the monarch as the embodiment of the unity of society, the reservoir of ultimate authority, and the instrument of society's willing and acting. But republics and city-states had also prepared the ground, in particular, by establishing a tradition of institutionalzied social willing and acting, the institutions consisting of individual members of society but having an independence and an authority which derived from their role as containers of the authority of society and as instruments of its willing and acting.

12.63. Any form of society may be organized statally. A family is not normally a state-society; but, in societies where the family is organized under the constitution in strict hierarchy (patriarchy or matriarchy, elders), a family is a form of state-society, with the specially responsible family-members willing and acting for the commonwealth of the family under authority derived from the continuing reality-for-itself of the family. An industrial or commercial corporation is normally a state-society, with the institutions of the corporation carrying the authority of the corporation as a whole, including authority to make legal relations for the corporation and its members, and authority to do all other willing and acting for the society and in relation to its commonwealth.

12.64. The government of a state-society comes soon to occupy an intermediate and intermediary position between the society and its members. It can, by its willing and acting, organize systematically the interaction of the willing and acting of citizens, if need be by estalishing legal relations conferring social power—in other words, exercising legislative power-rights. A government may use existing social power deriving from the legal constitution to modify the willing and acting of citizens, and the willing and acting of all other subordinate societies—in other words, exercising executive power-rights. A government may will and act to determine the social powers of others conferred on them by existing legal relations—in other words, exercising judicial power-rights. Given the generic principles of the constitution of any society, considered in Chapter 11, such willing and acting by the government, for society, can play a dominant role in a given society's struggle with the perennial dilemmas of society, in society's self-creating. The government of a statally organized society can, through all the forms of social power available to it, take control of the reality-forming processes of society, especially law and education, but also morality and history and art (including public entertainment). The government of a statally organized society may be in a position to determine the total social process and hence society's becoming.

12.65. The society (for example, a nation) which became a state-society, with an ultimate source of willing authority and with a government exercising authority on behalf of society, could thus become systematically very effective. The total social process, society's struggle with its perennial dilemmas, could be organized so that the willing and acting of a small number of members of society could modify the willing and acting of all. In particular, such a society was able to become very efficient economically, creating specifically the constitutional framework within which agriculture and industry and commerce could flourish. The social exchange of natural power for social purpose could, through appropriate systematic organization and social control, become an exchange containing and generating immense energy. The aggregated economic effort of the members of society, including the symbolic aggregation in the form of taxation, could be exchanged for the systematic ordering of society, each sustaining the other.

12.66. In the early modern period, the development of the state within certain large-scale nations alerted self-conceiving social consciousness to three evident, and evidently harmful, concomitants of that development. They were dangers which had been perfectly familiar to supersocializing theorists in ancient societies. They were the dangers of alienation, corruption, and tyranny.

12.67. Individual members of society, in exchanging nationality for citizenship, could easily feel threatened in their identity as individual human selves, threatened in their membership of many subjectively determined nations other than the new statally organizing nation of which they were citizens. The subjectivity of nationality, a feeling of belonging naturally, was not enough for the new form of society, whose citizenship had to be actualized in countless forms of subjection, stemming from law and from every other reality-forming system. And membership of some nations might come to be treated as incompatible with citizenship of the given state-nation, leading to persecution, and worse.

12.68. And, beyond alienation, there was, secondly, the lesson which all of past history had demonstrated—that those who exercise public power might come to identify social purpose with their own personal purposes, might abuse the public power made available to them. Corruption feeds on corruption. Corrupt bureaucrats rely on corrupt judges. Corrupt politicians rely on corrupt businessmen. Corruption can infect the public realm of a society like a contagious disease. Once corruption has taken hold of a society, it is extremely difficult to eradicate. The only members of society with the desire to eradicate corruption are those whose lives and interests are abused by the corrupt use of power, that is to say, the mass of the people. History shows that public power may be abused so effectively that the people, seemingly all-powerful in their massive potential energy, are rendered powerless, morally or physically or both.

12.69. And there was, thirdly, the age-old risk that the holders of public power might come to see that power as a personal possession, to be accumulated as if it were a form of wealth, might come to see the commonwealth as their own wealth, might come to see their own consciousness as an adequate arena for the total social process, might come to see the will of society as contained in their own personal will. The government might begin to see their possession of power as a primary social purpose in itself. Eventually society might come to seem residual to concentrated public power. Public power feeds on public power and grows into tyranny.

12.70. The human world was constituting itself as a world of states. But, from early in the modern period, supersocializing social theory remembered and recognized the dangers of alienation, corruption, and tyranny. It set about rescuing state-society from the threat of the usurping state, seeking to build defences against the dangers of state-organization while securing and enhancing its advantages. The redeeming of society was a long and painful process. To begin to understand that process is to begin to take power over the future of international society.

13 The Socializing of Modern International Society

13.1. The struggle to socialize society over the last five centuries can be considered in three aspects.

(1) Social consciousness generated within itself a pure theory for statally self-organizing societies, a theory contained in the word-idea-value which came to be the idea and the ideal of *democracy*.

(2) Social consciousness resisted the monopolization of power in the state-society and in international society by conceiving and reconceiving a rich profusion of subordinate societies, ranging from the society of the family to great world empires, organizing in an ever-increasing variety of social structure-systems the dramatically increasing levels of social energy, especially the energy of economic power.

(3) Social consciousness undertook the conceiving and the constituting of international society.

(1) THE IDEA AND THE IDEAL OF DEMOCRACY

13.2. The idea of democracy is a surpassing of the idea of sovereignty. Democracy is the dialectical successor of sovereignty. Sovereignty had provided a theoretical explanation of social power by suggesting that the source of all social power is a social power which is not itself derived from social power. Sovereignty conferred authority on the unwilled willing of the sovereign, on the making and the exercising of all social power. Under sovereignty the terms of the social exchange were fixed, and fixed in favour of the government of the state-society.

13.3. The idea of democracy eventually surpassed the idea of sovereignty by finding a basis of all social power not merely in the idea and the fact of authority but in the *constitution* of society, that is to say, in the very structure-system of society itself.

13.4. The struggle within social consciousness to surpass the idea of sovereignty was the long struggle of constitutionalism. It was the struggle to conceive of society not merely as a structure of actual power (real constitution) but as a reality-forming consciousness of what it is (legal constitution) and of what it might be (ideal constitution).

13.5. It is possible to reconstruct the process by which social consciousness formed within itself the idea of democracy.

13.6. Sovereignty as the source of internal authority (internal perspective of society) and sovereignty as the integration of authority at the level of the total society (integral perspective of society) were linked, through supersocialization, with the external perspective of society, its relationship to all that is beyond society. The being of a statally organizing society was seen as intrinsically an authority-being and hence the becoming of society was a becoming-under-authority. But the supersocializing of authority in its integral perspective necessarily opened up the question of the supersocializing of authority in its internal perspective, authority-as-process, how authority is applied as willing and acting. If the sovereign's role was to be regarded as supernatural, in particular as the unwilled source of the authority of the legal constitution and hence of all legal relations, then there still remained the question of the theoretical basis, and hence the possible supersocialization, of *law-making under that authority.*

13.7. As a matter of historical experience, such was the first step along the path to the democratization of the modern statally organizing society. Taking up a thread from the legal and real constitutions of pre-modern nations, social consciousness recalled that even a monarch might be required, in accordance with hallowed constitutional traditions, to consult with some of his subjects before making or applying the law, that is to say, before applying the legal constitution to make new legal relations and to execute power-rights, including both a power-right to levy taxation and a power-right to demand services, and might be required to exercise judicial power-rights—arbitrating conflicts between right-holders—according to settled procedures. History and legend attested to the fact that the formal installation of monarchs—involving a formality of election and/or an anointing and/or a coronation with coronation oath—had typically involved a submission, however formalized, to a constitution. It was thus by invoking an historically-based legal constitution that social consciousness was able to conceive of a basis on which the power of the sovereign, exercised under the real constitution, might be regarded as subordinate to an aspect of the very society which that same sovereignty integrated as a system.

13.8. A supersocializing of *constitutional sovereignty* was a first means by which theorizing social consciousness responded to, and tempered, a supersocializing-through-philosophy of *sovereignty*. A social exchange occurred at the level of theory. The self-contained social power acknowledged in the idea of *authority* was exchanged for the social purpose contained in the idea of *constitutional sovereignty*.

13.9. But supersocialized sovereignty provoked another form of response from social consciousness, a reaction with still more far-reaching consequences. Sovereignty might enable statally organizing society to conceive of itself as a coherent structure-system. In might enable such a society to conceive of how the real constitution, the willing and acting of the sovereign, was structurally related to the legal constitution and thereby to the very being of society. But sovereignty-as-structural-integration and sovereignty-as-ultimate-authority left unexplained sovereignty-as-system, the systematic aspect of the internal perspective of a statally organizing society.

13.10. In the terms of the present study, social consciousness had to enable itself to understand not only how sovereignty was subject to the constitution but also how the generic principles of a constitution, that is to say, the systematic principles of the constitution of any society, could be made compatible with the sovereignty of a statally organizing society. The matter was urgent, given that sovereign power was evidently capable of generating very great social power, including a power over consciousness itself, through its control of society's reality-forming, as well as the power to embody the values derived from such reality-forming in legal relations and to intepret and apply those legal relations authoritatively.

13.11. So it was that social consciousness addressed the unpromising paradox of *limited sovereignty*. Theory began to explore the idea that there might be *natural legal relations* which were supersocial to the actual legal regulations of society, and even supersocial to the actual power-rights of sovereigns and their servants and agents. Put in the terms of the present study, social consciousness came to understand that society is a system as well as a structure and that a system contains principles of its functioning, a constitution of its constitution, laws about law.

13.12. Once again, history was a convenient foundation for theory, in that, in the nations in question, there seemed to be an unbroken, if highly obscure and more than partly legendary, historical continuity, a past of which the present-here-and-now of society was evidently only a continuation, a latest resultant. Today's monarch under the real constitution—a particular human individual, together with his servants and agents—evidently only had authority as a result of the sum total of the past social process. And hence the sovereign had an authority whose limits were held in accumulated social consciousness, and could be specified, and, if need be, could even be put into words, in some great charter or other constitutional instrument.

13.13. Accumulated social consciousness, retained from a long process of social development, also lent support at the theoretical level. The idea of a *natural law*, supersocial to the law of a given society, a law-above-law, was evidently an ancient idea which had the extraordinary prestige of having been a common property of the social theorizing both of ancient societies (including societies for beyond the confines of Europe) and of the pre-modern societies of Roman Christianity. A law-above-law seemed, at the beginning of the modern period, an idea of exceptional evolutionary power, given that it had evidently been an idea conceived within the social consciousness of so many diverse societies at so many different periods of history, as their social processes generated their self-conceiving words and ideas and theories.

13.14. The idea of natural law, with its concomitant idea of natural legal relations (natural equality, natural freedom, and natural rights), embodied another social exchange at the level of theory. The social power acknowledged in the idea of *authority*, as modified by the concept of constitutional sovereignty, was exchanged for the social purpose contained in the idea of *limited sovereignty*. And such an idea was not merely an idea of theory. It was conceived also as a value, a possible ground for willing and acting by power-holders exercising all kinds of powers, including legislative and executive and judicial powers. In this way, the constraining constitution, the constitution of constitutions, containing law about law, was placed by social consciousness within the ideal constitution, determining the self-conceived possibilities of a statally organizing society.

13.15. There was a third self-correcting potentiality within the idea of the authority-based society, a potentiality which would transform one society after another in the following centuries. Although society might contain an authority-of-all-authority within society, closing the systematic structure of society, and although the legal constitution might embody the constitutional basis of actual sovereignty, and although the ideal constitution might set systematic limitations on all authority, and although this or that human being might exercise the rights, especially the power-rights, of the constitution under the real constitution, there always remained the question of the identity of the source of authority under the constitution in all its three aspects, *the identity of the sovereign*. Sovereignty seemed to imply a sovereign. But who was to be the sovereign?

13.16. Once again, historical experience showed that what was needed to provide the identity of the sovereign was something or someone who could be regarded as above the struggle of the total social process, who could be a supersocial embodiment of a society's sovereignty. The monarch, god, the law, the people—these had been the characteristic unauthorized authorities of countless societies. A *monarch* whose identity was precisely the identity of being unique, who was unique not merely within the given society but could be regarded as a member of some special supernatural order. A *god* whose will was all-embracing, embracing the willing of the society itself and the willing of the sovereign and of all that the sovereign willed, enabling the constitution to share in the prestige of the necessary order of the universe. The *law* as the living reality of the society's past, the supernatural inheritance of a society from its own origins and from the willing of the ancestors. The *people* whose voice was like the voice of a god, with the authority of those who could, ultimately by revolutionary force, create and destroy not only the sovereign, and all lesser authority, but the whole constitutional structure of society.

13.17. In the modern period, over the last five centuries, the increasing natural power of the people led to an increasing social power of society; and the increasing social power of society led to increasing possibilities for the natural power of the people. And this powerful intra-active development of the total social process led, on the one hand, to a greatly increasing social power of *government* within statally organizing society, and, on the other hand, to a greatly increasing power of the *people* as the source of the natural power without which there could be no social power.

13.18. Farmers, both landowners and peasants, were producing more and more beyond the requirements of subsistence. Merchants were discovering the multiplying power of money, the extraordinary power of wealth to generate wealth within appropriate social structures. Artists and intellectuals of all kinds were discovering the boundless natural power of human imagination and reason. Natural scientists were finding the apparently unlimited power of human imagination and reason to win a transforming power over the physical world, a power to transform the physical world into categories of consciousness, a power to use categories of consciousness to modify the physical world. Individual human beings were discovering individuality, the natural creative power of the individual human being, as maker of the individual self and as maker of

the self of society, including the family as society, and
including the power to respond, religiously or otherwise, to the
universe beyond society, up to and including the universe of
all-that-is, and including the power to educate their children
into the potentialities of the individual in society. All these
discoveries were rediscoveries of things not unknown to social
consciousness in many societies in many periods of their
history. But, in the early modern period, they generated the
special energy of the new.

13.19. The exchange between the people and society was
intensely dynamic. To society, the people could supply their
natural power, especially economic power, in order to serve
social purposes. From society, the people needed stability of
property relations, validity of contracts, reliability of money
and markets, security of the person, especially during travel,
libraries, schools, churches. And such people also needed the
confidence that social arrangements would enable a fair
distribution of society's burdens.

13.20. In this way, and not without endless conflicts and
setbacks, not without bloodshed and suffering of every kind,
the people gradually reasserted their social existence against
the state-society, the society organizing itself internally as a
state. The people as citizens were embodying themselves as
society. Society was coming to be a structure-system of
citizens. And the government was asserting itself as a specific
social sub-system with special responsibility for the willing
and acting of the public realm of society under the constitution.
The government with authority over the public realm was
embodying itself as the state.

13.21. In a fateful act of mutual self-creation, the people and
the government made each other, the one as the embodiment of
society, the other as the embodiment of the state. The citizens
surrendered to government, as government surrendered to the
citizens. Each, in so doing, empowered the other. Thus did the
state-society surpass itself as state-society.

13.22. So it was that the ancient word-idea-theory-value of
democracy came to take hold of social consciousness in one
statally organizing society after another in the modern period,

not only at the level of theory but in the constitution itself, including the systems of the legal constitution, and including, especially, the social purposes formed in the ideal constitution. The idea of democracy having been thought, it could not thereafter be unthought. Social consciousness could not now be led to forget the idea of democracy. Having conceived the idea of democracy as a possibility, having made of that idea an ideal, society was now in a position to make the ideal of democracy into the potentiality of every state-society.

13.23. When the idea of democracy has been conceived within social consciousness, as a matter of word and idea and theory and even value, it gives no guarantee that society will thereafter will and act so as to do good and avoid harm. The theory of democracy may be installed as part of the reality-for-itself of a society. But it is the total social process of a society which determines the actual life of society. The role of theory, of law, and of social systems is to modify the willing and acting of society and its members by modifying the reality-for-itself of society and hence modifying the range of its conceivable possibilities. But it still remains for society and its members to conceive its possibilities and to choose among possibilities, moment by moment, day after day, year in and year out.

13.24. In particular, historical experience has shown that the idea of democracy, even if it is contained in the ideal constitution of a given society, may actually facilitate the work of corruption and tyranny through the operation of the real constitution, that is to say, through the actual willing and acting of actual public power-holders.

13.25. The idea of democracy gives theoretical legitimacy to the state-organized society, adding the energy of value to the energy of efficacy, making the actual organization of power seem like an actualization of society's ideal purposes. The enhanced social power thereby made available to the government in a given society may overwhelm the natural and social power of its members. Individual power-holders and subordinate societies acting in the public realm may be able to use the exceptional energy and exceptional potentialities of a given state-society to do exceptional good for themselves, exceptional harm to others. They may take control of the reality-forming systems of society—from education to law, not to speak of will-forming sub-systems and the economic sub-systems.

13.26. The idea of democracy is able to release the boundless natural power of the people. The structure-system of a state-society harnesses that natural power as social power. The idea of democracy does not prevent the usurpation of state-power, a usurpation which may be made in the name of the people. Then the people's government becomes government of the people.

13.27. The idea of democracy having surpassed the idea of sovereignty, it thus became necessary to surpass the idea of democracy. Social consciousness took a fourth and final step in the redemption of society in the name of democracy. Again with great effort and at great cost and by dint of unrelenting revolutionary effort, social consciousness responded to actual historical experience of statally organizing societies, recognizing the potentiality of democracy as a legitimation of corruption and tyranny. The response of self-conceiving social consciousness was the supersocializing of democracy itself. Democracy was supersocialized in the name of social justice.

13.28. A statally organizing democracy came to conceive of itself as not merely a social structure-system in which the public realm is subject to the authority of the government, willing and acting under the constitution, deriving its authority from the sovereignty of the people. A democracy recognized itself as, first and foremost, a society, a socializing, a creating of itself through the total social process.

13.29. The pure theory of democracy was, necessarily, itself a product of the total social process of many societies over long periods of time. The idea of democracy emerged from the struggle of those societies with the perennial dilemmas of society. It was intimately involved in the establishing of their *identity*, their new identity as compared with their pre-democratic selves, their separate identity in relation to other societies, their distinctive identity in relation to other societies, their identity in relation to their members, the identity of their members in relation to the societies. It was necessarily part of the organization of *power* in those societies, as they organized the relationship of the one of society with the many of their peoples and subordinate societies, the one of each individual society-member with the many of the society. It was intimately involved with the organizing of the *will* of those societies, as they struggled to find a way of making the will of each into the will of all, the will of all into the will of each, to make government of the public realm into the self-government of the people, to make of the social process a means of universalizing values in society, and a means of particularizing society's values in the life of each society-member. It was necessarily part of the struggle for the stability-in-change, the struggle of *becoming*, as societies found ways of reconciling the endlessly dynamic social process with the maintaining of social structure, using the constitution, and especially the legal constitution, to carry the will of society from its past to its future, from its future to its past.

13.30. As a matter of historical experience, it took such societies time, what seems now like a surprisingly long period of time, to integrate the idea of democracy within the struggle of the perennial dilemma of *order* (justice and social justice). A democratic statally organizing society evidently could be an ingenious reconciliation of tyranny and anarchy in the form of a constitutionally limited sovereignty of the people. Such a society evidently could be very efficient in increasing the energy levels of society, socially organizing the ever-increasing natural and social power of society-members, especially economic power, generating vast surplus energy in society as a whole. And such a society could be extremely efficient in organizing the desire of its members within the reality-forming, and hence in serving the purposes, of the society. But it took time for such societies to make the well-being of their members into a primary social purpose.

13.31. In the end, social consciousness came to understand, in the nineteenth century if not later, that the social systems flowing from the pure theory of democracy are not merely well adapted to the pursuit of justice. They are perfectly suited. The pursuit of justice is inherent in the theory of democracy. Democracy, as a universalizing of particular wills in the willing of society, naturally seeks the universal purpose of all wills in society, naturally seeks to universalize all particular desire. Democracy, as the particularizing of the willing of society within the willing of each member of society, naturally seeks to make its purpose into the purpose of each of its members, naturally seeks to particularize universalized desire. Democracy seeks to make the individual society-member seek well-being in seeking the well-being of society. Democracy seeks to make society seek well-being in seeking the well-being of each individual society-member.

13.32. And well-being involves a relationship of order, a right relationship of each to all, a right relationship within the consciousness of each society-member, a right relationship of the self-creating self to itself, a right relationship between each society member and every other, a right relationship between each society-member and society, a right relationship between each society-member and the members of other societies up to and including every member of the international society of the whole human race, a right relationship of each society to every other, and a right relationship between every society and the world of non-consciousness, the physical world, the universe of all-that-is. At long last, social consciousness recognized that the ideal of democracy cannot be other than an ideal of order-seeking justice.

13.33. The re-conceiving of democracy as an instrument of justice had two fundamental effects on the theory of democracy. In the first place, it made possible the integrating of the public realm of society with the private realm into a single realm of universal value. There would be one and the same justice for society-as-state (including society's public servants) and for individual human beings, as such and as citizens. Law and morality, and the rest of social reality-forming, could be unified in a single order stemming from the single ordering of desire and obligation within the ultimate structure-system of society, and hence within the ordering of the impulse of life and of necessity within the order of the physical universe. The supersocializing of democracy had thus achieved the most complete form of supernaturalization available to philosophy (as distinct from the supernaturalizing of religion, mythology, and natural science). It allowed the total social process of a democratic statally organizing society to be conceived by society as a process of conforming to the *nature* of the human individual, to the *nature* of society, and to the *nature* of all-that-is.

13.34. Secondly, the idea of democracy as self-government could now become the idea of democracy as self-creating. Government of the public realm need no longer be conceived as intrinsically the exercise of authority. Authority could come to be conceived simply as the ordering aspect of the total social process. Government could be conceived simply as a way of organizing the participation of all members of society and of all subordinate societies in the reality-forming of society, in the will-forming of society. *Sovereignty as authority had evolved into sovereignty as self-willed order.*

13.35. Such was the self-forming of social consciousness in the modern period. Society conceived itself, at last, as society.

nation
|
sovereignty
(the unwilled willing of society's will)
|
authority
(willing as a function of sovereign power)
|
state-nation
(public realm under the authority of government)
|
constitutional sovereignty
(functional limits on sovereignty)
|
limited sovereignty
(constitutionalism—generic principles of the constitution)
|
popular sovereignty
(self-government)
|
self-willed order
(well-being through justice)

Fig. 9. The theoretical evolution of the idea of democracy

13.36. Such became the evolved ideal of democracy. An ideal democratic society is a society creating itself through the self-willing of its members in the name of justice and with a view to the well-being of the society and of all its members.

(2) THE FORMING OF SUBORDINATE SOCIETIES WITHIN INTERNATIONAL SOCIETY

13.37. One view of modern history has supposed that, from about the year 1500, a form of society known as the *state* or the *nation-state* simply emerged, as if by some natural and inevitable process, from the total social process of international society, and that the people of the world gradually, as if by some natural and inevitable process, aggregated into *states*.

13.38. The development of forms of social organization has, on the contrary, been an intense struggle in which no people and no region of the world has avoided the rough winds of endless change. At no time and in no place has it been the case that a specific people has found some natural and settled equilibrium in a specific state-society, that is to say, in a society organized as a state. Since every society is a process, not a state of affairs, and since there is no society whose members are not also members of other societies, historical experience of the last five centuries has been a sea which is never at rest, a scene of restless self-ordering energy. Forms of society, patterns of social membership, and patterns of social interacting between societies have formed and reformed through war, conquest, annexation, cession, treaty (voluntary or imposed), civil war, revolution, putsch, subversion, intervention, unification, federation, dismemberment, secession, colonization, decolonization, migration, forced movement of peoples, genocide, massacre, pogrom, persecution.

13.39. The fate of all subordinate societies, down to and including the family, has followed in the wake of the erratic movements of the larger societies of which they have been, from time to time, members and of the societies which have been, at one time or another and for one reason or another, in a position to affect their fate. The fate of *nations*, the subjectively determined societies of which we are members by birth, has been the most turbulent. Their powerful self-identifying and self-protecting energy has, again and again, met the powerful organizing energy of the state-society. Again and again, the two forms of energy have combined to form social entities of overwhelming power. Again and again, the two forms of energy have been in conflict, producing dramatic, and often devastating, effects.

13.40. The social experience of humanity over the last five centuries has included the development of state-societies, in which a public realm is under the authority of a government. It is by no means confined to such a development. In particular, nations (societies whose members consider themselves to be

---

1. *Statal society, other than a nation* (a society which is structuring itself as a state within another society).
2. *Non-statal society, other than a nation* (a society which is not structuring itself as a state).
3. *Non-statal nation* (a nation which is not structuring itself internally as a state).
4. *Statal nation* (a nation which is structuring itself internally as a state).
5. *Nationalizing state* (a society structuring itself internally as a state and whose purpose is to be a nation).
6. *Multinational nationalizing state* (a society structuring itself internally as a state and whose purpose is to be a nation containing several nations).
7. *Multinational statal society* (a society structuring itself internally as a state and whose purpose is to be a state-system for several nations).
8. *Multilocal statal society* (a society structuring itself internally as a state and acting within the constitution of more than one other society).
9. *Multilocal or international non-statal society* (a society which is not structuring itself internally as a state and is acting either within more than one other society or outside the constitution of any society other than international society).
10. *International statal society* (a society structuring itself internally as a state and acting outside the constitution of any other society other than international society).

Fig. 10. Forms of social development in modern international society

members by birth) have remained as significant and energetic forms of social organization. And the dramatic development of the economy has generated subordinate societies of many different kinds. At the risk of failing to do justice to the seemingly irreducible complexity of social experience in the modern period, it may be said that there have been ten forms of social development. See Figure 10 opposite.

13.41. Whether or not a particular society is developing in one or other of such ways is, for that society, a matter of that society's self-conceiving. The society's ideal constitution contains an idea of the direction of society's becoming, as conceived by the society itself. Through the legal and real constitutions, it creates the structures and systems appropriate to its idea of its possible self and distributes the appropriate social power. A society's development, so far as other societies are concerned, is a matter for their reality-for-themselves, including their words and ideas and theories and values. The mutual recognition of the social development of societies is part of the total social process of societies, especially as they struggle with the dilemma of identity (the self and the other). The conceiving of the social development of a particular society is also a matter for the total social process of international society, including international law, as international society forms its own reality-for-itself, including theory-forming about social development in general, such as the hypothesis proposed in the present volume.

1. Statal society, other than a nation

13.42. Any society, from the society of the family to the international society of the whole human race, may structure itself internally as a state, by conceiving of a public realm under the responsibility of a government willing and acting under the authority of society as a whole and on behalf of society as a whole. The government of such a society consists of individual human beings and subordinate societies exercising *public* social power under the constitution, including power contained in specific legal relations.

13.43. The government of a statally organizing society is accordingly a constitutional organ of the society having a specific place within the structure-system of the society. Whatever the status and social power of any particular such constitutional organ in any particular society, its status is necessarily also determined, like that of every other member of society, by the generic principles of a constitution which have been considered in Chapter 11. This consideration is of particular importance in the case of such constitutional organs, however, because the human beings involved in them lead two lives—their official life and their private life. The temptations of abuse of power (corruption and tyranny) are increased by this formal separation of the official and the private, with the danger that different realities (with different ideas and values) will condition official and private willing and action. It is the function of social and legal accountability to assert the integrity of society's reality-for-itself, so that its theories and values, in particular, apply equally effectively to all members of society.

13.44. Countless subordinate societies in a modern society, other than the superordinate society itself, are statally organizing: schools, churches, universities, professional associations, trade unions, political parties. But it is the industrial and commercial and financial corporations which have become the most significant. Particularly through the development of so-called capitalism, to be considered further in Chapters 17 and 18, such corporations have come to exercise very great social power, with the social power of the largest corporations exceeding the social power of many governments of state-societies. The government of such corporations is in the hands of officials and decision-making sub-systems and sub-societies, with the result that the human beings involved take on a dual existence closely analogous to that of government officials. The legal and, especially, the social accountability of such corporations is still relatively undeveloped. It will be developed, like that of governmental bodies, through the total social process of superordinate state-societies and the total social process of international society.

13.45. It is evident that a theory of international society and its law which does not take account of statally organizing societies of all kinds is not worthy to be a theory of the international society of the future.

2. Non-statal society, other than a nation

13.46. The societies which are not organizing themselves statally and which do not constitute a nation are countless in number and variety. They include all those societies and associations and clubs in which human beings come together for particular purposes, in the fields of politics, religion, sport, art, entertainment, leisure pursuits of all kinds. They include also loosely structured business and professional partnerships. And they include ethnic groups whose activities are essentially cultural in nature, not having structures of self-government.

13.47. Such societies are characterized by their informality, often by their transience. But it should be noted that even such societies are, in however simple a form, societies within the meaning of the hypothesis under consideration in the present volume. That is to say, they have a constitution to organize their social willing and acting, they have reality-forming processes which form, among other things, their ideas and values, so as to modify the willing and acting of the society and its members in their capacity as members.

13.48. Such societies are natural socialized democracies. Although the energy levels of modern societies of all kinds have tended to compel more and more societies to adopt aspects of statal structuring, with willing and acting on behalf of the society conducted by special constitutional organs, in the informal societies here under consideration the members participate naturally in all the willing and acting of the society, so that the general interest of the society and the particular interests of the members are naturally reconciled, within the scope of the purposes of the society, in its total social process which contains, as with any other form of society, a struggle with all the perennial dilemmas of societies.

13.49. Such natural societies can be regarded as a limiting case of all societies, reminding us that societies are not naturally systems of oppression but systems of co-operative endeavour for promoting the survival and prospering of the society and of its members in their capacity as members and within the scope of its self-conceived purposes.

3. Non-statal nation

13.50. A nation is a society which conceives of itself as a society on some specific ground, or on more than one specific ground (ethnic, regional, religious, linguistic, cultural), and whose members consider themselves to be members of the society by birth. A non-statal nation is a nation which is not organizing itself to have the characteristic structure-system of the state, namely, a public realm under the responsibility of a government acting on behalf of the society as a whole.

13.51. Such a nation may be a remote people who fall outside the state organization of all other societies at the relevant time. It may be a people, such as the aboriginal inhabitants of a territory, who form a subordinate society within some other society, integrated within the structure-system and the constitution of that society, but who nevertheless regard their specific national character as continuing to coexist within the superordinate society and, within their own self-conceiving at least, to have primacy over the superordinate society. It may also be a nation which extends across the territory of more than one other society, for instance a religious or ethnic nation, forming a subordinate society within more than one superordinate society, but similarly retaining its subjective specificity.

13.52. Non-statal nations have given rise to some of the most acute social problems of the last five centuries—and continue to do so to this day. Their participation in any superordinate society inevitably gives rise to problems as the larger society struggles to create itself through its struggle with the perennial dilemmas of society. Each of those dilemmas is liable to affect such a subordinate national society in critical ways, especially the dilemma of identity (as the nation and the larger society struggle to maintain their respective identities) and the dilemma of will (as the nation and the larger society struggle to retain their respective values).

13.53. As has been suggested above, there is nothing inherent in the structure-system of a society which prevents the functioning of the superordinate society in ways which continually increase the well-being of the whole society and of all its members, including subordinate nations. But, as has also been suggested, that increasing well-being is no automatic and mechanical consequence of the wonderful self-creating capacity of human social consciousness. Historical experience of the last five centuries—and, of course, experience of social organization as it is known to us from all earlier recorded history—witnesses to the all-too-human risk that the social system of the superordinate society may do great harm as well as good to such subordinate nations. Non-statal nations have experienced some of the worst suffering that human society can inflict on human beings.

13.54. The risk of harm to non-statal nations is even greater when they are present within a society which is statally organized. Statal organization is liable to give rise to ever more complex legal relations, modifying the willing and acting of citizens over ever larger areas of their lives and to ever greater degrees of intensity as the complexity of the society and the levels of surplus social energy increase. The most modern state societies require extensive and intensive lawmaking and administration (exercise of public power-rights) and high degrees of social conformity encouraged and enforced by very active social willing and acting. In these circumstances, a non-statal nation is liable not only to find difficulty in surviving as a distinct entity but also to be the subject of exceptional social activity by the superordinate society, activity which may well lead to harm being done to the non-statal nation. As ever, it is within the total social process that the position of the non-statal nation must be determined in a given society.

13.55. Especially acute problems arise where a non-statal nation is present within more than one superordinate society, especially if those societies are neighbours. Experience shows that, in such circumstances, the struggle for identity, autonomy, cultural values, social justice, for the very survival of the non-statal nation may seem to the government of the superordinate society as a threat to its social order, a threat which may be perceived as a threat of internal subversion and even as an external threat to the survival of the superordinate society.

13.56. A theory of international society and its law which does not take account of the situation of non-statal nations, the most ancient and the most heartfelt of societies, is not worthy to be a theory of the international society of the future.

4. Statal nation

13.57. Certain nations whose identity had been constructed on ethnic, regional, religious, linguistic, or cultural grounds developed more and more of the features of state-societies, by the process of statal development of societies in general which has been considered above. The forming of a monarch's will came more and more to be shared with his leading subjects and with persons from wider and wider classes within society. The expression of a monarch's will came to be embodied in more permanent and more objective forms, as legislation. The administration of justice more and more detached itself from the will of the monarch, with the objectification of the law and with the appointment of professional judges. The administration of the public property, including land and the fruits of taxation, became less and less the administration of the monarch's personal estate, more and more the administration of the *public wealth*. Appointment to public offices was less and less appointment to the monarch's household, more and more the appointment of servants of society. The monarch became the government.

13.58. Statal nations are thus nations which underwent a systematic transformation. Many had, as nations, pre-existed the modern period. Some, especially in Africa and Asia and America, were ancient and even pre-ancient. Some, especially in Asia and Mediterranean Europe, had long been statal in tendency. In the modern period, through emulation and through colonisation in particular, more and more nations were reconstructed statally, and more and more rapidly.

13.59. Nations which became part of superordinate societies which have been perceived as colonial empires—see further under (7) below—were normally organized in a way which combined the process of social development of the superordinate society and aspects of the traditional social development of the subordinate society. A particular process of development then began, specific to the society in question, generally with the growing statalization of the subordinate society, until the time when it became independent and took its place as a statal nation in its own right.

13.60. The most significant feature of statal nations, as opposed to other forms of statal society, is that they brought their old identity to their new status. That is to say, the identity which they had constructed, through the course of their total social process, often over many centuries, was brought into conjunction with their new statal organizing. The reality-for-itself of a national society is full of its own words and ideas and theories and values, its own realities of religion and mythology and history and art, its own law and morality and education, its own legal and real and ideal constitution. The intense energy of such an identity is then combined with the energy which flows from the process of statal organizing. In the particular case of certain European statal nations, in the modern period beginning in the late fifteenth century, such an intensification of social energy led to the social expansion which was imperialism. Other societies in earlier periods, back to the pre-ancient period, had shown similar expansionist energy in periods of high social organization.

13.61. Once again, a theory of international society and its law which ignores the phenomenon of the statally organizing nations, with their exceptionally high levels of self-identifying and self-defending energy, is not worthy to be a theory of the international society of the future.

5. Nationalizing state

13.62. The vagaries of the history of international society have led to the establishment of societies which were established in order to be statally organizing societies. Typically they are the result of secession from other societies, especially statal nations. It was in the late eighteenth century of the modern period that the stream of such new secessionist societies began to flow. It has continued to the present day. They are said to gain their independence. Their independence is their initial social purpose. They are said to seek self-determination. That is to say, they seek to construct a social identity, initially as a self in relation to the other from which they have seceded, but also in relation to the other of all other societies.

13.63. Such a statally organizing society gives birth to itself by adopting a so-called *constitution*. Such a constitution is a written document which is intended to embody the initial ideal and legal constitutions of the society. It is the life-giving act of the new society. Such a written constitution at once enters the total social process of the new society and becomes subject, in particular, to that society's struggle with the perennial dilemmas of society, including especially the dilemmas of identity (as it forges its selfhood) and of power (as it organizes social willing and acting). The written constitution thus at once becomes merely one part of the constitution of the society—one part of the legal and real and ideal constitutions which the society never ceases to form thereafter within the total social process.

13.64. Historical experience shows that the construction of the identity of such new non-national societies takes the form, from the very first, of self-nationalizing. That is to say, the new society seeks to become a nation. It seeks to create for itself a ground for existing other than the mere fact of its existence. It establishes membership of the society on the primary basis of birth within the society. It permits membership by those not born within the society, but does so by so-called naturalization, assimilating them to its indigenous members.

13.65. The new society sets about creating a powerful reality-for-itself, powerful enough to take precedence over the reality-for-itself of each of the societies (especially, national societies) to which its new members formerly belonged, and powerful enough to cause other societies and their members to recognize and respect the self of the new society. Normally, the indigenous people inhabiting the territory of the new society will have a history of their own. If their history has included a period of colonization (participation in the structure-system of another society), then that history will include the history of the colonial period but also the history of the pre-colonial period, which may be long and complex and culturally rich. If the new society does not have a ready-made history, it must set about the task of forming its history, making its past from its future in its present-here-and-now. Other reality-forming systems—language, religion, mythology, art, law, morality, education, natural science—contribute to forming the specific reality-for-itself of the new society, a reality which comes to be embodied in its own words and ideas and theories and values. The symbols of the nation—flags and anthems and symbols and rites and rituals and ceremonies—will foster the growth of the new identity for the society and its members and for other societies and their members as they find themselves relating to the new society. At last the new society will see itself, and be seen, as a new nation, with a ground of its existing other than the mere fact of its social organization.

13.66. The statal organizing of such a new society is necessary to the creation of the nation. It is the capacity of the state-system to act for society as a whole which enables the new society to take effective command of its own becoming as a nation, in all the working of its total social process. The written constitution of the society is available as a programme for those whose willing and acting on behalf of society as a whole will cause the total social process to generate that which is needed for the social development of the new society. The total social process needs the exceptional social energy which the state-system, so programmed, can generate. And the state-system, because of its relative objectivity and impersonality, can transcend the exceptional multiplicities of the new society, imposing unification, dominating the struggle with all the perennial dilemmas of society. The state-system generates and sustains the will to be a nation.

13.67. A theory of international society and its law which ignores the desire of peoples not only to be organized as state-societies but to acquire the social identity of members of a nation is not a theory worthy of the international society of the future.

6. Multinational nationalizing state

13.68. Some societies have sought to achieve three structural objectives simultaneously. They have sought to use a state-system to gather together a number of nations into a single nation, without those nations ceasing to be nations. In other words, the separate nations have a status in the superordinate society which is recognized in its constitution. Their relationship to each other, to their members, and to the society as a whole are regulated as constitutional relations, in addition to the working-out of those relations in every aspect of the total social process of the society, including all its reality-forming. The included nations have subordinate state-systems for forming the social will of the individual nations and they also participate in the will-forming state-system of the whole society. Such a situation is typically a federal state-system, but with the special characteristic that the subordinate states are nations.

13.69. The significant feature of such systems is that they also seek to establish a nation of all their nations. That is to say, they are nationalizing in the manner of the nationalizing states considered above. The constitution of the superordinate society enables the society to create itself in the manner of any society, to make its past from its future in its present-here-and-now. The state-system of the superordinate society enables it to dominate the reality-forming of the society in ways necessary to create the nation. It is evident that, given the level of social energy liable to be contained in the subordinate nations, the task of the state-system of the superordinate society is liable to be more difficult than in a nationalizing state. The subordinate societies are liable to be energetic simply because they are nations. But also they are liable to be exceptionally energetic as they create and project and defend their identity in relation to the other subordinate nations and in relation to the dominating society as a whole, the emerging superordinate nation.

13.70. The formation of a multinational nationalizing state is thus essentially a unifying event in social development. In the nineteenth and twentieth centuries there have been notable cases of such unifications. Historical experience shows that, on the one hand, remarkable levels of surplus social energy can be achieved at the level of the new unified nation, and, on the other hand, that it is exceptionally difficult to maintain the complex equilibrium of such a society.

13.71. Experience also shows that the rather unstable, exceptionally high energy of the society may be directed outside the society, presumably as a way of lowering internal energy levels and as a way of unifying the society in relation to external challenges. Such external activity may take the form of exceptional social activity of an economic kind or self-assertion through aggression, or both.

7. Multinational statal society

13.72. So-called imperialism was the gradual extension of the state-system of one society to embrace other societies, including non-statal nations and statal nations. The systems adopted by imperialism varied from society to society and varied over time. There was at no time a clear and settled pattern of imperial organization. It is only with hindsight that any sort of pattern can be imposed on such a disorderly process. But international society had known many so-called empires in the pre-ancient, ancient, and pre-modern periods. And the empires of the modern period had some characteristic imperial features.

13.73. The most important feature was that some part, often the principal part, of the public willing and acting of the subordinate societies became part of the public willing and acting of the imperial society. The public realm of the subordinate societies was, to a greater or a lesser extent, integrated with the public realm of the superordinate society. This had three fundamental consequences. In the first place, the energy of the state-system of the superordinate society, including the aggregated energy of the subordinate nations, could be very great and was in a position to achieve effects which would not otherwise have been possible. In particular, the production of surplus social energy through the economy, to be considered further in Chapter 17, was very greatly enhanced.

13.74. Secondly, the subordinate nations were to a variable extent disempowered, with their willing and acting no longer controlled by their own total social process. But, thirdly, statal organization was introduced to the subordinate society, leading to the development of the public realm of the subordinate society, and creating the potentiality for organizing the increasing surplus social energy of the subordinate society, especially economic energy, a potentiality which might be fully actualized only when the subordinate society ceased to form part of the imperial system. It may thus be said that the subordinate societies gained something from their participation in the empire and they lost something.

13.75. Such imperial societies did not have it as their purpose to become nations. That is to say, they did not seek to be unified societies in which the members identified themselves as members merely by birth and for whom their membership was a prime part of their self-identification. To put the matter crudely, imperializing societies may have feared an unacceptable dilution of their own selfhood, their own national identity. But the empires involved a great deal of what might be called *incidental nationalizing*—through the mere presence in the subordinate societies of the imperial legal system, language, educational system, economic system, armed forces, and through the impressive trappings of imperial power. The imperial power also normally either extended its citizenship to the members of the subordinate societies or created a special imperial citizenship. And, in time of war, it was expected that the peoples of the subordinate societies would come to the *self-defending* of the imperial society as a whole.

13.76. The imperial society thus used, more or less consciously, some of the energy of a nation to promote the survival and the prospering of the imperial system, without using the state-system to create a single unified nation. State-system imperialism ended finally in the twentieth century, as the subordinate societies asserted or reasserted their separate selfhood as nations.

13.77. By what may seem a bizarre conjunction required by social theory, there began in western Europe, coincidentally with the ending of state-system imperialism, what must be regarded as a social development of the same analytical character. The European Community is also a multinational statal society—auto-imperialism, as it were. The Community is a state-system, with the three Communities (the European Economic Community, the European Coal and Steel Community, the European Atomic Energy Community) forming part of a single social structure-system with one constitution. Under the Community state-system the public realm willing and acting of the member state-societies has become integrated, to a certain extent, in the public willing and acting of the Community state-system. A public realm of the Community has superseded, to an uncertain and ever-changing degree, the public realms of the member state-societies. The minimum extent of that transformation is determined by the constitutional instruments of the Community, which reflect its ideal and legal constitutions. The actual extent of such transformation is determined, day by day, through the total social process of the Community, in its real constitution.

13.78. The Community is a socializing by way of state activity. It is already a state-society. It does not presently have as its purpose its self-creating as a nation. It may be said to be a statal organizing not only of subordinate nations but also of one part of a wider, existing European nation. Like the former empires, it uses, intentionally and incidentally, some of the concomitants of a nation to create and maintain and develop and protect its identity. There is nothing in the state-system of the Community to prevent it from being a nationalizing state and becoming a statal nation. Such social development is a matter for the total social process of the Community, as it conceives of its possibilities in the future, and as it chooses among its possibilities in the present-here-and-now of its communal willing and acting. The European Community will become what it chooses to become.

13.79. Although the imperial form of social development is not likely to be repeated in the foreseeable future, the model of social development which is that of the European Community could well be followed elsewhere in international society. The search for well-being, to be considered in Part Three, is already leading, in the late twentieth century, to what will there be identified as an international public realm, integrating and superseding, to an ever-increasing extent, the public realms of all statally organizing subordinate societies. There is no reason why the international establishment of public realms (such as the constitution of the European Community) should not form part of the future general social development of international society.

8. Multilocal statal society

13.80. Much of human activity is naturally transnational, not naturally confined to any particular society. When that activity is organized through a society which is a statal system acting within several societies (with the *locus* of its willing and acting being in several societies), then that society is a multilocal statal society. The three leading categories of such societies in recent centuries have been—religious institutions, professional and trade and sporting associations, industrial and commercial and financial corporations (sometimes referred to as *multinational corporations*).

13.81. In the present and forthcoming development of international society, multilocal statal societies of an economic character are playing a leading role. The economy of a society is a system of systems of social power depending on legal relations, and hence depending on the constitution of the society, and forming an integral part of the total social process, including the society's pure and practical theories concerning its nature and purpose. The economy of international society, the world economy, is no different in principle in these respects. It will be considered further in Chapter 17. The subordinate systems of the international economy include societies of all kinds here under consideration. And they include, in particular, multilocal statal societies of an economic character, which exercise social power, including legal power, arising under the constitutions of several or many societies, whose activities form part of the total social process of several or many societies, whose activities are subject to the pure and practical theories of many societies, including theories as to the nature of the good life in general, as to the role of property in society, as to the social and legal accountability of individual holders of social power.

13.82. Multilocal statal societies of an economic character thus give rise to important problems of co-ordination which it is the function of the system of international society to deal with, under its own constitution, in the light of its own theories, within its own total social process. Although multi-local industrial and commercial and financial corporations give rise to the most evident problems of social co-ordination, other kinds of multilocal statal societies give rise to analogous problems. An international trade association co-ordinating the activities of ecnomic operators in several or many national societies, an international trade union co-ordinating the activi-ties of national trade unions, a religious institution with national affiliates and individual members within several or many national societies, a sports federation regulating sports carried out in several or many national societies—all these are willing and acting in the total social processes of subordinate state-societies, using social power, including legal relations, arising under the constitutions of such societies.

13.83. Multilocal statal societies are willing and acting also within the total social process of international society, as the society of all societies, affecting, often directly and powerfully, the survival and prospering of the whole human race. The powers of multilocal statal societies, including such societies of an economic character, are delegated powers, like the powers of any other society. They are delegated by international society and by the superordinate societies within which they will and act. Multilocal statal societies are statally organizing societies—that is to say, they are systems in which willing and acting are assigned to officials of the society acting on behalf of the society as a whole. It is for both international society and the national societies in which they will and act to assert the social interest in relation to their activities, to ensure social and legal accountability, in accordance with the generic principle of a constitution which have been considered in Chapter 11.

13.84. Accordingly, a theory of international society and its law which does not take account of the willing and acting of multilocal statal societies, especially those of an economic character, is not worthy to be a theory of the international society of the future.

9. Multilocal or international non-statal society

13.85. The realm of the international interaction of socially organizing private citizens and non-statal subordinate societies, like the realm of the societies considered under (2) and (3) above, is a realm of infinite variety and richness, as individual human beings pursue their private lives, in their families and in all the other forms of society which their desire and their natural energy may generate. Such societies seek to co-ordinate the willing and acting of their members, to aggregate the energy of their members, to apply communally the surplus social energy which they generate. Their systems are thus not conceptualized in terms of a public realm of social willing and acting, or are so conceptualized only in the most marginal way. If they have so-called decision-making sub-systems, then those sub-systems are conceived as directly representative, the many of the members being symbolically present in the one of the decision-making body. The function of such a restricted body is conceived as being essentially the practical one of ensuring continuity, efficiency, the representation of the society externally. Its function is not conceived as one of governing.

13.86. When such a non-statal society acts internationally, then it may do so either by establishing itself in more than one state-society (for example, an international association of like-minded political parties, an international environmental lobby, an international human rights lobby, a non-regulatory international professional association) or else it may be essentially international in its organization, acting both on the international plane and through branches or meetings within national societies (for example, a non-governmental organization in the field of humanitarian assistance or disarmament or education, or an association of persons working in a particular field).

13.87. Such forms of society have acquired a particular importance in the twentieth century, as the volume of energy in international society has greatly increased, and as the volume of statally organized activity, internal and external, has greatly increased, and as the democratic aspirations of citizens, their desire to participate in the willing and acting which determines their lives, have increased.

13.88. The activities of such societies are not merely parallel or alternative activities to the activities of the governments of state-societies. They may have it as their very function to affect governmental activity. They may conceive of their purposes as including the function of acting as a countervailing power, acting internationally in a way which is directly analogous to the function of non-statal societies within the total social process of state-societies, participating in reality-forming, in forming words and ideas and theories and values, in asserting social and legal accountability.

13.89. Thus the total social process of international society includes not only the activities of state-societies and their governments. It includes also the activities of all other statal and the non-statal societies which participate in the becoming of international society, which have international social power, including legal relations, under the international constitution.

13.90. It follows that a theory of international society and its law which ignores the role of private citizens and their non-statal international societies in the total social process of international society is not worthy to be a theory of the international society of the future.

10. International statal society

13.91. The increasing social energy of subordinate societies of all the kinds here under consideration as they developed in complexity and hence in energy led to a more than proportionate increase in the social energy of international society, the society of all societies. Such surplus energy within the total social process of international society led in turn to fundamental developments in the structure-system of international society.

In particular, it led to the formation of new subordinate societies of international society, specialized structure-systems designed to organize the willing and acting of international society in fields where the interacting energy of subordinate societies required such organization.

13.92. This need-led system-building within international society has by now generated a profusion of such new statal societies, responding to need in every field of inter-societal activity, from the most general economic fields of trade regulation and market-management to the most technical fields, comprising every kind of specialized activity from meteorology to metrology, from air transport to fish-stock conservation, from public health to the harmonization of law and law enforcement. Such societies have come to be called, (unfortunately, from an analytical point of view) international organizations or, more comprehensibly, intergovernmental organizations.

13.93. The first feature of international statal societies which distinguishes them from the category of *multilocal statal societies* is that they are delocalized, that is to say, they are, primarily and essentially, using social power and legal relations deriving not from some subordinate society of international society but from international society itself. It is for this reason that they are called *international*, although they are certainly not the only form of society acting internationally or participating in the international social process.

13.94. The second distinguishing feature of international statal societies stems from the fact that, as at present constituted, their members are typically state-societies in the narrow sense, that is to say, societies in categories (4), (5), (6) and (7) above. It follows from this that international statal societies of the kind here under consideration are essentially *public realm* societies. They are conceived as co-ordinating the functioning of the public realms of the state-societies through the interacting of their governments. (In the present volume, the expression *state-societies* will be used to refer, unless the context makes clear to the contrary, to societies in categories (4), (5), (6), and (7) above.)

13.95. However, as a third distinguishing characteristic, international statal societies, although they will and act outside the total social processes of their member state-societies, have substantial effects on the development of those social processes. The consequence is that a significant, and daily increasing, part of the activity of the internal public realms of the state-societies, especially in the economic field, is partially abstracted from internal social processes to be conducted by governments acting externally, thus giving rise to serious problems of social and legal accountability and, generally, to difficulties in the operation of the generic principles of a constitution, considered in Chapter 11 above. These problems will be considered further in the next section and in Chapters 15 and 16.

(3) THE SELF-CONCEIVING OF MODERN INTERNATIONAL SOCIETY

13.96. The ten forms of social development in modern international society, considered above, have in common the characteristic that they are the activity of a society (international society) creating itself like any other society. Self-creating international society conceives its possibilities, like any other society, in its words and ideas and theories and values, in its struggle with the perennial dilemmas of society, in constituting its constitution, in its total social process. International society, like any other society, is a process, a process of a struggle, a becoming, a structure-system constructing itself through the operation of its own structure-system.

13.97. The future of international society, as of any other society, is not simply its past transported through its present into the future. The future of international society, as of any other society, is the possibilities which it conceives within its conceiving of its own future, as they are transformed into its past through its willing and acting in its present-here-and-now. The future of international society is thus contained in its self-conceived possibilities and in the possibilities which it chooses to actualize. Its choosing, within the struggle of its total social process, is determined not only by what it has already become but also by what it conceives that it might become. That is to say, in the terms of the present study, its future is not only a function of its willing and acting under the real constitution, using social power, including legal relations deriving from its legal constitution. It is a function also of its self-conceiving in its ideal constitution, its idea of itself. International society can choose to become what it conceives it might be. To know the future of international society, it is accordingly necessary to know how it conceives itself in the present-here-and-now.

13.98. The self-conceiving of international society in the modern period (since about the year 1500 of our era) is a strange, not to say a tragic, story. It is a story which can be told in a single sentence. Tempted for a while to conceive of itself as a society, international society chose instead to regard itself as the state externalized, undemocratized, and unsocialized.

13.99. Early in the modern period, pressure from three directions led social consciousness to consider the theoretical problem of the systematic relationship among the subordinate societies of international society. The first pressure came from the rapidly increasing energy levels of the developing state-societies, an energy which was manifesting itself in power-competition of every kind, including economic competition and including frequent and ferocious physical conflict. Such instability called for some understanding of the nature of the relationship of the new state-societies. The second pressure came from the coming to consciousness of what was seen as a New World, a world in which Europe was re-conceiving itself as only one small part of an immense, complex world which was, nevertheless, evidently full of great new possibilities. The third pressure came from developments within social consciousness itself, as expanding consciousness was undertaking not only the task of re-supersocializing individual societies but also the task of re-supernaturalizing the physical world in the new natural philosophy (natural science). The human condition, including the international social condition, had to be re-conceived.

13.100. Quite specific theoretical questions had to be faced. Could there be found some sort of social system for organizing the power-competition among the rapidly developing new-old societies—or must they be regarded as being in a state of natural anarchy governed only by force? How were the inhabitants of the newly discovered or rediscovered lands to be treated—as sub-societal or pre-societal or non-societal outlaws or as fellow-members of some putative society, such as a society of the whole human race? Could there ever again be a unification of human social consciousness, given that a unification on the basis of a single religion was now no longer a practical possibility and given that the more that became known of the world, the more culturally diverse it revealed itself to be?

13.101. The theoretical supersocialization of international society became part of the total social process of international society, became part of the struggle of international society with the perennial dilemmas of any society. Contributions from many different countries interacted in a theoretical struggle which, even now, has a profound fascination for us, not only an intellectual fascination but also the ironical fascination of the spectator who knows how the drama will unfold and what extraordinary events would lie ahead, flowing from the vicissitudes of a debate so seemingly abstract in character.

13.102. In the terms of the present study, international society was re-socializing itself by means of pure theory. It was reconstructing its *self* in relation to an *other* which was a new world, a world which was new in so many different ways— geographical and cultural and social and economic and philo- sophical. International society was seeking to reconstruct itself as *one*, a total system of social power, in relation to the *many* of a world which was proving to be vastly more complex and diverse and disintegrated than had ever been known before, a world in which even old nations were closing in on themselves in newly conceived social structures, alienating themselves and their citizens from international society. International society was reconstructing its *unity of nature* in face of a seemingly uncontrollable *plurality of value* which had emerged from the disintegration of the pre-modern world-view and from the discovery and rediscovery of other worlds of value all over the newly known world. International society was reconstructing its idea of *justice*, the relationship of its order to the order of all-that-is, in a physical universe which was being re-supernaturalized by science in ways which were difficult to assimilate, reconstructing its idea of *social justice* in a social world which now contained levels of social energy and forms of social power which overwhelmed and far outstripped the possibilities of existing legal relations and existing ideas. International society was trying to control the overwhelming flood of change, to take control of the endless *becoming*, to reconstruct itself as a continuing structure-system, with laws which could exist as *old laws* for its countless *new citizens*.

13.103. The society of the whole human race struggled with the insoluble dilemmas of all societies always, but faced them in circumstances of exceptional urgency and intricacy and danger. Because we know the outcome of that struggle, over the last five centuries, and because we are living its consequences in the present-here-and-now of international society, we are able to see what might have been as well as what has been. And we are able to see what might be as well as what could be.

13.104. (1) A natural human society. (2) An international state of nature. (3) Statal nations under natural law. (4) Statal nations under customary law. Such were the theoretical options which presented themselves to international social consciousness from early in the modern period. The first option survived as a possible dominant pure theory of international society until the middle of the eighteenth century. Although it was by no means confined to Spanish writers, it may be referred to summarily as the Spanish tradition. (Its most notable exponents were Francisco de Vitoria [1492–1546] and Francisco Suarez [1548–1617].) The second possible theory rose to pre-eminence in the sixteenth and seventeenth centuries and, it must be admitted, survives to this day, especially among those who are theorists of international relations rather than of international law. Although it comes in many variants other than that associated with the name of Thomas Hobbes, it may be referred to summarily as the Hobbesian tradition. (Hobbes's best-known work is *Leviathan* [1651].) The third option was a resumption of a tradition from the theorizing of pre-modern and, especially, ancient societies. At some time in the eighteenth century, it ceased to be a possible dominant theory. Although the writing of Hugo Grotius represented only one, idiosyncratic variety of the natural law tradition, it may be referred to summarily as the Grotian tradition. (Grotius's most influential work was *Of the Law of War and Peace* [1625].) The fourth option, growing out of the ideas of Grotius, established itself as the dominant theory in the eighteenth century, especially with the work of Emmerich de Vattel. It may be referred to summarily as the Vattel tradition. (Vattel's main work was *The Law of Nations, or the Principles of Natural Law applied to the Conduct and to the Affairs of Nations and Sovereigns* [1758].)

13.105. The eventually dominant Vattel tradition is not merely a tradition of international law. It implies a pure theory of the whole nature of international society and hence of the whole nature of the human social condition; and it generates practical theories which rule the lives of all societies, of the whole human race. It is nothing but mere words, mere ideas, mere theory, mere values—and yet war and peace, human happiness and human misery, human wealth and human want, human lives and human life have depended on them for two centuries and more. The essential elements of the tradition are as follows:

(1) *The state turned inside out.* The state (public realm under the authority of a government) having developed as a way of internally organizing a certain sort of society, such state-systems came to be conceived also as the external manifestation of the given societies. The state was turned inside out, like a glove. The governments of the statally organizing societies recognize in each other that which is *state*, not that which is *society*. The powerful word *state* came to be used, sometime in the eighteenth century, to identify not only the governmental system of the internal public realm but also the *whole society* as it manifested itself internationally. Sinister synecdoche. Fateful ambiguity.

(2) *Sovereignty externalized.* The self-conceiving of statally self-organizing societies having been founded on authority conceptualized in the concept of sovereignty, the same conceptualization was applied to the externalized state-system in

its relations with the externalized state-systems of other societies. The governments of the new state-societies looked at each other and recognized the concept of sovereignty lodged in the self-conceiving of their respective internal orders. Sovereignty could unify conceptually the structure of the society as seen from outside, as it had been used to unify conceptually the structure of the society as seen from inside.

(3) *Interstatal society as interacting public realms.* Statally organizing societies having generated within themselves a public realm of governmental willing and acting on behalf of society as a whole, the area in which such societies met externally was, and is, conceived as being not an international society, but merely as an arena for the interacting of those public realms. It is an interstatal unsociety.

(4) *Diplomacy and war as the total social process.* The willing and acting of such societies in such an arena of public realms is conceived as the interacting of holders of public power-rights acting on behalf of the totality of their internal systems. The essence of the international unsocial process is conceived as the interactive willing and acting of governments in relation to each other (so-called diplomacy) and physical conflicts of differing degrees of violence between the state-systems or sponsored by the state-systems (so-called war or armed conflict).

(5) *The external public arena in the internal public realm.* The external representation of the society (the government willing and acting externally in relation to other governments) is conceived internally as a particular function of government, intrinsically within the internal public realm. The government willing and acting externally is merely carrying out its internal public realm activities externally. It not only represents the society externally but also organizes internal willing and acting with a view to its participation in external willing and acting.

(6) *Internal society and interstatal unsociety as separate worlds.* As a corollary of (1) to (5) above, the internal world of society and the international world of inter-state relations came to be conceived as intrinsically and radically separate. Each state-system is regarded as a closed system in relation to every other. The citizens participate in interstatal unsociety only

through the intermediation of their governments. Interstatal relations take place in a conceptual no-man's-land which is simply the empty space between the state-societies.

(7) *Internal social process not part of an international social process.* As a corollary of (6), the internal social processes of the state-societies came to be conceived as being entirely independent of the vestigial social process of the governments interacting externally. It follows that all the socialising of human beings in societies, all social reality-forming, is conceived as being a matter for each and every state-society independently. The interacting of the internal social process of one society with those of other societies is, as a consequence, haphazard, unordered, contingent, and peripheral.

(8) *International private realm non-societal.* All interacting of persons and societies other than the state-societies and their governments is conceived as being outside the vestigial social process of the interstatal unsociety. In particular, all economic interaction, other than the participation and intervention of governments in international economic interaction, is conceived as being outside the interstatal social process. All the dynamic interacting of non-state persons is conceived as being simply non-societal.

(9) *Separate development of the interstatal social process.* The vestigial interstatal social process is accordingly conceived as developing entirely separately from the national social processes. It is conceived as being a development entirely different in kind from the social development of the national processes, since the interstatal arena is not conceived of as a society. Its social development is that of the international relations of diplomacy and war, as the internal public realms lead their separate lives and interact only intermittently and more or less fortuitously. International social development has been simply the aggregation or resultant of such haphazard interacting.

(10) *Differential internal social development.* It followed that the internal social development of the different state-societies followed independent courses, as they organized themselves statally in different ways and to different extents, generating the idea and the ideal of democracy, if at all, in different ways and to different extents, socializing their

internal sovereignty (with a view to the actualization of justice and social justice) in different ways and to different extents, if at all. Interstatal unsociety came to contain state-societies at radically different stages of social development, especially economic development. There was, and is, no theoretical reason why, in the interstatal unsociety, they should not continue to be at different, even increasingly different, stages of social development.

(11) *Undeveloped interstatal sovereignty.* The concept of sovereignty having been transported from the internal to the interstatal world, the concept then did not share in the dramatic course of development followed by its internal progenitor and considered above. Sovereignty in the interstatal world came to be conceived simply as authority deriving from land-holding, a concept reminiscent of the so-called feudal systems of pre-modern societies. Land-holding within internal social systems was turned inside out to become so-called territorial sovereignty. However, as a species of property, so-called territorial sovereignty did not even follow the striking conceptual development of internal concepts of property. By comparison with corresponding internal concepts, interstatal territorial sovereignty remained and remains a pre-modern, essentially feudal, concept.

(12) *Sovereignty undemocratized.* The interstatal form of sovereignty remained untouched by the dramatic internal social developments which culminated in the idea and the ideal of democracy. Since interstatal unsociety did not have a total social process involving individual human beings and non-statal subordinate societies, there was no pressure and so no need for democratization and the idea and the ideal of democracy could not be generated. In a society which does not conceive of itself as a society, social revolution is impossible.

(13) *Sovereignty unsocialized.* Lacking a total social process, interstatal unsociety could not be socialized in the name of justice. The power used externally by the state-societies is not conceived as social power, because there is no conception of a society to delegate it as a social power. It is conceived as natural, unsocialized power, energy applied for a purpose. The purpose is not conceived as a purpose formed within a process of international reality-forming nor within a struggle with the

perennial dilemmas of society, including the dilemma of order (justice and social justice). The purposes of the interstatal unsociety are simply the aggregated purposes conceived within the government-controlled public realms of the state-societies, purposes related to the survival and prospering of each of those state-societies rather than the survival and prospering of an international society of the whole human race.

(14) *Interstatal unsociety as a realm of freedom.* Although interstatal unsociety was conceived as a system formed by the externalization of the concept of sovereignty, it was not itself to be a system integrated by sovereignty. There was to be no international government authority over an international public realm, willing and acting for a superordinate international society. Instead, it was to be merely an aggregation of sovereignties. The state-systems derived their external authority from their internal systems. Their external relationship was accordingly supersocialized as being a relationship of natural sovereignty, natural freedom, and natural equality (*natural*, in the sense of not being socially derived from a superordinate society). Such natural legal relations between states were not, however, to be derived from a natural law supersocialization, but rather simply as a logical corollary of the evident absence of an authority in interstatal unsociety. The state-societies are conceived to be free, subject to no constitution and no generic principles of a constitution, in their international interacting because they are free.

(15) *Interstatal law as the willing of states.* Such a conceptual structure of interstatal unsociety led to the conceptualizing of a so-called international law, as a law formed from the willing and acting of state-societies expressed in one of two ways: either immediate acts of will in the form of treaties or retained acts of will in the form of customary international law. Both are conceived as being generated in the only social process recognized by the state-societies, that is to say, as a by-product of so-called international relations. In the case of customary international law, the social process is specifically conceptualized as *state practice*. State practice generates retained acts of will when the acting of state-societies can be regarded as manifesting a will to give rise to legal relations (so-called *opinio juris*). In this way, state practice is conceived as

generating both the acting which constitutes the willed legal relation and the willing that such acting should become a legal relation.

(16) *The amoralization of interstatal unsociety*. Interstatal unsociety being a separate world from the internal world of the state-societies, and its social process being a separate social process from the social processes of the state-societies, the reality-forming of its subordinate societies is not regarded as flowing systematically into interstatal unsociety. All the varieties of reality-forming (religion, mythology, art, philosophy, history, science, morality, economy, law) find their way into interstatal unsociety incidentally, escaping or leaking from the state-societies in the interstices of so-called international relations. In so far as such reality-forming does take place internationally (for example, in religion and art and philosophy and science and economy) it does so not as part of any specific international social process but merely as the random interacting of the non-public realms of the subordinate societies of international society.

The immediate consequence of this is that internal law is intrinsically isolated from international law. But the most important practical consequence is that morality is discontinuous as between interstatal unsociety and its subordinate societies. The result is that governments, and the human beings who compose them, are able to will and act internationally in ways that they would be morally restrained from willing and acting internally, murdering human beings by the million in wars, tolerating oppression and starvation and disease and poverty, human cruelty and suffering, human misery and human indignity, of kinds, and on a scale, that they could not tolerate within their internal societies. Interstatal unsociety is a realm of unmorality.

13.106. Such was, and is, the Vattel tradition and the Vattel reality flowing from it. It is a reality which was welcome to the ruling classes of western Europe, the classes who still had most control over social reality-forming, including the self-conceiving of society in theory and including reality-forming far beyond the territorial limits of western Europe. It was most welcome of all to the political and administrative sections of those ruling classes, who could speak to each other and compete with each other and conflict with each other across frontiers, safe in the fastnesses of their self-contained internal–external state-systems.

13.107. It is a speculation of the most profound human interest to consider what the human world would have become if international society, in the eighteenth century, had not chosen the Vattel tradition but, instead, had forged a Rousseau–Kant tradition, and, in the nineteenth and twentieth centuries, had joined in the revolutionary development of national societies, if international society had had its 1789 or its 1917. It is a speculation which is not merely of intellectual and historical interest. It is actual and urgent.

13.108. The misconceiving of international society as a system of closed sovereignties, externalized state-systems, undemocratized and unsocialized, spread throughout the world. As nations and peoples sought to establish themselves as social selves in their own right, to liberate themselves from what they regarded as alien state-systems, to actualize their *self-determination* in place of their *other-determination*, their aspiration to freedom and independence interacted with their need to establish a new social order. The theory of a naturally free, naturally equal, naturally sovereign statal society, whose external existence could be closely controlled in a world of other statal societies, seemed to be an excellent way to actualize the ideal of independence and to meet the need for a new internal order. And, like the ruling classes who had led the way along the same path, the ruling classes of the so-called *new states* also welcomed a theory which could give such a convincing supersocializing explanation of their own personal power.

13.109. Misconceived international society became, as national societies had at one stage of their development, a world sovereignty-state-system, a world fit for governments. It is an unsociety ruled by a collective of self-conceived sovereigns whose authority is derived neither from the totality of international society nor from the people but from the intermediating state-systems. International society has condemned itself either to stagnate in such a condition or to live again the experience of national societies in which the evolving statally organizing societies discovered, painfully, the dangers of their evolving sovereignty-systems, and discovered, painfully, how to redeem themselves in the name of democracy and justice.

13.110. The people of the world are not in a position to make an international revolution. Overwhelmed by the power of governments and their bureaucratic battalions, they have, in many cases, little enough hope of redeeming their own state-society in the name of democracy and justice. They know little enough of its constitution, its systems, its possibilities. They know too little of the social struggle at the level of the total social process, too much of the struggle of their own daily living. The idea of a misconceived international society is an idea formed in and for the reality of the ruling-classes of their state-societies.

13.111. But it is more than an interesting thought-experiment to consider how the people of the world would conceive of the human world if they could express their anguish and their aspirations. We may speak hypothetically for the people of the world who cannot speak for themselves. What follows is speculation. The speculation is that the people of the world, however cautiously and however tentatively, see in international society dangers that they, and their predecessors over the centuries, see and have seen in state-societies. Specifically, they see: (1) alienation—the alienation of humanity from itself; (2) corruption—the corruption, in particular, of an unsocialized international economy; and (3) tyranny—the tyranny of physical insecurity.

(1) ALIENATION

(a) The people of the world understand the need for social organization, even for the remarkable energy-generating and energy-organizing capacity of the state-society. But the people of the world also know and respect and love the natural societies into which they are born and the societies which they make for themselves, societies whose limits frequently do not coincide with the limits of state-societies.

(b) What they do not understand is their enforced alienation from each other, the surrender of their natural affections and natural loyalties, their subjection to state-societies which require that they treat other human beings as *other*, merely because they are subject to another state-system. The people of the world meet as friends in countless worldwide human activities but meet only as fellow-aliens in international society as presently conceived.

(c) The people of the world feel a loving sympathy with their fellow human beings in their individuality, in their family-life, in all the striving of their personal lives. And they feel a loving sympathy with their fellow human beings in all their suffering, the suffering at the hands of social power and of natural forces. And they feel their love distorted by an international system which demands from them perverted ideas and values, other forms of loyalty.

(d) The peoples of the world are represented externally by their state-systems and by the governments which speak for them. But the idea and the ideal of democracy has evolved and the people have matured with it. They demand not merely to be represented but to participate in the willing and acting which is the willing and acting of their lives, their survival and prospering, their well-being.

(2) CORRUPTION

(a) As in the early days of statally organizing national societies, the most basic human social activity is alien to the system of international society as presently conceived. The world is a scene of economic activity of amazing energy, full of dynamic forces which are transforming the face of the earth and the lives of all the people of the world. And yet it is only the regulatory side of the international economy which is integrated into the international system. All the productive activity of farmers and manufacturers and traders, all agriculture and industry and commerce, is conducted on the periphery, in the interstices of an international system whose real business is conceived as being diplomacy and war.

(b) Not integrated into the state-system of international society, the productive aspect of the international economy presents itself as a sort of natural world, an environment, in which nonsocialized forces produce natural effects. The supersocialization of the international economy is a super-naturalization. The consequence is that the people of the world feel locked into a natural system of unequal development. It is an unsocialized system in which natural energy seems to remain natural, not transformed into social power performing a social function. It is accordingly a system in which social justice is achieved, if at all, by good fortune rather than by good choosing.

(c) The potentiality of the international economy has no known limits—a potentiality for good and for harm. The people of the world feel that the system, for all its remarkable achievements, is not making full use of its potentiality to generate human well-being and yet is imposing substantial burdens and costs on the physical world of the planet and on the moral world of humanity, burdens and costs which are growing rapidly but are beyond measurement and beyond control in the absence of systematic willing and acting by international society in the interest of the whole human race, including the interest of human beings yet to be born.

(3) TYRANNY

(a) The amoralization of international society has meant that so-called national interest may, one day, require the destruction of humanity itself. In other words, the self-conceiving of international society leaves the possibility, and may even require, that one state-society or a collection of state-societies destroy not only their own men, women, and children by the million but also men, women, and children over wider and wider areas of the world, may even threaten the lives of all men, women, and children everywhere. A society which conceives its survival as depending on threats of self-destruction is a society which misconceives its nature as a society. A society which conceives its own self-destruction among the possibilities which it might choose is a society which misconceives its potentiality as a society.

13.112. The people of the world live in a present-here-and-now in which they are obliged to see the future of humanity, its possibilities, in terms of these self-inflicted aberrations. An extraordinary effort of self-transcending is required from humanity, if it is to change the words and ideas and theories and values which are the reality-for-itself of a self-misconceiving international society.

14 Humanity and Law

14.1. The task of humanity now is to take possession of the waste-land of international society in the name of the people and in the name of justice, to redeem state-societies as systems for organizing the willing and acting of all human beings. It is through re-conceiving itself as society that international society may humanize the state-system. It is by re-conceiving international law that international society may set about the process of re-conceiving itself as society. In finding the human potential of international society through the human potential of international law, humanity may discover the human potential of society and of law. Humanity may discover a truly human law as the potential of all law in all society.

14.2. The human animal, like the chimpanzee and the termite, is a social animal. To be a social animal is to be law-abiding. The human being, endowed with consciousness, is able to present its socializing to itself as law. The self-redeeming task of the people of the world is to reintegrate the law of international society with the laws of all subordinate societies, including the state-societies, by re-presenting to itself the law of international society as the law of all societies and the law of the whole human race.

14.3. Law is a product of the total social process of the society of which it is the law. The total social process includes not only the law-making capacity of the society but every other form of reality-forming, the forming of its reality-for-itself. Law is a source, one among others but not the least, of the total social process of which it is itself a product. Through law society is able to organize the reality of its words and ideas and theories and values, to organize its struggle with the perennial dilemmas of all society. The total social process of international society makes the law of international society, the law of the society of all societies, the society of the whole human race. The law of international society participates, as creator and creature, in the social struggle of international society, the reality-forming of the total social process of international society, the reality-forming of the whole human race.

14.4. In the constitution society finds the means to establish itself as a structure and to organize itself as a system. In the legal constitution, social power is made available by society to enable society to direct the becoming of society. In the ideal constitution, society's possibilities are made available by society to enable society to choose its self-creating. In the real constitution, society uses social power to choose its future in its present-here-and-now. The legal relations which are contained in the legal constitution and are created under the legal constitution are society's constant willing of its future from its ever-present past. Through the making of international law under the international constitution, international society makes the legal relations by which it may constantly will the future of the human race from its ever-present past.

14.5. In law society finds the means not only to survive but also to prosper. Through law natural energy is transformed into social power. Through law natural power is exchanged for social power when social purpose is made a condition of the exercise of natural power. Law is the socialization of particular desire, the particularization of social desire. Law is the socialization of particular obligation, the particularization of social obligation. Law is the willing and acting of society in the willing and acting of the individual. Law is the willing and acting of the individual in the willing and acting of society. In international law the society of the whole human race may will and act not only the survival but also the prospering of the whole human race, universalizing all particular human willing, particularizing universal human willing.

14.6. In choosing to organize itself statally, a society finds a means to generate high levels of surplus social energies, especially in the economic aspect of their struggle to survive and prosper. By creating a public realm in which social power is exercised on behalf of society as a whole, society chooses to delegate the exercise of those powers to persons and subordinate societies appointed under the legal constitution. All public power is subject to the generic principles of a constitution, including the principle of delegation and the principle of the supremacy of the social interest. State-societies as subordinate societies of international society are delegates of international society. State-societies do not have any inherent legal powers, any legal powers which are above or beyond the law, any legal powers which are delegated other than with the condition of social purpose. To claim a legal power, as much for a state as for any private citizen, is to acknowledge social purpose.

14.7. In generating the pure theory which contains the idea and the ideal of democracy, a society seeks the means to enable the people, the members of society, to embrace law as their own, not merely because they may conceive of themselves as its authorizing source but because they may will and act the law in their participation in the total social process which forms it. In choosing to conceive of their society democratically, the people may choose to will their own past in willing their own future. International society, in conceiving itself democratically, seeks to become the self-creating of the people of the world through their own willing.

14.8. In generating the pure theory which contains the idea of the socialization of democracy, a society seeks the means to integrate the ideal of justice into the becoming of society. Through socialized democracy the people seek to will not only their future but also their future well-being. In the democratized and socialized state-society the people choose to use the state-system as the intermediary between themselves and society, as their instrument in aggregating their energies in the actualizing of justice. In conceiving itself democratically and socially, international society seeks to become the intermediary between every human individual and the whole human race, to become the instrument of all human beings in aggregating their energies with a view to the actualizing of justice.

14.9. In taking power over its becoming through the work of imagination and reason as they conceive the structure-system which are societies, humanity has found a means to choose the future well-being of a society and its members. In conceiving the structure-system of international society, the society of all societies, humanity may find a means to choose its own future well-being. Nothing more nor less is required than a self-willed change in human consciousness. A revolution, not in the streets but in the mind.

Part Three   *Well-being*

Government is a contrivance of human wisdom to provide for human wants.

> Edmund Burke, *Reflections on the Revolution in France*, (12th edn., London [1793], 88).

*

Where one's mind is attached—the inner self
Goes thereto with action, being attached to it alone.

> *Brihad Aranyaka*, IV. 4. 6.
> (in R. E. Hume, *The Thirteen Principal Upanishads*, Bombay [1954], 141).

15 International Order I: Social Order

15.1. In seeking well-being society seeks order as precondition and product of its well-being, precondition and product of its survival and prospering. To speak of *order* is to speak in terms of pure theory or in terms of practical theory, or both. That is to say, the word may be used to convey a supersocializing theory of the nature of society. For example—*society is naturally order-seeking*. Or else the word may be used to ground ideas of value with a view to modifying willing and acting within a given society. For example—*in this society, we choose order as a social purpose (or good order, peace, good government, law and order)*. Or else the word may be used to invoke the nature of society as a ground for modifying willing and acting. For example—*in this society, we choose as a social purpose the order of a self-ordering society.*

15.2. In terms of the hypothesis set out in Parts One and Two, a society is by its nature self-ordering in the sense that: (1) society is creating itself as both structure and system; and a structure and a system are an ordering. They are the continuing process of ordering. A society is also by its nature self-ordering in the sense that: (2) a society's socializing through the struggle of the total social process is an ordering, as society seeks ceaselessly to resolve the perennial dilemmas of society. That process of struggle can itself be seen as a searching for order, both within the struggle of each dilemma and as the changing totality of all such striving.

15.3. It also follows from the hypothesis set out above that: (3) society is by nature self-ordering as it forms its constitution and, in particular, as it creates social power in the form of legal relations. The constitution, as it enables the society to transform its future into its past through willing and acting in the present-here-and-now, gives to society a means of directing its own becoming. Its becoming, the emerging resultant of its interacting internalities and externalities, is ordered by the constitution, as society's possibilities are conceived by its consciousness, and selected by its willing and actualized by its acting. Through legal relations the willing and acting of individual members of society is integrated with the willing and acting of other members and the willing and acting of society as a whole, within the systematic process contained in the constitution, generically as a constitution, specifically as the constitution of a particular society.

15.4. It also follows from the hypothesis set out above that: (4) social consciousness itself is by its nature a self-ordering of society, as society transforms the reality of all-that-is into a reality-for-itself, using words and ideas and theories and values to create its own world of consciousness, including the great idea-structures of religion and mythology and philosophy and history and art and natural science and economy and morality. That world of consciousness, created by imagination and ordered by reason, is the world in which human willing and acting takes place. The world made by consciousness is the world where we live. In relation to the endlessly changing flow of the physical world beyond consciousness and of individual and social willing and acting, it is a world of ordering and of relative order.

15.5. It follows, finally, from the hypothesis set out above that: (5) a society is ordering itself in seeking not only its survival but also its prospering, in seeking not only its being but also its well-being. In forming its reality-for-itself, society conceives the possibilities of its future. In seeking its well-being, it chooses among those possibilities, forms its purposes. And its purposes draw it into its future through its willing and acting in the present-here-and-now. Whatever particular choices it may make in actualizing its future, society's system is thus ordering its becoming in the direction of its self-conceived possibilities. To choose a future is to order the present and the past in terms of that future.

15.6. In conceiving of itself as society, society thus conceives of itself as self-ordering. But a particular society may go further and choose self-ordering as value, as a ground for its choosing, as a social purpose modifying all its willing and acting. It may do so by translating the idea of order as a hypothetical idea into the idea of order as a prescriptive idea, by allowing the idea of order to flow from pure theory (as to the nature of society) into practical theory (as to the aims of the given society). In recognizing order as an aspect of its nature, society may choose self-ordering as an aspect of its self-creating.

15.7. The self-ordering of international society in what has here been called the modern period, the period of the last five centuries, has been a function of international society's self-conceiving. That is to say, it has been a function of international society's self-misconceiving. International society has conceived of its own nature as being a non-societal system for the tempering of natural disorder among statally organizing societies, the self-restraining of interacting externalized public realms. Because international society has had little or no consciousness of itself as a society, international society has had little or no consciousness of itself as a self-ordering society. Not knowing itself as a self-ordering society, it has not been able to choose order as a social purpose.

15.8. However, from the vantage-point of the end of the twentieth century, it is possible to perceive the activity of international society in the last five centuries, especially its activity in the twentieth century, as the pre-natal ordering of a society which was yet to be born into the world of its own consciousness, as the unselfconscious self-socializing of a society which did not yet know itself as a society. It is possible to say, with the benefit of hindsight and hypothesis, that international society has been ordering itself in spite of itself. International society has been not merely a self-misconceived unsociety but a pre-society instinctively or spontaneously seeking to become a society. International society has been readying itself for a metamorphosis, for the sloughing of its self-unknowing. If so, it is also possible to suppose that international society, as it comes to conceive of itself as society, may at last find itself able to choose order as a social purpose.

15.9. The anticipatory self-ordering of a potential international society may be considered in the following aspects:

(1) War and peace.
(2) Diplomacy.
(3) State sovereignty.

The specifically legal self-ordering of international pre-society will be considered in chapter 16 below.

(1) WAR AND PEACE

15.10. It is hard to imagine that any sane human being could regard war as a means of bringing about order. And yet there have been those who have conceived of war as a social purpose which a society may choose from time to time, as another means available to a society in its willing and acting, another form of a society's self-ordering. Human experience has another conception of war. The order that war brings is the order of death and destruction. To choose war is to choose death and destruction. To choose war is to choose uncontrolled and unmeasured suffering. It is hard to imagine that any thoughtful human being could regard war as natural. Natural disasters are conceived as being natural because they seem to originate in the necessity of the physical world, not in the choosing of the world of consciousness. War is made nowhere else than in the world of consciousness, through the willing and acting of human beings. War is chosen. War is chosen by conscious human beings as they use the energies of the physical world to kill and to maim conscious human beings, to bereave and to orphan conscious human beings. To suffer death is of the nature of all living things. To choose to kill in the public interest is human.

15.11. To commit war could be regarded as natural only on the basis of a pure theory of humanity which sets a limit on the capacity of human imagination and reason. And such a pure theory which sets natural limits on human imagination and reason would, in turn, have to depend upon a transcendental theory which showed how human imagination and reason could conceive of their own limits. And even if there were such a pure theory and even if there could be such a transcendental theory, they would, as theories, be met by other theories which diametrically opposed them, such as the theory outlined in the present volume, suggesting that human consciousness makes itself as human beings make it, that human society makes itself as human beings make it, that we are the authors of our willing and our acting, that we can always and everywhere will and act for our own survival and prospering, that we can be the makers of our own well-being, that we are responsible as human beings for human survival and prospering.

15.12. To regard war as natural because there have always been wars, or because individual human beings frequently use violence against each other, would be to rely on a pure theory which asserted that human beings are doomed to be as they have been. And, once again, such a pure theory would have to depend on a transcendental theory which explained how human beings can know that they cannot be other than they have been. By what form of experiment or inference or theorem would such a theory be established? It would be a theory which would make of human science a science which surpassed natural science, since not even the transcendental theory of natural science claims that science knows what the future of the physical world will necessarily be.

15.13. To regard war as natural is thus, in short, to choose precisely to disregard the wonderful capacity of human consciousness to make the future other than it has been, the wonderful capacity of human consciousness to choose its future from all the possibilities which imagination can conceive and which reason can order. We are no more doomed to die in war than we are doomed to die by disease. War is no more necessary than it is natural.

15.14. War is human failure—a failure of imagination, a failure of reason, a failure of learning, a failure of theory, a failure of willing, a failure of acting. In the pre-societal self-conceiving of international society, war has been conceived as the seeking of order only in the sense of a seeking of order through disorder, when imagination and reason have proved incapable of bringing about order by choice. War is suicide masquerading as self-creating, a form of ordering not found in the lowest forms of animal or vegetable life.

15.15. War is an education in crime. The example of international society is an example of lawlessness which pollutes the minds of the citizens and, worse, the public officials of state-societies. When public officials see that the crime of war is treated as a natural and inevitable event in international society, it is hardly surprising if they see violent crime as a natural and inevitable event within a state-society. If the most sophisticated calculations of the most privileged classes of national societies lead them to the point of believing that mutual mass-murder may be not only natural but also useful and necessary in the social interest, it is hardly surprising if the same people, as the ruling class of a national society, calculate that crime, especially the corrupt abuse of their social power, may be useful and necessary in their personal interest. Still less is it surprising if the least privileged members of those societies make the same calculation. An amoral international society breeds amorality throughout the world. It will not be possible to rid national society of its addiction to violence until international society is cured of its addiction to war.

15.16. War has no place in the words, the ideas, the theories, the values of a society ordering itself in consciousness. The word *war* (and its hypocritical periphrasis *armed conflict*) will disappear from the vocabulary of international society. The category of war will disappear from international law. War will go the way of slavery, the killing of unwanted children, exile, vendetta, blood-feud, trial by ordeal, trial by fire, putting to the question, judicial maiming, outlawry, and lynching. The idea of war, as old as recorded human history, will wither away in a new international society, an idea which could not adapt itself to a society which has taken control of its future, of its survival and its prospering. The withering-away of war, as it becomes part of our self-conceiving, will be our purpose. Self-creating precludes the choice of self-destroying. Where there was *war* there will be the crime of war. Where there was war there will be law.

15.17. The word *peace* will disappear from the vocabulary of international society. The category of peace will disappear from international law. The idea of peace as the absence of war will wither away with the withering away of the idea of war. It is said that the people of the world long for peace. Such a statement is a hypocritical travesty of the truth if it is supposed to mean that the people of the world long for greater intervals between wars. What the people of the world long for is a world without war. What the people of the world long for is an end to the self-inflicted terminal insecurity of their lives and their possessions. What the mothers of the world long for is an end to the periodic mass-murdering of their sons. What the world longs for is a new kind of peace. The age-old illusion of peace will evaporate and a new word-idea-value of *peace* will enter human consciousness—peace as the self-creating of society, peace as the struggle for justice within the framework of legal order, peace as the ordering of human desire with a view to the survival and prospering of the whole human race, peace as the ever-increasing well-being of every human being. Where there was *peace* there will be peace. Where there was peace as truce, there will be peace as growth.

15.18. The words *use of force* will disappear from the vocabulary of international society. To rationalize the use of physical force as a general form of social power is to deny the societal character of society. In society natural power, including physical force, is transformed into social power through the activity of the total social process, including the economic system and the law. Law transforms natural power into social power by means of legal relations which determine when and how natural power may be used for a social purpose, by whom and in relation to whom. Physical force is not some natural residual power available to any society-member, unsocialized but socially accepted, to be used at will, even if only in the last resort.

15.19. In society the last resort is law and legal power. To consecrate the use of physical force by making of it some general theoretical category of social and legal power is to consecrate anti-social behaviour. To articulate social power in terms of the use of physical force is to form a social reality in which violence is conceived as being natural. Society cannot educate its least socialized members out of small-scale anti-social behaviour when its most socialized members conceive social possibilities and purposes, plan social development, in terms of anti-social behaviour on a world-scale. National society will not rid itself of an unsocialized underclass devoted to crime until international society rids itself of a privileged overclass devoted to organized mass-violence. Where there was *use of force* there will be the exercise of social power under the law.

15.20. The words *self-defence* will disappear from the vocabulary of international society. The law may allow a subject of law to use physical power to preserve the existence of the self in circumstances determined by the law. To rationalize self-defence as a natural residual power to act outside the law in more or less subjectively determined extreme circumstances is to deny the societal character of society. The natural impulse to create the identity of the self—whether of an individual human being or of a society—is so great, the natural impulse to create and protect the identity of the *self* at the expense of the *other* is so great, that one of society's most fundamental functions is precisely to socialize the struggle of interacting self-creating and self-defending. Self-defence is not natural or residual or marginal in a society which conceives itself as a society. It is an integral part of society self-creating and society self-socializing. It is at the heart of all legal relations, as they particularize society's social willing and as they universalize the willing of its members. It is an aspect of the exercise of all social power, in international society as in any other society, as society integrates its self-creating with the self-creating of its members. Where there was *self-defence* there will be the exercise of social power under the law.

15.21. And the transformation has already begun. In the twentieth century, human experience of the disgrace of total war (world-scale mass murder in the public interest) has combined with human experience of national societies democratizing and socializing themselves. Each form of experience has energized the other, to produce within human consciousness the idea that war and the unsocialized use of force and the unsocialized use of self-defence are unsocietal. The socialization of the use of force through the Charter of the United Nations has combined with a growing recognition of constitutional principles within national societies, including the principle of the supremacy of law over all social power, to produce within human consciousness the idea that, even in the international society that does not yet know itself as society, a social purpose of international well-being is incompatible with a practical theory of individual self-help.

15.22. And yet if such ideas have begun to find their way into the international legal and ideal constitutions, they are far from being actualized in the international real constitution, as the threat of unsocialized force and the use of unsocialized force remain everyday choices of governments, day by day and year in and year out. The social process which includes the law and the systems of the United Nations, let alone the social process which includes the diplomatic interaction of third-party governments, is thus far only able to modify marginally and intermittently the willing and acting of the governments parties to actual conflicts. But they have changed the form of the debate, changed the tone of the rhetoric, created some small inhibition in the minds of some public officials and some more thoughtful members of the ruling class. Thus does a new reality begin to form itself.

15.23. The process of socializing the use of natural force has begun in international society, the social exchange of power for purpose. The power in question is the aggregated power of all human beings. The purpose is the well-being of international society, the society of all societies and of the whole human race. The spirit of the true peace of a true society is rising from the graves and the ashes of an exhausted world.

(2) DIPLOMACY

15.24. Diplomacy developed as the statally organizing nations found an increasing need to communicate with each other, ruling class to ruling class, government to government, public realm to public realm. Diplomacy is the dialogue of a stunted society, the dignifying of human desolation. Diplomacy is a dismal charade, with its panoply and protocol, its rituals and formalities, its treaties and communiques and *bouts de papier*, its sounds-bites and photo-calls of conniving politicians, its diplomatic emotions which are said to be warming or cooling, its tiffs and reconciliations, its infantile world of enemies and friends. Elegant diplomacy and espionage, its half-witted underworld crony, play the grown-up game which begins in whispering and ends in suffering, which begins in deception and ends in war.

15.25. The people of the world are obliged to witness in long-suffering unbelief the theatre of the absurd which is diplomacy. From time to time the drama bursts the bounds of the gilded conference-chambers and the electronic chattering, and the people of the world are swept into some new collective fantasy or some new unnatural disaster contrived by the monarchs and the presidents, the ministers and the ambassadors and the under-secretaries, as they choose the future of the human race. The people of the world must wait, like children, as their lives are determined by people they are obliged to trust, by means they cannot comprehend, on grounds they cannot know. Diplomacy is a social process whose nature is to be unsocial.

15.26. Diplomacy has spawned a phantom social process known as *international relations*. International relations are the unsocialized interacting of the public realms of statally organizing societies. Each such society has what are called a *foreign policy* and a *defence policy*. Foreign policy and defence policy are generated within the total social process of each society in the systems created by the constitution, using legal relations established under the legal constitution. They are then projected externally by each society to interact with the foreign and defence policies similarly formed and similary projected by other societies. Such policies are liable to lead to willing and acting by the societies concerned, individually and jointly or collectively. Such willing and acting is liable to affect the well-being and ultimately the survival of the members of the societies in question, possibly even the well-being and survival of human beings everywhere.

15.27. So-called international relations are articulated on the basis that each society is a unit as viewed from another society, a closed system, and on the basis that each society is, first and last, responsible for its own well-being and the well-being of own its members. Each society is a unit of what is called *power*. But it is power in the unsocialized sense—energy applied for a purpose. It is not power exchanged for social purposes, transformed into social power under the constitution of an international society. Each unit of power is regarded as having a natural tendency to prefer and to seek its own so-called *interest*. In short, international relations treat state-societies as if they were unsocialized human beings. The phantom society which state-societies are regarded as forming is simply the aggregation of the interacting of their independent willing and acting.

15.28. On such a view of international society, *calculations* of power and interest are clearly vital to each society, since power and interest are seen as expressions of the possible effect of one society on another. Governments in their external aspect are mechanisms designed to calculate so-called power and interest. In conceiving the possibilities of a society with a view to choosing its so-called policies, a government calculates its possibilities as a function of its own power (capacity to will and act) and the power of other societies which may be in a position to affect it, and as a function of its own interests (purposes in willing and acting) and the interests of other societies which may be in a position to affect it. Policy-making thus comes to be a system acting in two modes—*advantage-seeking; equilibrium-seeking*. Foreign and defence policies come to be either a calculation of the circumstances in which an advantage in well-being of one society may be gained at the expense of another, or else a calculation of the willing and acting needed to avoid or neutralize the possible effect of one society on another through matching perceived power with perceived power. And international relations become the fortuitous aggregation of such unilateral calculations. So it is that unwilled wars may occur. So it is that all parties to a war may conceive themselves as defending their respective selves.

So. it is that international society is incapable of choosing to promote its own survival and well-being.

15.29. Diplomacy is an education in deceit. It sets before the people an example of practical amorality, the pursuit of any profitable end by any practical means. The public imagination is caught by the world of espionage, lying and cheating and stealing in the public interest. But every word and every act of diplomacy is objectively a deceit, since a government speaks and acts in relation to another government in order to produce a particular effect, and not for the sake of doing good. The effect may or may not be justified by the morality recognized by the members of one or both governments, and such justification, or lack of it, may even be used as a further form of acting by one or other government, as a rhetorical weapon in the second line of attack or defence. And the so-called moral dimension may be used to justify the action in relation to a society's own citizens, to encourage them to give up their property or their lives in the social interest. But the consciousness of people, including the consciousness of public officials, is formed not only by the words that are spoken to them. It is formed also by the actuality of the total social process, the history of the willing and acting of state-societies in relation to each other. For every word that they hear spoken in the so-called moral dimension of international relations, they have heard ten words of deceit and they have seen ten acts of immorality. International relations are a world-wide school of advanced immorality undoing the work of countless local schools of social responsibility.

15.30. The modes of willing and acting which are amoralism and selfishness, advantage-seeking and equilibrium-seeking, leave little room in international society for another mode of willing and acting—social struggle with a view to the improvement of universal well-being. Such a mode occurs almost by chance, as a by-product, especially when more than one society is said to take a *longer-term view* of its own interest. A society is then said to form a view that its own survival and prospering may depend in the long run on the survival and prospering of one or more other societies, perhaps even of other societies in general. The outcome may be universalizing for particularizing purposes, unsocialized social action, paradoxical socialization.

15.31. As seen from the vantage-point of the end of the twentieth century, and with the benefit of hindsight and hypothesis, it is possible to see diplomacy and international relations as constituting a form of instinctive self-ordering, the rudimentary self-ordering of a society which still does know itself as a society, first steps in the education of social consciousness, the self-exploring and the other-exploring of a child. This hypothetical possibility has become more evident in the experience of the intensity of international relations in the twentieth century, as statal interacting has increased so much in volume and complexity that it is difficult any longer to disentangle the strands of calculating self-interest, and as economic interaction has overwhelmed in volume and almost in significance the interacting foreign and defence policies of governments. Governments are being swept up into self-socializing by the flood of their own activity. It seems possible now to say that through diplomacy and international relations, slowly and laboriously and ironically, it is being learned, first, that interests can be reciprocal and, then, that there can be a universal interest which transcends particular interests, and that there can be a particular interest which may be served by the universal interest—in short, the lessons of a society socializing itself.

15.32. Even the concept of the *balance of power*, that venerable device of the diplomatic stock-in-trade, the traditional foreign-policy formulation of the strategy of equilibrium-seeking, could be regarded as having had an educational effect. To balance power and to calculate competing interests, however crude a social purpose it may be, at least involves the identification of power and interest. It sows the seed of the idea of the reciprocity of social power. To recognize the reciprocity of social power is a first step towards recognizing the total social reality of a society. And, as multilateral diplomacy and even a form of parliamentary diplomacy have developed in the twentieth century, in countless intergovernmental organizations and intergovernmental conferences, the calculations of power and interest have come to be ever more sophisticated, the radical and irreducible mutuality of all international willing and acting becoming an unmistakable reality of international society.

15.33. The social function of diplomacy, within the evolving history of international society, may thus now be seen to be not merely advantage-seeking and equilibrium-seeking but the social education of public officials. Diplomacy is transforming itself into a school in which the public officials of statally organizing societies are learning two lessons: that there are other societies with other selves, locked also in the struggle of social self-creating; and that no society's struggle of self-creating is isolated from the self-creating of every other society. Those two lessons are elementary lessons in the re-conceiving of international society as society. At the end of the twentieth century, it is possible to suppose that they are lessons which are being learned, more and less well, by public officials all over the world. Diplomacy is coming to be the first-grade school of a society learning to be a society.

(3) STATE SOVEREIGNTY

15.34. The frenetic forming and reforming of societies of all kinds all over the world in the last five centuries has led to the emergence of statally organizing societies, and especially national and nationalizing state-societies, as the dominant form of social organization. Such a process has had a revolutionary aspect, as the idea of sovereignty has been used, again and again, not only to restructure the will-forming systems of existing societies, but also to form one society from several societies and to establish the independence of one society from the system of another. Great increases in social power have been made available to the external statal self-creating of individual societies, in so-called war-making and peace-making, and also to their internal self-creating through the social organization of human energy in their economic systems.

15.35. The dangers of alienation, corruption, and tyranny have become realities again and again as statally organizing societies have turned their aggregate power on to their own citizens.

The people of the world have been herded like cattle into states. By sword and rifle and whip and truncheon and boot and fist, they have been forced to choose the rule of those with power to rule them or to choose death. And, coralled here, they have seen other herdsmen come from there, to destroy their home, to divide their family, to silence their language, to suppress their religion, to stamp out their identity. They have been forced to become the society of state-systems made by and for the state-makers. They wait with the patience of those who know that their own society will outlast any usurping state. They wait with the tears of those who must, in the meantime, live in fear for the well-being of their children and of their children's children, knowing that they can rely on receiving nothing from society but the prolongation of suffering. They are the citizens and the victims of the same society.

15.36. The self-conceiving of international society was able to offer them no consolation. On the contrary, that self-conceiving provided a whole series of concepts perfectly suited for the construction of impregnable walls of indifference around the citizen-victims—the concepts of sovereign equality, territorial integrity, political independence, domestic jurisdiction. Each state-system was conceptually the equal of every other, each was master in its own land-domain. In a realm of natural freedom, each had a natural right to will its own system internally and to act externally in pursuit of its own well-being. Collectively the state-systems did not recognize any wider social process from which they could derive limits and purposes controlling the exercise of their internal powers. They recognized no wider social process in which the pursuit of the well-being of each could be reconciled with the pursuit of the well-being of all. They recognized no total social process in which they could form a social reality-for-themselves full of reality-forming structures and systems to form their social willing and acting. There was only the social process of licensed gang-warfare, the legitimation of force and the ultimate arbitration of war in their ceaseless conflicts of power and interest. Between wars, there was, so far as the less sophisticated sort of politician was concerned, only an unintimidating rag-bag of law-like ideas called customary international law supplemented by a miscellany of treaty obligations which were sustained by the kind of hypocritical sanctity which is, in another context, called honour among thieves.

15.37. Such a system certainly had the advantages of comprehensibility and administrative convenience, quite apart from the personal pleasure and profit which might be derived from it by those whom it privileged in each society. If you can comprehend the idea of property or the idea of slavery, you can easily comprehend the idea of sovereignty. Like sovereignty, property and slavery both involve the ideas of exclusion and of authority—property involving the exclusion of anyone not authorized by the property-owner from the enjoyment of the thing owned; slavery involving the will-determining authority of the slave-owner over the slave. And sovereignty was certainly convenient in organizing the willing of a whole society within a single comprehensible structure-system. Such convenience could also easily be relative efficiency, as the social task came to be a task of organizing an ever-more-complex economic system.

15.38. And, by the process considered in Chapter 13, a statally organizing society could, even if at substantial cost, socialize itself by reconceiving itself as a society in the name of the idea and the ideal of democracy. By such means it could seem to transcend its own nature, property and slavery seeming to transform themselves into constitutional power and self-governing citizenship.

15.39. All government is conspiracy. Democratic government is a conspiracy in which the people are co-conspirators. During the nineteenth and twentieth centuries, as the idea of self-democratizing statally organizing societies within an unsocialized international society spread throughout the whole world, a phantom international orderliness seemed to acquire the substance of some definitive social order. For the grateful ruling classes around the world, for specialists in the study of so-called international relations, even for some social philosophers, and for countless poorly informed citizens, a miracle of self-deception has been consummated. The unnatural has become not only natural but also rational. Humanity is societies not society, some societies are better than others, some societies are worse than others, some people are prospering, some people are not prospering. Given human history, what more could reasonably be expected? It is, surely, only natural and, therefore, rational?

15.40. No place on earth from the polar ice to the desert, no human activity from conception to brain death, is exempt from the willing and acting of statally organizing society. And the public realm has come to take into itself every aspect of reality-forming, not only law and morality but also religion and philosophy and even art. Consciousness, not only social consciousness but even individual consciousness, has become the object of the willing and acting of the state, filling the minds of the citizens with public information and public fantasies in the public interest. The reality-for-itself of a statally organizing society is the reality-for-the-state of that society. Not only the good but also the true have become the good-for-the-state and the true-for-the-state. The good and the true have become instruments of government. Politics, like diplomacy, has become a school of deceit. Every word uttered by a government is objectively a lie. Every deed done by a government is objectively immoral. The reason is that a government and its agents do not speak or act for the sake of speaking the truth or for the sake of doing what is right. They speak and act in order to produce an effect. That effect is necessarily part of the socializing of society, part of society's self-creating. It may be lawful, in conformity with relevant legal relations under the legal constitution. But it is not necessarily a good effect in terms even of the morality of the given society, let alone the morality of another society, let alone the morality of international society. The people of the world are learning from their governments how to do well without doing good.

15.41. So it is that an international society which is conceived as being merely the unsocialized interacting of statally organizing societies can be dynamic, can be efficient, but is prevented from being a society by two great impediments—the amoralizing tendency of statally organizing societies and the lack of reality-forming, including morality-forming, at the level of international society. Such a non-societal international society may, on balance and as a net result, promote the survival and prospering of the human race, but it does so not as a purpose but as an incidental effect. And even positive balances and favourable net effects are second-best social outcomes. They could always be better. And they necessarily include a quantity of the negative and the unfavourable. But so far as human society is concerned, the second-best and the negative and the unfavourable are experienced as the *actual* suffering of *actual* human beings.

15.42. So it is that a non-socialized international society institutionalizes human suffering by institutionalizing the state-societies which institutionalize human suffering. Governmental oppression and lack of social progress become natural effects of an unsocial system that conceives itself to be natural and rational and inevitable. State-societies, as members of such a non-society, can organize their own total social processes in order to reduce the human suffering and increase the human well-being of their own citizens but they do so by a perverted form of social exchange. They gain the power to determine exclusively the lives of their own citizens in exchange for surrendering the power to improve the lives of the citizens of other subordinate societies of international society, including nations contained within superordinate state-societies.

15.43. The power to improve the lives of the citizens of other subordinate societies of international society would flow from the participation of all societies in forming a reality-for-itself of international society, as the society of all societies, a reality which contained words and ideas and theories and values which rejected human suffering as a natural product of any acceptable social purpose, wherever it occurs on the face of the Earth, whatever the citizenship of the human beings who are suffering, a reality-for-itself which embraced all human beings as fellow members of a single society, all equally worthy of the love of their fellow human beings, all equally entitled to social justice in the name of justice.

15.44. And, once again, it is possible to say, from the vantage-point of the end of the twentieth century and with the benefit of hindsight and hypothesis, that the total social process of international society is beginning to socialize international society, in a way which it itself hardly recognizes. International society, interstatal unsociety, is a society which does not yet know itself as society, but which is beginning to behave as society. It is the non-socialization of international society which is leading it to socialize itself in spite of itself, and may yet bring it to know itself. The self-ordering of international society through the self-ordering of its countless subordinate societies, including the sovereign-equal state-societies, is being transcended by a new form of self-ordering. That spontaneous and tentative self-ordering is manifested in three developments in modern international society:

(1) *The international public realm.*
(2) *Human rights.*
(3) *International reality-forming.*

(1) THE INTERNATIONAL PUBLIC REALM

15.45. The international public realm of the interstatal unsociety has been the external interacting of the public realms of the state-societies. In the twentieth century, an extraordinary thing has been happening to the international public realm. More and more of the internal public realm of state-societies has been externalized in the international public realm. More and more of the international public realm has been internalized in the public realm of the state-societies. A public realm of international society is forming itself.

15.46. International relations had, until well into the present century, consisted almost entirely of so-called diplomatic incidents, alliance-making, war-making, and peace-making. All of these could give rise to so-called differences and disputes and conflicts, which might or might not be resolved by so-called negotiations, but which might also lead to the use of physical force, which might or might not turn into so-called war. The history of a given society, especially a nation or nationalizing statally organizing society, was seen as proceeding along two tracks which were only parallel in the long term. In the short term, internal social history and external diplomatic history were conducted as separate games, interacting with each other, but played according to different rules.

15.47. The total social process of a given society was the source of both the internal and external social developments. But the external social development involved interaction with the total social processes of other societies, so that it was claimed by governments, and normally accepted by the people, that external social action, including especially so-called foreign and defence policies, was a special case, entitled to a special place in the constitution of society, calling for special legal powers for those carrying the special responsibility. The special responsibility was treated as being an especially heavy responsibility, since it seemed that the external activity of the society went to the root of the very identity and the very survival of the society. Outside the society there were other societies which might harm the identity, take away the independence, threaten the existence of the society. It was obvious that not only special skills but also special powers were needed to defend society itself against other societies. And those other societies, rivals when they were not enemies, in any case fell beyond the pale of the reality-forming of our society, outside the benefit of our religion and morality and law.

15.48. It was in this way that the external relations of democratizing societies came to be isolated even from the development of the idea and the ideal of democracy. What was projected beyond our frontiers was our public realm, naturally a matter for the exercise of the powers of the government. What was projected beyond our frontiers was foreign and defence policies which were not about the relationship between our society and its citizens. What was projected beyond our frontiers was our struggle to survive and prosper as state-society in relation to other societies, not our struggle as human beings in relation to each other.

15.49. From time to time we, the people, might become involved, in financing some foreign enterprise of our society, in taking up arms against some foreign enemy. From time to time, we might be called upon to contribute our consciousness specifically to the development of social consciousness concerning some external matter, judging and condemning the immorality of some activity of a foreign society, such as slavery or genocide or the mistreatment of a fellow-citizen of ours. From time to time, we might be called upon to demonstrate the strength of our national feeling, as a reassurance to our government in its external activities or as a warning to the government of some other society. But, at all other times, we, the people, were nothing but spectators of the international scene.

15.50. It was capitalism and capitalist imperialism which first learned the lesson that the internal fate of a society is as much determined by its external situation as by its internal life. It learned the lesson not by philosophical contemplation but by practical experience. In the nineteenth century, the development of societies internally required a development of international society. And the development of international society required a development of societies internally. The internal development of a society at one end of the world could directly depend on the internal development of a society at the other end of the world. Raw materials required for manufacturing. Foodstuffs to feed a growing population. Markets to buy the products of manufacturing. Investment to make use of the profits of industry and trade. The world entered into a cycle of economic energy each part of which was necessary to all others. And, if it was to be a cycle of ever-increasing economic energy, always producing and consuming more and more, then it required the necessary forms of social development to occur all over the world, and that social development meant the internal social development of societies everywhere. In other words, the developing world economy demanded not merely the development of international relations, not merely the development of the interacting public realms, but also the development of the whole internal realm of societies as a function of the development of international society.

15.51. The result, in the nineteenth century, was that the public realm of societies everywhere had to expand to take command of more and more of the total social process in the interest of the survival and prospering, especially the economic survival and prospering, of the society. The development of the idea and the ideal of democracy made possible, and was made possible by, the development of the public realm. As societies became aware of themselves as societies, involving the interaction of all society-members, a sharing of each in the fate of all, a sharing of all in the fate of each, as democracy installed itself in the ideal constitution of one society after another, it became possible to create within the legal constitution legal powers of government far surpassing those which had been claimed by the most tyrannical rulers known to human history. Those societies would be the most successful which proved able to harness most effectively the whole energy of all the people in promoting the well-being of the whole society.

15.52. The greatly increased internal role of the public realm manifested itself in every aspect of internal social development. Every aspect of social life was reformed and organized to make possible the new sort of society. Schools, universities, the court system, the legal professions, a professional bureaucracy, police, prisons, public health systems. Vast networks of new legal relations were created in family law, property law, corporation law, criminal law, factory law, employment law. Every form of industrial and commercial and professional activity was the subject of regulatory legislation. It was found that not only was it necessary to create the legal basis for the economy. It was necessary to create a settled structure in society as a whole. The whole of society had to be organized to be a successful economy. And there had to be the development of public law—a fundamental development of the legal constitution designed to subject power to power, to subject social power in the public realm to the social power of the law, including the social power of the individual citizen affected by the exercise of public power.

15.53. And the success of a society now came to include, not least, success internationally in relation to other societies. As a result, the social process of international society took on a strange character, a character which we may now identify as *transitional*. There were, in the first place, international relations in the traditional sense, the dangerous game of foreign and defence policy conducted through diplomacy. There was, secondly, international economic activity, conducted by non-governmental agencies, especially statally organizing non-governmental societies (corporations), and, later, conducted also by governmental and quasi-governmental agencies behaving like corporations (state-trading enterprises). And there was, thirdly, the activity of the public realm of one statally organizing society interacting with the activity of the public realms of other such societies.

15.54. These interacting public realms at first conceived themselves in traditional terms, conducting an international economic policy analogous to foreign and defence policies, advantage-seeking and equilibrium-seeking, posing threats to other societies, countering threats from other societies, using economic phenomena as if they were forms of physical force, to attack, to defend, to retaliate. To the traditional causes of diplomatic incidents and disputes and conflicts there was now added a new dimension of international economic rivalry, into which some of the ferocious self-identifying and self-defending vigour of traditional international relations was poured.

15.55. Pure theories of economics were formed, as to the nature and functioning of the economic activity of society. And then practical theories about economic activity were formed within the struggle of the total social process of each society, calling for this or that development of the constitution, especially in relation to legal relations of property and the control over the economic process, and the distribution of wealth. Revolution and counter-revolution attended the development and the implementation of such practical theories. The pure theories were extended to the international economy, explaining its nature and functioning. And the practical theories were also extended internationally. And international relations had found a new component of foreign and defence policies, the propagation of practical economic theories and the willing and acting that they entailed, if need be by force and war.

15.56. We can now see, from the vantage-point of the end of the twentieth century, that what has happened is that international society has called forth the necessary international public realm to contain the interacting national public realms of all the societies of the world. And that new international public realm is not merely an arena of international relations. The new international public realm is not merely an interacting of internal public realms. The new international public realm is a realm of and for international society itself.

15.57. The amazing growth of the national public realms and the internationalization of the social struggle to survive and prosper have necessitated a development of international society closely corresponding to the development which national societies have undergone. It became necessary for the public realms, acting collectively, to organize more and more of international life. In this way, the national public realms have come to be more and more subsumed into an international public realm. In this way, too, the self-conceived international society of sovereign independent statally organizing societies has simply ceased to match the international reality. The world has changed and the world has hardly noticed it.

15.58. There is now hardly an area of human social activity which does not have an international dimension. And that dimension includes the exercise of public social power through international governmental activity. So-called intergovernmental organizations have been identified in Chapter 13 as *international statal societies* because they are the activity of a statally organized society externalized, taking place within international society. The interstatal unsociety formed itself, in the modern period (since about the year 1500), by turning sovereignty inside out. What has happened in the later twentieth century is that the internal public realms have been turned inside out, and governmental activity is now conducted internally and externally in a single continuum, which is the beginning of a true international public realm. The atomic sovereign states are becoming cellular societies surrounded by permeable membranes, societies whose life is organized by systems contained within their cells but whose life depends also on the participation of the cells in higher systems whose effects flow into and out of the cells.

15.59. In the international economy, in particular, which will be considered further in Chapter 17, a functional integration of state-societies is taking place, not only the integration of practical economic activity, but the integration of all the reality-forming of the economy, together with the public willing and acting required to make possible, and to support, the economy as reality and as system. National public realms are becoming residual to the international public realm. And yet the international public realm is still the public realm of a society which does not know itself as a society, and which is accordingly barely capable of supporting it as reality or as system. The result is that humanity is passing through what is presumably a transitional period in which the international public realm is forming itself but is still unrooted, alien, isolated, unnatural, unintegrated in either the structure-systems of the state-societies or in any substantial international social structure-system dedicated to the survival and prospering of humanity as a whole.

(2) HUMAN RIGHTS

15.60. Within the development of the idea and the ideal of democracy, a supersocializing pure theory of society generated the idea that the individual human being was the beneficiary of natural legal relations which logically, if not historically, existed prior to the legal relations created by the law of a given society. The purpose of such a theory was to set a limit to the law-making power of society, even to the law-making of a sovereign whose authority was otherwise conceived of as being ultimate and total. Once again, social consciousness had sought to gain for society the benefit of the energizing power of a unified social system (a *one*) without the burden of the total negation of the autonomous willing and acting of individual human beings (the *many*), to gain the priceless value of the power of the individual human being (the *one*) and also the amazing power of the members of society acting together (the *many*). The idea of human rights is the squaring of a very difficult theoretical circle. They establish a form of individual social power which relates the individual citizen to the whole of society (limiting the law-making power of society). They establish a form of collective social power which relates the whole of society to the individual (protecting the willing and acting of every individual).

15.61. Such *natural rights*, of the *one* individual/of the *many* individuals, served a revolutionary purpose in challenging the old regimes of undeveloped societies and served as a foundation for the new orders of the post-revolutionary societies. But the concept was destined to play a second role in the twentieth century. The intensely dynamic development of the new public realms of the statally organizing societies created the possibility of alienation, corruption, and tyranny, on an unprecedented scale, as the many were herded into the new societies, into their new coal-mines and factories and offices and armies, and, if need be, into their concentration camps and labour camps and war cemeteries. In the twentieth century, humanity experienced unimagined horrors flowing from the dynamic development of the public realms of state-societies.

15.62. The direct outcome was that the pure-theory concept of natural or human rights was revived and, this time, was installed not merely in the constitutions of national societies but in the constitution of international society itself. It is fortunate that the essential significance of the idea of human rights is that the idea should exist. The precise content of the rights and the mode of their enforcement are secondary matters. In the terms of the present study, the idea of human rights is a matter of pure theory rather than of practical theory, and hence is well adapted to transcend the differences between national societies.

15.63. In international society the idea of human rights began to participate in the social struggle with the dilemma of power, of the one and the many. But the idea of human rights also entered into international society's struggle with the dilemma of will—unity of nature, plurality of value. The idea of human rights reconciles the willing of all human societies with the willing of all human beings by asserting the unity of human nature without transcending the plurality of human values. When the idea of human rights is inserted into the constitution of a particular society, including its written constitution, then it comes to share in the practical theory of that society, liable to affect all willing and acting under that constitution. But the idea comes trailing its supersocial origin, always proclaiming as its very function the transcending of all forms of social power deriving from the constitution. Human rights are a permanent witness to the possibility of values which transcend the values of a given society.

15.64. But the role of the idea of human rights in the total social process of international society is not confined to its participation in the struggle of the dilemmas of power and will. It plays a forming role in the struggle of the dilemma of order— the struggle of justice and social justice. The idea of human rights, present in the pure theory of society, provides a model or pattern or formula for all law-making. Human rights provide a model or pattern or formula of the reconciling of the good of each member of society and the good of society within a good which transcends society. Human rights are not a mere mechanical reconciling of the one and the many, of the unity and the plurality of value. They exist to be themselves perceived of as a good, as a social purpose for any society, modifying the willing and acting of any society as it chooses its possibilities, as it creates itself in socializing itself, as it makes its past from its future. They are the pattern or the model or the formula, as conceived by pure theory, for the realizing of justice within the realizing of social justice in every society.

15.65. In short, human rights are an expression of humanity's discovery from its own social experience that among the possibilities it can choose is to live in society, given that a society is neither a unity nor a multiplicity of power, neither a unity nor a plurality of value, neither a realization of justice nor merely a realization of social justice. In the second half of the twentieth century, this piece of human self-discovering was extended to the self-discovering of international society.

15.66. But, as so often in human social experience, the installation of human rights in the international constitution after 1945 has been paradoxical. The idea of human rights quickly became perverted by the self-misconceiving of international society. Human rights were quickly appropriated by governments, embodied in treaties, made part of the stuff of primitive international relations, swept up into the maw of an international bureaucracy. The reality of the idea of human rights has been degraded. From being a source of ultimate anxiety for usurping holders of public social power, they were turned into bureaucratic small-change. Human rights, a reservoir of unlimited power in all the self-creating of society, became a plaything of governments and lawyers. The game of human rights has been played in international statal organizations by diplomats and bureaucrats, and their appointees, in the setting and the ethos of traditional international relations.

15.67. The result has been that the potential energy of the idea has been dissipated. Alienation, corruption, tyranny, and oppression have continued wholesale in many societies all over the world. And in all societies governments have been reassured in their arrogance by the idea that, if they are not proved actually to be violating the substance of particularized human rights, if they can bring their willing and acting within the wording of this or that formula with its lawyerly qualifications and exceptions, then they are doing well enough. The idea of human rights should intimidate governments or it is worth nothing. If the idea of human rights reassures governments it is worse than nothing.

15.68. But, once again, there is room for optimism, on two grounds. (1) The idea of human rights having been thought, it cannot be unthought. It will not be replaced, unless by some idea which contains and surpasses it. (2) There are tenacious individuals and non-statal societies whose activity on behalf of the idea of human rights is not part of international relations but is part of a new process of international reality-forming.

(3) INTERNATIONAL REALITY-FORMING

15.69. As they organized themselves as states, societies used every available means to construct the *self* of the new form of society and to construct the *other* which was outside the limits of the society. From the first statally organizing nations of the modern period to the most recently established or re-established state-societies, it has been necessary to set about the task of forming a reality which gives substance to the identity of the new society. Every kind of reality-forming is used for the purpose. Every assertion of the self is an assertion of the other, of the foreign and the strange, of the rival and the enemy. Every assertion of the other is an assertion of the self, of belonging, of the true and the loyal.

15.70. Each newly self-conceiving society must take a view of history, of mythology even, to conceive of the society as a natural development of a naturally existing society, and preferably of a naturally superior pre-society. History must be seen as the gradual actualizing of the potentiality of some original or pre-historical or putative society, the actualizing of the unique capacities of a particular people. Very often the history of a dominant nation within the new state-society can be used as the history of the new society, often at the expense of the histories of the non-dominant nations included within the new state-society.

15.71. The new society must resolve any internal conflict of languages, to find a dominant language or languages, since social reality is expressed so much through language and since language is such a convincing identifier of the other, within and beyond the frontiers of the new society. The installation of the dominant language or languages, the exclusion of subordination of alien languages, the forming of linguistic orthodoxy are matters to be regulated under the legal constitution, to be enforced through education, through all forms of cultural activity and, especially, literature. Arts and crafts of all kinds, including such things as costume and folk-songs, styles of house-building, styles of furniture and furnishing—all of these are appropriated to form the ethos of the new state-society, directing great accumulations of social power within the consciousness of the people to fill the reality of the new society with passionate nationalizing energy.

15.72. The new society must resolve any religious uncertainty, both because religion is liable to generate morality, and thereby affect every aspect of individual and social willing and acting, and because religion, with all its inward certainties and outward manifestations, is another striking self-identifier and other-excluder. Especially in the early modern period, an integral part of the development of the new societies in the early modern period was precisely a domestication of religion, an exclusion of foreign domination of religion, the establishing within the legal constitution of not only the organization of religion but even of the determination of religious orthodoxy, an attempt directly to control the most fundamental words and ideas and values of the citizens by means of legal relations.

15.73. The new society must take command of education, primary and secondary and tertiary, because it is through education that the social formation of willing and acting is achieved more effectively than through the mere handing-on of traditions and customs and folk-wisdom, the ancient informal means of socialization. The making of the citizens of the new societies requires not only that they accept as a matter of habit and superficial assent the values and theories of the society but also that they be imbued with those theories and values in the depths of their consciousness. There might come a time when they would have to sacrifice their lives for the new society. And, in the meantime, they might be required to devote the greater part of their individual energy, directly or through taxation, to working on behalf of the society, rather than merely in their own interest.

15.74. The new society must therefore, to take command of the economy of the society to organize all the mental and physical activity of the citizens with a view to the survival and prospering of the new society. This requires that the theories of the new society, pure and practical, are coherent and powerful enough to generate the necessary values of self-dedication, self-denial, and self-motivation in the citizens. History contains examples of human individuals being forced to work for society *en masse*, as slaves and helots. But the more sophisticated the economy of a society the less could it rely merely on force to cause the willing and acting of individuals. Society had to make individual citizens *want* to work for society, had to prepare their wills so that they willed freely to work for society. It has been the development of the idea and the ideal of democracy which gives to individual citizens a sufficient ground for such self-willed social action. They could now believe that in working for society they were working for themselves. The result is that such a modern society could now build pyramids and temples reaching to the skies, could clear jungles and move mountains and change the course of rivers, could turn night into day, all by co-operative effort and at relatively little human cost—all the product of some successful reality-forming by statally organizing societies.

15.75. It is law which has made possible the self-creating of the new societies. The structure-system of a complex self-contained modern state-society requires a powerful constitutional structure. The rise of constitutionalism, symbolized by the adopting of written constitutions from the late eighteenth century, was a necessary concomitant of the self-creating of the new societies. The constitution must not only exist within the depths of the consciousness of each citizen. It must be visible and impressive. It must be seen to be strong and enduring. The written constitution has come to be the outward, almost physical manifestation of the society, an exoskeleton of the social structure-system. It is the almost physical manifestation of the past and the future of society in its present-here-and-now, proving as powerfully as possible to every citizen that the present-of-society is nothing other than the actualization of its past possibilities and the actualizing of its future possibilities. To make the new society requires the citizens to share an idea of that past and that future, of what the society has become and of what it could be. With the idea of sovereignty, the constitution could acquire the necessary coherence and completeness in the consciousness of the citizens. So the making of the constitution, from day to day, is wholly involved in the total reality-forming of the given society.

15.76. Unfortunately, from the point of view of the ruling-classes of the new statally organizing societies, reality-forming within human consciousness can be modified but cannot be wholly determined. Dissent, heresy, impiety, disloyalty, and subversion are, in the end, irrepressible, not to speak of selfishness and individualism. And, worse still, the reality-frontiers of a given society are not impermeable. There are further and further reality-horizons to which human consciousness can look, up to and including the reality-of-all-that-is, but including also the reality of international society, the society of the whole human race.

15.77. The result has been that reality-forming has been a difficult task for the new societies. The more they succeed in forming their own reality, the more they endanger it. Their total social process, their self-creating through self-identifying, includes an internal *other* and an external *other* of alarming proportions. The internal other is all that had to be modified and suppressed to form the new reality, especially suppressed nationalisms and religions and languages, internal aliens of all kinds. The external other is all that the people of the society share with the people of other societies but which is not incorporated in the exclusive reality of the new society, all the rest of the universal human condition, all the rest of human consciousness, individual and social consciousness.

15.78. In the twentieth century, and especially in the latter half of the twentieth century, it has begun to seem that the exclusive reality-forming of state-societies cannot be maintained for much longer. *Governments are losing control of the minds of the citizens.* Suppressed nationalisms, including passionate regionalisms, are asserting themselves everywhere. Suppressed religions are reasserting themselves. Class-structures are changing with the changing structures of national economies, especially as urbanization accelerates all over the world and as proletariats break up, to become more differentiated and, in the case of some societies, to decline in numbers and significance in the face of a sort of mass declassification or reclassification. The mass media, within societies, have taken over the leading role from formal education in the reality-forming of the mass of the people. In those societies where the government does not choose to control the mass media using legal powers, reality-forming thus becomes a much more complex product of the total social process, more or less beyond the control of holders of governmental power or even of an otherwise dominant ruling class. In such situations, there is nothing to prevent the mass media from becoming a form of dis-education or anti-education, modifying individual and social willing and acting in ways contrary to those proposed by formal education.

15.79. But the external aspect of the loss of control over reality-forming creates an even greater difficulty for the governments of statally organizing societies. Through the international economy, through the mass-media of communication, and through travel, social reality now floods through the world's consciousness like the weather-systems of the earth's atmosphere. World social reality is a world climate, ultimately beyond the control of governments. Words and ideas and theories and values move round the world and make their way into human consciousness through a thousand unofficial channels. More and more, the people of the world are singing the same song. And it is a song that they have not learned at their mother's knee or in the class-room. Imagination and reason, the common inheritance of all human beings, are generating a common experience of all human beings, an international consciousness.

15.80. It is a consciousness which is acquiring distinctive features. It perceives the world as a unified environment, the shared arena of all human willing and acting, and an arena shared with all other living things. It perceives the humanity of human beings everywhere, responding with spontaneous human feeling to the experience of other human beings which it can recognize and understand, recognizing also wants and needs—physical, psychological, spiritual—shared by all human beings everywhere. It is beginning to conceive of standards, purposes, ideals which transcend the ideas of any particular society, but which are an amplification and a completion of the ideas which are the foundation of familiar, everyday values.

15.81. It is too soon to predict with any reasonable degree of assurance the consequences for the ordering of international society of the internationalization of human consciousness. It is possible already to discern a relative decline in the power of governmental systems, at least in relation to other forms of statally organizing society, especially industrial and commercial and financial corporations. It is possible, too, that *politics* in the form which has become familiar in recent centuries is in relative decline—that is to say, politics as a special part of the total social process devoted to a competition within a ruling class for control of certain legal powers under the real constitution of a society. Politics is apparently being assimilated to other forms of mass communication, with the mass of the people forming a political will to approve or disapprove potential power-holders and their programmes in much the same way as they process any other form of choosing, including the willing and acting connected with the economy, the identifying and the satisfying of material wants.

15.82. Such changes could lead to a cascade of changes in the self-conceiving of all state-societies, and thus of international society. The theoretical element of *authority* would disappear with the practical reality of authority. With the disappearance of authority from society, sovereignty would finally fall away as the key element in supersocializing theory. *Freedom* might then cease to be conceived as an absence of constraint, as a defence of the self against the totalizing power of society. Freedom might, instead, come to be simply an expression of the inherent nature of human consciousness within the order of society and of all-that-is, the freedom of choosing which is at the intersection of *desire* and *obligation*.

15.83. Furthermore, *power* in society might cease to be an expression quantifying the perceived capacity of one person or one society to affect another. And relations between societies might cease to be seen as a calculating of power relationships with a view to gaining an advantage or maintaining an equilibrium. Instead, power might come to be conceived as *social power*, the conferring of society's possibilities in exchange for the the subordinating of particular forms of human and natural energy to society's purposes. And, at last, society itself might come to see itself as a structure and a system for organizing the willing and acting of human beings with a view to their survival and prospering, through the constituting of social power in the form of legal relations.

15.84. Such free-flowing speculation goes beyond the legitimate extrapolation of the new phenomenon of international reality-forming. But it is safe to predict, in the light of the present state of development of international society, that the structure-system of international society will not continue for much longer to be what it came to be in the modern period and especially in the period since the eighteenth century. As war and the use of force and self-centred self-defence wither away in the real constitution of international society, as diplomacy and international relations come to an end, as the international public realm comes to supersede the individual national public realms, as international reality-forming disempowers the reality-forming of state-societies, international society will have become new, whether or not it has chosen its newness in choosing new theories of its self-conceiving. Like any other society, international society will have created itself anew in its own present-here-and-now from the possibilities which it has itself found in its own self-conceived future.

16 International Order II: Legal Order

16.1. Only international law is left speaking to governments the words that governments want to hear. International law assures the governments of state-societies that things are as they were, that all is for the best in the only possible world. Conceived as the externalized law of feudal land-holding state-societies or the public law of interacting public realms, international law has continued as the law of an old regime, faithful to the old dispensation, the old constitution, the old order. Its interest and its charm are those of precious survivals, of those rites and rituals which can move us, but only mildly, on account of their exceptional capacity for survival and because they do not threaten us.

16.2. International law, in what has been referred to above as the Grotian tradition and subsequently in the Vattel tradition, was conceived as the tempering of the interacting of the public realms of the statal societies. It was conceived as the tempering of their willing and acting as so-called *sovereigns* of their so-called *territories*. Hence the legal relations of international law were and are essentially the legal relations necessary to temper the public interactive willing and acting of the governments of statal societies as that willing and acting affects their sovereignty over territory. They were empowered and obliged by legal relations to will and act in ways which were specifically agreed among themselves or which had been determined by their previous willing and acting.

16.3. The role of a misconceived international law within a self-misconceived international society has been marginal, residual, and intermittent. It has been one element in the willing and acting of the state-societies as they made their fevered calculations of so-called *power* and *interest*, as they sought one advantage after another, one equilibrium after another. International law has been neither very threatening nor very useful to the politicians and the diplomats. It has seemed to be little more than a neutralized diplomacy, international relations half-set in amber, a more or less safe refuge within so much international turbulence, a set of relatively fixed points for taking political measurements, some common ground from which to launch flights of rhetoric, the modest voice of common sense in the midst of rampant unreason. It has performed the role of an old servant in a family of ancient lineage, a venerable legal adviser to great landowners whose most treasured possession is now a colourful past, full of glory and shame. International law is the faithful friend of a family overtaken by time.

16.4. It follows from all that has been said above that the place of *law* in society is anything but marginal, residual, and intermittent. The legal constitution of society carries society's structure from its past into its future. Law is the self-directed becoming of society, the order of the self-ordering of society. Legal relations embody relations of social power among the members of the society to enable natural energy—human energy and the energy of the physical world—to be applied for the purposes of society. Legal relations make possible the integrating of the willing and acting of individuals with the willing and acting of society, the willing and acting of society with the willing and acting of individuals. Law is the particularizing of the universal and the universalizing of the particular, as society struggles to create itself in its words and ideas and theories and values, as it forms its reality through the struggles of the total social process. Law is creator and creature in the total social process, formed from the past of the total social process, forming the future of the total social process, the intersecting of the ideal and the legal constitutions as they form the willing and acting of society's present-here-and-now.

16.5. It follows also from what has been said above that, since society creates itself within consciousness, within individual and social consciousness, society's ideas of itself are part of society's self, and society's forming of its ideas is part of society's forming of its self. Society cannot be better than its idea of its self. Law cannot be better than society's idea of itself. Given the central role of law in the self-ordering of society, society cannot be better than its idea of law. International society's existing idea of itself and its law is, like an infant's view of its family-world, an unstable illusion which lived reality will destroy.

16.6. A conception of law which was not adequate to a less complex condition of society will be still less adequate to a greatly more complex condition of society. As the total social process of international society carries the whole of humanity into its future in an ever-accelerating flood of social change, as the new self-ordering of international society becomes at last a self-reconceiving of international society, a conception of international law which was always inadequate proves itself at last to be worse than inadequate. It is a conception which is preventing international society from conceiving of its own possibilities and from actualizing its own possibilities. International law, as it has been and as it is, cannot function as the legal system of an international society which is learning to know itself as a society. International society will create an appropriate legal system for itself in conceiving of itself at last as society. Each will create the other. Or else each will destroy the other.

16.7. The systematic weakness of international law is demonstrated most eloquently by the fact that every single fundamental operational sub-system of modern international society law is uncertain and incoherent and anachronistic. Such operational sub-systems are the reflection within the international legal system of the generic principles of a constitution which have been considered in Chapter 11. They are the generic principles of a constitution as seen through the distorting lens of international society's self-unknowing. But in every aspect of the operational weakness of international law as a system are to be found also the possibilities of its self-reconceiving and thereby of the self-recreating of international society.

16.8. *Law is part of the total social process. Principle of integration.* International law is a mystery to international society. The people of the world do not know themselves as participants in its making, only as participants in its effects. It seems to be the business of a foreign realm, another world, in which they play no personal part, but in which everything is done in the name of this state-society or that, of which they happen to be citizens. The total social process of international society has generated a form of law which depends on the acquiescing of the people of the world in a partial social process, the social process which is conceived as the interacting of the governmental public realms of the state-societies as units of willing and acting, mathematical points with location but without extension. Such a phantom total social process has then generated a phantom international society, the interstatal unsociety of the state-societies. And international law has come to be, at least in the consciousness of the members of the ruling classes of the state-societies, the law formed within the phantom social process of a phantom society. It is not surprising if such international law fails adequately to perform the role of law in society.

16.9. Because it is conceived as the law of a society which is not the society of the whole human race but as a law which nevertheless affects the survival and prospering of the whole human race, international law has given rise to insurmountable theoretical problems in explaining its nature and functioning. Its failure to generate a satisfactory pure theory of itself has meant that international law has not been able to take root in any satisfactory practical theory, even the practical theory of the phantom international society of the state-societies, let alone of the international society of the whole human race. A social system which is not explicable within a society's theory of itself can hardly function as a social system at all, let alone as the leading system of society's self-creating structure-system.

16.10. The phantom international law of the phantom international society has not been able to establish any theoretical basis for itself. It does not know whether its so-called rules should be observed because they have the authority of custom or because they have the authority of a promise, or both, or neither. If, as suggested above, law is a set of legal relations not a set of rules, the self-questioning is, in any case, misconceived.

But the self-questioning stems from a more profound misconception. If law within a state-society is conceived as the willing of a sovereign, then law within a society which is not subject to a sovereign must, it seems, be conceived in some other way. If international society has been conceived, in what has here been called the modern period, as a collection of state-societies, all sovereign and equal and independent, themselves not subject to any sovereign, then there is not much choice other than to conceive of interstatal law as the product of the willing of those state-societies.

16.11. The more or less articulated assumption of those whose willing and acting is affected by international law has been that customary international law is to be conceived either as a product of the universalizing will of state-societies or as a product of express or tacit promising by state-societies, or both. The *universalizing will* is the characteristic conception of customary law systems, the conception that a member of the society may, in willing and acting, not only will the action but may also will that the principle of the action should become law for society as a whole. Such a universalizing will has been referred to in the self-conceiving of international law as *opinio juris*. The willing of the particular action is thus both law-applying and law-making at the same time. The willing of the particular action is both the exercise of a legal power to do the action and the exercise of a legal power to legislate further legal relations. The legal relation which gives rise to the power to do the action itself forms part of a legal relation which gives rise to a power to participate in legislating new legal relations. Within such a conception of customary international law, so-called *state practice* is the arena in which law-applying is law-making, law making is law-applying. State practice is, in other words, a phantom law-making process of the phantom international society. Within such a conception, the subjects of the law (participants in legal relations) are also the authors of the law. Or, in other words, the state-societies legislate for themselves in participating in their phantom social process.

16.12. *Express or tacit promising* is a conception which is taken over from other forms of social reality-forming to become a central conception of the making of new legal relations. *Express* promising takes the characteristic form of the undertaking, the agreement, acquiescence, or compromise (non-legal reality), the declaration, the contract, the treaty, the conveyance, cession, or estoppel (legal reality). *Tacit* promising arises from a course of conduct which creates mutual expectations. Mutality and reciprocity, mutual reliance and reciprocal benefits and burdens, may, within the constitution of a particular society, create inferred legal relations. The relation is established as a legal relation by the co-action of the willing and acting of the legal persons involved in particular transactions. Once again, the subjects of the law (participants in legal relations) are conceived as being also its makers. International law is then regarded as *voluntary law*—a phrase which is not seen to be a daring paradox but is supposed to be a simple statement of history. Law-making is seen simply as a series of acts of will of the subjects of the law, the law being formed by a certain sort of coincidence between particular acts of will.

16.13. The theoretical alternatives of the formation of law as custom and the formation of law through promising have been reflected in a generally accepted classification of international law into two varieties, known as customary international law and treaty law. Their bases of authority are conceived either as intrinsically different from each other or as being two aspects of a single source of law, which is itself then conceived as being either customary or consensual in nature. And it is sometimes supposed that the customary and consensual sources must then themselves be derivatives from a single source which lies in the collective and communal willing of the sovereign states, willing in the exercise of their sovereignty. Such theoretical problems are left unresolved because the idea of sovereignty seems to dissolve all problems, offering an ultimate explanatory source which seems to be located outside and beyond the international legal system, in the constitutional systems of the state-societies, and in the hard facts, the supposed reality, of international society. Believe that the sovereignty of states is part of the reality of international society, and problems of theory apparently become otiose.

16.14. Theoretical conceptions of custom and promise are by no means out of place in the self-conceiving of the legal system of any society which is not conceived in terms of sovereignty, that is to say, any society which does not place the ultimate legal power to make law in the unwilled will of the legislator. There have been, and are, countless societies in the world in which law-making is essentially non-sovereign and customary or voluntarist in character. The difficulty caused by such conceptions in international society is precisely that they have been made to be an adjunct of the conception of *sovereignty*, that they have been conceived as the law-making of legal persons who are also conceived as *sovereigns*. This resulting conception, placed as the impossible foundation of a pure theory of international law, has been a collection of sovereignties which are self-limiting. In that lies the theoretical incoherence and the practical impotence of international law.

16.15. Sovereignty is not a phenomenon of the physical world. It is not even some sort of necessary and ineradicable idea within consciousness. It is a word-idea formed, like any other word-idea, from and in human consciousness. Sovereignty is not a fact but a theory. It is a theory which a society may generate in the course of specific historical developments within the reality-forming of its total social process. Sovereignty has meaning only within the total social reality which forms it and which uses it. The sovereignty of state-societies, which they are supposed to use when they make international law and which they are supposed to limit by making international law, is only the externalization, as a result of the social development considered in Chapter 13 above, of particular theories of society developed in a particular period of history in particular social circumstances. When sovereignty found itself present in international society, as the self-conceiving of certain of the subordinate societies of international society (the statal organizing societies), it thereby came into contact with the total social reality of international society. It had been formed within the total social process of the state-societies and then came to be part of the total social process of international society, a process which had existed for thousands of years before the introduction of the idea of sovereignty but which was to be profoundly altered by its introduction.

16.16. Once introduced into the social reality of international society, it would have been possible for externalized sovereignty then to democratize and socialize itself, in the way discussed in Chapter 13, in parallel with the democratization and socialization of state-societies. It would have been possible for international society to develop a theory of *representation*, to articulate the way in which the state-societies aggregated the willing of their citizens in order to will and act internationally as the representatives of their citizens. Instead, the consciousness-controlling activities of government, and their supporters, ensured that sovereignty would be externalized into a society which was conceived as being a society containing only sovereigns, a society which would contain no theory of representation, which would leave obscure and unexplained the sense in which the people of the world might be virtually present in international society by reason of the participation of the state-societies. The result was the stunted and primitive reality of an international society in which only the voices of governments are heard, and those voices evoke only a weak and distant resonance of the infinitely rich internal social processes of the state-societies, of the self-creating willing and acting of the internal social process of the state-societies.

16.17. So it was that international society had to order itself, not by the self-creating of law-making through the total social process of international society, as all the people and the peoples of the world interacted with each other, but through the self-limiting of their governments, as their respective public realms interfered and conflicted with each other. International law is a reality-forming of international society which does not recognize the reality of the total social process by which all reality is formed. It chooses to recognize only the social process of the interacting of the governments of state-societies, as if they constituted a self-contained and self-caused social process, as if they constituted the whole of the total social process of international society. An international law which is conceived as the product of so limited a part of the international social process is not able to become a leading participant in international reality-forming. It is doomed to be what is has been—marginal, residual, and intermittent.

16.18. *Law is dynamic. Principle of transformation.* The self-disabling of international law, the conceiving of international law as the self-limiting of equal sovereigns in their externalized public realms, meant that international society deprived itself of the capacity to use law as the main instrument of its self-creating, the means not only of its survival but also of its prospering. It deprived itself of the wonderful power of legal relations to create an intensely dynamic human reality, matching the dynamic of the physical world, incorporating the dynamic of the physical world and of the world of human consciousness, creating the system by which the whole of reality, physical and human, may be transformed with a view to survival and prospering. If a legal system is conceived as being merely the tempering of the interacting of neighbouring land-holders, then that legal system is not likely to lead those land-holders, let alone the human beings who live from the land, to aggregate their possibilities in a shared system of social self-creating, of ever-increasing well-being.

16.19. What is worse, the self-limiting which flows from a legal system whose function is conceived as primarily particularist is not the self-limiting required for the making of a society of ever-increasing general well-being. Even neighbouring land-holders may recognize the need to be restrained from destroying the value of their own land. Such restraint can be generated by self-interest or by a sharing of parallel self-interests. But such unilateral or multilateralized self-interest is only the beginning of social empowering through law. When law becomes not merely the multilateralization of individual purpose but the universalization of social purpose, it transcends self-interest and becomes the self-creating of a society. It becomes a reconciliation of every kind of interest (the economy versus the environment, the wealth-creating of the few versus the wealth-creating of the many, the practical versus the aesthetic, the material versus the spiritual) within the ultimate struggle of society with the self-creating perennial dilemmas of society. And it becomes the reconciliation of the past and the future (the depletion-rate of natural resources, the creation of long-term hazards, saving versus consumption, education versus indoctrination). Through the establishment of legal relations arising out of the total social process, such reconciling can become the substance of society's most dynamic self-creating. International law, conceived as the self-limiting of land-holders or of interacting public realms, has deprived international society of its potentiality for self-creating through law.

16.20. Another consequence of international society's self-disabling is that, in the international society of the second half of the twentieth century, the organization of social power throughout the world has taken forms which aggregate but are not seen to cohere as a system of systems—the activity of the international economy, including especially the activity of statally organizing corporations (so-called multinational corporations) and of non-statal societies and individuals; the activity of governments in controlling the internal aspects of the international economy (for example, protecting the environment and protecting the consumer by means of national law); multilateral governmental activity, seen simply as the multi-lateralization, usually through treaties and the decision-making of intergovernmental organizations, of such internal activities; non-governmental activity by lobbies and pressure-groups.

16.21. The need has created these disparate means of meeting the need. They are the fruit of need not the fruit of purpose. In the absence of any general social process other than the interaction of the public realms of state-societies, there is no means to generate the purposes of international society, transcending the purposes of the individual state-societies. It follows that the social exchange at the root of all social power is distorted and impeded. The transformation of natural power by the acceptance of social purpose is, in the phantom international society of the state-societies, an exchange of *unnatural* power (the so-called *power* of the societies organized around their so-called *sovereignty*), for *unsocial* purposes, formed from interactions within the fantasy-process of so-called *international relations*.

16.22. In such a distorted system, international law plays no leadership role. The transactions of such an international society may emerge as uncertain, faltering legal relations, but they are legal relations which seem to be anything but the work of the real constitution of international society, using the law-making powers of the legal constitution in fulfilment of the purposes of the ideal constitution. They are legal relations which do not seem themselves to be playing a leading part of the self-creating process of a society making its own structure-system, making its future from its past, its past from its future. They are playing no significant part in international society's struggle with the perennial dilemmas of society, as it makes its *identity*, organizes its structure of *power*, constructs the grounds of its *willing*, establishes its *order of justice*, takes control of *becoming*. They are the work of *de facto* sub-systems of a social structure-system-in-waiting, waiting to come to consciousness, waiting to be part of the total social process of a reality-forming international society, a society in which international law would at last play the dynamic transforming role of law.

16.23. *All legal power is delegated power. Principle of delegation.* International law has told the state-societies that their power is not delegated but original, natural, and inherent. It has said that the pure theory which subtends their internal authority is sufficient to support their external authority as the law-makers and the subjects of the international legal system. It has said that no one but states and the international statal societies which they create (so-called intergovernmental or international organizations) are participants in international legal relations, let alone in international law-making. It has said that international society is not a society of five billion human beings and countless subordinate societies but a society of some one hundred and seventy state-societies and an uncertain, but small, number of international organizations.

16.24. These ideas have left in penumbral uncertainty most of what has above been considered as the emerging social process of international society. They have placed the governments of state-societies in the extraordinary position of being the sole attorneys of all their citizens in the law-making of international law. They are certainly not the sole attorneys of all their citizens in the rest of the reality-forming of international society. Less and less are they even the dominant force in the reality-forming of national societies. A result is that international law has created for itself an irreducible tension between so-called *recognition* and so-called *self-determination*. In other words, international law has been unable to determine why it is that this particular state-society and its government are entitled to act as participants in the phantom social process of interstatal international society and hence are entitled to determine the survival and prospering of this or that collection of their so-called citizens.

16.25. By the concept of *recognition*, state-societies have assumed a power in the legal constitution of international society to act under the real constitution of international society to determine the actual participants in international society at any particular time. A statally organizing society (a so-called *state*) is said to *recognize* a particular stage of development of another society, the stage of development when another society has, in the course of its social development, taken on the character of a *state*, and hence has become a subject of international legal relations. But even the power of recognition is subject to a whole series of unresolved, but fundamental, uncertainties which flow directly from the misconceiving of international society and international law.

16.26. International law, in its present form, makes no clear provision: (a) as to when a society is to be regarded as achieving the legally necessary characteristics of a *state*; (b) as to whether the *recognition* of other *states* is a precondition of such achievement or even an element therein; (c) as to whether the existing *states* have a freedom-power to make judgements in the matter, or whether they are subject to constraint-liability of any kind in making such judgements (including obligations of, and attaching to, non-recognition); (d) as to whether the same or similar or any legal relations apply to the achieving by the society known as an *international organization* of the status of being a subject of international law; (e) as to whether the same or similar or any principles apply to the power of a *government* to act as the willing and acting organ of a *state* within international society; (f) as to whether such *recognition* is an instance of, and hence is systematically linked with, a wider concept of recognition of legally significant events in international society (for example—acquisition or loss of territory, acquisition or loss of nationality, the existence of an identity-threatening condition of so-called *war* or an identity-respecting condition of so-called *neutrality*); (g) whether a state-society from which a new state-society is formed by separation has special powers and obligations as regards the *recognition* of the new state-society; (h) whether a state-society may forfeit its status as a state-society, for example, by reason of some specific internal development; and (i) above all, whether the will of the members of the recognized or unrecognized society, their determintion of their self-as-society, is a legally significant factor in the achievement or non-achievement by that society of the privileged status of being a so-called *state*.

16.27. In an international society which conceives of itself as limited in its membership to so-called *states* (and the statal societies which they form) and conceives of those *states* as the exclusive participants in legal relations, such questions will be of fundamental importance. And yet international society, after four centuries, has not resolved, or found a means of resolving, such ultimate problems of its systematic structure.

16.28. International society will not solve its three fundamental structural problems (as to the nature of an international legal system in an international society, as to the process by which international legal relations are formed, as the determination of the actual participants in legal relations under the real constitution) until it recognizes its own universality.

(1) Every legal power in every society in the world is connected with every other legal power in every other society in the world through the international law of the international society, the society of all societies, from which all law-making power is delegated.

16.29. International society will not take command of its own self-creating until international law at last finds itself able to tell the governments of the statally organizing societies about the particular nature of the so-called *state*.

(2) State-societies are nothing more nor less than a particular form of subordinate society of international society, identified by the form of the internal self-organizing of their public realms.

(3) State-societies, and the state-societies which they themselves form (so-called international organizations), are constitutional organs of international society within the legal constitution of international society. They hold particular powers under the international constitution and participate in particular legal relations for the purpose of organizing the public realm of international society within the total social process of international society.

16.30. International society will not be able to integrate its law into the total social process of international society until it conceives of the forming of state-societies as one instance of the forming of any kind of society.

(4) State-societies are formed through the total social process of international society as part of the self-identifying of individuals in the societies to which they belong and the self-identifying of societies in relation to their members and in relation to other societies.

(5) The participation of the people of the world in the making of the state-societies to which they belong as citizens is the same as their participation in the making of all other societies, including the nation-societies of which they consider themselves to be members by birth. The peoples of the world form the state-societies as they are formed by them.

16.31. It follows that none of the innumerable subordinate societies of international society, including the state-societies, has legal powers which are original, natural, and inherent. To speak of legal powers which are original, natural, and inherent is to utter a contradiction in terms. Legal powers arise from the legal constitution of a society which is part of the constitution of the society which is formed from the total social process of that society, operating over time and operating uniquely, specifically for that society. Legal powers, far from being original and natural and inherent, are socially derived and socially formed and socially delegated. Societies which are organizing themselves as states—with a public realm under the authority of a government—are, in this respect, no different from any other form of society. They certainly do not, through their own social development, turn themselves into some unique class of supersocial societies.

16.32. Such state-societies have an *external* status, a constitutional relationship with each other and with all the other subordinate societies of international society, and hence legal relations, deriving from the constitution of international society, and hence from the total social process of international society. And such state-societies have an *internal* status, a constitutional relationship with their members (citizens and subordinate societies), and hence internal legal relations, deriving from a constitution which is formed within their internal social process but which is itself an integral part of the international constitution formed within the total social process of international society.

16.33. The role which international society has appointed for the state-societies, as constitutional organs participating in the system of its public realm, is analogous to the role assigned to the constitutional organs within a society—head of state, the government, the legislature, the courts of law, political parties, a religious establishment. That is to say, the legal relations in which such organs and their members participate are specifically designed to fit their role in relation to the public realm. But every single legal relation in which any society of any kind, including a state-society, participates, or in which any human individual participates, is a relation created by delegation from international society. This is true of every legal relation from a power-right to make law for the whole world to a power-right to cause the installation of a particular traffic-light at a particular road-junction.

16.34. From a change of self-conceiving will come a change of vocabulary. From a change of vocabulary will come a change of self-conceiving. States are not sovereign. States do not have sovereignty. The words *sovereign* and *sovereignty* will disappear from the vocabulary of international society and international law, together with the words *war* and *peace* and *use of force* and *self-defence* and *international relations* and *diplomacy*, as redundant anachronisms, no longer required in the self-conceiving theories of international society and international law.

16.35. *All legal power is limited. Principle of the intrinsic limitation of power.* International law has told the state-societies that not only are their powers original, natural, and inherent. They are also in principle unlimited. That is to say, in the misconceived international society and international law, a misconceived pure theory suggests that the so-called states limit by their own willing and acting an otherwise total freedom of action, their so-called sovereignty. As the idea and the ideal of democracy took root in national societies, the word *freedom* became, once again, a word of great power within human consciousness, a word to fling at reaction from the barricades of oppression. It was a word which played, and plays, other roles in human consciousness, especially in pure theories of individual consciousness—the so-called *freedom of the will*. It was a word which had taken on the rich evolutionary significance of all words which have seen action in countless social struggles over very many centuries.

16.36. The word seeped into the social consciousness of international society. When the internal social development of statally organizing society was turned inside out to form the international society of interacting public realms, the idea of democratic freedom accompanied the transformation. An aroma of freedom filled the nostrils of the governments of the so-called *states* as they met in the dignified halls of an international society from which the people were, fortunately, excluded. The so-called *states* found themselves to be free. They were free in relation to each other, none having authority over any other. And, still more attractively, they were free in relation to their own peoples. Sovereign equality, political independence, territorial integrity, domestic jurisdiction. Such were the slogans and the legal guarantees of the supposed natural freedom of the so-called states.

16.37. So it came about that international law led governments to believe that the state-societies which they controlled had legal powers which were limited only by voluntary subtraction from an integral freedom. So it was that international law came to be conceived as obligation-by-subtraction-from-freedom. And the constitutions of the state-societies consecrated this conception by conceiving of their national legal systems as theoretically autonomous, owing nothing to international society, certainly owing no obligation to international society, unless the state-society in question had accepted limitations by the willing and acting of its government within the special world, the phantom society, of international society.

16.38. The absurdity of the idea of legal relations as freedom-limited-by-voluntary-subtraction has been demonstrated with overwhelming effect in the twentieth century, when the energy levels of national and international society and new forms of social interaction have led to a vastly increased capacity of the natural power of individuals and societies to affect the lives, and even the existence, of other individuals and societies. In particular, human and social power over the physical universe, through the application of science in technology, has given to every human being and, still more, to every society immensely increased possibilities for producing effects which can determine the life of one individual person and effects which can determine the lives of all human beings, to affect all living things, everywhere. And the effect on the lives of human beings everywhere now includes effects on the consciousness of human beings everywhere, on the very process of willing, on the process of conceiving and choosing possibilities—through the media of mass communication, through the spread of pure and practical theories of society, through the forming of human wants in an integrating international economy. And the effects of willing and acting today are effects which may be felt over longer and longer periods into the future.

16.39. Any society, and now quite evidently international society, is an inextricable network of interacting effects, an integrated but ultimately indivisible structure-system. It is precisely a function of the structure-system of society to organize the interacting social process. And it is the function of legal relations, including legal power-rights, to organize that interacting at the level of willing and acting, to affect all willing and acting within society with a view to organizing the effects of willing and acting for the purposes of society. The legal relation establishes a link between the willing and acting of the two or more participants in the legal relation such that their willing and acting may be modified in the light of the social purposes which are reflected in the legal relation.

16.40. Every legal power under international law, including powers to legislate internally within a state-society and powers to cause effects on other state-societies, is thus a shared power—shared with the other participants in the relation, whose own rights and liabilities are determined by the content of the legal relation, and shared with the rest of international society which has caused the legal relation to be created. To have a legal power under international law is thus necessarily to have a limited power, a power limited by its content and limited by its interrelationship with all other legal powers, with the contents of all other legal relations. If you claim to have a legal power, if you seek to act on the basis of a legal power, you acknowledge the legal system which creates the power and which confers it on you, and you acknowledge that the power is in principle limited, and you acknowledge the specific limits of the power.

16.41. It is international society which determines, through the creation of social power in the form of legal relations, the extent to which a state-society may exercise natural power (the mental or physical energy of its members and subordinate societies, the energy of the physical universe) as a legal power, the circumstances and conditions in which the state-society may exercise that power, the persons or societies which may be affected by such exercise of power, the effects which the exercise of power may have on any or all human beings and on international society itself and on all its subordinate societies, the methods by which the exercise of the power may be reconciled with the exercise of their powers by other persons and other societies, the methods by which the content and the limits of the power may be determined, the consequences of the abuse of the power.

16.42. So much for the supposed *natural freedom* of states. States are naturally free only to obey international law.

16.43. *All social power is under the law. Principle of the supremacy of law.* International society, as presently conceived, is a society without a socionomy. That is to say, it does not present itself, to those who participate in it, as a structure and a system of desire-modifying obligation, as a structure and a system ordering itself in and through a constitution.

16.44. Since they conceive of their social existence as flowing not from international society but from their internal social structure-systems, from their own constitutions, the state-societies do not conceive of that existence as being formed by the constitution of international society. They conceive of their social existence in international society as secondary and derivative in relation to their internal social existence. They conceive of the structure and the system of international society as being nothing other than a side-effect of their willing and acting, an aggregation, a secretion, a residue. International law connives at, and sustains, this unsocial world-view of the state-societies by every one of its fundamental structural postulates—by establishing the state-societies as the authors of their own law, by confining legal relations under international law to legal relations in which the state-societies and their so-called international organizations participate, by treating the interaction of their public realms as the arena of the only international social process from which international law springs, by regarding the state-societies as having a natural freedom and inherent powers, by treating international law itself as a set of self-willed restrictions upon that freedom and those powers, by conceiving of the sovereignty of states as being essentially a sovereignty over a particular area of the earth's surface, by treating international legal responsibility as being nothing other than the consequence of a wrong caused by one state-society to another.

16.45. From time to time, the governments meet together to co-ordinate their willing and acting for social purposes in specific fields (political, economic, social, military). The executive branches of the state-societies communalize, for a while and to a certain extent, some part of their executive activity. That communalizing may sometimes be in aid of causes which are likely to be welcome, in principle, to the people of the world—economic planning and economic development, crisis control and conflict resolution, arms limitation or reduction, protection of the environment, the prevention of disease, educational development, the relief of starvation or poverty. Sometimes such communalizing takes the form of phantom constitutional systems within so-called international organizations, with a phantom executive branch (a *council* or an *international commission* or a *secretariat*, for ·example), a phantom parliamentary body (a *general assembly* a *general conference*, perhaps, but composed of politicians and diplomats and civil servants rather than elected representatives of the people), and even with a phantom judicial branch (a *court* or a *tribunal* or some other *dispute-settlement* subsystem).

16.46. Such spurious international constitutional systems create an illusion of constitutionalism. The participating state-societies may form groups (Group of 77, less-developed-countries, advanced industrialized countries, geographical groups, non-aligned countries) with some of the attributes of political parties, coagulating what are regarded as relevantly assimilable economic and/or ideological and/or regional interests. They hold debates, trade texts, make compromises and concessions, hold votes and make explanations of vote, all as if they were the elected representatives of the peoples of the world. Their deliberations may lead to the creation of legal relations, new rights and liabilities, conferred on and accepted by state-societies through the willing and acting of their governments brought together in the willing and acting of governmental agents.

16.47. In a development full of the most painful irony, the governments of the state-societies have in this century even begun to conceive of themselves as law-makers in the most straightforward sense. In special international conferences and in the framework of international organizations, their representatives meet as if they were the parliamentarians of international society. They consider draft laws, to be adopted as treaties, designed to create legal relations in abstract form, like national Laws or Acts of Parliament or Acts of Congress. And the governments have even appointed a body, within the structure of the United Nations, to prepare the ground for what is called *the codification and progressive development of international law*, as if there were such an activity distinct from the process of *law-making or legislation*. They have given themselves an International Law Commission, as any well-ordered society should have its law-reform process. Experts in international law, often having long experience in the business of international relations and diplomacy, excogitate the common interest of the state-societies, as perceived by the governments of the state-societies, in a form apt to become the self-chosen and self-limiting law of the state-societies. They supply the simulacrum of a draft law to be turned into the simulacrum of law by means of a process which is a parody of legislating.

16.48. And the peoples of the world are presumably somewhat grateful for the devoted work of their governments and their servants and agents, remote and incomprehensible as it may seem to be. The peoples of the world know too well that there are many less desirable ways in which the governments of the world, and their servants and agents, could occupy their time and their talents. The appearance of law-making is better than the reality of war-making. However, the peoples of the world are also presumably puzzled by two aspects of the process. In the first place, such international law-making is still presented by governments to their respective peoples as if it were merely the pursuit of national interest by other means. Secondly, the people of the world are not directly involved in such law-making, and are only indirectly involved to the extent, if any, that they are involved in forming the foreign and defence and international economic policies of their respective state-societies.

16.49. The risk for governments is that activity on their part which looks like constitutionalism and behaviour which looks like law-making behaviour are liable to lead to rising expectations of law. And, at the end of the twentieth century, it is possible to say that such rising expectations of law in international society are becoming a reality which governments will not, for much longer, be able to dispel with the tricks and illusions of the theatre of diplomacy. Governments are generating a socionomy in spite of themselves. Governments are generating an international Rule of Law, whilst still conceiving of themselves as masters of the Rule of Power. In the phantoms of international constitutionalism and international law-making are the seeds of an international law which is the law of an international society which is a society.

16.50. The Rule of Law will not be established in international society until international society comes to understand its non-legal reality. Law, as part of the total social process of a society, is not an insignificant part of that process. It is structurally fundamental and dynamically determinative. But law has no meaning and no effect except within the structure-system which transcends it and which organizes all the reality-forming which forms, among other kinds of reality, the reality which is the law. Law and the rest of the social process are not independent or parallel or merely interacting. In accordance with what has been considered above as the Principle of Integration, law and the rest of the social process are integral to each other. Law and religion and mythology and history and morality and art and natural science are all integral to each other. Law and the willing and acting of all subordinate societies and other members of society are integral to each other in a given society. The supremacy of law—its role as the ultimate arbiter of the distribution of social power—depends upon its theoretical integration in the whole of social reality and its practical integration in the working of the total social process, both of these things being achieved through the structure and the system of the constitution.

16.51. Law and the rest of social reality are integral to each other even in statally organizing societies. The mere fact that in a state-society a public realm of willing and acting is formed under the authority of specific constitutional organs, comprising the so-called government, does not remove that public realm from integral involvement with the rest of social reality. In particular, the development of what have been called above the democratization and the socialization of state-societies has precisely been the organizing, as theory and ideal, as process and actuality, of the structural-systematic relationship between the public realm and the rest of social reality.

16.52. The principle of the Supremacy of Law does not assign to law a society-transcending role in society. On the contrary, it is a relational principle, identifying a special role which law plays as the bearer of society's constitutional structure-system from its past to its future, as the special means by which the universal and the particular are reconciled in the willing and acting of society and its members, as the voice which speaks the last word on behalf of society before the moment of choosing, when consciousness seeks to reconcile obligation with desire, in each particular act of willing.

16.53. In a self-misconceived international society, in which there is no conception of an international social process or international reality and reality-forming, in which there is no conception of an international constitution, and in which there is no international public realm but only the interacting of a number of individual public realms, there can be no conception of the supremacy of law. There is nothing transcendent into which law can be integrated, no transcendent structure-system, no transcending structures of theory and value. And where there is no conception of the supremacy of law, there can be no adequate conception of the reality of non-law, including especially morality. When law has no established place in the systematic relationship between individual and social consciousness, morality cannot find an established place in the systematic relationship between individual consciousness and the reality of all-that-is. The misconceived international society is a desert in which neither law nor morality can take root and flourish.

16.54. To establish the supremacy of law in international society is to establish the reality of non-law in international society. To establish the reality of non-law in international society is to establish the supremacy of law in international society. Within the democratizing and socializing of the state-societies, an activity know as *politics* has been identified as an aspect of the governing of their public realms. Its function is to generate a range of ideas—known as *policies*—which are a product of the interaction of society's theories, pure and practical, with actual social reality. They are a product of the real constitution, as the participants in the total social process use social power with a view to forming the willing and acting of society, including the particular form of willing and acting which is the making of the law.

16.55. The systematic structure of the governing of the public realm is specific to each society. The participants and their respective contributions to the process are specific to each society. The outcomes of the political dialectic are specific to each society. However, in many modern state-societies the politics of the public realm is a multiple dialectic involving four interacting sub-systems—a governmental system, a deliberative body, interest-groups, public opinion. Social power concentrates in such sub-systems and the systems acting together are able to choose, from all the possibilities made available by the total social reality, those possibilities which will be made actual through willing and acting under the constitution, including law-making.

16.56. Because international society does not know itself as society and cannot find within itself even the possibility of systematic politics, it is not only international law which is a puzzle and a mystery to the participants in international society. The bilateral and multilateral and communal relations of the state-societies, including their relations within the so-called international organizations, also seem incoherent and unordered. When those relations are not capable of being characterized as law-making, they seem to have no meaning, to belong to no known category. They seem to be a form of unpolitical politics, the non-governing of a realm which is not a realm of governing, the half-forming of a formless social reality.

16.57. Even in the United Nations, which comes closest to being the general social process of a pre-social international society, the activity of the delegations of the Member States seems, to many of the participants themselves and to most outside observers, to be feckless and irrational and even illegitimate when it is not activity specifically implementing legal powers or activity specifically directed to spurious law-making. Governing (willing and acting in the public realm under actual legal relations conferring authority) and law-making (the creation of new legal relations by virtue of old legal relations) seem to them, conditioned by the reality of their internal state-societies, to be naturally meaningful and purposeful and self-justifying activities. International policy-making seems to them to be a contradiction in terms.

16.58. A similar phenomenon plagues the European Community which comes closest to being a genuinely unified public realm transcending the internal public realms of a number of state-societies. Despite the inclusion in the Community system of a directly-elected parliament and despite countless efforts to stimulate actual Community-reality-forming, there is only a very partial Community social reality. Three of the four estates of the social process of a modern socialized democracy are present to a significant degree—a government, a parliament, and influential interest-groups. The fourth estate—influential public opinion—is hardly present at all. As a consequence, the Community system is obliged, like the United Nations system, to focus most of its attention on its activity as law-executor and law-maker, leaving reality-forming to be a by-product of Community government and of the inadequately interacting non-law realities of the Member States.

16.59. International society, when it conceives of itself as society, will have its own specific sub-system which will be international politics. In becoming a society, international society will at last recognize that the relations between states are not merely the interacting of internally generated foreign and defence and international economic policies but the forming of law in the process of forming non-law, and the forming of non-law in the process of forming law, as the rich and complex dynamic dialectic of international society generates the policies which may, under the real constitution of international society, actualize themselves in many forms, including the form of law.

16.60. As it comes to recognize the relation of law-reality to non-law reality, international society will find itself liberated from a self-imposed tyranny, a self-constraining which directly stems from its self-conception as the piecemeal interacting of statal societies. Because the interaction between the self-recognized members of non-social international society is conceived as being limited to an interaction of their public realms to an extent controlled by them through their separate foreign and defence and international economic policies and through the self-limiting concession of specific legal relations, it is difficult for the dynamic possibilities of non-law reality to flow into the development of international law and for the dynamic possibilities of law-reality to flow into international non-law. Even here, however, there are signs that, over recent decades, social creativity is beginning to flood into international society. The number of different forms of legal act has greatly increased. And, still more important, international society has begun to generate forms for containing *policy*. These forms, which have been disparaged and misunderstood as *soft law*, closely resemble similar forms which have been generated within the state-societies. The function of such para-legal acts is specific and essential. *Para-legal acts enable social policy to modify the willing and acting of the holders of legal power-rights.*

16.61. Para-legal acts may take different actual forms—final acts, declarations, resolutions, codes of practice, understandings, recommendations, decisions, and other forms *ad libitum*. Whatever their actual form, they are designed to be less merely potential than ideas and less actual than legal relations. They have an effect in two quite different directions. (1) They are the means by which a rudimentary social reality is being formed in international society, as international society slowly and painfully finds its own words and ideas and theories and values, its own purposes and its own ideals, its own policies. (2) They provide value grounds on which the legal powers of members of international society (the state-societies, other subordinate societies, human individuals) may be exercised in conformity with the social consciousness of international society. They are early evolutionary traces of an international society which is beginning to socialize and democratize itself.

16.62. Following the experience of modern state-societies, international society will also develop new forms of specifically *legal* act. Even if the main sources of law continue to be a *customary* form (accumulated through the law-making which takes the form of law-applying) and a *deliberative* form (the intentional creation of specific legal relations), it is inevitable that both forms will develop in flexibility and sophistication, as government of the public realm of international society develops. In particular, the deliberative form will take on a more and more statutory form, as international society comes to legislate for itself as society. Such a development will only be possible if the constitutional structure of international society provides the means for relating international law to the whole of an international reality-for-itself, if the constitution of international society becomes its means of reality-forming, if international law at last comes to embody the supremacy of law in society.

16.63. *All legal power is power in the social interest. Principle of the supremacy of the social interest.* International law tells governments that they are the government of states whose sovereignty is in essence a sovereignty over territory, whose sovereignty over territory is a species of property, whose relations with other states are the relations of property-owners, whose freedom is a freedom to exercise exclusive authority over a territory and over all that is within that territory, whose citizens have their birth in that territory as their primary self-identifying as citizens.

16.64. A state-society which is also a nation (a society whose members regard themselves as its members by birth) or is a nationalizing society (seeking to become a nation-society) is able to make use of the attachment of the people to their fatherland, their motherland, their homeland, their home, their land, their own country, their ancestral lands, their tribal lands, the land of their fathers. And any state-society, whether or not it is a nation or nationalizing, is capable of using, more or less cynically, such territorial attachments of the people, attaching the people to the territory of the state-society of which they are citizens.

16.65. Furthermore, because international law allows it to regard its state-territory as a species of property, the state-society is able to invoke the ideas and the feelings which support the idea of property in individual and social consciousness. Whether or not the practical theory of a given society supports the possession by the citizens of *surplus property*, property beyond their everyday needs, there seems to be an ineradicable idea in every human being that personal possessions, the hearth and the home and, perhaps, a small parcel of land, are an integral part of human self-identifying. However modest such personal possessions may be, they seem to be worth defending with a determination closely akin to the need to defend life itself.

16.66. One way or another, therefore, a state-society is able to generate powerful emotions in its citizens in conducting its struggle to identify itself by asserting its rights over territory and to defend its identity by defending those rights. Loyalty to the state-society and its government has been connected with love of country, with love of the most personal of possessions. And since the state-society has identified itself by so-called sovereignty, an original and natural and unlimited authority, it has seemed only natural that sovereignty over territory should be conceived as being as aspect of sovereignty and hence of the very identity of the state society.

16.67. The outcome has been that sovereignty over territory has taken on a supersocial character, has entered the realm of the kind of social theory which links the phenomena of society with things which transcend society, up to and including the natural order of all-that-is. Sovereignty over territory has taken on the character of a supernatural attribute of the state-society.

16.68. Since the idea of property seems necessarily to imply exclusion, sovereignty over territory conceived as a form of property has also fused naturally with that aspect of the theory of state-sovereignty which postulates the exclusive authority of the structure-system of the state-society within its own society. State-sovereignty makes each society into a closed system, conceptually integrated by the idea of sovereignty as an ultimate source of authority, making possible all law-making, including all constitution-making, within the society. The idea of property seems similarly to imply that the property-owner has power-rights to exclude others from use of the property, to benefit from the use of the property to the exclusion of others, or in preference to others, to dispose of the property at will, regardless of the interests of others. State-sovereignty fused with sovereignty over territory seems necessarily to justify the holding of such seemingly *natural* power-rights in the state-society as a member of international society, in its relations with other state-societies.

16.69. This in turn means that the function of an international law of such territorially-sovereign state-societies would have as its natural aim the regulation of the interaction of the exclusivities of the state-societies—the exclusivity of their constitutional authority within the society, the exclusivity of their territory-holding in relation to other societies. And such, indeed, has been the content of international law in what has been referred to above as the modern period, since the fifteenth century. International law has been the minimal law necessary to enable state-societies to act as closed systems internally and to act as territory-owners in relation to each other.

16.70. Such also had been the conception of law *within societies* all over the world in many periods of their history. The power of the most powerful members of society had been based on land-holding or, at least, land-control. The function of law had been to provide the means by which their power could be related, on the one hand, to the structure-system of society as a whole through its constitution and, on the other hand, to the power of those who lived and worked on the land and who might be called upon to defend the status of the property-owner and, thereby, the means of their own subsistence.

16.71. The economic structure of many such societies developed in complexity and energy. Ideas were generated which challenged the equation of the exclusivity of property-holding with the exclusivity of social power. Gradually and in parallel with the democratization of social power, the holding of land was socialized, each sustaining and reinforcing the other. The legal system changed in corresponding ways. Its function came to be the organizing of a much more complex and variegated social structure-system, in which the social aspect of all legal power, including property-power, came to be a determinative aspect of all law, from the legal constitution down to individual property-rights. The self-reconceiving of societies all over the world came to be a reconceiving of the power which society delegated through the legal system. That reconceiving was a relativizing. To different degrees in different societies, depending on practical theories as to the nature of society and of social justice, all legal power was recognized as having a social component. It has been suggested in Chapter 13 that such an idea is, in any case, systematically necessary within any theory of law which understands law as the basis of the structure-system of a society. But history shows that not all societies at all times have chosen to recognize that necessity within their own pure and practical theories of society, within their own social reality.

16.72. To put the relevant development of social consciousness in other terms, it was a recognition that the authority conferred by sovereignty within the society could legitimately (in terms of the ideas and theories and values of the society) be exercised to control property-holding in the social interest. And, once that idea was accepted, it was a matter for the total social process of a given society to determine the extent of the socializing of property, as society struggled with each and every one of what have here been called the perennial dilemmas of society.

16.73. In the present century, international society has begun to experience a dramatic development in complexity and energy, strongly reminiscent of the development of many of its subordinate societies all over the world. International relations and diplomacy have responded in the ways considered above, especially by a partial and intermittent communalizing of the governmental process, bilaterally and multilaterally and in so-called international organizations. But much of international social development has occurred in the *other international society* of the non-state and para-statal societies, especially through the development of the international non-governmental economy. Only international law has failed to respond. It knows that it cannot respond without destroying the only structure-system it knows, the structure-system of sovereign states having sovereignty over territory.

16.74. General international law has continued to be a law of delicts, a law of property and a law of contract. That is to say, it has continued to be a law primarily concerned with establishing bilateral and multilateral legal relations among the discrete participants in the legal system and with correcting unlawfulness as it occurs in the bilateral and multilateral relations among the participants in a particular legal relation. It is true that, because such relations are legal relations, they necessarily embody the social interest, as a tacit third party of every legal relation, in accordance with the generic principles of a constitution. Even the most detailed legal relation between two parties is created by society through law and includes within it the relevant interest of society determined in and through the operation of the total social process of society, including necessarily society's struggle with the dilemma of justice and social justice.

16.75. However, the history of the statally organizing societies shows that a legal system based primarily on the creation and enforcement of such legal relations is not capable of organizing the complexity and the energy of a modern society. The development of the role of government in such societies has enabled society to intervene as a third party in any bilateral legal relation, not merely in creating and enforcing the legal relation but as an active participant in legal relations through the exercise of public power. The public realm of a state-society is precisely the area in which the public realm is integrated into the private realm of particular legal relations, so that the implementing of the legal relations becomes an integral part of social willing and acting, of the willing and acting of society as a whole. Society is enabled to actualize its purposes not merely by creating the appropriate legal relations but also by intervening in the implementation of particular legal relations. By this means modern complex societies have found another way, born of theory and necessity, to use the law to universalize the particular and to particularize the universal. Through the public realm all particular legal relations are made into general social relations.

16.76. By this means, legal power came to be conceived as being not merely delegated by society, as all social power is delegated. All legal power came to be seen as being directly related to the power of society as a whole exercised through its constitutional organs, the organs of so-called government. Once again, it has been a matter for each state-society to explain such a development to its own satisfaction, as an aspect of its own pure and practical theories of society. In particular, one society may choose to regard public powers as a limitation on non-public powers, while another society may choose to regard non-public powers as a subtraction from, or a limitation on, public powers. Whatever theoretical explanation is used, the net result is that society has come to assert the social interest not only in the making of law but in the exercising of social power itself.

16.77. The development of public law was a dual development, as society itself came to be a participant in more and more legal relations (through the wholesale creation of public power-rights) and as society then found it necessary to create a meta-public law (administrative law) to control the exercise of public power-rights. Such changes were revolutionary in character, quite as revolutionary as the rearrangement of power within and between the constitutional organs themselves. Such state-societies directly incorporated the willing and acting of society as a whole into the legal system, whereas formerly it had been located primarily within the other reality-forming systems of society (religion, mythology, history, morality, philosophy, natural science, art) and, within the legal system, primarily in the form of the creation and enforcement of private bilateral legal relations.

16.78. Not knowing itself as society, international society has not been able to see, or else to understand, that it is following the same course of development. As the state-societies come to be recognized as constitutional organs of international society, their characteristic legal relations can at last come to be seen for what they are—not as relations of property law or the law of delicts or contract law, but as *relations of public law*. International law delegates to the state-societies power-rights and confers on them constraint-liabilities, in relation to certain events and persons, not as an incident of their land-holding but as an aspect of their governmental responsibility in the public realm of international society. Their primary governmental responsibility is very rarely a responsibility not to commit a delict (tort), very rarely a responsibility to act as a good property-owner. The general responsibility of the state-societies under international law is to act in the social interest of international society in the exercise of the powers which international law has delegated to them in relation to the public realm of international society and thereby in relation to the public realms of their own societies.

16.79. All the fundamental trends in the development of international society which have become familiar elements in international social consciousness over recent decades are outward signs of this natural and inevitable self-reconceiving of international society and its law. The transformation of international relations and diplomacy into a communalizing of government, the sharing of a public realm. The elimination of war and force as structural categories of international society. Concern for the world environment as the living-space of life on earth, including human life, rather than as the arena and the residuum of human interacting. Concern for human rights as the natural limits on public power everywhere. Concern for economic development as a human need shared by all human beings everywhere, a need to use natural and social power to overcome starvation, poverty, disease, and indignities of every kind. Concern for human spiritual welfare, for the reality-forming which determines all social possibilities and hence the future of humanity as a whole. All these developments are the development of international society as a society, a society in which all members of society, including the state-societies, are able to participate in creating themselves and creating society through the dedicating of natural energy to social purpose in the form of social power, including the power of the law. International society is recognizing itself as a society in which the state-societies are agents and instruments of the survival and prospering of the human race.

16.80. *Sovereignty over territory* will disappear as a category from the theory of international society and from its international law. It will join the other redundant words which are no longer required by an international society which is a society, words which can serve no further useful purpose in an international law which is the public law of such an international society. With the exclusion of the concept of sovereignty over territory, international society will find itself liberated at last to contemplate the possibility of delegating powers of government not solely by reference to an area of the earth's surface. Such a liberation will enable international society to do two things, in particular, which will open up rich new possibilities for its self-ordering. (1) International society will be able to see international organizations at last as true international societies in their own right, not merely as co-operative ventures of the state-societies. (2) It will be possible for two or more state-societies to share in organizing the public realm of one and the same territory or of one and the same nation.

16.81. (1) So-called international or intergovernmental organizations have been formed by state-societies as a means of communalizing some aspect of their public realm. The communalized aspect is one of those in which the public realm of one state-society flows into the public realm of another, so that both together form part of the international public realm. The necessity for communalizing stems from the fact that the willing and acting in the area in question extends beyond the limits of any one state-society. The organization so formed is a new subordinate society of international society, having its own total social process, its own struggle with the perennial dilemmas of society, as it establishes its identity, organizes its structure of power, organizes its own capacity to will and act, organizes its own internal order in relation to the order of all that transcends it, organizes its surviving as it transforms its future into its past. The international organization is thus not merely an aggregating of the activity of its member state-societies. It is a structure-system for governing one part of the international public realm, with its own willing and acting, with its own reality-forming systems, its own reality of words and ideas and theories and values. An international organization is, like a state-society, thus a constitutional organ of international society with its own legal relations delegated by international society by means of international law, legal relations which may affect willing and acting within state-societies, including the willing and acting of their constitutional organs and of any or all of their members.

16.82. (2) An international society which recognizes itself as a society having power to delegate powers to constitutional organs for the purpose of governing its public realm need not consider itself obliged to ensure that one state-society is solely and exclusively responsible for the government of any one area of the earth's surface. Accordingly, such an international society need not consider it essential that any particular nation (a society to which its members consider themselves to belong by birth) should be a participant in only one state-society or that a particular state-society should not contain more than one subordinate structure-system to accommodate its different constituent nations.

16.83. In this way, international society will be able to remove the greatest cause of war and of interminable self-destructive social struggle. Endless international and internal conflicts, costing the lives of countless human beings, have centred on the desire of this or that state-society to control this or that area of the earth's surface to the exclusion of this or that other state-society, the desire of this or that nation to be or not to be part of the structure-system of this or that state-society. International law has contributed next to nothing to the avoidance and the resolution of such conflicts. On the contrary, it has fueled them with the perverted passions generated by its primitive categories of *sovereignty* and *sovereignty over territory*.

16.84. There is no reason why, in an international society which is a society, there should not be an unlimited number of further alternatives beyond the binary choice of *state-society* or *international organization*. There need be no theoretical limit to the possibilities of complex power-holding in relation to the same area of territory or the same group of individual human beings or the same function of government. There is no reason why international society should not extend substantially the communalizing of government on a functional basis, the building of horizontal public realms joining rather than isolating the social processes of different state-societies. The test of what forms of organization are necessary and useful, the inspiration for the ceaseless self-reordering of international society, is nothing other than the social interest of international society, that is to say, of the whole human race, discovered and actualized through the total social process of international society.

16.85. An international society which is freeing itself from so many obsessions and neuroses (*war* and *peace* and *force* and *self-defence* and *international relations* and *diplomacy* and *sovereignty* and *sovereignty over territory*) is an international society free at last to create itself without forever threatening to destroy itself.

16.86. *All social power is accountable. The principle of social responsibility.* Of the two forms of accountability in society, a self-misconceived international society knows only a rudimentary version of legal accountability, and knows next to nothing of social accountability.

16.87. In default of the most rudimentary system of social accounting, international society has appeared to make much of legal accounting. In conformity with international law's conception of legal relations, legal accounting has taken the form of what is called the *international claim*. The international claim is the exercise of a power-right of one state-society to oblige another state-society to justify some particular act as a matter of international law. The making of the claim, assuming that the so-called claimant state has the necessary power-right to do so, creates a constraint-liability on the claimant state to take steps to show that the act in question violates some right possessed by the claimant state and that the act is attributable to the so-called respondent state. The claim then imposes on the respondent state a constraint-liability to take steps to show that the act in question was done under some right possessed by the respondent state. In other words, the international claim is articulated, in claim and defence, in terms of a set of legal relations in which the two states participate.

16.88. The claim and the response are made through the process of diplomacy. The matter is resolved, one way or another, by the process of negotiation. The respondent state concedes and gives satisfaction to the claimant state. Or else the claimant state withdraws the claim. Or else some third form of resolution is found to their mutual satisfaction. If no mutually satisfactory resolution is found, the matter remains in issue and remains part of the regular business of international relations, as each state uses any form of legal or non-legal social power available to it to further what it conceives to be its interest in the matter. In traditional international relations, the issue might ultimately be submitted to the so-called arbitration of force.

16.89. The whole process is thus predicated on the bilateral legal relations of the parties and is conducted through the medium of their bilateral international relations. The social interest of international society is embodied in the process only through the legal relations which have been placed, by the parties themselves, at the centre of the issue between them, given that those legal relations are relations of international law created by the law-making process of international society and hence, in that way and to that extent, embody the social interest of international society. However, the perception of the matter as raising a legal issue, the identification of the legal issue, the identification of the relevant legal relations, the resolution of the issue, the consequences of the non-resolution of the issue—all these matters are in the hands of the parties. The social interest of international society does not directly determine their willing and acting in such matters.

16.90. Experience of international society over recent centuries has shown that even the state-societies have found it necessary to modify this fundamentally bilateral system of legal account-ability, in three significant directions. (1) The state-societies have found it useful to involve third-parties in the determination of the legal aspects of their claims. Conciliation, mediation, arbitration, claims commissions, other specialized settlement procedures, the International Court of Justice. An extraordinary variety of forms of third-party involvement have been devised by the governments of the state-societies, which are able to perceive subtle distinctions of interest and advantage between them in relation to particular forms of claim. (2) The state-societies have found it useful to use communal international systems, especially international organizations, as forums within which to conduct some part of their international relations with a view, among other things, to reducing the risk of creating socially disruptive, especially war-threatening, disputes and situations. In some of these, most notably the League of Nations and the United Nations, constitutional organs have even been given power-rights to will and act in the name of international society as a whole to prevent and to mitigate such disputes and situations. (3) The state-societies have found it useful to create special mechanisms within their international organizations to resolve disputes arising in relations to willing and acting within the organization. Once again, they have been imaginative in developing a wide range of different kinds of procedure, from the most court-like to the most informal, designed to suit the nature and the needs of the particular part of the international public realm with which the organization is concerned.

16.91. Such developments reflect a dawning sense, however tentative and however unarticulated, in the governments of the state-societies that there may be a third party interest in all two-party disputes, namely the social interest of international society, an interest which may go beyond the satisfaction of *claims* and the avoidance of *disputes* to include *situations* of more general concern and involve *decisions* in the name of a wider society than that of two disputing states. The result is that contemporary international society and contemporary international law contain yet another fundamental tension which may yet prove productive of much new self-ordering, including a more developed system of social accountability. The tension is between what has been the intrinsically *bilateral* character of international legal accountability and an incipient international *social* responsibility.

16.92. The essentially bilateral character of international legal accountability flows directly from the essentially bilateral character of international legal relations. If unlawfulness in the international public realm is misconceived as being essentially a matter of a trespass or a delict or a breach of contract, it is not surprising if legal accountability is essentially confined to determining and correcting such wrongs. It is not surprising also if, in the more developed international society of the twentieth century, with its ever-increasing communalization of the government of the international public realm, the governments of state-societies continue to perceive of unlawfulness as essentially arising when one state violates a right of another state. Sovereignty and sovereignty-over-territory— exclusivity and freedom in relation to a particular territory— still dominate the conceptualization not only of the legal relations but also of the nature and consequences of a breach of law.

16.93. A consequence of this form of legal accounting is that the isolation of a set of relevant legal relations between the parties involves the elimination from their legal dispute of all their other legal relations, of all their non-legal relations, of all the legal relations of other parties which may be affected by the dispute but which are not parties to the proceedings, and of all the non-legal relations which may be affected directly or indirectly by the dispute and its resolution. International law has delegated to the state-societies the settlement of their disputes, as if their disputes were their own business.

16.94. Another consequence of essentially bilateral legal accounting is that it requires that a claimant state should be able to prove that it has the relevant right and that the respondent state has a corresponding liability. And that requires that the claimant state should not only show that such a right has been conceded either by treaty or by the law-making process of customary international law. The claimant state must also be prepared itself to acknowledge that such a right has either been conceded in the treaty also in favour of the respondent state or has been established in general international law, and hence that a similar claim may be brought against it (the claimant state) in other circumstances by the respondent state or by another state (if the treaty is a multilateral treaty or the right is claimed under general international law). States thus have an incentive to moderate their claims against other states to claims in respect of generally acknowledged rights and rights which they would themselves acknowledge in favour of other states.

16.95. The inhibition is reinforced by the consideration, which state-societies cannot ever ignore, that, in all that they do in the way of law-applying and law-enforcing, they are also law-making. The assertion of legal claims and the determination of legal claims by negotiation or by a third-party are the two most privileged and potent forms of the *state practice* from which customary international law is formed. The inhibitory effect of this consideration is not an incidental effect in a customary law system. It is of the essence of it. The effect is precisely that of causing the individual law-subject, in willing and acting, to will and act as if the principle of that willing and acting will form the content of legal relations applying to law-subjects in general.

16.96. In a customary law system the underlying conception of legal relations is thus especially critical in the development of the system, since it constrains its possibilities of development. The essentially bilateral character of the relations of international law, its delict-property-contract ethos, have made it impossible for international law to develop in the ways that are demanded by the development of international society. Two modern structural developments in legal accountability illustrate these constraints. The attribution of individual legal responsibility for events connected with a particular so-called war—responsibility characterized as so-called crimes against the peace, war-crimes, and crimes against humanity—was made possible only by the use of actual physical power flowing from the successful use of physical force against the so-called criminals. The attribution to individual human beings of human rights, including procedural rights to obtain legal accountability for the willing and acting of constitutional organs which violates those rights, was made possible only by embodying such rights and their enforcement within traditional forms of law-making and law-enforcing, in treaties concluded among state-societies, in constitutional organs created and controlled by the governments of the state-societies.

16.97. In other words, the price extracted by the structural nature of international law was the exceptionalizing of war crimes and the bureaucratization of human rights. Since no government ever regards itself as an aggressor, since every government has a dozen rationalizing explanations for its barbarities, the deterrent effect of such exceptionalized crime is negligible. Since no government need fear that bureaucratized human rights will lead to internal revolution sparked from outside, need ever risk losing control of its constitutional right to oppress its people, the deterrent effect of bureaucratized human rights is negligible.

16.98. There is little or no prospect that customary international law, as at present conceived, could generate general law covering the crime of public mass murder (formerly known as *war*) or of conspiracy to commit public mass murder, or of failing to prevent public mass murder. There is little or no prospect that it could generate torts / delicts of gross negligence by governments, gross dereliction of public duty by governments, gross misfeasance in public office by governments—in causing or allowing public mass murder, in causing or allowing mass starvation or mass poverty or mass disease or other human indignities on a mass scale, in causing or allowing large-scale damage to the world environment, in causing or allowing large-scale degradation of the human spirit, of human consciousness. There is little or no prospect that international law, in its present form, could generate a land-holder's responsibility to put first the interest of international society in the use of land, a conception of trespass to all land everywhere, of trespass to the whole planet Earth.

16.99. International law will not be able to respond to the new international society and to create adequate legal accountability until it reconceives itself, in its application to the state-societies, as a system of *public law*. The essential characteristic of the international law of an international society which conceives itself as a society is that it imposes legal accountability on the exercise of social power, that it is able to identify and correct, not merely delicts and torts and trespasses, but *abuse of power*.

16.100. The concept of abuse of power turns every international wrong into a wrong against the whole of international society. It means that any willing and acting anywhere in the world, but especially willing and acting by and on behalf of the state-societies and international organizations, as constitutional organs of international society, is of concern to every member of international society, that is to say, of every other subordinate society and every other human being. The concept of abuse of power means that the function of international law is not merely to prevent bilateral torts, to regulate land-holding, to redress breaches of contract. The function of international law is to organize the distribution of legal relations, and especially power-rights, throughout the world in the social interest of the whole of international society—and to control the implementation of those relations, including especially the exercise of power-rights.

16.101. It follows, further, from such a conception that international law-making—whether in the customary law form or in any number of statutory forms—can at last be conceived as essentially the constant self-creating of the international legal constitution and the exercising of law-making power under that constitution with a view to actualizing international society's ideal constitution, transforming the unlimited natural power of the human race into social power, as international society embodies *its purposes* in every form of social power, including the legal power of legal relations.

16.102. From a reconceived legal accountability will come a reconceived social accountability. Social accounting can be released from the inhibitions and constraints imposed on it by the rudimentary character of international law and international legal accounting. The concept of *abuse of power* is a concept of social accounting as much as of legal accounting. Legal accounting applies the generic principles of a constitution to every form of legal power. Social accounting applies all of society's words and ideas and theories and values to judge the exercise of all forms of social power. It is the reality-forming of international society as it reforms the willing and acting of all

338   *Eunomia*

members of international society, as it actualizes all the possibilities of the future of international society in its present-here-and-now. In reconceiving legal and social accountability, international society takes control of its own self-ordering.

16.103. *New international order.* The new self-ordering of the new international society may thus be represented in diagrammatic form as follows:

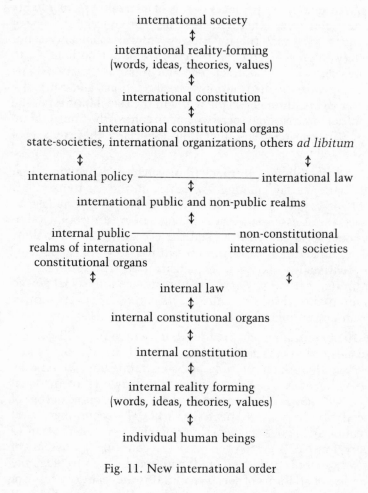

Fig. 11. New international order

16.104. *New international law.* The new international law of the new international society may be represented in diagrammatic form as follows:

international reality-forming
(social purpose-forming)
↓
international legal constitution
↓
international law-making and policy-making
by constitutional organs
↕
international law
(constitutional law, administrative law, trade law, commercial law, environment law, transport law, telecommunications law, etc.)
↓

customary international law	statutory international law (treaties, other forms)
↓	↓

legal relations
↓
power-rights (among others)
↓
exercise of power

↓	↓
social accounting	legal acounting
↓	↓

international reality-forming
↓
international legal constitution
↓
and so on again, as above

Fig. 12. New international law

17   International Economy

17.1. The economy is the social transformation of the physical world. Every society, from the society of the family to the international society of the whole human race, is, as part of its socializing, an economy. The economy is the intersection of social consciousness and the physical world. In the economy, society systematically transforms its physical situation, like all other living things, as the process of its living, as the substance of its becoming. In the economy, society transforms the physical world in and through human consciousness, as human beings do and as other living things do not. In the economy society lives humanly as part of the living world, seeking to survive and prosper through transforming the physical world. The economy is humanity seeking its well-being as part of the physical world.

17.2. The transformation of the physical world in the economy is the combined work of mind and matter, a work of physical effort and of the effort of consciousness, of the human body acting as a part of the physical world and of human consciousness acting as the self-causing cause of social and individual becoming. The economic transformation of the physical world takes five forms:

(1) a social transformation into an object of labour;
(2) a social transformation into an object of use;
(3) a social transformation into an object of desire;
(4) a social transformation into an object of property;
(5) a social transformation into an object of trade.

The economy of a society organizes such transformations systematically, in order to serve the purposes of society through the generation of self-creating *surplus social energy*.

(1) OBJECT OF LABOUR

17.3. A thing is transformed into an object of labour when human willing and acting is applied in relation to it with a view to transforming it into another thing. A thing to be transformed into an object of labour may be a part of the physical world which has not yet been an object of labour—minerals in the earth, plants and animals, naturally occurring electromagnetic fields. Or it may be a thing which has already been an object of labour—extracted minerals, plants and animals which have been raised or harvested, timber, paper, cloth, iron, steel, sound or light generated by other labour. And it may be events in the brain, either events occurring spontaneously as reactions and reflexes and feelings or events occurring as words and ideas transformed by previous mental effort.

17.4. The thing is transformed into an object of labour as a result of willing by a human individual or by a society, choosing the possibility of applying energy to the thing with a view to transforming it, and then acting accordingly to transform it. The transformation is thus as much the work of the energy of consciousness as it is the work of physical energy. It is consciousness which conceives of the thing as a possible object of labour (abstracting it conceptually from all the undifferentiated mass of the physical world), which conceives of the possibility of applying transforming labour to it, which chooses the possibility of applying transforming labour, which directs the application of the transforming labour, which conceives of the thing as a thing transformed by labour. An object of labour is thus the sum-total of: *a conceiving by consciousness of a thing as a possible object of labour + the willing of labour + the acting of labour + the conceiving by consciousness of the thing as transformed.*

17.5. A person totally isolated from human society could make objects of labour. When they are made by persons who are members of a society, then social reality enters decisively into each stage of the process of transforming a thing into an object of labour. All of the reality-forming of society may affect the process, including all the forms of reality which affect the conceiving of the reality of the physical world (for example, religion or mythology or natural science or philosophy or art), all the forms of reality which affect the conceiving of the process of transformation itself by all those who participate in it and who observe it (the ordering of consciousness in words and ideas and theories and values), and all the forms of reality which affect desire and obligation (for example, modifying the will through religion and morality and economy and law).

(2) OBJECT OF USE

17.6. A thing is transformed into an object of use when it is conceived in consciousness as a possible object of further transformations. It is consciousness which isolates the thing from the rest of the physical world, which identifies it as a particular thing. And it is now consciousness which adds to that identity a particular possibility. An object of use is an object which has been transformed by consciousness into a potentiality, which has been reconceived in relation to the future, in relation to its becoming and to the becoming of consciousness.

17.7. Tree-branches are parts of trees until they are conceived as possible fence-posts. Logs are dead trees until they are conceived as possible timber. A fish is a fish until it is conceived as possible food. Words are words until they are conceived as possible poetry. A person is a person until conceived as a possible friend.

17.8. Possible uses (possible further transformations) are as various as the necessary order of the physical world (as conceived by consciousness) allows, and as various as human imagination (ordered by reason) can conceive. Individual and social consciousness conceive of uses as a function of all of society's reality-forming. An object of use is thus the sum-total of: *a thing as conceived by consciousness as a possible object of use + the conceiving by consciousness of a particular possible use + the conceiving of the thing as a possible object of that particular use.*

(3) OBJECT OF DESIRE

17.9. A thing is transformed into an object of desire when it is conceived in consciousness as a possible object of our willing and acting. It is an appropriation which does not yet make of it an object of property, but which makes it no longer an object of indifference to us. It is the physical world seen in the light of our desire. It is the physical world seen in the light of the possibility of our willed action. It is the world as a world of our wants and needs. It is the world as the scene of our possible self-creating, as the raw material of our self-creating. It is the world conceived as the world which we may consume in order that we may live. It is the world conceived as the world of our possible world survival and prospering.

17.10. In transforming a thing into an object of desire, consciousness acts on the world like light. Without the physical world, there would be no thing to desire. Without desire, there would be no thing desired. As we do not see the light which lets us see all that we see, so we do not experience desire except as the transforming of the thing desired. The transforming of the thing into an object of desire is not the application of specific physical energy, other than the energy expended in the human brain during the physiological events corresponding to desire. It is the application of the energy of consciousness, that is to say, the systematic activity of the brain as it presents to itself its own activity—specifically, its activity in conceiving of the thing desired in the light of the possibility of our willing.

17.11. Desire sees the world only as possibility, but as a possibility within those which are the possibilities of our willing and acting. It places the object of desire in a particular relationship to the whole of the reality within which we conceive of our willing and acting. It follows that all reality-forming participates in the making an object of desire. It follows also that social consciousness is present, inevitably and intrinsically, in the transforming. Social consciousness is present in every way in which it can affect our willing and our willed action, as it conceives of the impulse of life which causes us to cause our becoming, of the necessity of the physical world which limits our possible action, of desire as it shapes our willing, of obligation as it constrains our willing.

17.12. Particular timber is desired as timber for our house. A particular fish is desired as our food. Particular words are desired to make our poem. A particular person is desired as our friend. An object of desire is thus the sum-total of: *a thing conceived in consciousness as a possible object of desire + the conceiving of the possibility of our willing in relation to that thing + the conceiving of that thing as a possibility of our willing.*

(4) OBJECT OF PROPERTY

17.13. A thing is transformed into an object of property when it is installed in a relationship between two or more members of society (individual human beings or subordinate societies of the society). Such relations are created through the application of social power under the constitution of the society. The social power takes the form of legal relations, if the object of property is present, in abstracted form, in a particular legal relation. The social power takes a form other than that of legal relations, if the relevant relationship of the society-members concerned is determined within some other reality (for example, religion or morality or economy).

17.14. Property thus establishes a relationship which is a structure-system integrating four or more relators—the two or more society members involved in the property-relation; society itself; the thing which is the object of the property relation. It is a *structure* in so far as it persists over time and constitutes a more or less settled framework in relation to which the rest of the willing and acting of those involved takes place. It is a *system* in that it enters into the willing and acting of those involved in relation to each other. An object of property affects the transformations which society members make in relation to each other and in relation to some part of the actuality of the physical world.

17.15. The relationship involves the physical world in two senses. The object of property may be a physical thing, a part of the physical world conceived as a thing by consciousness which isolates it from the rest of the otherwise undifferentiated physical world. But the object of property may also be something conceived in consciousness as an object of property, something which is caused by consciousness to be treated as if it were part of the physical world. In other words, anything which can be an object of labour or use or desire can be an object of property.

17.16. An object of property is thus the sum-total of: *the conceiving by consciousness of a species of things as possible objects of property + the conceiving of social relations applicable to that species of things + the conceiving of particular society-members as participating in such social relations + the conceiving of a particular thing as a member of the relevant species of things.* It is apparent that the whole structure-system of society enters into the transformations of things into objects of property, not only society's reality-forming of all kinds but also society's constitution and its subordinate structures and systems. It is apparent also that it is in the total social process of a given society, including its struggle with the perennial dilemmas of society, that potential and actual transformations of things into objects of property take place.

(5) OBJECT OF TRADE

17.17. A thing becomes an object of trade when an object of property is installed in a relationship with other objects of property. Anything that may be an object of property may be an object of trade. The transformation occurs when consciousness conceives of a particular thing—not merely as an object of *labour*, but as the product of an act of labour which has produced a thing which has a relationship to other economically transformed things; not merely as an object of *use* capable of further transformations, but as a thing capable of being transformed into an object of trade; not merely as an object of *desire* subject to my willing and acting, but as a thing capable of being transformed by me into an object of trade; not merely as an object of *property* subject to my social relations with other society members, but as a thing to which those relations can be applied to transform some other object of property.

17.18. A piece of paper may be used to light a cigarette. The same piece of paper may be displayed in a museum. The same piece of paper may be money. A collection of words may be used to praise God. The same collection of words may be set to music and give rise to aesthetic pleasure in an audience. The same collection of words may be copyrighted. The transformations involved take place within consciousness as it conceives of reality (physical reality, social reality, human reality), as it conceives of its relationship to reality, as it conceives of relationships within reality, as it conceives of relationships between consciousnesses and within social consciousness. And the consciousness involved is not only the consciousness of the relevant members of society (individual human beings and subordinate societies) but also the shared consciousness of the society.

17.19. The transformation of a thing into an object of trade thus involves, as in the case of the making of an object of property, the whole structure-system of society and all its reality-forming. However, in the case of an object of trade society generates a particular reality which enables a thing to have an identity which is *intersubjective*. That is to say, it creates structures and systems within society which enable a given thing to be conceived as an object of trade by an unlimited number of members of society. Objects of property are evidently intersubjective in a more limited sense—they must be conceived by more than two members of society as being subject to a given property-relation. And, especially in the case of legal relations of property, they must also be capable of being so conceived by other particular kinds of society-member, especially those administering and enforcing the law.

17.20. In the case of objects of trade, the relevant social structures and systems generate an intersubjectivity which is unlimited in extent. An object of trade is already an object of trade when it is conceived by two persons as having a particular relationship to one other object (barter in its simplest conceivable form). But when more than two persons are involved, society makes it possible that those involved conceive of classes of objects of trade in relatively uniform and persistent ways. To make possible the intersubjectivity of economic transformations, society creates *economic value*.

17.21. Pure and practical theories of society include theories of the economy. The supersocialization of society, the explanation of society in terms of that which transcends it, has been a feature of economic theory, as much as of all other forms of social theory. In particular, economic theory has sought to supersocialize *economic value*. Economic value has seemed to be an essential key to the making and remaking of societies, through the making and remaking of their economies. Through the idea of *value*, attempts have been made to find a supersocial basis for measuring that which is added to a thing by acts of transformation and hence a way to value all the activity which human beings contribute to the social structure-system which is the economy.

17.22. Economic value is one species of *value*. That is to say, its function is as a ground of willing and thereby of acting. Like all other forms of value, it is formed within all the reality-forming of society within the struggle with the perennial dilemmas of society and with a view to reconciling desire and obligation within human consciousness.

17.23. It is evident from all that has been said above that the value added by acts of transformation must be determined by society's reality-forming both as it leads to acts of transformation by society itself and as it modifies the consciousness of individuals and subordinate societies as they carry out acts of transformation. Externally measurable value can be created only as part of the pure and practical theories of a society, as it determines what is of value for that society by forming all of society's words and ideas and theories and values. Internally measurable value is a function of the conceiving of each form of transformation—labour, use, desire, property, trade—and may seem non-contingent to those involved in the process of transformation. But, for other consciousnesses, it is contingent on their conception of the conceiving of those involved in the transformation. The value of a transformation of the physical world is a function of the theories within which the transformation is conceived. And those theories may include scientific theories as to the nature and functioning of the physical universe, theories as to the religious or aesthetic or moral significance of human becoming, theories as to the nature and purpose and functioning of society itself. And the relative values of particular forms of transformation of the physical world may vary substantially over time.

17.24. If the value added by an economic transformation is necessarily contingent, the *price* of an object of trade is also a resultant of many relativities. The price is expressed as a relationship between particular objects of trade, which may themselves vary in perceived value and in price. The price is also relative to the consciousnesses of the seller and the buyer, for whom the same nominal price may have a very different subjective significance in further relation to other things which they value. The price will also be subjectively different for the seller and the buyer if they perceive the object of trade differently, with one perceiving it merely as an object of property and an object of trade while the other perceives it also as an object of use and / or an object of desire. And the price will be present very differently in the consciousness of third parties who observe a transaction of trade and who see the price in terms of their own multiple relativities. The possible perceptions of value and price by third parties may themselves be a factor affecting the price as perceived by the trading parties.

17.25. It follows that the economic structure-system of a society must include some system for establishing value and price so as to make trade possible as a mode of functioning of the society. It must make it possible to stabilize the radical instability and intersubjectivity of value and price so far as objects of trade are concerned. It must, in other words, use social power, and legal relations in particular, to create an artificial structure of value and price. It must use legal relations of all kinds, every aspect of the legal system, to create the social conditions in which trade between trading parties is possible.

17.26. In particular, it must use the legal relations of the so-called law of contract, to create a temporary mutual power-system for the trading parties within which their willing and acting is modified in the social interest, to create relative foreseeability and reliability and certainty. And it must use the law of property to give to the trading parties the degree of control over the object of trade which is necessary to enable their interactive willing and acting to actualize a possible transaction of trade. In making transactions of trade possible on the scale necessary for the survival and prospering of society, society necessarily opens up the economy to all the rest of society's reality-forming, as it uses society's practical theories to form the purposes incorporated in the social power, including the legal relations, which it distributes, including the social power and legal relations necessary to socialize and to stabilize value and price. Value and price thus become part of the most fundamental self-creating of society, part of society's struggle with its perennial self-socializing dilemmas, including the dilemma of justice and social justice.

17.27. To survive and prosper as a society by transforming the physical world, society makes its economy. To make its economy, a society must structure and systematize three things:

(1) the application of natural energy to make transformations of the physical world as necessary for the survival and prospering of the society and its members;

(2) the creation and application of the social power necessary to make possible the transformations required for the survival and prospering of the society and its members;

(3) the forming of the reality within which social and individual willing and acting can occur in fulfilment of (1) and (2), including the reality of economic value.

17.28. As a structure-system within the structure-system of society, the economy is organized under society's *constitution*. Through the legal constitution, the economy forms part of society's structure as it is carried from its past to its future. Through the real constitution, the economy is part of the systematic willing and acting of society in its present-here-and-now, as it chooses among its possibilities and uses its system to actualise those possibilities as transformations of the physical world. Through the ideal constitution, the economy is conceived as possibility, an aspect of society's possibilities which flow from society's own idea of itself, as society knows its world-transforming possibilities.

17.29. As a structure-system under the constitution, the economy is an organization of *social power*. By the *social exchange*, society socializes the natural power of its members (individual human beings and subordinate societies), the natural energy which they can use to make transformations of the physical world. Society gives social power in exchange for the dedication of the natural power to the purposes of society. In so doing, it enables the willing and acting of its members in the transformations of the economy to be integrated with the willing and acting of society. It enables the particular transformational willing and acting of its members to be universalized so as to become the economic willing and acting of society. And it enables the willing and acting of society to be particularized in the most particular economic willing and acting of each of the members of society.

17.30. As a structure-system under the legal constitution, the economy is organized through *legal relations*. By legal relations under the legal constitution, social power is conferred on the constitutional organs of society to create law relating to the economy. The law then creates legal relations to modify the economic willing and acting of the members of society (including the constitutional organs and other subordinate societies), modifying their desire through their conceiving of obligation, empowering their desire through the obligation of others, installing social purpose in all their willing and acting, imposing legal accountability on all their acting. By legal relations, the actuality of the economy is placed in the possibilities conceived by economic actors in society, as they choose to make the transformations which, by their willing and acting, will bring about the survival and prospering of society and its members.

17.31. The economy has come to occupy a dominant place in the structure and the system of societies because the social transformation of the physical world generates an extraordinary phenomenon. A familiar feature in society's self-knowing for thousands of years, it is reflected in various concepts of pure and practical theories of economics: *division of labour, the invisible hand, cumulative causation, the multiplier effect, surplus value.* It reflects the special capacity of a society as a *structure-system.* In the physical transformation of the world, the social aggregation of individual energy can produce effects greater than the sum of the energy introduced into the system. *In the economy a society integrates energy systematically in order to produce surplus social energy.*

17.32. The surplus social energy which is greater than the sum of the input-energies is a product of certain particular features of the economy as a social structure-system. (1) There is a social *momentum* which is caused by the action of energy on energy. Each transformation of the physical world can be made to interact with an unlimited number of other transformations through the systems of society. (2) Energy can be *aggregated* in systems which are capable of making transformations of the physical world which would not be possible for individual members of society, by causing an interaction between the capacities of one member of society and the capacities of others. (3) Energy can be *accumulated* in social systems to be carried from the past into the future, in the structure-systems of all the subordinate societies of society including, for example, industrial and commercial and financial corporations. (4) Society can cause or allow the creation of unlimited forms of subordinate society, each such subordinate society being capable of *intermediate universalizing,* generating possibilities in the social interest, that is to say, both the social interest of the subordinate society and the social interest of the superordinate society which allowed the subordinate society to be created to serve a purpose of the superordinate society.

17.33. (5) Through the *organization of social power,* society as a whole can maximize the social advantage of the interaction of transformations of the physical world, making trnsformations which individual human beings and subordinate societies could not, or would not, make—the provision of the physical infrastructure of society, public services, external defence, and so on. (6) Through the *distribution of social power*, especially in the form of property-power, society is able to organize the interaction of transformations of the physical world, inserting the social interest into all such transformations, ensuring that the application of energy by each individual member of society (human being or subordinate society) serves two purposes at once, an individual and a social purpose. (7) Since so much of the activity of the economy is activity in the human mind, the work of individual and social consciousness, society can use its powerful *reality-forming* capacity to generate the conceptions which give rise to the most socially advantageous transformations of the physical world, for example, by specifically modifying desire (demand, wants, needs, aspirations, ideals) and obligation (duty to work, taxation, charity).

17.34. (8) Society can draw on the *impulse of life* of all its human members, generating in its members a desire to use natural energy for the benefit of society as a whole as well as for individual benefit. By identifying (through reality-forming) individual survival and prospering with the survival and prospering of society, society is able to aggregate and accumulate in the social interest the wonderful and terrible life-creating and life-preserving power of human desire. (9) Through science and technology, society is able to draw on *the necessity of the universe*, the transformations which the physical world makes without human intervention but which can be made to serve social purposes through the reality-forming which is natural science and through the large-scale organization of natural transformations which is the social power of technology.

17.35. The surplus energy produced from the social systematization of energy is reintroduced into the system and contributes to the generation of further energy, including surplus energy. So the cycle is endlessly repeated and, in principle, society can generate ever higher levels of social energy to be applied for social purposes. Society can *develop*, as it is called. It can forever increase in complexity and sophistication, forever increase the generation of surplus social energy, forever carry out more and more of its self-conceived purposes, forever satisfy more and more of its self-conceived needs and wants, forever actualizing more and more of its possibilities as a society. The economic system of society can develop itself progressively in accordance with the purposes of society. By means of its economy, society can increase its own well-being, subject only to limits imposed on itself, by its own self-conceiving, its own capacity to create itself as a structure and a system within consciousness. Society has power over its own well-being, a power which is self-determined as it creates its self.

17.36. So it is that the economy of a society may be seen as a particular structure-system within the general structure-system of society whose function is to organize the transformation of the physical world in the social interest—(1) through the conceiving of society's reality-for-itself, which enables society to operate the economy in and through consciousness, generating the words and ideas and theories and values which the economy requires, including the valuation of different forms of economic transformation; (2) through the constitution, including the distribution of constitutional power to the organs having authority in the public realm of society and including the system for creating the legal relations necessary for the economy; (3) through the delegation of social power of all possible kinds, including the delegation of property-power in an unlimited range of possible forms to an unlimited range of possible power-holders, subject to an unlimited range of possible terms of delegation, as the social interest requires; (4) through the making of the actual legal relations required to modify the willing and acting of members of society (human individuals and subordinate societies) with a view to bringing about the transformations which the economy requires and with a view to the interacting and aggregating of such transformations; (5) through the total social process of society, as society struggles with its perennial dilemmas to determine the actual delegation of actual social power, including the struggle to reconcile justice and social justice. Such is the economy of any society, from the society of the family to the international society of the whole human race, the society of all societies.

17.37. In a misconceived international society, there cannot be other than a misconceived international economy. In a misconceived international economy, international society cannot organize the social transformation of the physical world for the survival and prospering of the whole human race. In the self-conceiving of international society as an interstatal unsociety, the international economy is conceived as a residual and non-systematic anomy.

17.38. (1) The international economy is conceived as *residual*, because international society itself is conceived as the interacting of the public realms of the state-societies, accompanied by a non-socialized interacting of the non-public realms of the state-societies. In such a conception, the transforming energy present in the international economy is an externalization, a set of external effects, deriving from a set of intrinsically independent, non-international structure-systems of economic transformation. International economic transformation is merely an aggregation of the epiphenomena of state-society economic transformations which happen to have cross-frontier effects.

17.39. (2) The international economy is conceived as *non-systematic* because international society, not conceiving of itself as a society, does not conceive of itself as having the capacity to form the multiple reality-for-itself without which the organization of social transformations of the physical world is impossible. An economy is a sub-structure-system of the structure-system of a society and can function as such only within the total social process which the society generates.

17.40. (3) The international economy is conceived as an *anomy*, because international society, not having the capacity to form a reality-for-itself, is not capable of forming the pure and practical theories which would enable it, in particular, to determine its purposes. And hence it is unable to generate social power through the social exchange (the socializing of human transforming energy in exchange for the acceptance of social purpose). And hence it has been unable to establish an economy-embracing socionomy, a structure of social obligation as conceived within a society, including the legal relations necessary for the universalizing of particular economic willing and acting, the particularizing of universal economic willing and acting.

17.41. The international economy as residual, non-systematic anomy has thus been prevented from generating the ever-increasing surplus social energy which is generated by an economy as it makes use of the inherent possibilities of its structure-system. The international economy has been unable to ensure the sustained and accelerating *development* of all its subordinate societies, the ever-increasing *well-being* of the whole human race.

17.42. An economy depends, above all, on law. The legal system embodies the products of society's struggle with its perennial dilemmas in forms which enable the economy to contain within itself both stability and change. The law enables the economy to carry in the very structure of society the products of past social transformations of the physical world, in the form of constitutional power and property-power but also in the form of all other legal relations of the economy. But the law also enables society to contain in its very system the dynamic self-creating and self-developing power of social transformations of the physical world, organizing the willing and acting of every organ of the society, every subordinate society, every individual human being who is a member of the society.

17.43. The inadequacy of the misconceived international economy has intersected with the inadequacy of misconceived international law to disable international society as a structure-system of human well-being. The actual lived reality of the international economy has become a scene of disordered, not to say frenzied, social energy, particularly through the effects of international capitalism (to be considered in Chapter 18). But international law has not only failed to bring order to such developments. It has contributed to the disorder. It is possible to construct an image of the anomy of the international economy by recalling a series of fundamental and notorious problems which the international economy has posed for the self-conceiving of international society and its law. They are symptoms and symbols of the underdevelopment of international society as a society, of the international economy as an economy, of international law as a legal system. (They are stated below in the conventional terms of contemporary international law, rather than in the light of the conceptions of the New International Law proposed in the present study.)

(1) EXPLOITATION OF THE INTERNATIONAL DEEP SEABED

17.44. Since the international deep seabed is, as a matter of contemporary international law, said to be outside the territorial sovereignty of all of the states, is any one of those states, and its nationals, entitled to extract and exploit, unilaterally and at will, the natural resources of the area? If so, is there any obligation on the state concerned to share the benefits of the resources with others? Or are the resources of the area in some sense the common property of humanity? If so, how are they to be exploited communally and how can they be protected from abusive exploitation?

(2) EXPLOITATION OF OUTER SPACE

17.45. Since outer space, including the other planets and the Moon are, as a matter of contemporary international law, said to be outside the territorial sovereignty of all of the states, is any one of those states and its nationals, entitled to exploit outer space militarily or scientifically or commercially, unilaterally and at will? If so, is there any obligation not to exploit outer space in certain ways or to limit the terrestrial effects of such exploitation or to share the benefits of such exploitation? Or is outer space in some sense the common property of humanity? If so, how can it be exploited communally and how can it be protected from abusive exploitation?

(3) SOVEREIGNTY OVER NATURAL RESOURCES *VERSUS* THE WRONG OF EXPROPRIATION

17.46. Do the sovereign rights of a state in the natural resources contained in the territory of which it is sovereign include a sovereign governmental power to nationalize or otherwise expropriate the investment (contractual rights and / or quasi-property rights) or a foreign investor lawfully extracting or otherwise exploiting those natural resources, so that a right of the national state of the investor is not, in principle, violated if the territorial state exercises such a governmental power? Or is such nationalization or expropriation in principle a wrong (violation of right) committed by the territorial state against the national state of the investor?

(4) STATE CONTRACTS

17.47. When a state concludes a contract with a non-state body (for example, an industrial or commercial or financial enterprise; for example, a concession agreement to exploit natural resources or an investment agreement to establish a capital project or a loan agreement), does the contract modify the state's inherent rights of government in its own territory or do those rights remain unmodified or are they modified to a certain extent? If so, to whom is the modification of right owed as an obligation—the investor or the investor's national-state or both? Under what legal system is such modification enforceable—international law, the law of the contracting state, some other legal system?

(5) STATE IMMUNITY

17.48. Given that, in principle under contemporary international law, one state is not subject to the jurisdiction of another state's courts (because of the sovereign equality of the states), does a state lose that immunity if it engages in an economic transaction which is of a kind which a non-state person engages in, even if the transaction is of a kind perceived by that state as an aspect of its governmental function?

(6) LIMITS TO NATIONAL JURISDICTION

17.49. Given that the concept of territorial sovereignty means that a state's inherent powers, legislative and executive and judicial, may, in principle, only be exercised in respect of events occurring in its territory, and given that economic transactions may take effect in more than one state's territory, should a state be prevented from controlling economic transactions which have an effect in its territory but which are the product of activities conducted elsewhere? Or should a state be entitled to control such transactions, even if it thereby controls activities taking place within another state's territory?

(7) CROSS-FRONTIER DAMAGE

17.50. In the event that damage is caused in the territory of one state from a cause occurring in a neighbouring state (assuming that it is a cause which the government of the neighbouring state could have prevented by the exercise of internal sovereign powers), how can international law give to the injured state a right to compensation for damage to its territory, without giving the neighbouring state a right to justify its own action on economic grounds (cost of preventing the cause of damage, economic freedom of the actual originator of the damage)?

(8) ECONOMIC AND SOCIAL HUMAN RIGHTS

17.51. Given that international law has assimilated the idea of human rights, albeit government-conceived and government-controlled human rights, and given that economic and social structures are an integral part of the social structure of a state, how can international law give effect to political and civil human rights without giving effect to economic and social human rights? But how can international law give effect to economic and social human rights without first establishing a common conception of the economic and social structure of which they are an integral part?

(9) WORLD ENVIRONMENT

17.52. Given that the land- and the sea- and the air-spaces of the planet Earth are shared, and are not naturally distributed among the states of the world, and given that world-transforming activities, especially economic activities, can have effects, directly or cumulatively, on large parts of the world environment, how can international law reconcile the inherent and fundamental independence of the states with the inherent and fundamental interdependence of the world environment? How could legal control of activities adversely affecting the world environment be instituted, given that such activities may be fundamental to the economies of particular states?

(10) UNEQUAL EXCHANGE *VERSUS* ECONOMIC SELF-DETERMINATION

17.53. In the international economy, the value and the price of a commodity are often determined in market-places not controlled, or even influenced, by the states in whose territory the commodity is produced, when they are acting as sellers; and, when they are acting as buyers, the value and the price of the commodities which they buy are often determined in market-places which they do not control or even influence. How can the inherent sovereignty of such states be reconciled with their inherent economic dependence?

(11) UNEQUAL ECONOMIC DEVELOPMENT

17.54. Within a state, the constitutional structure of the state and the particular structure of its economy may bring about a distributive effect, so that the outcome of the exercise of political and economic and legal power in relation to economic transactions is determined not only by interactions between non-state persons but also by governmental policy designed to produce what is conceived as a fair society. Such an effect may call for the exercise of governmental powers in relation to the economy as a whole (taxation, interest rates, wage and price controls, subsidies, regional aid, social legislation). How can such a distributive effect by governmental action occur in the international economy, given that the inherent powers of individual states are powers in relation only to the part of the international economy which is within their respective individual sovereignties and given that there are no international constitutional organs with distributive economic power?

(12) THE USE OF ECONOMIC FORCE

17.55. Given that international law has established some legal controls on the use of physical force in international relations and has achieved some socialization of the physical use of force in the general public interest, how can international law regulate uses of economic power which can have adverse effects on the survival and prospering of states as significant as the use of physical force (boycotts, embargoes, economic counter-measures, discriminatory trading conditions, differential consumer protection, discriminatory investment policies, trade protection, non-tariff barriers to trade, the manipulation of intellectual property rights, dumping, predatory pricing, seller- and buyer-monopolies, producer and consumer cartels)? But how could international law identify illegitimate uses of economic power when international society, communally, could not identify legitimate uses of economic power?

17.56. These twelve problems of the international economy, as it intersects with international law, are characteristic problems of a society as it struggles to create itself, to socialize itself, to form and to realize its purposes, as it struggles with each of the perennial dilemmas of society. They are typical problems of any dynamic society anywhere. They are essentially dilemma-problems, in the sense that they cannot have definitive solutions. They must be dealt with on a continuing basis, dialectically, as all of society's reality-forming, all of its words and ideas and theories and values, interacts with the lived reality of everyday life, interacts with actual human wants and needs and aspirations. In an international economy which is not the economy of an international society, using an international law which is not the law of an international society, they must be faced non-systematically, piecemeal, pragmatically.

17.57. It is instructive to see the way in which international society since 1945 has dealt with such fundamental and structural problems. It is eloquent testimony to both the inadequacy and the potentiality of an international economy-in-waiting within an international society-in-waiting. The expedient solutions which have been generated by misconceived international society and its law are impressive in their imaginative diversity. Taken together they may seem to form a golden thread leading to a new conception of the international economy:

(1) *International organizations.* As considered in Chapters 13 and 15 above, so-called international organizations have been a form of communalizing of the interacting public realms of the states, especially in matters relating to the international economy, a communalizing which is tending to the formation of an independent international public realm.

(2) *General Agreement on Tariffs and Trade.* At a particularly propitious moment, a group of state-societies which had played a leading part in the development of the international economy, agreed an international policy concerning national policies on inter-state trading restrictions. They gave legislative effect to that policy in treaty-form, creating appropriate legal relations, including enforcement procedures.

(3) *International Monetary Fund.* At the same propitious moment, a group of state-societies agreed an international policy concerning national policies on the stabilization and control of currency-values. They gave legislative effect to that policy in treaty-form, creating appropriate legal relations and appropriate institutional arrangements.

(4) *Commodity organizations.* In relation to trade in certain basic products, the communalizing of intergovernmental action has gone further than in relation to trade in general, to include a form of communal organizing of the relevant product-market through international policy-making and communal intervention in the market. Again, the agreed policy was given legislative effect in treaty-form, creating appropriate legal relations and appropriate institutional arrangements.

(5) *Development assistance.* The lack of an overall capacity to redistribute wealth in the international economy has led to *ad hoc* arrangements of many different kinds (loans, grants, investment guarantees, subsidies, technical assistance, trade preferences), created by the state-societies by unilateral action (under national legislation), by bilateral and multilateral agreement, and communally through international organizations.

(6) *New International Economic Order. Charter of Economic Rights and Duties of States.* An effort has been made to agree communally a world economic policy in relation to the problem of unequal economic development in the international economy. It consists of policy goals, policy targets, and policy commitments. Its purpose is to form a basis for the willing and acting of state-societies, individually and communally, and for the formation of specific legal relations.

(7) *Economic unions.* Neighbouring state-societies have formed economic systems (free-trade areas, customs unions, economic unions, the European Community) which transcend their national economies and which involve communal policy-making, leading to the communal formation of specific legal relations. They have done so on the basis of legal relations under international law, legislated in treaty-form. In the case of the European Community, the legal relations of the treaties, and further legal relations made by delegation thereunder, have direct internal effect in the member states, with the result that the Community forms a communal public realm, especially in the economic field, shared by a number of state-societies.

(8) *World physical environment.* The state-societies have acknowledged a communal responsibility for the world physical environment, including the acceptance of elements of world environment policy and the creation of institutional arrange-

ments making possible the agreeing of further environment policies and the formation of specific legal relations.

(9) *Law of the Sea*. The state-societies have legislated in treaty-form, creating joint policies and specific legal relations and communal institutional arrangements governing every aspect of the oceans of the world as an intrinsically shared area and shared resource and establishing a communal regime for the exploitation of the international deep seabed.

(10) *World commercial and financial markets*. The overwhelming surplus energy of socialized economic activity has generated world markets in every traded physical object of trade and world financial markets in every non-material object of trade. They have given rise to international means of payment (either national currencies treated as international currencies or cross-frontier payments which do not enter any particular national economy). Although such markets and such transactions have their roots in the policy and the law of particular state-societies, they behave as socializing institutions of a world-wide economy. They are not substantially under the control of any one state-society, its social process and its legal system.

(11) *International contracts*. The special nature of complex international transactions has led to the development of a species of international contracts, between state-societies and non-state persons and between non-state-persons, creating a system of legal relations applying to the parties but which are either entirely delocalized (not purporting to be created under the legal system of any particular state-society) or are artificially localized (deemed to be created under the legal system of a particular legal system chosen by the parties).

(12) *Multinational corporations*. The internationalization of the production and distribution of objects of trade has led to the development of industrial and commercial and financial corporations which are themselves aggregations of corporations formed under the legal systems of several state-societies. The resulting multinational corporation, although its roots may be substantially in one particular state-society, forms its policy and hence its legal relations in the light of its international situation. They are not substantially under the control of any one state-society, its social process and its legal system.

(13) *World technology.* The transformation of the physical world by the application of science in the form of technology is a capacity shared by the whole of humanity. The development of technology has taken on an overwhelming momentum, transforming the whole world through the development of methods of agricultural and industrial production and methods of commerce, through medicine, through the production of objects of mass consumption, including mass entertainment. Even if it may have particular roots in this or that national economy and its legal system, the development and application of technology is now intrinsically international in organization and effect.

(14) *World mixed economy.* The international economy is accordingly a mixed economy in two important senses. It is partly an economy organizing the transactions of non-state actors, determined by their policies and legal relations; and it is partly an economy organized by the state-societies in their interacting public realms. It is also an economy which contains many subordinate economic systems, of many different kinds, at many different stages of development, pursuing many differing kinds of policy in the light of diverse ideas and theories and values (especially practical theories of society and the economy), each having its own legal system with its own ethos and its own legal constitution and its own structure of substantive legal relations.

(15) *World economic environment.* The international economy is accordingly now an economic environment which is shared by every state-society and every other form of subordinate society of international society and hence by every human being. As in the case of the world physical environment, the state-societies recognize as a matter of practical policy, if not as a matter of social theory, that all subordinate economies of the international economy are interdependent, so that not only small-scale events and transactions interact with each other over long distances, but also large-scale developments, including so-called economic crises, affect the whole world.

17.58. International society since 1945 has thus been a scene of intense *ad hoc* social engineering within the echoing waste-land which is the international economy. The international economy will become the economy of a society like any other in the course of time. In the reconceiving of international society there will be contained, as an essential part, the reconceiving of the international economy.

17.59. Remove the metaphysical partitioning of the imaginary state-frontiers from the face of the Earth and what is to be seen? The human species multiplying, rapidly. The human species transforming the whole Earth into an object of labour through the application of human energy. The human species using the energy of the Sun and the energy contained in the Earth to transform the whole Earth into an object of use, a second world created for human use from within the mind of humanity. The human species imagining—recreating the whole universe as a possible arena for human willing and acting, as an object of desire. The human species reasoning—co-ordinating and organizing its Earth-transforming activity to make the whole Earth into an object of property. The human species co-operating—generating unlimited surplus social energy from the interacting of its world-transforming efforts, transforming the whole Earth, everything on it and in it, into an object of trade.

17.60. And yet it is generally supposed that the conceiving of the international economy as the economy of an international society which is a society cannot be among the possibilities which humanity can make into one of its purposes, cannot be a possibility which humanity can choose to actualize. It is generally supposed that, in the case of the international economy, there are insuperable obstacles in the way of its being conceived as an integral part of humanity's self-socializing.

17.61. A particular obstacle is thought to be that, given the central role that property has played in the conceiving of national economies, there is no possibility of ever conceiving of an idea of *property* capable of forming the conceptual basis of an international economy. And such an obstacle is also commonly conceived in more general terms. It is thought that, given that the economy is an integral part of the total self-creating of a society involving all of its reality-forming, there is no possibility that a world characterized by opposing *economic ideologies* could ever become a world which is able to form the single systematic reality of a single international economy.

17.62. The idea of *property* has played a major part in social self-conceiving, in constitutional struggles, in revolutionary social change, in the struggle of societies with their perennial self-socializing dilemmas. Property has been used by societies to establish the power-structure of their economies, as an essential part of the structure of the economy which enables the system of the economy to be conveyed from society's past to its future through the present-here-and-now. Property has played a leading role in society's struggle to find its theories, pure and practical. It has played a leading role in each particular society's struggle with the perennial dilemmas of social self-creating. And it has played a leading role in real-world historical struggles to make and remake constitutions through the total social process and through counter-constitutional activity, including the use of force to bring about and to resist constitutional change. Property has thus played a major part (1) in social theory-making, (2) in constitution-making, and (3) in the distribution of power in the name of social justice.

17.63. (1) In the struggle of theory, property has, again and again, been the subject of supersocializing. Particular pure and practical theories of society have contained the idea that property is not merely the creation of a given society as part of its self-creating but is something having a basis beyond any given society, in the nature of all society, or in so-called human nature, or even in the nature of the order of the universe. The idea that property is thus in some way supernatural is then made available either to defend the existing system of property in a given society or as a ground for altering the existing system of property in a given society. Very often, it is used to do both things at once—to defend the existing system of a given society, to condemn the system of property in another society; to condemn the existing system of a given society, to extol the system of property in another society.

17.64. One feature of the supersocializing of property has been a tendency to hypostatize property, to conceive of it as having substance, to conceive of it as something other than a word referring to certain forms of social power. *Rights in property, real and personal property, tangible and intangible property, industrial and intellectual property, property-holder, property-owner, property transfer, public property, private property, state property, law of property.* Such phrases generate the idea that property is something analogous in its reality, in its substance, to the physical land or the physical object in respect of which property-power is held. Such an idea can then form a part of this or that social theory, designed to make property seem as natural and solid as the physical world, designed to make a particular distribution of property-power seem to be a product of, or a violation of quasi-natural laws of the physical world. When the idea of property takes on a quasi-material character, it is liable to become a part of the self-identifying of members of society, to call for self-defending as much as the personality, the body, the hearth and home. It is liable to attract to itself the ideas and the passions which are generated by the idea not merely of prospering but even of survival.

17.65. (2) The reason for the remarkably theoretical and remarkably violent character of the struggle of property-power is partly tactical. Those seeking to defend or to overthrow the existing distribution of property-power are liable to invoke theory to justify fundamental change and to resort to force, if theory is not powerful enough to bring about change. But a further reason for the exceptionally high energy-levels attaching to the idea of property is that property-power seems to be involved with constitutional power, with power over the public realm, the willing and acting by certain members of society in constitutional organs, in the name of, and on behalf of, society as a whole. Property seems to be involved in the distribution of ultimate power in society.

17.66. It is a tribute to the central role of the economy in the self-creating of a state-society that the struggle to control the government of the public realm can seem to be a struggle to control the economy, and vice versa. As society's structure-system for transforming the physical world in the social interest, the economy has to be a major part of a society's legal system, and the legal system has to play a major part in organizing society's economy. It is particularly in the legal constitution, and in the legal relations made under the legal constitution, that the structure and the system of the economy is embodied, since it must be carried from society's past into its future. The unique contribution of the law, as one form of social power, to the system of the economy is that law is social power from the past, which presents itself to present willing-and-acting as a relatively ineluctable fact (in comparison with other social phenomena), beyond modification in the present-here-and-now, except as part of universalizing willing on behalf of society as a whole. Since the generation of surplus energy by the economy is dependent on its structure and its system, it follows that the law plays the privileged role of embodying the established structure-system within which the energy of the economy is organized systematically.

17.67. (3) By placing a supernaturalized idea of property in the pure theory recognized by a given society, it becomes possible to place one or other derived idea of property in the practical theory of that society, and hence to make property a matter of internal contention, theoretical and practical, within the total social process of that society. In particular, within a statally organizing society with a public realm subject to the authority of government, property is a major element of the dialectic of politics, as the members of society take part in society's struggle with its perennial dilemma of *justice and social justice.*

17.68. Property is power over the physical world socialized, but socialized as part of society's system. Property is a delegation of power by society which causes the energy of the property-holder to be integrated with the energy of other society-members. Property is thus at the root of the systematic organization of energy which is the economy of a society. Like all other legal relations, the legal relation which is described as property-holding is a network of legal relations, a network which cannot be stated completely unless it is a statement of all other legal relations in society, up to and including the legal relations of the legal constitution. Since all legal relations in society are necessarily connected with all others in the system of the legal constitution, the legal relations of property have effect as an integral part of the whole structure of legal relations. Property-relations are power-relations, modifying the willing and acting of all members of society in relation to each other.

17.69. Property-power may be distributed in any form to any member of society. Property-power may be distributed, to this or that extent, to individual human beings and to subordinate societies of any kind, including public-realm bodies and non-public-realm bodies. In other words, society may confer property-power on bodies acting for and in the name of society as a whole, or on bodies acting on their own account, or on bodies acting both for society as a whole and on their own account (industrial and commercial and financial corporations, nationalized industries, state-trading enterprises, public authorities, collectives and communes, charities, non-profit bodies, and so on *ad libitum*).

17.70. Property-power may be delegated in relation to anything which can be the subject of transformation in and through human consciousness. It can apply to the most literally physical of transformations, such as the use of the land to produce crops and animals for human consumption. It can apply to the most abstract of transformations, such as the generation of ideas of theory. The world can be reconceived in consciousness, as necessary to make possible the delegation of the social power of property. A person may be reconceived as a slave or an employee, metals and paper reconceived as money, land reconceived as an estate, a physical object reconceived as a work of art, electrical impulses reconceived as a television programme. And the delegation of power may constitute any form of human society as a power-holder, from the society of the family to the international society of the whole human race, and including every conceivable kind of intermediate constitutional organ, public authority, company, corporation, enterprise.

17.71. Whatever the nature of the particular property-power or the particular property power-holder, the property-power is delegated by society, so that the social interest is included in the delegation. The terms of the delegation may include either that the transformations generated by the exercise of the property-power are benefits of society as a whole (that they become the property of society as a whole) or that they are benefits of the power-holder (that they become subject to further property-power of the power-holder). In the latter case, it is determined, in conferring the property-power, that the social interest may be achieved by allowing the property-holder to continue to apply energy to make transformations under the property-power, subject always to the assumption that society may choose to derive benefit from such further individual application of energy.

17.72. By taxation society is able to share in delegated property-power. By taxation society takes a part of the benefits accruing from the transformations generated by the exercise of the property-power delegated by society. Taxation was thus conceived, from the earliest days of human society, as a means of socializing individual effort. A share in those benefits is retained by society to be applied elsewhere as property-power, through the creation of some social system which itself socializes some aspect of energy, or through a transfer of the property-power, in the form of a social benefit, to a member of society other than the original property-holder.

17.73. Because the idea of property has played so central a role in the social struggles of subordinate societies of international society, especially in the development of the state-societies, taking on the aura of a veteran warrior of countless social struggles, it has generated a trauma in the ruling-class of all societies, for whom the defence of so-called property-rights or else the revolutionary reassignment of so-called property-rights is central to their conception of the social interest and of social purposes. For those who exercise governmental power in the state-societies, property is an idea which cannot be allowed out on its own in a dangerous world. Not only may it escape the control of suitable reality-forming, necessary to give it a satisfactory content. But also it may return changed by its experiences of the outside world. Having left home as a friend of power, it may return home as a subversive.

17.74. The result is that the social power of property is a necessary and fundamental feature of the actual functioning of the international economy and yet the idea of property is not integrated into the self-conceiving of international society. The only form of property known to misconceived international society is the false-property of so-called sovereignty over territory which, as noted in Chapter 16 above, has used the aura of property to sustain and enforce within consciousness the structure of the international society of the so-called states.

17.75. The consequence of this discontinuity in international society (presence of the actuality of property / absence of the idea of property) is that all of the international economy which is not part of the interacting of the public realms of the state-societies is not integrated into the conception of international society and international law. And this means that most of the social power which is exercised internationally is neither socially nor legally accountable within international society.

17.76. If the nature and function of property in international society is conceived in the same way as the nature and function of property in any society, which has been considered above, then the trauma of property in international society can be overcome. All property is power. Property-power is social power which may take the form of legal relations. This is true as much of property in international society as of property within subordinate societies of international society, including the state-societies. All property-power is delegated, in international society as in national society, by society in the social interest, in the same way as all other forms of social power, all other forms of legal power. The social interest, of international society as of national society, is that the individual power-holder should be able to will and act individually, serving an individual interest, but in ways (determined in the delegating of the power) which contribute eventually to the social interest, to the survival and prospering of the whole society and of all its members. The individual willing and acting in the exercise of property-power, as of any power, is accountable socially and also legally (in the form of determinations as to the legal limits of the power and as to whether specific willing and acting is within those limits). The exercise of all international property-power is similarly accountable.

17.77. Because the international legal system ignores the existence of social power other than the power of the state-societies, the exercise of international property-power by non-state actors is not legally accountable to international society, and is socially accountable only in a very weak form. This means that all the economic power exercised by non-state actors, including industrial and commercial and financial enterprises of all kinds, is legally accountable, if at all, only through national legal systems. National legal systems, as systems of subordinate societies of international society, have it as part of their function to serve the social interest of international society. But the social interest of international society can only be served partially and intermittently and unreliably and unsystematically by such residual legal accountability. International society cannot take control of its survival and prospering unless it takes control, in consciousness, of the total reality of the international economy, as a structure-system of the structure-system of international society.

17.78. International law, as properly conceived, must therefore control all the property-power which is exercised internationally in the form of legal relations. It follows that, like national legal systems, international law must abandon the conceptual category of *subjects of international law*, the words which have been used to identify the participants in international legal relations. The law of the subordinate societies of international society, including the state-societies, applies to all those to whom it applies—that is to say, to all those who participate in legal relations under the legal system. Those persons may include citizens of the state-society, but they may also include any other person who, by physical presence within a given area or otherwise, participates in legal relations under that system. And the participants in legal relations may be individual human beings or any other kind of person or society as determined by the legal system itself, as it chooses to delegate legal power in the social interest.

17.79. Thus international law also does not have *a priori* subjects of international law. The two supposed kinds of subject of international law—so-called *states and international organizations*—are only two among the countless participants in international legal relations. It would not be possible to list definitively the participants in international legal relations. It can only be said that they are as numerous and various as the needs of international society demand and the actual legal relations of international law recognize.

17.80. As constitutional organs of international society, the state-societies and the international organizations formed by the state-societies play, within the current constitution of international society, an exceptional role in governing the public realm of international society and, in particular, in law-making, in the creating of new legal relations, both the legal relations of international law and the legal relations of their respective societies. But, especially in the international economy, the exercise of property-power by non-state actors, including legal property-power, is at least as important in determining the survival and prospering of the international society of the whole human race. It is at least as important that there should be social and legal accountability for the activities of the non-state actors as for the activities of the state-societies and of international organizations.

17.81. The developments referred to in paragraph 17.57 above show that a new international law is developing in spite of itself, an international law which concerns itself naturally with every aspect of the international law economy, regardless of the status of the actors involved. Nothing in the international economy is alien to the new international law. International law will develop the substance and the system of every area of law which affects the actual international economy, which affects the actual survival and prospering of humanity, as each state-society has had to develop one area of law after another to respond to the needs of developing national economies— property law, contract law, corporation law, commercial law, fiscal law, insurance law, intellectual property law, consumer protection law, environment law.

17.82. In so doing, international society will transcend so-called ideological conflicts. The deceptive and dangerous word *ideology* is used to refer to the particular amalgam of theories— practical and pure and transcendental theories—which determines the reality-for-itself of a given society. The word is used, like the word *property*, to suggest that such theories have taken on a hypostatic substance within a given society, to suggest that they are so fundamental a part of the structure of a given society that they transcend the total social process of that society, that they are, in some sense, prior and decisive in relation to all other social reality-forming. Such a linguistic tactic is used both by those within the society who have an interest in supersocialising a particular set of theories, and by those outside a society who have an interest in making the society into an irredeemable *other*.

17.83. Following the view of the nature and functioning of a society which has been proposed in the present volume, it is not possible to regard any particular reality-for-itself of a society as beyond redemption, beyond change. On the contrary, the total social process inevitably leads to perpetual change of the social reality-for-itself. The function of all society's reality-forming processes is not merely to transport the past into the future but also to actualize the possibilities of the future, transforming them into society's past through the social process of the present-here-and now. Even the legal constitution, with its function of carrying the structure-system of society from the past into the present, is itself a part of the perpetual struggle of society's self-creating.

17.84. International society, like any other society, is able to live with the diverse realities of its subordinate societies, each a reality-for-itself within the reality-for-itself of the subordinate society. But the diverse subordinate realities themselves change. There could, in the future, as well be post-capitalism and post-socialism as there could be any other new reality. And there could be a reality which is neither socialist economics nor capitalist economics but simply international economics. International society cannot avoid having its own reality-for-itself. International society already has its own reality-for-itself, transcending all the different realities of its subordinate societies, including the state-societies. It already has its own theories, including its theories of the international economy, whether or not it recognizes them as such and whether or not it has taken control over their development, as part of the total social process of international society. International society already has an international economy. It is an international economy which is waiting for an international society which knows itself as a society.

18 International Culture

18.1. The *culture* of a society is the society seen as a whole, all that it has made of itself as actuality, all that it has conceived of itself as possibility. Its culture is not something conceived within the society as part of its reality-for-itself. The culture of a society is not part of its total social process, as it struggles with the perennial dilemmas of society to create itself as society. It is not part of such things, because they are part of it. The culture of a society is the reality of society's reality-for-itself. It is the totality of all the processing of society's total social process, the imagination of its imagining, the reason of its reasoning. The culture of a society is the society as *spirit*.

18.2. *Spirit* is a hypothesis which remains necessary when a particular thing has been explained in terms of its structure and system. When willing and acting is explained as a function of consciousness which enables human beings, as living things, to transform the world with a view to human survival and prospering, and when survival and prospering is understood in relation to purposes which human beings and societies extract from among their self-conceived possibilities, which they choose in the present-here-and-now as they make the future into the past, and when social self-creating is explained as the creating by imagination and reason of a reality-for-itself (of religion, mythology, philosophy, history, art, science, morality, economy, law) within which possibilities have value, and when the becoming of society is explained as society's endless socializing struggle with the perennial dilemmas of society within the total social process—when all these things are explained, there remains the question of society as *totality*, the total effect of the structure-system of a particular society, the effect which surpasses all actual conceiving and self-conceiving in society, all actual self-creating and socializing, that which makes a particular society into a unique society, with a unique identity. There remains the question not of society-through-itself (society created by itself) nor of society-for-itself (society conceived by itself) but of society-in-itself (society conceived as totality).

18.3. The culture of a particular society is not only spirit as totality. If it also spirit as *self-transcendence*. Human consciousness, as it forms and is formed by society, is nevertheless able to transcend itself and society. It is not only able to do so. It is unable not to do so. It is able to do so, by the power of an imagination and a reason which do not know their own limits. It is unable not to do so, because it cannot prevent itself from conceiving of a world which is not simply the product of human willing and acting. The world of human willing and acting, through individual and social consciousness, does not exhaust the world conceived by consciousness. There is the physical world within which human consciousness places the human being as body, with brain and nervous system, and to which much of human reality-forming is devoted. But there is also the totality of the all-that-is which includes, but surpasses, human consciousness and of which our reality-for-ourselves, all the work of accumulated social consciousness, is some sort of a shadow or reflection or intimation.

18.4. The totality of all-that-is is a reality about which we may maintain a respectful silence, because it is beyond our conceiving. Or else it is a reality about which we may form unlimited realities-for-ourselves in mythology, religion, philosophy, art, natural science, and economy, adjusting our willing and acting accordingly. Or else it is a reality which we can simply ignore, conducting our lives as if there were no reality beyond the actual contents of individual and social consciousness. But whichever practical strategy we adopt, it is a reality which will never cease to present itself to human consciousness, so long as human consciousness has imagination (to create conceptions of the universe) and reason (to order its conceptions of the universe). The world beyond the world made by human consciousness is a world which, since it is not a world made by human willing and acting, is a world without time and without space. And so it is a world which consciousness cannot inhabit and appropriate, but which consciousness cannot leave.

18.5. The culture of a particular society is not merely spirit as totality and spirit as self-transcendence. It is also spirit as *self-judgement*. The self-transcending of a society's totality is not merely a form of freedom, not merely a social freedom-of-the-will, liberating us, in the last resort, from the constraints of the social structure-system, as freedom of the individual will is conceived by consciousness as liberating individual human beings from the mere physiology of the body. It is certainly a form of empowering, but it also a form of constraining participation, as consciousness shares in the necessity of a world which surpasses it. Consciousness is obliged to transcend itself. To be conscious is to be conscious that we are not conscious of everything. To be conscious is to be conscious that either our consciousness is part of some consciousness which far surpasses it or else that our consciousness is one aspect of something which far surpasses consciousness.

18.6. The consciousness of a world beyond consciousness introduces an additional dimension into all human socializing. It is the dimension of *relativity from beyond-relativity*, the dimension of judgement. It is the dimension which makes every human measurement relative and provisional and partial, because it is a dimension which is beyond human measurement. It is the dimension which makes it possible to see that even society and even human consciousness are limited, finite, and bounded. It is the dimension which makes it possible to see society as a whole, as if we were seeing it from outside. As a structure-system, society is hypothetically closed, using its own reality to make itself grow as an organized whole in relation to other societies, including co-ordinate and super-ordinate societies, in relation to the rest of the physical world, and in relation to its own idea of the rest of all-that-is. But all of the self-creating of a society is also activity within a world which is outside the range of society's willing and acting but which is not a matter of indifference to society.

18.7. It is the aspect of the spirit of a society as judgement which suggests to us also that all social activity is determined by dilemmas which will never be finally resolved, full of paradoxes and mysteries and uncertainties which will never be finally elucidated. As each peak of unknowing is conquered, another comes into view. The self-judging spirit of society suggests to us that society is necessarily and permanently imperfect and incomplete, always developing. It does these things by enabling us to conceive, in a world beyond society, of what it would be to be more perfect, more complete, more developed, as human individuals and as societies. The spiritual dimension of a particular society, which that society makes but does not choose and cannot escape, is the dimension of the ideal, the idea of all our ideas, the potentiality of all our possibilities, the direction of all our becoming, the ultimate source of all our imagining, the ultimate order of all our reasoning.

18.8. The culture of a society is spirit—totality, self-tran-scendence, self-judgement. The culture of a society is not hypothesis. It is an available actuality, available to human consciousness. It is available to those outside a given society, available to the *other* of a given society—co-ordinate societies, superordinate societies, human individuals outside the society. The internal perspective of a society is also, necessarily and unavoidably, an external perspective. The society as a whole, its culture, is available outside the society. It is available to become part of the reality-forming of other societies and their members, as they make their own selves, as they become their own cultures. And, because it is available to the *other* of the given society, it enters into the forming of that society's *self*. In forming its self it cannot avoid forming a conception of its self as it presents its self as a culture to that which is not its self.

18.9. And the spirit of a society is available as actuality in another way. In every society, from the society of the family to the international society of the whole human race, there is a consciousness which is not finally and wholly absorbed by society—the consciousness possessed by the human individual. Individual human consciousness, formed by the societies it forms, is, from the moment of birth to the moment of death, a part of social consciousness. But it also continues to be, from birth to death, a consciousness apart from social consciousness, a unique totality, a spirit of its own.

18.10. When the human individual has been explained in terms of the union of two aspects, body and consciousness, of willing and acting with a view to individual survival and prospering, of willing and acting as a part of the physical world of non-consciousness and as a member of countless societies, from the society of the family to the international society of the whole human race, there remains the question of the total effect of the structure-system of a particular individual, the effect which surpasses all actual conceiving and self-conceiving in society, all actual individual self-creating and self-socializing, that which makes a particular human individual into a unique individual, with a unique identity. There remains the question not of self-creating personality (the individual-through-the-individual and the individual-through-society) nor of self-consciousness (the individual-for-the-individual and the individual-for-society) but of the individual conceived as totality (the individual-as-individual). There remains, in other words, the question of the individual as spirit.

18.11. Just as a given society is also society-as-spirit, so a given human being is an individual-as-spirit—a totality which surpasses the individual's actual becoming and serves as a permanent external dimension of self-judgement. The individuality of a human being is, as it were, the culture of that human being. The culture of a society is, as it were, the individuality of that society.

18.12. Society-as-culture is thus the social reality which is always one step beyond social reality-forming, always just beyond the grasp of social willing and acting. It is society's own image reflected in a mirror which society holds up to itself but which society has not itself chosen to make. It is society's shadow thrown by a light within society which society cannot see. It is a reality formed by society which society does not choose to form. It is society participating in a world of the spirit whose nature is to be always a world beyond society. Society-as-process makes its spirit as a secretion from all its becoming. Society-as-spirit secretes itself in every pore and fibre of society-as-process.

18.13. In willing and acting to cause the survival and prospering of itself as structure-system, society wills and acts in conformity with itself as being. In conceiving of time and space as the co-ordinates of its willing and acting, it conceives of itself also as that which wills and acts, as that which uses time and space for its willing and acting, as that which is not itself in time and space, as a being in spirit. The dimension of the total and self-transcending and self-judging spirit of society's culture is the fifth dimension of all society's willing and acting in time and space.

18.14. The culture of a society, as totalizing and self-transcending and self-judging spirit, is the reality within which society forms its reality-for-itself, through all its reality-forming processes. It is the metaphysical aspect of all the practical functioning of its structure-system. The physical, non-conscious world *makes* the hypotheses of natural science by the mere ordering of its structures and the functioning of its systems. Human consciousness *conceives* those hypotheses within consciousness as the hypotheses which the natural world would conceive if it were conscious of its own order and functioning in the form of human consciousness. It is for this reason that the natural world seems to *obey* the hypothetical laws of science.

18.15. However, in the world of consciousness, human consciousness is both observer and observed of its own order and functioning, in individual and social consciousness. In the culture of a society, human consciousness *makes* the hypotheses of the order and functioning of that society by the mere ordering and functioning of its structure-system, and of all its subordinate structure-systems. Human consciousness *conceives* within individual and social consciousness, in the form of its reality-for-itself, the hypotheses of its own order and functioning in the reality it forms, in its words and ideas and theories and values. In all its self-creating and self-socializing, society is not only actualizing its self-conceived possibilities in accordance with its self-determined purposes. It is also willing and acting in accordance with the laws of its own order and functioning contained within its culture, the laws which human consciousness would make for itself if it could ordering and functioning of a society, its spirit is manifested as its spirit is formed.

18.16. In the culture of international society, *humanity* knows itself as spirit. In international society, in the society of the whole human race, humanity comes face to face with humanity as a self-transcending and self-judging totality. Given the painfully ambiguous legacy of human social experience, all the grandeur and all the misery, it is not wholly surprising if humanity is reluctant to conceive of itself as society, to see humanity in the mirror of social humanity. In a society which dares not know itself as society, the fifth dimension of the spirit is necessarily distorted. The distorted spirit of international society distorts all the functioning of the structure-system of society. It disables the society in all its willing and acting. It deranges every word and idea and theory and value of the society. It disorientates all the becoming of society. It stands in the way of all its progressive self-development. It makes society into the enemy of its own being.

18.17. The effects of the distorted culture of international society are evident enough from all that has been said in the present volume.

18.18. (1) International society presents itself to humanity as a *semi-natural world* beyond the limits of the denaturalized social worlds of the subordinate societies. It is a realm where natural forces seem to predominate over social forces. It is a place where extraordinary occurrences happen which, although the work, in whole or in part, of human consciousness, take on the character of natural events, the pseudo meteorological phenomena of international society—wars, civil wars, genocide, famine, epidemics, oppression, exploitation, social indignities of all kinds, destruction and waste of the world physical environment, cycles and crises and other large-scale phenomena in the world economic environment.

18.19. Because unsocialized international society seems to humanity to be a semi-natural world, humanity is hardly more surprised at such phenomena than it is when it sees similar phenomena in the natural world, plague or drought or hurricane. And it is only a little more ashamed of such phenomena than it is of wholly natural calamities. And it is as little confident that such things will ever be eradicated in the semi-natural world of international society as it is confident that calamities will cease in the wholly natural world. It is less confident of its capacity to alter the semi-natural course of the becoming of the society of the whole human race through the power of consciousness than it is confident of its ability to alter the course of the wholly natural world, through science and technology. Depriving itself of the strength of its spiritual being, of the power to transcend itself in self-judging totality, humanity weakens its own will to survive and prosper, its will to create itself in accordance with its self-conceived possibilities.

18.20. (2) Without an idea of its culture as spiritual being—total, self-transcending, and self-judging—unsocial international society presents itself to humanity as a *marginal society*, a frontier outpost, on the fringe of organized society. It is a society in which social behaviour and unsocialized behaviour are in simple conjunction, simply ordered, easily comprehended, quickly judged. Because the totality of the social structure is remote, it impinges little on the everyday life of the marginally social society. Its impact is so slight and so intermittent that it is easy to believe that the total society does not exist or, at least, that the marginal society is not an integral part of any total society, a total society which is too remote and uncertain to comprehend and to respect.

18.21. Or else it is easy for the marginal society to believe that the total society itself must be nothing but the marginal society on a large scale. To a marginal frontier society, all society seems to be a frontier settlement—impermanent, precarious, and close to nature. For a semi-social international society, all the world is the Wild West.

18.22. (3) The absence of the totality of an international society, as self-transcending and self-judging spirit, spreads *social degradation* like an infection to its subordinate societies, especially the state-societies. One social perversion is added to another to form societies whose actual achievement is not the survival and prospering of the society and its members but self-maiming and increasing misery. Corrupt administration, corrupt politics, corrupt religion, corrupt ideology, civil strife, economic corruption and inefficiency, spiritual and moral degeneracy, socio-natural disasters of famine and epidemic, political and social and economic aggressions from outside the society— such can be the actual social process of individual societies and the actual daily life of the human beings who are condemned to suffer as their citizens.

18.23. From an international society which itself has no spiritual dimension, such suffering societies, and suffering humanity in general, can expect no rescue and no redemption. A semi-natural, semi-social international society can offer no consolation but the consolation of recognizing and accepting the supposedly natural and the supposedly inevitable. In an international society which cannot transcend itself as society, there is no hope that its subordinate societies will learn to find self-transcendance within themselves. A semi-social, semi-natural international society does not merely fail to enlighten. It is an education in evil. It legitimates, by naturalizing, even by supernaturalizing, the willing and the acting of the corrupt, the inefficient, and the wicked manipulators of rotten societies.

18.24. (4) An international society which is not a spiritual totality generates *international hypertrophies* of all kinds, to fill its spiritual emptiness. International society is swept by intermittent and unpredictable paroxysms of wild energy.

There are world-scale *events*—world wars, cold wars, local wars of world-wide significance, summit meetings of so-called world statesmen, so-called nation-making and alliance-making and peace-making, natural and semi-natural and social disasters of all kinds.

There are world-transforming economic phenomena—mass industrialization, mass urbanization, mass production and mass consumption, mass excess and mass penury, crises and cycles and failures, the life-transforming and life-threatening discoveries and inventions of science and technology.

There are the world-scale phenomena of consciousness itself, the phenomena of mass communication, of mass fantasy—waves of fashions and fads, of mass entertainment, and of sport—tides of erratic popular sentiment attaching to this or that object of excitement or hope or anxiety or compassion, a new invention, a charismatic person, a piece of diplomatic paper, the pathetic victims of one disaster or another.

There are the world-scale phenomena of militarism—the ultimate hypertrophic symbols of non-social international society, the instruments of mass destruction, the mountains of cryptophallic weapons of death and destruction, filled with insane technological magic, the sacrifice of human lives and human dignity and the human spirit, the devotion of human energy and human ingenuity and natural resources to actualizing the pathological fantasies of the holders of great political and economic power.

18.25. Because of the intense energy which they accumulate as they sweep across the world, such monstrous pseudo-social manifestations have overwhelmed countless local phenomena. They have altered and even destroyed countless local cultures, altering and even destroying the self-transcending spiritual totalities of countless societies all over the world. Cultures which have accumulated over long periods of time, cultures of splendid complexity and sophistication, cultures full of the individuality of isolation, cultures with unique forms of social reality in the way of religion and mythology and history and law and morality, cultures giving priceless self-identity to proud nations, cultures full of precious and subtle human qualities of dignity and affection and consideration and respect and responsibility. The juggernaut of mass international unculture has swept such cultures aside, enslaving and exploiting and changing human beings as effortlessly and as thoughtlessly as it has cleared forests, moved mountains, polluted the atmosphere, drained the Earth of irreplaceable resources.

18.26. At the end of the twentieth century, it may be too late to stop, still less to undo, the havoc caused by international unculture. It is on world-wide capitalism that a unique responsibility rests. If world-wide capitalism is not socialized within a social international society, there will soon be not only no international culture but also no local cultures anywhere in the world. A world in which there is only an unsocialized capitalism acting as the pseudo-culture of a semi-social international society, and in which there are no individual and indigenous cultures of subordinate societies, will be a world well prepared to destroy itself sooner rather than later, a world set to destroy itself not only as a physical world but also as a human world. Humanity will, by its own deranged behaviour, destroy the three worlds—of the individual, of society, of the planet Earth—which have made possible the interesting experiment which is human life.

18.27. Capitalism is an inappropriate name given to an economic system which generates surplus social energy on a vast scale by systematically transforming objects of desire into objects of property, objects of property into objects of desire, attaching desire to products, attaching property to wants. Through the medium of money, which is the archetype of desire made property and property made desire, it distributes social power which is not only economic power but also political power, determining the total social process of whole societies. Capitalism is an economic sub-system of society in which the primary distribution of economic power is through the medium of property.

18.28. The remarkably dynamic character of capitalism stems from the fact that, by linking social power so directly with desire through the medium of property, society is able to harness the impulse of life of all its members and, by organizing that energy in social sub-structures (in particular, as industrial and commercial and financial enterprises of all kinds), it is able to generate great quantities of *surplus social energy*, the energy which comes from the functioning of a society's structure-system, as it organizes the otherwise fragmented energies of its participants. In this way, the natural human energy which seeks the survival and prospering of the individual is directly harnassed by society, as the individual identifies and conflates individual survival and prospering with the survival and prospering of society. In this way, for my society to survive and prosper is for me to survive and prosper; for me to survive and prosper is for my society to survive and prosper.

18.29. Capitalism is the most complete and sophisticated and enduring form of totalitarianism which human social consciousness has yet devised. The only freedom guaranteed by capitalism is the freedom to acquire property. The fate of the individual is totally determined within the fate of society. The will of the individual is totally subsumed within the will of society. The values of the individual are totally dominated by the values of society. And capitalism must naturally tend to take the whole world into its system. Not only is there no natural limit (say, at the frontiers of a given state-society) to the capitalist system. There must always be a need to transform everything which desire can desire and property can control. Capitalism has no inherent limits other than the inherent limits of human desire and of human physical power.

18.30. Because capitalism seems to respond so directly to natural human desire, to serve so faithfully the natural human purpose of survival and prospering, it is difficult for human consciousness to resist it as an economic system. It seems too natural and too useful. Consciousness is presented with an agonizing choice—on the one hand, foregoing a possibility of dramatic world-transforming economic development; on the other hand, submitting to an organization of energy which swamps all other aspects of social self-creating. At the end of the twentieth century, humanity itself is facing such a dilemma as the idea of capitalism spreads like fire across the whole world.

18.31. The socializing of capitalism seems, in principle, to be a difficult, if not impossible, task. It seems to be doing what capitalism already does or else to be undermining capitalism in what it does best. Capitalism already socializes all human economic effort. What more can it ask for in the way of socializing? Capitalism requires that all human economic effort be subordinated to its values. How can it tolerate other values?

18.32. The solution to the problem of socializing capitalism will be found in a reconceiving of capitalism, a reconceiving which is both theoretical and historical. It is a reconceiving which also leads to a reconceiving of its apparent antithesis, and eventual antagonist, socialism. It is necessary, in the first place, to dispel the magic of the word *capitalism*. Capitalism is a magic name which was applied to certain developments in the unending and unbroken story of the distributing of economic power in society, developments characterised by a particular form of *devolution of economic power*. And the devolution of economic power, apparently characteristic of capitalism, can now be reconceived as a particular form of the socializing of economic power. Secondly, it is necessary to reconceive the history of all such economic developments as an integral part of the history of the distribution of *social power* in general, including not only economic power but also political power (public-realm power under the constitution).

18.33. In the history of the last two centuries, both capitalism and socialism came to have a profound effect on the development of international society. They flooded into the cultural vacuum of the non-social international society of the state-societies. Then, as phenomena of the unsocial international society, they have flowed back into the social development of subordinate societies, causing economic and/political transformations, by revolutionary violence or otherwise, which have altered the cultures of countless societies which are united now only by their subjection to the distortions of international unculture.

18.34. An outline hypothesis for the reconceiving of such developments is suggested below in the form of four historical phases.

(1) FROM 1770 TO 1870

18.35. Late in the eighteenth century, the idea asserted itself strongly in the social consciousness of many societies that the products of the scientific revolution of the modern period (since the fifteenth century) could play a major part in the development of society as a whole, making available to society a greatly increased power to transform the physical world socially through the economic system. The discoveries of science and the inventions of technology would enable society to generate levels of surplus energy which were without precedent and which were without necessary or apparent limit. The so-called Industrial Revolution was part of a continuing revolution which had begun with the modern revival of science and technology. The Industrial Revolution was the socialization of science and technology through society's economic sub-system.

18.36. With the publication of Adam Smith's *Wealth of Nations* in 1776, there also became available to social consciousness in some societies the idea that individual economic energy could be organized, especially through the medium of property, so as to generate substantial surplus social energy, thereby making possible the generation of still greater individual economic energy, through the reinvestment of one part of the social energy in the activity of the individual economic operator and the investment of another part of the social energy in the socializing of society as a whole (to provide a general social framework helpful to the new economic system). Social consciousness became able to form pure theories of society, and in due course practical theories, incorporating so promising and so potent an idea in the actual self-creating and socializing of one society after another. Words and ideas and theories and values were produced in profusion to explain and to organise the practical application of the idea.

18.37. The idea of the economic appropriation of the products of science and technology thus formed a powerful alliance with the idea of the socialization of individual energy through the individualization of social energy. Together they have made possible the dramatic political, economic, and social developments of the nineteenth and twentieth centuries.

18.38. The organization of the new economic system of society depended centrally, in ways which have been considered above, on the concept of *property* and hence on the development of a more and more complex and efficient legal system to make property possible and reliable. However, to use the concept of property as a fundamental part of the economic structure-system, society needed more than a development of its legal structure-system. It needed practical theories to determine the appropriate devolution of property. It needed practical theories to determine the actual distribution of property-power between society as a whole (social property-power exercised within society's public realm) and individual property-owners (subordinate societies outside the public realm, such as joint-stock companies, human individuals). And it needed practical theories to determine the terms and conditions on which property-power would be delegated by society, and on which the exercise of property-power (social and individual) would be socially and legally accountable. In other words, the development of society through the devolution of economic power depended on the appropriate development of the total structure-system of society, not merely on the development of its economic and legal systems.

18.39. Great struggles took place in the nineteenth century, struggles which have continued into the twentieth century in societies all over the world, struggles to establish new pure theories of society (in particular, to supersocialize the new forms of devolved property-power) and to establish practical theories of particular societies, establishing the words and ideas and values necessary to organize the social struggle of each society as it integrated the devolution of property-power within its self-creating and self-socializing. Great struggles took place at all three levels—establishing pure theories, establishing practical theories, applying the practical theories within and between societies. The struggles frequently took a revolutionary or near-revolutionary form. In some cases, violence was used again and again as societies conceived their new possibilities and made choices among their newly conceived possibilities. In other cases, a sort of permanent revolution was staged, as everyday politics (the social struggle of the public realm) continually brought theory into the everyday process of social distribution.

18.40. In other words, the development of what has normally and unfortunately been called *capitalism* and the development of what have normally and unfortunately been called *socialism* and *communism* were responses at the level of theory to a continuing and dynamic process of reorganizing the devolution of economic power in many different societies. And that reorganizing was itself part of a general reorganizing of society, which went far beyond the economic sub-system to include every aspect of the structure-system of society, the constitution in all its aspects, all aspects of reality-forming. Typically, the outcome of the struggles of the nineteenth century was a form of mixed economic sub-system (neither strongly capitalist nor strongly socialist) which sought a balance between the individualization of property-power (law making society safe for individual property-power) and the socialization of property-power (law making property-power serve the social interest).

18.41. The reorganization of the total structure-systems of the societies in question included, above all, the reconceiving of the constitutions of those societies. That is to say, it included a reconceiving and a redistributing of social power of all kinds, not merely property-power. Given the dependence of the new economic system on property-power, given the dependence of property-power on the legal system, given the dependence of the legal system on the organization of the public realm, given the dependence of the legal system and the public realm on the constitution, given the place of the constitution in the total structure-system of the society, it was inevitable that economic reorganization would form part of a general reorganization of society. The distribution of power among the constitutional organs of society, the reconceiving of the public realm of society, the reconceiving of the relationship of society as a whole to its members (subordinate societies, human individuals) and of the members to each other, all of these things required substantial development of the pure and practical theories of every society, including the practical application of reconceived concepts of so-called popular sovereignty.

18.42. The question had to be asked and answered yet again of how to organize the system by which new legal relations are created, including the legal relations of property-power, the ideas and theories and values which such new legal relations were to embody, the forms of legal and social accountability to be applied to the creation and application of such new legal relations. Who; whom? The ultimate constitutional question of every society at all times had to be asked and answered yet again, if need be, through the use of non-constitutional energy.

(2) FROM 1870 TO 1945

18.43. Late in the nineteenth century, the social struggle in many societies was leading to an aberrant phenomenon which was, however, predictable and predicted—the concentration of economic power, the concentration of constitutional power. They were two sides of a single coin. The *desire* which is embodied in property-power is liable to lead the power-holder (landowner, entrepreneur, investor, state bureaucrat, corporate bureaucrat) to want more and more property-power, up to a limit which can be controlled only by the *obligation* embodied in the rest of society's reality-for-itself, including the legal system. The theories of the relevant societies did not directly, or indirectly through the constitution and the legal system, prevent the accumulation of ever greater economic power in ever fewer economic operators and the accumulation of ever greater public-realm power in ever fewer participants in the constitutional organs. Such totalitarian tendencies were intrinsic possibilities, necessary risks, of a political-economic system which depended on the powerful alliance between the individualisation of social power and the socialization of individual power.

18.44. The effects of the new constitutional-legal-political-economic system had come to be felt world-wide. Its amazing capacity to generate surplus social energy and to bring about profound social transformations was being demonstrated all over the world, as production and trade came to be organized, more and more, on a world-wide basis. There would soon be no society anywhere in the world which had not felt the effects of the new system. And now the quasi-natural hypertrophies of the new economic system were also to be felt world-wide, as the concentration of economic and political power led to far-reaching economic and political imperialism and expansionism of all kinds, and to uncontrollable rivalry and antagonism between holders of greater political and economic power. In the twentieth century, the gross aberrations of the new systems threatened the survival of whole societies, whole continents, a large part of the whole world, and the whole of the international economy, during thirty years of social atavism, consisting of two periods of unprecedented public mass murder punctuated by a period of economic and social anarchy. The system destroyed its excesses by almost destroying itself.

(3) FROM 1945 TO 1971

18.45. With the end of the Second World War, a new period of power-devolution began, using hard lessons learned from terrible experiences. Within societies, economic power was reorganized, with much property-power socialized, in one or both of two ways—in the form of the reassigning of property-power from individuals to subordinate societies under the direction of the public realm (nationalization); and in the form of the socializing of individual power (through taxation, legal regulation, control of land-development and land-use, competition policy, consumer protection, environmental protection). At the same time, the political system was reorganized by the development of the idea of human rights (setting a limit on all public power in the name of the ideal constitution of a society), by the development of the legal accountability of public authorities (administrative law), and through the development of political accountability, in the form of the institutions of mass democracy (universal suffrage, public education, media of mass communication).

18.46. In the interacting public realms of the international society as then conceived, steps were taken, of an exceptionally imaginative and practical kind, to organize the interaction of the public realms of the national economic sub-systems, especially through the medium of international agreements and by the formation by the state-societies of so-called international organizations. Some attempt was even made to socialize at the international level legal accountability of a wider kind, in the form of the development of the internationalization of human rights. And, in the United Nations, there was even created a form of social accountability of a more general kind, with the public realm of one state-society accounting to the public realms of the others.

(4) FROM 1971

18.47. From 1971, the post-war structure began to give way within societies and internationally. Internally and internationally, the balance between the individualization of social power and the socialization of individual power began to change yet again. Internally, there was a new devolution of property-power, through the reassignment of property-power (privatization) and through the de-socialization of property-power (de-regulation of economic activity). Internationally, there was a weakening of the commitment to the organizing of the international economy through agreed regulation, agreed policies, and communal public-realm activity in organizations.

18.48. The integration of the national economies in the international economy had taken on a new form, as compared with the corresponding period in the nineteenth century. In the first place, there were now many more powerful participants in the international economy (in itself, a form of devolution of international property-power). Secondly, the energy-levels of the world economy were now vastly greater, thanks to the ever-improving techniques of mass production, the application of ever more powerful effects of science and technology, an enormous increase in world-wide demand for products and services. Thirdly, the internationalization of all economic activity (production, distribution, finance) had made seemingly separate national economies fundamentally dependent upon each other.

18.49. Such developments, in the period since 1971, have led to a reaction. The emergence of the idea of *the environment* has been as much a development in the social consciousness of international society as in the social consciousness of individual subordinate societies. In this respect, it is analogous to movements of social consciousness in the nineteenth and early twentieth centuries against slavery, on behalf of ethnic minorities and indigenous peoples, in favour of the self-determination of nations. In the same respect, it is analogous to the re-emergence of the idea of human rights after 1945.

18.50. There are now signs that such national-international movements of socializing consciousness may go further than issues of the environment and so-called Green politics and may be the outward sign of a more fundamental change in human reality-forming.

18.51. Supporting evidence for this might be found in the fact that developments analogous to those noted above in relation to capitalism have taken place in relation to the practical application of *revolutionary socialism* (as practical theory) and *marxism-leninism* (as pure theory). A period of fundamental social reconstruction in the societies concerned, through the redistribution of property-power and associated with fundamental constitutional change, was followed by a period of aberrant totalitarianism which is now being followed by a period of social regeneration, including a new redistribution of property-power associated with fundamental constitutional changes.

18.52. The differences in the case of revolutionary socialism have been that the periods of time involved have been much shorter, and the international significance of the social developments in question has been quite different from the international significance of evolving capitalism. Revolutionary socialism acquired its identity by dialectical opposition to capitalism. The internationalization of capitalism, and its overwhelming power in the international economy, left revolutionary socialism with three courses of action—(1) to isolate itself from the rest of the international economy; (2) to seek to disseminate revolutionary socialism as a theory, especially in state-societies whose social and economic structures were relatively undeveloped (that is to say, in particular, those societies which had not managed to reconceive themselves within the idea and the ideal of socialized democracy); (3) to take practical steps to bring about revolutionary change in such societies, especially with a view to disrupting international capitalism.

18.53. There are signs now that both capitalism and revolutionary socialism are beginning to seek their self-identifying otherwise than by dialectical opposition to each other. It is possible that they are beginning to identify themselves in relation to what is coming to be called the *quality of life*. International social consciousness has, on this view, progressed to the stage of believing that humanity has the means to direct the becoming of society with a remarkable degree of efficiency. That efficiency stems from the practical social power made available by science and technology, the efficiency of mass communications over all reality-forming in society and hence over individual and social consciousness, and the improvements in human self-understanding which have accumulated over the centuries and which it has been the purpose of the present volume to seek to identify.

18.54. It may further be suggested that this development in international social consciousness has generated the further idea that the future development of society everywhere depends not only on the practical achievement of social change but on solving the problem of what social change is desirable. The issue of the *quality of life* is then a subsidiary issue within the more general problem of the meaning of *the good*, when society is conceived as a *communal pursuit of the good*.

18.55. The developments discussed above may be represented in diagrammatic form as follows:

	Economic sub-system	Political sub-system
from 1776	capitalism (devolved economic power)	popular democracy (collective political power)
	↓	↓
from 1870	monolithic capitalism (concentrated economic power) (economic imperialism)	totalitarianism (concentrated political power) (political expansionism)
	↓	↓
from 1945	economic socialization (and world economic organization)	mass democracy, human rights (politics-by-television, *glasnost*)
	↓	↓
from 1971	new economic devolution (deregulation, privatization, *perestroika*)	? new democracy (communal pursuit of the good, new international order)

Fig. 13. Economic-political development

18.56. Such developments within human social consciousness are giving rise to a new tension, a new dialectical opposition. It is a tension from which much may be expected. *Humanity, as it becomes aware of its ever-increasing power over the future of human society, feels less and less certain of its purposes and, therefore, of its values.*

18.57. So it is that the transcending of capitalism and revolutionary socialism comes to seem not only possible but necessary. So it is also that the question of the nature and the future of international society takes on a central role in determining the future of humanity. And so it is that the redeeming of international capitalism, with its ever-increasing dominance not only over the international economy but also over all of human consciousness, becomes a central challenge in determining the future of humanity. And, because of their dialectical relationship, the redeeming of capitalism will necessarily be a redeeming of revolutionary socialism.

18.58. Capitalism, which had grown as a complex system within the development of complex societies, was externalized into an international society which was not a society fit to receive it, a minimal international society of the interacting public realms of supposedly sovereign states. Capitalism, which had depended on the development of ever more sophisticated constitutional structure-systems and legal relations, democratizing and socializing it, found itself in a society which did not even have a conception of its own constitution, which contained only the most rudimentary of legal relations, which had only a minimal capacity for socializing self-creation. Capitalism found itself, naked and alone, in a society which was not a society, within a culture which was not a culture.

18.59. A series of specific consequences flowed from this misfortune. (1) Unsocialized capitalism came to behave as a fact rather than as a theory in international society. Its complex social roots could not be reproduced internationally. All that was apparent internationally was its activity. So it came to seem acultural, self-contained, culturally neutral, unsocialized, intrinsically individualist in character. In other words, it seemed to be a version of capitalism which no longer existed within state-societies. (2) Primitive capitalism, with all its dynamic energy, became one of the over-energetic international uncultural phenomena, transforming the culture of one subordinate society after another. (3) Capitalism, which had inspired a revolutionary-socialist antithesis within state-societies, an anthithesis which had altered its character internally, found opposition to itself in a number of state-societies in different parts of the world, such opposition being in the name of practical theories based on socialism and Marxism. (4) But socialism was not able to rival capitalism internationally, because the deliberate socialization of property-power depended on appropriate social structure-systems, which could not be reproduced in an international society which did not conceive of itself as a society and which could not conceive of its own constitutional organs, let alone of its own total social process.

18.60. (5) With primitive international capitalism, there came what might be called the *hardware* values of capitalism, those associated with the individualization of property-power, those associated with the functioning of capitalism as a structure-system of economic transformation, those flowing from the practical theories of primitive capitalism (the market, market forces, supply and demand, comparative advantage, value determined by price, economic development determined by rate of profit, economic freedom). What might be called the *software* values of developed capitalism (economic and social policy, public accountability, the public interest, legal regulation) were only vestigially present. (6) The worst of all situations resulted. The socialist resistance to capitalism inspired capitalism to present itself internationally not merely as an economic sub-system, supported by a practical theory of the economy, but as if it were in itself a practical theory of society as a whole and even, since 1945, as if it were a pure theory of society. Such inflation of capitalism was accompanied by an inflation of socialist economic theory into a supposedly rival theory of society, practical and pure. (7) International society came to seem to be an arena in which two lonely giants, Capitalism and Socialism, would fight out their final struggle.

18.61. (8) After 1945, the unculture of international society came to be characterized by a terrible duality—the non-culture of international capitalism imposing its non-social values on societies all over the world; the all-or-nothing rivalry of two practical theories of economics masquerading as world-views. (9) In due course, the unculture of international society began to give way to a culture of ultimate irony, as humanity at last began to see itself as one, united at last and at least in the possibility of its own self-destruction.

18.62. (10) Through all this time, capitalism was also acquiring a practical hegemony over natural science. Judging from actual social experience, science can serve four kinds of purpose—

(a) it can serve purposes conceived within the public-realm of state-societies, including military purposes (*governmental science*);

(b) it can serve purposes conceived within the economy of a society, including industrial purposes (*economic science*);

(c) it can serve purposes conceived within the total social process of society, including life-enhancing medical and agricultural purposes (*humanitarian science*);

(d) it can serve a purpose which is not a purpose beyond itself, reflecting nothing but its intrinsic progressivity, its dynamic tendency to surpass itself constantly (*disinterested science*).

18.63. In the course of the twentieth century, capitalism has extended its power and influence beyond economic science into governmental science and humanitarian science, even becoming the patron of otherwise distinterested science. Such a relationship between capitalism and science has served not only to enhance the practical achievement of both science and capitalism. It has also had an important effect within international social consciousness, allowing capitalism to share in the prestige of science, allowing the bright light of science to shine on capitalism, to make capitalism seem as natural, and as naturally right and reasonable, as science. It has lent dignity to the ethos of primitive capitalism as it permeates international social consciousness.

18.64. The pseudo-naturalism of the international economy, apparently functioning without any social superstructure, has given to humanity yet another of the *human gods* which it has so prolifically created for itself through the whole course of human social experience. Fate, Fortune, Nature, History, the State, Sex—and now the Market. Such word-idea-theory-values have shown themselves to have an overwhelming power over human consciousness. They empower and disempower in ways which human consciousness apparently finds exceptionally acceptable and useful. They empower by seeming to provide a one-word explanation of otherwise overwhelmingly vast and obscure phenomena. They disempower by seeming to identify the source of those phenomena in something which is beyond the control of human willing and acting.

18.65. Such ideas act as axioms, leading to an unlimited series of ideas-by-deduction. And they act as spurs to the imagination, producing rich crops of ideas-by-association. Such derived ideas may include purposes, values, moral precepts. Primitive capitalism carries with it, in particular, a penumbra of ideas which combine a theoretical function with a quasi-moral dimension—enterprise, initiative, efficiency, invention, innovation, novelty, reward, profit, wealth, success, demand, want, property, freedom, self-interest, competition. Accumulating within international social consciousness, they begin to add up to a practical international quasi-morality formed from the ethos of primitive capitalism.

18.66. The ethos of primitive capitalism is the ethos of *obligation in the service of desire*. Through the international success of primitive capitalism and the international impotence of socialism in a non-social international society, the unculture of international society has become a culture-by-default, a *de facto* culture, a vacuum filled by the ethos of obligation-in-the-service-of-desire. In an international society which does not know itself as society, in an international society which accordingly cannot know its own socionomy (a society's totality of obligation conceived within the society), in an international culture which accordingly cannot see itself as culture (the totality of a society seen, as if from outside itself, in the form of spirit), unrooted capitalism has become the unsocial dynamic of an unsociety, fuelling desire with desire, ordering desire only by reference to the needs of the economic system, treating the apparently natural necessity of the economic system as all that there is of desire-ordering obligation.

18.67. In an unsocial international society dominated by unsocialized capitalism, to want is to need, to desire is a duty, to live is to consume.

18.68. The socializing of capitalism and the democratizing of socialism will start from the proposition that economic theories and economic systems are theories and systems of social power. All economic power is social power. Delegated social power is exercised by the management of a capitalist corporation or of a socialist enterprise whenever decisions are made on investment plans, on research and development plans, on the location of a factory, on production schedules and marketing strategies, on labour numbers and grades, on salary- and wage-levels and non-financial benefits for management and employees, on the pricing of products, and decisions on a merger of enterprises, the winding-up on an enterprise, the closing of a factory, the termination of a line of production, the laying-off of labour, the raising of prices. Delegated social power is also exercised by other enterprises when they respond to such decisions. Delegated social power is exercised by organized labour and trade associations and professional associations when they will and act to influence the decisions of enterprises.

18.69. All such decisions, just as much as the economic decisions of government agencies acting under their public-realm responsibilities, are using social power derived from society in a way which forms part of the total social process of society, directly determining the lives of members of society. And other members of society, individual human beings and other subordinate societies, when they are willing and acting as employees and consumers, are also exercising delegated social power as part of society's total social process.

18.70. There has been a phantom democratization and social-ization of the economic aspect of the total social process, separate from the democratization and socialization of the public-realm (political) aspect of the process. In the case of capitalism, *the market* is treated as a form of natural democracy, in which all participants are naturally free and equal. The natural economic democracy is then supposed to be socialized (in the pursuit of social justice) through the intervention of public-realm decision-making. In the case of socialism, *planning* is treated as a form of technical democracy, in which all participants are treated as equal beneficiaries of rationalized decision-making. The technical democracy is then supposed to be socialized (in the pursuit of social justice) through the activity of the public-realm in controlling the plan of all plans, as it were, organizing the interacting of economic sub-systems through central planning.

18.71. The problem of the international economy of an unsocial international society is thus an aspect of a problem which goes to the root of all economic structure-systems of both capitalism and socialism. How would it be possible to democratize and socialize an international economy which knows only the pseudo-natural democracy of *the market* and which could not, at least in the foreseeable future, generate *a plan of all economic plans*? That is a specific challenge facing international society at the end of the twentieth century. It is the challenge of forming a post-capitalist and post-socialist *practical theory* of the international economy.

18.72. In forming a pure theory of international society, such as that proposed in the present volume, international society may take the first and prerequisite step in its social struggle to meet such a challenge. In other words, the first and prerequisite step is the coming-to-consciousness of international society as a society.

18.73. In an international society which comes at last to know itself as society, the international economy will take its place within a self-creating and socializing struggle which will far transcend the struggle to organize the economic sub-system of international society. There will become available to international society the immeasurable wealth of human values of all kinds, the wealth of human experience contained in the culture of every subordinate society, accumulated over all the long history of human social experience. Humanity will remember all its rich diversity and all that it shares. It will remember that it has generated, and can continue to generate, great human realities which transcend societies, which transcend time and place—realities of religion, mythology, art, philosophy, history, science, economy, morality, law. International society will set about forming its own reality once again, forming practical theories in the light of its new-found pure theory of itself, the pure theory of international society as society. In rediscovering what it is, international society will be able to become what it might be.

18.74. In an international society which comes at last to know itself as society, humanity will discover its law, a new international law, which is the collective self-creating of all human beings everywhere, the self-directed becoming of the society of all societies, the society of the whole human race. And the pursuit of social justice, for all people everywhere, will take its rightful place in relation to the justice which connects human self-ordering with the order of all-that-is. The Human City begins with me and my neighbour. The Universal City begins with me and my neighbour.

18.75. In an international society which comes at last to know itself as society, humanity will be able at last to conceive itself in the self-transcending and self-judging totality of its spirit, beginning to become its true being. It will be a culture in which humanity discovers and rediscovers its *humanity*, what it is to be human, the species-characteristic of all human beings. New-old words and ideas and theories and values will flood the social consciousness of the whole of humanity, like undammed streams flowing again into some great river. *Community, co-operation, trust, concern, compassion, need, justice, duty, self-fulfilment, self-giving, self-discipline.*

18.76. International society will be a society in which the word *love* will, once again, have a meaning unconnected with trade and property. Love as the reconciling of desire and obligation, the reconciling which human consciousness seeks in the life of the individual human being and in the life of society. Love as the reconciling of the impulse of life and the necessity of the universe, the reconciling which all living things seek, as participants in the mysterious unfolding of a

universe which contains, among other mysteries, the insignificant but very ambitious microcosm which is the international
society of the whole human race.

18.77. In a social international society dominated by human
love, to want is to hope, to desire is to create, to live is to
grow. In a social international society, the ideal of all ideals is
eunomia, the good order of a self-ordering society.

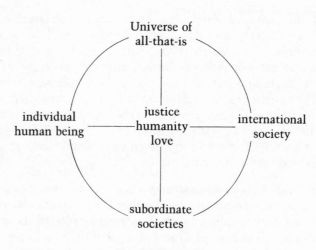

Fig. 14. Eunomia

19 Humanity and its Future

19.1. Halfway between the ape that it was and the being that it could become, the human being must each day choose its future. Matter among all the matter of the universe, the human being will share in the future of the universe. A living thing among all the living things of the Earth, the human being will share in the future of life on Earth. A conscious being among conscious beings, the human being will have the future chosen by human consciousness.

19.2. Inhabitant of three worlds made by consciousness, the human being will inhabit the future of the worlds which consciousness makes. In the *physical* world made by consciousness, the human being has found means of transforming that world by treating it as a world ordered in the dimensions of consciousness, time and space, and as a world which respects the ordering projected onto to it by the self-ordering of consciousness. In the *social* world made by consciousness, the human being has found means of integrating natural human energy into structures and systems which reproduce the self-ordering of consciousness to serve purposes conceived by consciousness as human survival and prospering. In the *individual* world of the consciousness of each human being, consciousness orders itself into the structure and the system which is the unique identity of each human being, as each human being seeks survival and prospering—as individual, as a member of societies, as self-differentiated particle of an undifferentiated universe.

19.3. When, in the course of the evolution of living things on Earth, the human being found itself to be a system which is able to contain an idea of itself as system within its functioning as a system, the human being became conscious. That evolution, seen as the actualization of possibilities in the physical world of living things, is seen as such by the very same system which became conscious and chose to treat all the physical world as being a system with a future which becomes a past, a system which has possibilities which are actualized.

19.4. Since the possibilities of the system of living matter which included the possibility of human consciousness could not themselves be possibilities chosen by human consciousness, the human being created hypotheses to explain the actualization of the possibility of consciousness. In the theory of the natural selection of species (evolution), the human being found a hypothesis which suggested that the development of consciousness, like all other developments within living things, was an integral part of the functioning of a physical universe conceived by human consciousness as a world of order, a world in which universal (natural) self-ordering made a choice among possibilities (selection).

19.5. In this way, human consciousness was both differentiated from the rest of the physical universe and integrated into it. The self-ordering of the human system-of-order (consciousness) was conceived by human consciousness as part of the self-ordering of the system-of-order of all-that-is.

19.6. So it was that the future of the human species came to be conceived by human consciousness as the interacting of two systematic processes—the process of the physical universe as a whole and the process of self-ordering human consciousness.

19.7. The interacting between those two processes has, for two reasons, proved exceptionally difficult for human consciousness to explain. In the first place, consciousness has enabled the human being to make transformations of the physical universe through choices made by consciousness, including choices made within the reality formed by *natural science.* It follows that the interacting of the two processes may be disproportionately affected by one of the two processes. It follows further that consciousness may have become able to interfere with the evolution-by-natural-selection not only of the human species, but also of all other living things on Earth.

It may be that human consciousness, and not Nature alone, will select the further evolution of living things on earth.

19.8. Secondly, human consciousness is able to conceive of realities which go beyond the reality of the physical universe and beyond the reality of human consciousness as the self-ordering of a self-differentiated particle of the undifferentiated physical universe. In the reality-forming of religion, mythology, art, philosophy, history, natural science, economy, morality, and law, human consciousness can create possibilities for future human development which are not merely those offered by the possibilities of the system of the physical universe. In other words, evolution-by-natural-selection has evolved a creature which can conceive of its own future development in terms other than evolution-by-natural-selection. Humanity can conceive of its future in terms of evolution by human selection.

19.9. Within the reality formed by natural science, such a development does not contravene the *laws* of the physical universe, since it is the physical universe which has engendered the conscious human being. Human consciousness and all the realities which it forms are, within the reality of natural science, themselves aspects of the systematic self-ordering of the universe of all-that-is.

19.10. Natural science cannot exclude as hypothetically impossible any particular reality which human consciousness chooses to form. Such choosing is merely the activity of a physical system which has acquired the possibility of containing an idea of itself as system within its functioning as a system, the possibility of choosing its future. On the contrary, natural science is presumably constrained to regard all such realities formed by human consciousness as natural and inevitable, in accordance with its own fundamental assumption (that is, within that part of its own reality which it cannot itself have made), namely, the assumption of the explicability of all phenomena, the orderliness of the universe as a whole.

19.11. The realities which human consciousness forms for itself as to the nature and functioning and purposes of its three worlds—the world of the individual, the world of society, the world of all-that-is—are systematic products of the system of human consciousness functioning as a system. From a theory explaining subatomic particles through a theory of democracy to a theory of the Will of God, they are phenomena generated by the self-ordering system of human consciousness as part of the self-ordering system of the universe of all-that-is.

19.12. And they are not phenomena formed once and fixed for ever. They are themselves part of an endless process of self-ordering consciousness, a process which consciousness conceives, in time and space, as the conceiving of possibilities, followed by a choosing among possibilities, following by an actualizing of a chosen possibility. This process of willing-and-acting is the systematic functioning of the system of human consciousness as it transforms its self-conceived future in its self-conceived present-here-and-now into its self-conceived past.

19.13. The process of self-ordering human consciousness is thus part of the process of the self-ordering universe of all-that-is. It is the form which the self-ordering of the universe of all-that-is takes within the system-for-itself which is human consciousness.

19.14. So it is that the future of the human species is both a future which is contained in a book of universal self-ordering which humanity has not written and a future which is a blank page on which humanity must write.

19.15. Humanity, having the burden of consciousness, has no choice but to take responsibility for creating itself within the self-creating of the universe of all-that-is.

19.16. In all its reality-forming (religion, mythology, art, philosophy, history, natural science, economy, morality, law), humanity is seeking to read the book of universal self-ordering with a view to writing on the page of its own future. In all its self-ordering (as individual, as society, as world-transforming physical system), humanity is creating itself within the self-creating of the universe of all-that-is.

19.17. The functioning of human consciousness at any given time thus determines not only the possibilities of humanity's future. The current state of human consciousness determines its future state and thereby the future of humanity. At the end of the twentieth century, it is possible to say that human consciousness is threatening the survival and prospering of humanity in its future. It is possible also to see human consciousness as containing, at last, the possibility of its own self-redeeming through self-surpassing.

19.18. At the end of the twentieth century, humanity finds itself overwhelmed with the products of its own consciousness. Through its own extraordinary efforts it has exceeded the possibilities of its own self-creating. In seeming to lose power over itself, humanity seems to have lost power over its future.

19.19. Through the wonderful development of *science and technology*, humanity has given to itself a very great power over the physical world which is also a power over humanity's future as part of the physical world. Through the wonderful development of *society*, it has given itself a very great power in the collected energies of human beings, up to and including the collected energies of the whole human race. Through the wonderful social development of its own functioning (*imagination and reason*), it has given itself a very great power over consciousness itself, the consciousness of individual human beings and the consciousness of masses of human beings.

19.20. And yet humanity in general feels as little confident as ever in its own capacity to take command of its own future. Through the very successes of its power of *imagination*, it seems to have made itself a victim of its imagination, ruled by fantasy and pathology and more or less unspecific despair. Through the very successes of its power of *reason*, it seems to have undermined its own capacity to reason, to have disordered its capacity of self-ordering. Humanity seems to have become for itself a sort of natural system which it must inhabit, as it inhabits the physical universe. It is a natural system which, like the physical universe, may generate events which reflect some ordering which is more or less beyond human control, an ordering which is not capable of being contained within human self-ordering. Humanity seems to humanity to have become inhuman.

19.21. The consequence is that generations of children are coming to maturity with a disabling conception of humanity and its possibilities. They are conscious only of their own spiritual and moral and intellectual confusion and impotence. Human beings are being bred who are uncertain of their own humanity. Uncertain of their own humanity, they are uncertain of humanity's capacity to create itself in accordance with its own self-ordering capacity. If humanity loses its self-ordering capacity, it will lose its reason for existing. If humanity ceases to be a system ordering itself in accordance with its own conception of itself as a system, it will cease to be humanity. Humanity will cease to be.

19.22. There is no reason to suppose that the human experiment is close to some natural conclusion. On the contrary, there is good reason to suppose that humanity is close to the beginning of its self-controlled development.

19.23. At the end of the twentieth century, the necessity and the opportunity exist to reconceive humanity in its totality within the totality of the universe. It has been the purpose of the present volume to suggest such a reconceiving at the level of theory. Humanity as a self-ordering system within the ordering of the universe of all-that-is finds its intermediate self-ordering in the structure-system of society and in the structure-systems of each individual human being.

19.24. The system of a self-creating structure-system is its law-for-itself. The law-for-itself of the human individual is the system of human consciousness. The law-for-itself of society is its legal system. The law-for-itself of humanity is the system of human consciousness as humanity creates itself within the ordering of the universe.

19.25. Such a theory is a *pure theory of social idealism* which humanity has the *opportunity* to adopt at the end of the twentieth century, as it reconceives human existence. It is a theory which *necessity* now demands as a *practical theory of social idealism* on which humanity must base its willing and acting if it is to survive and to prosper in its self-creating future. And the theory of social idealism, pure and practical, must become the basis for a *new international law* which humanity will construct as the law of a *new international society*.

19.26. So it is that our definitions must become not only axioms of humanity's self-conceiving theories but also purposes of humanity's self-creating through willing and acting.

19.27. (1) *Society is the collective self-creating of human beings.*

(2) *International society is the society of the whole human race and the society of all societies.*

(3) *Law is the continuing structure-system of human socializing.*

(4) *International law is the law of international society.*

(5) *Eunomia is the ideal order of self-creating humanity.*

20 Synopsis

PART ONE. SOCIETY

Chapter 1

20.1. We put the world in words. We put our lives in words. Words and their meanings have lives lived alongside the lives we live in our own consciousness and in the consciousness of the societies to which we belong. Long-lasting words with rich histories—like *society* and *law*—contain our past and our possibilities.

Chapter 2

20.2. We make ideas from words and from other elementary units of consciousness. Ideas contain the fusion energy of all the consciousness which they contain and of the order which they are. With ideas we construct the structures in which we live our social lives. Using our imagination and our reason to generate and to order our ideas, we make a self-ordering world of consciousness.

20.3. Our idea-structures include the reality-forming structures called *theories*. Our theories of religion, mythology, art, philosophy, history, science, economy, morality, and law are the substance of the reality-for-itself within which a society creates itself. Those theories are *practical* when they are the theoretical basis for our willing and acting. They are *pure* when they are the explanation of our practical theories. They are *transcendental* when they are our theoretical explanation of theory itself.

Chapter 3

20.4. As part of the physical world, we are a reconciling of the *impulse of life*, which we share with all living things, and the *necessity* of the universe, which we share with all matter. As human beings, we are a reconciling of *desire*, which causes us to will our acting, and *obligation* which causes us to will as self-ordering systems.

20.5. When we will and act, we choose among our self-conceived possibilities and act to actualize the chosen possibility. The basis of our choosing is *value*. Our values depend on the realities within which we live, including the whole reality-for-itself of each of the societies to which we belong, from the society of the family to the international society of the whole human race.

Chapter 4

20.6. A society makes itself a society, socializes itself, not only by forming its realities-for-itself but also by struggling with a set of inherent dilemmas which stem from its nature as an intermediary between the consciousness of the human individual and the totality of all-that-is, the totality of a universe which contains not only matter but also consciousness.

20.7. In its struggle with the dilemma of *identity* (the self and the other) society seeks to make itself in relation to that which is not itself. It makes itself from day to day, never achieving a settled identity, always surpassing itself, always resisting and responding to identity-threatening from within and without. In its struggle with the dilemma of *power* (the one and the many) society seeks to make itself a structure of structures, a system of systems, always an aggregating of willing consciousnesses which are not wholly subsumed in the willing consciousness of society, always a totality for which to be a unity is to be a society.

Chapter 5

20.8. In its struggle with the dilemma of *will* (unity of nature, plurality of value), society seeks to reconcile its value-generating reality with the value-generating realities of its members and with the value-generating reality which transcends it, including the reality of the physical universe and the reality of all-that-is. In its struggle with the dilemma of *order* (justice and social justice), society seeks to reconcile its internal self-ordering with the ordering of that which transcends it, including the ordering of the universe of all-that-is (all matter and all consciousness and all that contains them both). In justice society sees its own order in the order of that which transcends it and it seeks to make that order the justice of its own self-ordering.

Chapter 6

20.9. In its struggle with the dilemma of *becoming* (new citizens, old laws), society seeks to survive as a structure and a system. Its reality-forming is also a structuring and a system-atizing. *Religion* seeks to reconcile all value with the value of all reality. *Art* explores the presence of consciousness in material reality, the presence of material reality in consciousness. *Mythology* seeks an explanation of what society is in an explanation of why society was. *History* seeks an explanation of what society is in what society was. In *natural science* the physical world is recreated as a world of consciousness in which human beings can act as if they belonged merely to the physical world. In *morality* social consciousness speaks of obligation within the individual consciousness of its members, modifying their desire as they will and act, in order that they should will and act as members of society. In *economy* society makes the world—the physical world and the world of consciousness—into a world fit for social transformation through the exercise of social power. In *law*, society carries its past willing into its future willing. It thereby wills that it, as it has made itself, should exist as a structure and a system in the future as well as in the past.

20.10. By the interacting of its activity as it struggles with the perennial dilemmas of any society, a given society becomes. Like a human brain, a society is a structure-system which makes itself unique by the activity of that which it shares with all societies.

Chapter 7

20.11. International society is the social becoming of five billion human beings and of uncounted subordinate societies.

PART TWO. CONSTITUTION

Chapter 8

20.12. To make the universe a place fit for human willing and acting, human consciousness makes of it a process in time and space. It is a process in which possibilities of willing and acting are conceived (the *future there*) and are chosen and actualized through willing and acting (the *present here*) in order to become the conceivable possibilities of further conceiving and further willing and acting (the *past there*).

Chapter 9

20.13. The *constitution* of a society is that society's idea of itself as structure and system in time and space. The *legal* constitution carries that idea from society's past to its present in the form of legal relations, that is, as retained acts of social willing. The *ideal* constitution presents to society its idea of its possible self-ordering, in the perspective of all its reality-forming, all its words and ideas and theories and values. The *real* constitution is society as it knows itself in its self-conceived present-for-itself, exercising its function and its responsibility to order its becoming.

Chapter 10

20.14. Society becomes by transforming natural power into social power in a *social exchange* which involves the adding of social purpose to natural power. Social power includes the power contained in *legal relations* which seek to determine the interaction of the willing and acting of members of society in order that their interactive willing and acting should serve the self-creating and socializing purposes of society. By the social exchange in the form of legal relations, society is able to universalize the willing of its individual members and to particularize its own willing within the willing of its members.

Chapter 11

20.15. Societies share the systematic characteristics of all societies. Those characteristics, which make possible the systematic self-creating of a society as a continuing structure, are reflected in the systematic characteristics of the constitution of a society. Those characteristics may be presented as a set of seven *generic principles of a constitution.*

Chapter 12

20.16. Societies make themselves within the structure-system which they share with all societies and the structure-system which they have made for themselves. Societies may do harm to themselves and to their members. That harm may arise from the very process of reality-forming through theory-making, since so much else in a society's becoming depends on its self-made theories.

20.17. A feature of pure theories of society is that they seek to explain the particular arrangements of a given society in terms of something which transcends the society. They tend to *supersocialize the social.* Within the development of societies over the last five centuries, a particular form of supersocializing has caused the idea of *sovereignty,* conceived as a source of unwilled willing in society. It gave rise to the idea of a *state-society* in which a public realm of socializing is conceived as being under the authority of a *government.*

Chapter 13

20.18. Through the idea and the ideal of democracy and through actual experience in the reality-forming of actual societies, sovereignty was socialized. It became possible to recognize that society, including its legal sub-system, was a self-willed ordering, in which the self-creating of the members of society and the self-creating of society could be reconciled.

20.19. Actual social experience generated societies of many different kinds throughout the world, from the society of the family to international society, the society of all societies. The state-society was to be only one form of society, among many other forms. In particular, *nations* (societies to which their members considered themselves to belong by birth) continued in vigorous life alongside state-societies, within state-societies, and as an aspiration for self-creating state-societies.

20.20. International society had to find its own theory. It chose to see itself as a collection of state-societies turned inside-out, like a glove. It chose to be an unsocial society creating itself separately from the development of its subordinate societies, ignoring the idea and the ideal of democracy, depriving itself of the possibility of using social power, especially legal relations, to bring about the survival and prospering of the whole human race.

Chapter 14

20.21. There is no reason why international society should not reconceive itself as a society, using social power, and especially legal relations, to bring about the survival and prospering of the whole human race.

PART THREE. WELL-BEING

Chapter 15

20.22. Society is a self-ordering. International society is a self-ordering of the whole human race and of all subordinate societies. In the non-social, undemocratized and unsocialized, international society, self-ordering has taken aberrant forms. Force and the threat of force have been used as substitutes for self-ordering. The social process has been a stunted process of interaction between the public realms of state-societies, so-called international relations conducted through a vestigial will-forming system called diplomacy.

20.23. The idea of state-sovereignty had been used to super-socialize the non-social international society. But actual social experience has, especially in the twentieth century, been struggling against the theory, creating a tension which cannot be resolved except through new theory. In particular: the substantive development of an *international public realm* (not merely the interacting of externalised national public realms); the development of *human rights* as a first democratizing and socializing of all subordinate societies by will-forming in international society; the development of *international reality-forming*, as governments lose control of the consciousness of human beings, lose the ability to confine reality-forming within the structures and systems of their own society.

Chapter 16

20.24. International law has been the primitive law of an unsocial international society. Itself a by-product of that unsocialization, it has contributed to holding back the development of international society as society. Failing to recognize itself as a society, international society has not known that it has a constitution. Not knowing its own constitution, it has ignored the generic principles of a constitution.

20.25. In an international society which knows itself as a society, state-societies have no natural and inherent and unlimited powers. Like any other of the myriad societies of international society, they have only the legal relations, including powers and obligations, conferred by the international constitution and by international law. Their particular status is as constitutional organs of international society, having special responsibility for the organization of its public realms, including the public realms of their own societies.

20.26. State-societies, like all other members of international society, have social power, including legal power, to serve the purposes of international society, to will and act for its survival and prospering, that is to say, for the survival and prospering of the whole human race. They are socially and legally accountable for the exercise of their powers and the carrying out of their obligations. Non-statal societies, including industrial and commercial and financial enterprises of all kinds, exercise social power and carry out obligations on the same conditions.

20.27. The new international law will be as dynamic and as rich as the law of any subordinate society, organizing human willing and acting in every field which concerns the survival and prospering of the society of which it is the law.

Chapter 17

20.28. The economy is the structure-system of society for transforming the human worlds—the physical world and the world of consciousness—through human willing and acting. The social organization of energy produces surplus social energy which society applies to the survival and prospering of society and its members.

20.29. In the economy society creates a reality-for-itself in which all transformations are given an economic value which stems from the whole of society's reality-forming and which re-enters society's reality-forming as economic transformations are made. In the economy, social power is distributed in all forms, including in the forms of legal relations. Legal relations sustain, in particular, the idea of property, the means by which society delegates a social power to will and act in order to produce economic transformations of the human worlds.

Chapter 18

20.30. The culture of a society is the society as a totality within the totality of all-that-is. It is society conceiving itself as spirit, transcending all human consciousness, judging all human consciousness. Society makes its culture inadvertently, as a resultant from the whole of its total social process through time and space. But, as it is made, society's culture feeds back its self-transcending and self-judging reality into all that society wills and acts.

20.31. Contemporary international society has an unculture of its unsocial becoming. That vacuum is being filled by a culture of primitive capitalism, dominating an undemocratized and unsocialized international system. An international society which is at last a society will have as its ideal the word-idea-theory-value of *eunomia*, the good order of a self-ordering society.

Chapter 19

20.32. Humanity must take command of its future, which is the future of the human species. It will do so by conceiving of itself as a species endowed with imagination and reason and with the capacity to create itself through creating itself as society. It will make of itself an international society which is at last a society, a society whose purpose is the survival and prospering of the whole human race, that is to say, its self-selected evolution as a species.

Here my powers rest from their high fantasy,
   but already I could feel my being turned –
   instinct and intellect balanced equally
as in a wheel whose motion nothing jars –
by the Love that moves the Sun and the other stars.

Dante, *Divine Comedy: Paradise*, canto XXXIII,
ll. 142–146 (tr. J. Ciardi, New York, [1961], 365).

*   *   *

Into the foul water
Falls a camellia flower,
Making a hollow.

Takahama Kyoshi (in R. H. Blyth, *A History of Haiku*,
Tokyo [1964], ii, 119).

Index

References are to the number of the chapter and paragraph in which a discussion of the topic in question is contained or in which a discussion is initiated.